CW00669904

CARING AND THE LAW

Caring and the Law considers the law's response to caring. It explores how care is valued and recognised, how it is regulated and restricted and how the values of caring are reflected in the law. It does this by examining the law's interaction with caring in a wide range of fields including family, medical, welfare, criminal and tort law. At the heart of the book is the claim that the law has failed to recognise the importance of caring in many areas and in doing so has led to the costs and burdens of care falling on those who provide it, primarily women. It has also meant that the law has failed to protect those who receive care from the abuse that can take place in a caring context. The book will promote an ethic of care as providing an ethical and conceptual framework for the law to respond to caring relationships.

Caring and the Law

Jonathan Herring

·H A R T·
PUBLISHING
OXFORD AND PORTLAND, OREGON
2013

Published in the United Kingdom by Hart Publishing Ltd
16C Worcester Place, Oxford, OX1 2JW
Telephone: +44 (0)1865 517530
Fax: +44 (0)1865 510710
E-mail: mail@hartpub.co.uk
Website: http://www.hartpub.co.uk

Published in North America (US and Canada) by
Hart Publishing
c/o International Specialized Book Services
920 NE 58th Avenue, Suite 300
Portland, OR 97213-3786
USA
Tel: +1 503 287 3093 or toll-free: (1) 800 944 6190
Fax: +1 503 280 8832
E-mail: orders@isbs.com
Website: http://www.isbs.com

British Library Cataloguing in Publication Data
Data Available

ISBN: 978-1-84946-106-1

Typeset by Compuscript Ltd, Shannon
Printed and bound in Great Britain by
MPG Books Group Ltd

To Kirsten and all those who care

Preface

Not long ago it was reasonable to suggest that carers were ignored and invisible in society. That can no longer be said. It is widely acknowledged that we are facing a crisis in care, and one which, without rapid action, will escalate. There is growing recognition that care work is essential to ensure the wellbeing of the most vulnerable in society. Further, the failure of the law and society more generally to recognise and value care has led to significant disadvantage for women. This book explores the law's response to care work.

It argues that not only must the law find a way to support, reward and acknowledge care. It needs to rethink the values that underpin the law, moving from a more individualised conception of rights and interests to one which acknowledges the importance of relational values. It is hoped this book might provide a sounder theoretical basis and some practical recommendations for the promotion of a society and legal system which puts care at its heart.

I am grateful for the team at Hart publishing who have been exemplary. I would like to thank many people for their care friendship and support during the writing of this book. In particular, Se-shauna Wheatle, Sandra Fredman, Charles Foster, Stephen Gilmore, Alan Bogg, Julie Wallbank, Shazia Choudhry and Michelle Madden Dempsey. Above thank you to Kirsten, Laurel, Joanna and Darcy who have provided ceaseless care of the highest standard.

Contents

Table of Cases

Table of Legislation

UK Statutory Instruments

European Union

International Conventions

Caring

I. Introduction

Everyone cares. Everyone is cared for. Yet caring receives surprisingly little
attention from lawyers. The law degree is replete with cases about people
making money, losing money and claiming money. The business office; the
computer; and the racecourse feature prominently. The day care centre; the
nappy changing table; and the care home bypass most undergraduate students,
however. The well-dressed businessman with his rights of autonomy; freedom
of contract; and presumption of innocence can be well advised by our law
graduates. The exhausted mother of the disabled child, with little autonomy,
freedom or innocence, cannot. She is an anomaly, outside the norm. Not
even, perhaps, of particular interest to lawyers. After all, she will not be able
to pay any fees. Yet everyone cares. Everyone is cared for ...

Caring easily disappears from the picture when the production of economic
value becomes a national obsession. Economic forecasts and share price
changes are major stories in the media. The successful outing with the autistic
child or the happy haircut of the demented woman is not. Economic indicators
are linked inevitably to the well-being of the nation. 'It's the economy, stupid'
has become widely recognised as one of the greatest electioneering statements
ever made.[1] As Martha Fineman notes:

> The Dow Jones average is reported daily (even hourly on public radio) as though
> this reflected our country's health and wealth, an economic indicator substituting
> for other forms of evaluation of national standing such as the equitableness of the
> distribution of the wealth the society is producing or the well being of the most
> vulnerable of our citizens. We seem blinded in a reverie of self satisfaction even
> as the position of our children and the historically disadvantaged subgroups in

[1] The phrase originates from the remarks made by James Carville, a strategist for
Bill Clinton.

society deteriorates both from where they were a few decades ago and relative to the positions of these groups in other industrialized democracies.[2]

Perhaps the lack of attention paid to caring by the law is unsurprising. Law is best designed to deal with precise disputes: who did what to whom and when? Caring is about relationships. Individual acts of care can only be understood in the context of the relationship between the parties. Law is about enforcement; while caring is about the voluntary performance of acts motivated by love. Who would want to be cared for by someone who was only doing so under threat of court sanction? Law deals with people who are in dispute and need, in some sense, to be kept apart. Caring is about people being brought together.

These points reveal misguided presumptions about the nature of law and personhood. They do not show us that law and caring are incompatible, but simply that with certain ways of looking at the law and using certain principles to underpin the law, caring will not fit. They do not show that in their very essence caring and law are simply incompatible. This will be a major theme of chapter three.

A central theme running through this book is the argument that caring is an essential aspect of human existence. From our earliest days we are in caring relationships which are crucial to our survival; emotional well-being; and psychological identity. Caring is hardly some kind of luxury hobby or activity ancillary to other more important activities. It is central to our humanity. Feeding, bathing, changing, comforting, transporting, and nurturing are essential activities. Even if at times when we might feel we are independent and not in need of care, in fact we are dependent on others for the provision of food, transport and power. More importantly, we are dependent on others for comfort, company and identity.

The law for too long has been arranged around the vision of an able, autonomous and unattached adult. The law's role has been to enable him to retain his ability, autonomy and freedom. His rights are powerful tools to keep others out: rights to autonomy, privacy and liberty are used to maintain this character. Limitations on freedom need to be justified, typically by being chosen by the individual. This book argues for a different vision: one which starts with recognising that our identities, values and well-being are tied up with our relationships and the responsibilities that come with them. If the caring of dependents is accepted as central, then the values of autonomy, freedom and justice need to be used to enable and support caring.[3] Our starting point focuses on interdependent relationships and not the isolated individual.

---

[2] M Fineman, 'Contract and Care' (2001) 76 *Chicago-Kent Law Review* 1403, 1436.

[3] M Eichner, 'Families, human dignity, and state support for caretaking: why the United States' failure to ameliorate the work-family conflict is a dereliction of the government's basic responsibilities' (2010) 88 *North Carolina Law Review* 1593, 1618–619.

Taking such a view has a significant impact on what we regard as the central role of the law and the state. A central role for the state must be to ensure that the dependency needs of individuals are met. Without that people cannot live dignified lives.[4] Care cannot be dismissed as a private activity of no interest to the state. As Maxine Eichner puts it:

> The care that children and other dependents receive from family members is inextricably intertwined with state policies. This care takes place in a matrix of constraints and entitlements that affect family members' ability and opportunity to care for other members. The existence or nonexistence of minimum wage laws, union rights to bargain, and overtime provisions affect parents' ability to meet the financial needs of their children and other dependents. Welfare reform laws requiring recipients to work in order to receive welfare subsidies affect parents' ability to care for those with dependency needs. Family leave laws influence parents' opportunity to stay home with their children. The stability and security of a parent's job affects stress levels in the household, which also affect the quality of parenting. In these circumstances, the family has no 'natural' manner of functioning that it can be left to 'apart from' the state. Nor does the modern administrative state have a neutral, isolated position it can assume while leaving families autonomously to deal with their own affairs. Instead, the state is always and continually influencing how families conduct their affairs. The issue is not whether state policy will influence families but whether it will be formulated with this inevitable influence in mind. When it comes to the ways families function, no family is an island.[5]

This is not to say that care is only a matter for the state. Families and friends are well-suited to providing intimate care because, as I will argue in chapter two, relationships are central. Yet families and friends are not able to provide the broader social support necessary to ensure that caring can take place effectively and that mitigates the disadvantages that flow from care. To quote Eichner again:

> Determining that the state and families are both conjunctively responsible for meeting dependency needs does not mean that the state's role should be identical to families'. Rather, each should bear responsibility for the area in which it has greater competence. This means that families should bear responsibility for the day-to-day caring for (or arranging the care for) children and others with dependency needs. Meanwhile, the state should bear the responsibility for structuring institutions in ways that help families meet their caretaking needs, and that support human development. This includes ensuring that families have safe and affordable caretaking options, as well as structuring other societal institutions, such as schools and communities, in ways that foster children's and other dependents' development and well-being. This division of responsibility recognizes the malleability and contingency of institutional structures. It does not artificially separate state action from the realm of families or presume that completely clear boundaries can be drawn between them, but it does assume certain spheres of authority will exist between the two.[6]

---

[4] Ibid, 1619.
[5] Ibid, 1618–619.
[6] Ibid, 1618–619.

Currently, the state is failing to adequately support carers. In this book we will find plenty of examples of cases where the interests of those in caring relationships are ignored or excluded, and where legal styles of thinking fail to produce solutions that work for caring relationships.

One of the most powerful contributions to the inequality of women has been the devaluation of 'women's work' and the exaltation of 'men's work'. The classification of care work as private or a labour of love has left its significance unrecognised and unrewarded. One of the ironies of modern life is that women's increased opportunities in the 'workplace' has only been possible because other women have taken on the role of providing caring services such as child care, cleaning and the like. The children and dependants of the lowest paid workers are the ones who bear the cost of that.

II. Title

The title of this book is *Caring and the Law*, rather than the more obvious *Carers and the Law*. This is deliberate, for reasons elaborated on in chapters two and three. I will summarise those reasons now though, because they involve some of the central themes of this book. The more common terminology of discussing 'carers' and 'cared for' has received some justifiably trenchant criticism from disability rights advocates. It presents the person needing care as being the passive recipient of a kindness from the other. It perhaps also captures a rather patronising attitude towards those needing 'looking after'. However, the preference from many writing from a disability rights perspective of using the language of help and the carer being a personal assistant fails, I suspect, to capture the reality of many caring relationships. This contains three features which I suggest make it preferable to talk of caring relationships rather than carer and cared for, or disabled person and assistant.

First, in a caring relationship the interests and identities of the two people become intermingled. Their interests become interdependent. It becomes impossible to consider the welfare or rights of the one in isolation. Hence the focus must be on the relationship, rather than the individuals.

Second, the language of 'carers' is generally taken to refer to those who are caring for older people or disabled adults. The unfortunate consequence of this is that it sidelines the many other forms of caring that take place, be that of children, friends or partners. While the appropriate legal response to different caring relationships may vary, it is important to recognise the broader range of care work that takes place.

Third, and flowing from the previous point, the language of 'carer' and 'cared for' ignores the fact that we all need care. We are all vulnerable and rely on others to provide for our needs. To divide society up into those providing care and those needing care disguises the vulnerability that we all face.

Further, for many people in the course of a relationship they will at some point be regarded as a 'carer' and at another point a 'cared for'; and often both at the same time. To separate the parties in a relationship into carers and recipients of care oversimplifies the complexities of many relationships.

III. Ethic of Care

Many of the arguments in this book will be based on an ethic of care. This will be defined in chapter three. Ethic of care has received attention from writers from a broad range of disciplines including economics,[7] education,[8] law,[9] sociology,[10] philosophy,[11] social policy[12] and politics.[13] One of the aims of this book will be to explore how an ethic of care might be applied in concrete legal proposals. This is not straightforward because much of the law is based on principles which are antithetical to an ethic of care approach. It is not surprising, therefore, that many writing on an ethic of care have avoided using it to produce concrete solutions. Our society and legal system would be very different if based on ethic of care principles. The journey to the ideal legal system looks to be a very long one, but I will suggest how changes can now be made to the law in this book.

IV. Real Life

Government publications on carers are typically accompanied by pictures of attractive, smiling and calm carers. The reality can be rather different. Caring is extremely hard work. In his book, *The Selfish Pig's Guide to Caring*, Hugh Marriott, clearly a devoted carer himself, has this to say:

> We didn't apply for the job. Most of us don't have a vocation for it. We've had no training. We're certain we aren't much good at it. Plus, and this is the nub of the matter, we've got our own life to lead. Are we expected to throw that away because of somebody else's disability? We've got things to do, places to go. And now it looks as if we might not be able to.

---

[7] Eg N Folbre, *Who Pays for the Kids? Gender and the Structures of Constraint* (Routledge, 1994).

[8] Eg N Noddings, *Caring: A Feminine Approach to Ethics and Moral Education* (University of California Press, 1984).

[9] Eg M Fineman, *The Autonomy Myth: A Theory of Dependency* (New Press, 2004).

[10] Eg A Hochschild, *The Time Bind: When Work Becomes Home and Home Becomes Work* (Owl Book, 2001).

[11] V Held, *The Ethics of Care* (Oxford University Press, 2006).

[12] Eg S Sevenhuijsen, *Citizenship and the Ethics of Care* (Routledge, 1998).

[13] Eg B Hobson, *Gender and Citizenship in Transition* (Macmillan, 2000).

But aren't we just as important as they are? Why are we expected to sacrifice ourselves for somebody else? And yes, I mean sacrifice. We're not talking about giving up five minutes of time once or twice a week. Or putting off a holiday from this year to next. We're talking about changing our entire way of life. The old one wasn't perfect, but it was the best we could do. This new one isn't even ours. It's somebody else's life. And it's one that doesn't suit us at all.[14]

As Laura Kessler puts it, care 'can be self-annihilating, mind deadening, and repetitive. Caregiving can be dream deferring and socially isolating.'[15]

It is easy, and appropriate, to paint a gloomy picture of those undertaking caring relationships. Carers UK and the Carers Trust have quite rightly highlighted the disadvantages suffered by those undertaking care work. A survey by the Carers Trust reported that a third of carers feel so bad they do not want to wake up in the morning[16] and 45 per cent said they felt so depressed they could not cope. In the same survey the level of financial disadvantage was highlighted, with 53 per cent borrowing money because of their caring role and 45 per cent cutting back on food and heat to make ends meet.[17] Caring can cause ill-health, with carers being twice as likely as others to have mental health problems.[18] We will explore the disadvantages suffered by carers later in chapter two.

Carers UK estimates that there are 6.4 million people providing unpaid care.[19] By 'carer' they mean 'unpaid care by looking after an ill, frail or disabled family member, friend or partner'. Over the next 30 years, it is predicted that the number of carers will increase by 3.4 million (around 60 per cent).[20] Currently, around 12 per cent of the adult population are caring. Around 1.25 million people care for more than 50 hours a week.[21] The 2001 Census suggested that 58 per cent of carers were women. Notably many carers are older, with the peak age for caring being between 50 and 59, with more than 20 per cent of that age group providing care.[22] Young people undertake significant levels of care, with 174,996 carers under the age of 18 providing care according to the 2001 Census, and 13,029 of them providing at least 50 hours a week.[23] A disproportionate number of these young carers are from certain ethnic minority backgrounds (including Bangladeshi, Black African, Black Caribbean and Pakistani).[24]

---

[14] H Marriott, *The Selfish Pig's Guide to Caring* (Piatkus, 2009) 209.
[15] L Kessler, 'Is there Agency in Dependency? Expanding the Feminist Justifications for Restructuring Wage Work' in M Fineman and T Dougherty (eds), *Feminism Confronts Homo Economicus* (Cornell University Press, 2005).
[16] BBC News Online, 'UK Carers "Desperately Worried about Finances"' 23 September 2010.
[17] Carers UK, *The Cost of Care* (Carers UK, 2012).
[18] Carers UK, *Facts About Carers* (Carers UK, 2009).
[19] Carers UK and Leeds University, *Valuing Carers* (Carers UK, 2011).
[20] Carers UK, *Key Facts About Carers* (Carers UK, 2012).
[21] Carers UK, *Facts About Carers* (Carers UK, 2009).
[22] Ibid.
[23] Ibid.
[24] Equality and Human Rights Commission, *How Fair is Britain?* (EHRC, 2012).

In the popular imagination carers tend to be presented in one of two ways. On the one hand there is the picture of the exhausted carer, which has effectively been portrayed by organisations seeking to promote carers' rights. Typical would be the description in *The Guardian* of carers who 'face financial ruin, stress and exhaustion as they battle to cope with the demands of 24-hour care and a bureaucratic system that makes their lives a misery.'[25] On the other hand carers are presented as self-sacrificing paragons of virtue. As a recent White Paper puts it, 'The Government recognises and values the contribution of carers. By caring for people in their own time and supporting other people's independence, carers embody the spirit of the Big Society.'[26]

Mothers in particular are glorified. George Washington's comment is still typical today: 'All I am I owe to my mother. I attribute all my success in life to the moral, intellectual and physical education I received from her.'[27]

While not wanting to mock or downplay the significance of mothers, there are serious dangers with the glorification of motherhood. Three will be seen in this book. The first is that anyone who falls short of the highest standard is seen as a failure. In chapter seven we shall see the extraordinarily high standards to which the criminal law can hold mothers. The second is that the care of mothers is assumed. Just as the teenager who treats the family house like a hotel with no apparent awareness of the work behind the scenes, the state takes for granted the care provided by mothers and others. The third is that the care of others who do not fit within the traditional model of motherhood or family life is discounted. Hence, for example, the care in same-sex relationships or care by children is overlooked in discussions or presentation of care.[28] This sidelining of care can even be found in academic writing. In his influential study of ethics, David Heyd explains that his ethical analysis will not cover mothers who make sacrifices for children because that belongs to 'the sphere of natural relationships and instinctive feelings (which lie outside morality)'.[29] Although to give him credit, at least caring gets a mention. In many other works of political and moral philosophy caring is simply ignored.

---

[25] T McVeigh, 'Is This Any Way to Treat Our Nation of Carers?' *The Guardian* 14 September 2008.

[26] HM Government, *Recognised, Valued and Supported* (The Stationery Office, 2011) 3.

[27] Quoted R Kaufman Kitchen, 'Eradicating the Mothering Effect: Women as Workers and Mothers, Successfully and Simultaneously' (2011) 26 *Wisconsin Journal of Law, Gender and Society* 167.

[28] J Manthorpe, 'Nearest and Dearest? The Neglect of Lesbians in Caring Relationships' (2003) 33 *British Journal of Social Work* 753.

[29] D Heyd, *Supperrogation: Its Status in Ethics Theory* (Cambridge University Press, 1982) 134.

V. Politics and Care

Previously caring was seen as an issue of little relevance to political campaigning, but now that is very different. In 2008 the Government produced *Carers at the Heart of 21st-Century Families and Communities*, a major re-examination of the relationship between carers and the state. In its introduction Gordon Brown declared:

> Caring for our relatives and friends when they are in need is a challenge that the vast majority of us will rise to at some point in our lives. At any one time 1 in 10 people in Britain is a carer—the majority of them, of course, still women. It is a testimony to the importance of families that so many of us are prepared to make the personal sacrifices that caring can involve in order to help our loved ones lead fulfilling lives even in the face of incapacity or disability. Our support and appreciation for carers is therefore not just fundamental to ensuring that those of us in need of care are able to receive it, but goes right to the heart of our values as a society and our ambition to create a fairer Britain.[30]

Care has become a major political issue. Sadly, it is economics which has largely driven the sudden interest in care. Due to a range of social changes, including work patterns, family breakdown and changing demographics, an increasing number of people are becoming dependant on state care. The cost of this on the state and on individuals is huge. The state is worried by the growing cost of care and the middle class is concerned that their legacies will be eaten up with care costs. The Dilnot Report,[31] designed to deal with this concern, has received considerable attention. As we shall see in chapter four, governments have consistently failed to deal with the complexities of the economic costs of care.

The think tank, the New Economics Foundation carried out research on the true economic value of the work performed by various careers. Much media attention greeted its finding that hospital cleaners contributed more to society than bankers.[32] As they point out, tax accountants, although richly rewarded, contribute negatively to the overall wealth of the country. While slightly tongue in cheek, what such studies show is that the rewards our society gives are not necessarily governed by logic. No one would die or suffer unbearably if

---

[30] HM Government, *Carers at the Heart of 21st-Century Families and Communities* (London, The Stationery Office, 2008) 2. For a broader discussion of the role of Government in meeting the needs of carers, see F Carmichael, G Connell, C Hulme and S Sheppard, *Meeting the Needs of Carers; Government Policy and Social Support* (University of Salford, 2005).

[31] Department of Health, *Commission on Funding of Care and Support* (Department of Health, 2011).

[32] New Economics Foundation, *A Bit Rich? Calculating the Real Value to Society of Different Professions* (New Economics Foundation, 2012).

accountants, journalists or professors stopped work for a few weeks. However, they would if carers stopped caring. That is perhaps a 'cheap point' but it highlights the need to rethink what it is that we value in society. Care has not been seen as a major marker of a good society for too long. We need to elevate care to being recognised as a major requirement for a successful state.

VI. The Structure of the Book

Chapter two will explore the meaning of care and what is meant by a caring relationship. This will include an exploration of the lives of those in caring relationships. The chapter will describe the struggles facing those in caring relationships and attempt to identify the amount of caring that takes place in the UK currently.

The third chapter will define an ethic of care. It will set out some of the key principles underpinning the approach. However, this will not be an uncritical analysis of an ethic of care. There are serious difficulties with aspects of ethic of care and there are undoubted tensions that arise when it is put into practice. These are particularly apparent for lawyers because an ethic of care abjures abstract principles and instead focuses on finding solutions that are appropriate in the particular context. The chapter will argue that, appropriately understood, an ethic of care provides a powerful way of reorganising society and law in a way which puts caring centre stage.

The fourth chapter will examine the state's response to care. As already mentioned in this introduction, there is increasing political interest in care. There is still much debate over the role of the state in care. The chapter will look at the provision of payments and services in cases where care is needed. The chapter will explore the inadequate current response of the state to caring relationships and consider how that might be improved. It will also analyse the recent proposals for reform that the Government has put forward.

The book then turns to some particular areas of law to examine how caring relationships are accommodated. Chapters five and six explore family law and medical law respectively. One might suspect that these would be areas of the law where caring relationships would receive particular recognition and attention from the law. They do not. We shall see, even in these areas of law where relationships are so important, a fixation on individualised legal personhood and individualised models of rights. Hence, in medical law the legal approach is still very much based on a single patient before a single doctor. The interests of those in relationship with the patient are utterly eclipsed by talk of my right to make my decisions about my body. In family law, while relationships are central to the topic, the law privileges particular kinds of relationship. These tend to be sexual relationships, rather than relationships based on care. I argue in this chapter for a rethinking of this area of the law and recommend a family law which is less sexy and more careful!

Chapter seven looks at other areas of the law and their relationship with caring. It considers human rights law, employment law and tort law as examples where caring often goes unrecognised and unvalued. These areas highlight the way that the law makes assumptions about what we can expect from an employee and what is economically valuable, all of which downplay the importance of care.

Chapter eight acknowledges the 'dark side' of caring, namely that of abuse within intimate relationships. The chapter highlights the dangers that an ethic of care can valorise caring relationships but fail to recognise the need for protection. However, it argues that proper support and valuing of caring relationships requires an effective legal response to protect people in them.

The final chapter seeks to bring out some of the key themes in the book.[33]

I hope to change the way caring and the law are viewed through the arguments in this book. There is a way to make caring the central principle of the law. The law in all areas can be rewritten with caring as the underlying tenet. Money and individual rights, while important, are a sandy foundation, but caring is the rock on which society stands.

---

[33] B Sloan, *Informal Carers and the Law* (Hart, 2012) provides an excellent discussion of the detailed law on carers.

The Nature of Care

I. Introduction

Caring is a most basic human need.[1] A life without care would be a shallow one, indeed it would be an impossible one. Our gestation, birth and early years care cannot be done alone. Care is an inherent part of our humanity and we cannot avoid it. It is central to our flourishing.[2] Caring relationships are a source of meaning and value to life; a source of joy. Yet, care is also a source of severe disadvantage, social isolation and deprivation. Within apparently caring relationships grave abuse can take place. In a caring relationship one can find the joy of life or lose it.

This chapter will consider the nature of care: its definition; its place in society; and the impact of caring on individual lives and the different kinds of care that are provided.[3] For a long time carers have been 'ignored and invisible'.[4] But, recent governments have been keen to be seen to recognise the value of carers. Typical are the following comments from the forward to the 2010 paper, *Recognised, Valued and Supported: Next steps for the Carers Strategy*:

> Many of us will be carers at some stage in our lives. It is a role that can come unexpectedly out of a crisis; it is a role that can creep up on you. Being a carer provokes a complex mix of emotions. It can be both rewarding and frustrating. It can be costly in life chances, financial security and health.

---

[1] K Lynch, 'Affective Equality: Who Cares?' (2009) 52 *Development* 410.

[2] E Feder Kittay, *Love's Labor: Essays on Women, Equality and Dependency* (Routledge, 1999).

[3] For work on carers from sociological perspectives, see J Read, *Disability, the Family and Society: Listening to Mothers* (Open University Press, 2000); J Read and L Clements, *Disabled Children and the Law: Research and Good Practice* (Jessica Kingsley, 2001); and K Stalker (ed), *Reconceptualising Work with 'Carers'* (Jessica Kingsley, 2002). For a theological discussion, see R Groenhout, *Theological Echoes in an Ethic of Care* (Erasmus Institute, 2003). For a discussion of the legal issues, see L Clements, *Carers and their Rights* (Carers UK, 2011) and J Herring, *Older People in Law and Society* (Oxford University Press, 2009) ch 4.

[4] M Henwood, *Ignored and Invisible* (London, Carers' National Association, 1998).

> The Government recognises and values the contribution of carers. By caring for people in their own time and supporting other people's independence, carers embody the spirit of the Big Society.
>
> Supporting carers' well-being is therefore in all our interests. There are key issues— employment, support, respite—that carers are likely to face in their caring role. But the circumstances of every carer are unique, and that is why there is an overriding need to personalise support to fit around individual and family preferences.[5]

The increasing political and social significance of care work was reflected in the fact that the position of carers became one of the major themes of the 2010 Election.[6] The issue of care and the costs of care have been a major theme of debate in the media. Victoria Yates puts the increased attention paid to the rights of carers down to economic pressures operating through and in tandem with the following factors:[7]

(1)   Budget-led rather than needs-led social care management.
(2)   The push for deinstitutionalisation and community care.
(3)   Increased risk of mental and physical health problems in the carer population itself.
(4)   The social inclusion agenda's emphasis on encouraging people back to work and off welfare benefits.
(5)   The development of a human rights and antidiscrimination culture (epitomised in the establishment under the Equality Act 2006 of the Commission for Equality and Human Rights).
(6)   The adoption of the social model of disability.
(7)   The campaigning efforts of various carer representative groups such as Carers UK.
(8)   The need to recognise and support those carers' interests which may be compromised by the caring role.[8]

The fact that the issue of care has become part of a wider public debate over a 'work/life balance' could be added to this list.[9] Increasing working hours and the tensions in balancing work and home life have become an aspect of daily life for many. We will return to some of these themes in chapter four, but it important to notice how the personal, social and political influences can all impact on caring practices. Before exploring some of these themes further, I will examine the definition of care.[10]

---

[5] HM Government, *Recognised, Valued and Supported: Next Steps for the Carers Strategy* (HM Government, 2010) 3.

[6] Carers UK, *Recognition in Election* (Carers UK, 2010).

[7] V Yates, 'Ambivalence, Contradiction and Symbiosis: Carers' and Mental Health Users' Rights' (2007) *Law & Policy* 435.

[8] Ibid 445.

[9] A Hochschild, *The Time Bind. When Work Becomes Home and Home Becomes Work* (Owl Books, 2003).

[10] J Phillips, *Care* (Polity, 2007).

II. Terminology

Producing a definition of care is far from straightforward.[11] Interestingly, many of the official definitions seek to define a carer rather than care. This is significant, and will be criticised shortly. The Government uses the following definition of a carer:

> A carer spends a significant proportion of their life providing unpaid support to family or potentially friends. This could be caring for a relative, partner or friend who is ill, frail, disabled or has mental health or substance misuse problems.[12]

This is a notably narrow definition. First, it is restricted to those who spend a significant portion of their life caring. Second, it only applies to those who are unpaid. Third, it is limited to family and only 'potentially friends'. This is surprising because the nature of a caring activity does not change simply because of the presence or absence of a blood tie between those involved. Fourth, it is restricted to those who need care due to one of the listed causes. Fifth, although not explicit, the definition was intended only to apply to people caring for adults and not children.

In the social security legislation, the definition of a carer is limited to a person caring for a 'disabled person'. Disabled people are those who are 'blind, deaf or dumb or who suffer from mental disorder of any description, and other persons aged eighteen or over who are substantially and permanently handicapped by illness, injury or congenital deformity'.[13] The very fact this language seems archaic is revealing. It comes from a 1948 statute. The difficulty in defining care is reflected in the fact that no attempt has been made to update it. It is more restrictive than the Government definition as it only covers those who are caring in cases of substantial and permanent 'handicap'.

These narrow definitions can be contrasted with Harriet Lefley's broad definition of carers as 'individuals whose own happiness is entwined with the well-being of people who are dear to them'.[14] Another broad definition is that of Berenice Fisher and Joan Tronto's who claim caring is 'a species activity that includes everything that we do to maintain, continue, and repair our

---

[11] J Finch and D Groves, *A Labour of Love* (Routledge, 1983).

[12] HM Government, *Carers at the Heart of 21st-Century Families and Communities* (The Stationery Office, 2008) 18. If the definition was interpreted literally, it would include parents caring for children, but that is not how the Government intended it to be understood.

[13] National Assistance Act 1948, s 29. Much of the language used in that definition would not be used by those working in the area.

[14] H Lefley, 'The Impact of Mental Disorders on Families and Carers' in S Thornicroft (ed), *Textbook of Community Psychiatry* (Oxford University Press, 2001).

"world" so that we can live in it as well as possible'.[15] This definition would appear to cover a vast range of activities.[16] Care under such a definition might be thought to become so vague as to be of little practical use. Notably, it seems to focus on the emotional aspects of a relationship rather than to performance of tasks. Other definitions seek to list the kinds of activities which might be regarded as care:

> washing, feeding, getting in and out of bed, assistance with toileting, giving medication, changing dressings, giving injections or catheritistaion, dealing with incontinence, assisting with paperwork and personal business including managing money, negotiation and liaison with 'professional' caring agencies and staff, providing transport and undertaking household tasks.[17]

It hardly needs to be said that there is no 'correct' definition of care. Much depends on the context within which the term is being used. If one is looking for a definition of a carer for the purposes of the provision of benefits, one might have a very different concept from if one was considering the psychological impact of care. One of the difficulties in producing a definition, at least if it is not to be utterly vague, is that care takes place in so many different contexts and has so many levels that a bright line definition is unhelpful.

My approach to defining care will start by setting out what I think are the four key markers of care. These may be exhibited in different degrees. While not providing a definition as such, they provide an indication of the extent to which an activity is or is not care. Where all four markers are clearly present there is undoubtedly care. When these markers are shown to lesser extent the behaviour moves away from the central understanding of care.

A. The Four Markers of Care

I suggest the following four markers of care:[18]

— Meeting needs.
— Respect.
— Responsibility.
— Relationality.

These terms need further explanation.

---

[15] B Fisher and J Tronto, 'Towards a Feminist Theory of Caring' in E Abel and M Nelson (eds), *Circles of Care, Work and Identity in Women's Lives* (State University of New York Press, 1990) 40.

[16] P Meyers, 'The "Ethic of Care" and the Problem of Power' (1998) 8 *Journal of Political Philosophy* 142.

[17] M Barnes, *Caring and Social Justice* (Palgrave, 2006) 6.

[18] For an alternative analysis see J Tronto, *Moral Boundaries: A Political Argument for an Ethic of Care* (Routledge, 1983) 127–34.

i. Meeting Needs

We all have fundamental needs. Nearly all of us rely on others to meet our needs. Caring relationships of the most value involve, therefore, the meeting of people's needs.[19] I would reject the argument that caring is about a feeling, rather than activity. Caring involves the actual giving of care, and the giving of care effectively. Here it is useful to draw on the distinction drawn by many care writers between caring *about* and caring *for*.[20] Caring about something can be seen as essentially an attitude of mind, whereas caring for involves doing something. One can readily imagine a person who claims to care about all manner of things, but fails to put those feelings into practice. I might claim to care about the homeless, but do nothing to improve their position. That, I would argue, is not true caring.[21] The failure to act in the face of need, in fact, casts doubt on the claim to have a caring attitude. If care is to be regarded as something of particular recognition and value it must be more than a feeling.

Caring relationships usually involve an action.[22] Usually, not always, because there are some cases in which the caring thing is not to act. If a frail person is seeking to make you a cup of tea, not assisting might be caring, if they would find it distressing to be helped. Usually care involves doing something. It does not, however, necessarily involve direct interaction with another. Supervision or anticipating harms and seeking to avoid them would be caring, but would not involve direct interaction.[23] Sitting silently together, making arrangements so another can avoid an uncomfortable encounter, and doing the laundry can all be caring, even though they are not directly seen as 'body work'.[24]

Joan Tronto makes the somewhat controversial point that caring in an incompetent way may not constitute caring.[25] This suggests the 'success' of caring in meeting needs is part of good care. Others, especially those who see caring more in terms of a virtue, might be less concerned with the end product than the motivation. One may be caring, even when one fails to meet the other's need. We shall explore this link between care as a virtue and as a practice in chapter three. However, I suggest that a person who is seeking to care for another but consistently fails to meet the person's need, fails to provide care. For example, the person who despite their best efforts to cook

---

[19] S Clark Miller, 'Need, Care and Obligation' (2005) 57 *Royal Institute of Philosophy Supplement* 157.

[20] J Tronto, *Moral Boundaries: A Political Argument for an Ethic of Care* (Routledge, 1983) 127–34.

[21] K Lynch, 'Love Labour as a Distinct and Non-Commodifiable Form of Care Labour' (2008) 55 *Sociological Review* 550.

[22] A Barnes, 'Am I a Carer and Do I Care?' (2004) 7 *Medicine, Health Care and Philosophy* 153.

[23] M Nolan, G Grant and J Keady, *Understanding Family Care* (Open University Press, 1996) 2.

[24] J Twigg, C Wolkowitz, R Cohen and S Nettleton, 'Conceptualising Body Work in Health and Social Care' (2011) 33 *Sociology of Health and Illness* 171.

[25] J Tronto, *Moral Boundaries: A Political Argument for an Ethic of Care* (Routledge, 1983) 127–34.

a nutritious meal for the other, keeps burning it, would fail to care, at least not in its ideal form.[26]

If, therefore, care requires a successful application to needs, this still leaves the question of precisely what needs must be met to amount to care. I argue that care should be understood broadly to include the meeting of a full range of a person's needs. These include not only basic biological needs such as food and shelter; but also broader social needs for emotion, relationships and play.[27] Part of care work can therefore involve controlling professional care; managing financial issues; and working through bureaucracies.[28] It may involve helping another relate to other people or to be able to communicate. It can also involve emotional support and comfort. A study of carers of those at the end of life highlighted the complex role that carers may have to perform, from advocating for the individual, waiting with them, keeping illness at a distance, to liaising with professionals. That study highlighted the expertise that carers have about the individual needs of those they are in caring relationships with.[29]

Daniel Engster takes a narrower view and suggests caring should be seen as 'helping individuals to meet their basic needs and to develop and sustain those *basic or innate capabilities* necessary for survival and basic functioning in society, including the ability to sense, feel, move about, speak, reason, imagine, affiliate with others, and in most societies today, read, write, and perform basic math'.[30]

Engster's definition seems focused on bodily and rational activities, and excludes emotional well-being, although this possibly fits within his reference to affiliation. Although I would define care more widely, Engster's approach is helpful if we are seeking to define the kinds of caring relationships that are particular worthy of state support. The closer they are to meeting what society regards as the basic needs of individuals, the stronger the case for state support. My concern with Engster's approach is that if we are seeking through caring relationships to promote well-being, we should not restrict that too narrowly to the physical and rational, but must include emotional welfare.

In her excellent book *Care, Gender and Justice*, Diemut Bubeck argues for further restrictions on the meaning of care:

> Caring for is the meeting of the needs of one person by another person where face-to-face interaction between carer and cared for is a crucial element of the overall

---

[26] S Luo, 'Relation, Virtue, and Relational Virtue: Three Concepts of Caring' (2007) 22 *Hypatia* 92.

[27] M Nussbaum, *Women and Human Development: The Capabilities Approach* (Cambridge University Press, 2000).

[28] A Bookman and M Harrington, 'Family Caregivers: A Shadow Workforce in the Geriatric Health Care System?' (2007) 32 *Journal of Health, Politics, Policy and the Law* 1005.

[29] J Inger, A Birgitta and B-M Ternestedt, 'The Encounter between Informal and Professional Care at the End of Life' (2009) 19 *Qualitative Health Research* 258.

[30] D Engster, 'Rethinking Care Theory: The Practice of Caring and the Obligation to Care' (2005) 20 *Hypatia* 50.

activity and where the need is of such a nature that it cannot possibly be met by the person in need herself.[31]

It is worth emphasising two restrictions raised by Bubeck. The first is the restriction of 'face-to-face' interaction. This is clearly an attempt to exclude from the definition care through indirect means, such as providing money and arranging for another to provide care. I am not convinced by the need for such a hard line. True, most caring falling within my requirements will be face-to-face, but caring can involve arranging another's life. Indeed in some caring relationships, giving the other space; arranging things so they have increased independence will be the most caring way of treating them. I do not therefore include this as a requirement for care.

The other restriction is that the person cannot meet the need by themselves. Here, Bubeck draws a distinction between care and service. A wife who cooks a meal for her husband for when he returns home is providing a service because, presumably, he could have prepared that meal for himself. By contrast, preparing and serving food to a toddler, could be caring. While this factor could be significant in determining whether or not the care is of the kind that could be supported by the state, I do not think it can be used to produce a sharp definition of care. To use Bubeck's example, the toddler in fact might well be able to feed himself, but it would have been a messy, unhealthy production. Maybe the husband would have been able to cook his meal, but he would not have been able to stop in on his elderly mother and give her her medication if he had. The provision of her 'service' was done to enable care. I use these examples simply to show that it is not straightforward whether a person could have provided the care for themselves. Key, I suggest, are the elements of relationality and respect, which I raise shortly. Relationships in which one party meets the needs of another, all or most of which they could have met themselves, may not be relational or respectful. I would argue that these requirements meet Bubeck's concerns.

There is another reason why it is important to emphasise the practical nature of caring. In her writing, Julia Twigg[32] has done much to emphasise that care work is bodily.[33] She argues that much care involves negotiating nakedness, touch, dirt, disgust, and intimacy. Care work challenges the bounded nature of bodies. Bad odours not only leave one body but enter another. The foulness of the one body enters and interacts with her body. She suggests the fact it is 'dirty work' explains the low esteem in which it is held. Her argument is reinforced by the high respect given to doctors whose bodily work is limited to diagnoses,

---

[31] D Bubeck, *Care, Gender and Justice* (Clarendon Press, 1995) 129.

[32] J Twigg, 'Carework as a Form of Bodywork' (2000) 20 *Ageing and Society* 389.

[33] J Twigg, C Wolkowitz, R Cohen and S Nettleton, 'Conceptualising Body Work in Health and Social Care' (2011) 33 *Sociology of Health and Illness* 171; C Stacey, 'Finding Dignity in Dirty Work: The Constraints and Rewards of Law-Wage Home Care Labour' (2005) 27 *Sociology of Health & Illness* 831.

or mediated through machines, or performed in sterile environments, meaning that the dirtiness is avoided. Emphasising the activity in care work makes it clear we are not talking about high minded emotions, but hard work.

Clare Ungerson suggests that its bodily nature explains why care work has been seen as women's work. She argues that women are seen as appropriate dealers with bodily waste, reflecting assumptions that women's bodies are polluted. The fears and concern about the leaky body become connected to the 'disgusting' care work that is done.[34] Body work is seen as restoring a person to a desired state, so that we can maintain beliefs about the integrity of the body. As Julia Twigg puts it, 'women's work is here constructed out of the rejected and unacknowledged aspects of men's lives'.[35] This is why it is unacknowledged and unrewarded. We will return to some of these themes in chapter three.

ii. Respect

Respect is the second marker of care. It involves being alert to what the other needs and responding to those needs appropriately. It is not about treating the other as an object, but recognising them as a fellow human being with whom one is in a relationship. Robin Dillon[36] captures this with the word attention and argues:

> The term 'care' denotes here an epistemic attitude, understood as a moral ideal of attention: a commitment to attend, with intensely focused perception to all aspects of the irreducible particularity of individual human persons in their concrete contexts.[37]

There are four interconnected themes here that need to be unpacked.

First, respect involves recognising the fellow humanity in another. This involves not treating them in terms of categories or formulas, but recognising they are a unique individual. This means that caring involves a degree of empathy and anticipation.[38] These are needed to ensure that non-obvious needs are appreciated.

Second, respect involves listening to the other and ensuring, where possible, there is consent. It involves accepting that what most people might want in a particular case is not necessarily what the individual necessarily wants. They should be treated as an individual, not just a person with a particular condition.[39] Seeking out the particular needs and wishes of the other and seeking to meet them are an essential part of care.

---

[34] K England and I Dyck, 'Managing the Body Work of Home Care' (2011) 33 *Sociology of Health & Illness* 206.

[35] J Twigg, 'Carework as a Form of Bodywork' (2000) 20 *Ageing and Society* 389.

[36] R Dillon, 'Respect and Care' (1992) 22 *Canadian Journal of Philosophy* 105.

[37] Ibid 128.

[38] L Blum, *Moral Perception and Particularity* (Cambridge University Press, 1994) 30–61.

[39] V Dalmiya, 'Why Should a Knower Care?' (2002) 17 *Hypatia* 34.

Third, respect requires treating a person in a dignified way and respects their innate humanity. This may involve, for example, ensuring more intimate aspects of care are done in private and showing due respect for their abilities. This is separate from the previous requirement, because there may be a case where a person lacks capacity and is not objecting to the form of treatment, but to do it in public or in that ways undermines core notions of dignity.[40]

Fourth, respect requires an awareness of how the other person is experiencing the care. This involves interaction and engagement with the individual. Obviously care provided with no thought to the response of the person receiving it is in danger of objectifying the person receiving the care.[41]

This notion of respect shows why the emotional element is central to care. Imagine, for example, that there were mechanical or robotic devices available that could perform tasks that might otherwise be done by other humans. Apparently a human-washing machine, known as an 'assisted-care bath' has been created. Let us assume for a moment that a robot could be devised to carry out certain tasks, it is not clear that the level of care understood in the round would improve. The lack of social interaction and connectedness would be lost.[42]

I have used the word respect to describe the attitude reflected in good care. To some that may seem to be a word which lacks emotional warmth and they may prefer a word like affection or fondness. That, I suggest is inappropriate. While love and affection may well be involved in a caring relationship, it is not necessary. We will return to these themes when we discuss the relational aspect of care next.

iii. Responsibility

The best caring involves assuming a responsibility to care for another. Caring only when it is convenient is not the highest kind of care. That involves accepting a willingness to care, even where that was not one's preference. Of course, it may be that an individual is facing competing caring responsibilities and may not be able to meet all of them.

Caring, therefore, involves an acceptance of responsibility. In part this is because if one person enters a caring relationship with someone, others may not then offer care for that person. They may assume that any needs are met within that relationship. The parties in the relationship may not seek care from others, relying on each other to meet their needs. This is particularly likely to happen because a person's capacity to offer care is limited and inevitably can only be focused on a finite number of people.

---

[40] C Foster, *Human Dignity in Bioethics and the Law* (Hart, 2011).

[41] D Engster, *The Heart of Justice* (Oxford University Press, 2007) 55.

[42] J Parks, 'Lifting the Burden of Women's Care Work: Should Robots Replace the "Human Touch"?' (2010) 25 *Hypatia* 100.

There are, however, dangers in this kind of argument. Simply because two people are in a caring relationship does not thereby deprive others of any responsibility. The state would have an obligation to intervene if it was aware that the relationship was abusive. Others need to ensure an appropriate sharing of the burdens of care.

iv. Relationality

A central value in caring is that it should never be seen as uni-directional. Caring should be a relationship and therefore will require the person providing care to be open to receiving care.[43] Caring relationships require both (or all) parties to be open to receiving the support and help of the other.[44] Caring should be about a reciprocal relationship and not a one way street.[45]

Too much academic writing and the public discourse divides people up into 'carers' and 'cared for'. Carers UK, an excellent charity, focus on promoting the rights of carers. The Government produces documents promoting policies for carers.[46] Much of the academic writing on caring focuses on the work of carers. This creates an artificial divide between those who are carers and those who receive care. It overlooks the powerful disability critique of care, which we shall explore later. That argues that the emphasis on carers reduces the 'cared for' to a passive role.

Peter Beresford has captured the concerns over the idea of care well:

> ... The reality seems to be that while care might be regarded by many of us as a good idea in principle and something that some people might need at some time, few of us identify with it for ourselves and actually want to be 'cared for' in this sense. There is a strong reluctance to see ourselves or to be in this position, because it implies dependence. Care is a concept that is primarily associated with children. Models for adult caring have tended to be borrowed from childcare and grow out of the unequal relationships associated with looking after children. This has been the basis for many people's assumptions and understanding of such care.[47]

Whether care necessarily has these negative connotations may be questioned. There are certainly dangers, especially when the 'cared for' become reduced to no more than the object of receipt of care. This is why it is so important that we focus on caring relationships. When good care is seen as involving enabling and empowering both parties, some of the negative connotations fall away.

---

[43] V Dalmiya, 'Why Should a Knower Care?' (2002) 17 *Hypatia* 34.

[44] M Nolan, G Grant and J Keady, *Understanding Family Care* (Open University Press, 1996) 39.

[45] T Hassan, 'An Ethic of Care Critique', http://dspace.sunyconnect.suny.edu/bitstream/handle/1951/43954/An_Ethic_of_Care_Critique.pdf?sequence=1; S Ruddick, 'Care as Labor and Relationship' in J Haber and M Halfon (eds), *Norms and Values* (Rowman and Littlefield, 1998).

[46] HM Government, *Recognised, Valued and Supported: Next Steps for the Carers Strategy* (HM Government, 2010).

[47] P Beresford, *What Future for Care?* (Joseph Rowntree Foundation, 2008).

I would contrast an approach based on 'activity caring' and one based on 'relational caring'. The activity-based approach to care is likely to understand caring as involving 'doing something for someone else'.[48] The role of 'carer' and 'cared for' are clearly differentiated. Eva Feder Kittay, for example, states that care means 'the support and assistance one individual requires of another where the one in need of care is "inevitably dependent" that is, dependent because they are too young, too ill or impaired, or too frail, to manage daily self-maintenance alone'.[49] Hence she describes care as dependency work. This is not a distinction I would seek to emphasise. For me relationality is central to care. As Carol Gilligan writes, 'The ideal of care is thus an activity of relationships, of seeing and responding to need, taking care of the world by sustaining the web of connection so that no one is left alone.'[50] The relational view of care would emphasise interdependence over dependency; and mutual vulnerability over the frailty of one person. The relational approach is likely to see care in the context of the relationship between two people in which each is contributing care to the other: be that in terms of psychological, emotional or physical sense. Michael Fine and Caroline Glendinning capture this importance of the relational aspect of care in these words:

> Recent studies of care suggest that qualities of reciprocal dependence underlie much of what is termed 'care'. Rather than being a unidirectional activity in which an active care-giver does something to a passive and dependent recipient, these accounts suggest that care is best understood as the product or outcome of the relationship between two or more people.[51]

Activity caring regards the person needing care as being a problem, which the carer solves. This has the potential to glorify the 'carer' role, while downgrading the 'cared for' role. It produces an unequal relationship where the 'carer' has disproportionate power, over the dependant.[52] It is in danger of regarding dependency as a bad thing, with the aim of care to achieve independence for the person needing care. Michael Fine and Caroline Glendinning write of dependency:

> This has proved a complex concept. It has been seen by some politicians as a sign of moral weakness: 'the dependency culture'. By some sociologists it has been seen as a social construction of groups to permit paternalistic interventions; for others it

---

[48] C Ungerson (ed), *Gender and Caring: Work and Welfare in Britain and Scandinavia* (Harvester Wheatsheaf, 1990).

[49] E Feder Kittay, 'Dependency, Difference and the Global Ethic of Longterm Care' (2005) 13 *The Journal of Political Philosophy* 443.

[50] C Gilligan, *In a Different Voice* (Harvard University Press, 1982) 73.

[51] M Fine and C Glendinning, 'Dependence, Independence or Inter-Dependence? Revisiting the Concepts of Care and Dependency' (2005) 25 *Ageing and Society* 601, 619.

[52] J Orme, *Gender and Community Care* (Palgrave, 2001).

is what justifies intervention. It is interesting that independence is assumed to be an automatic good. It is linked to autonomy and that must be a good thing.[53]

In fact, as will be explained in chapter three, there is nothing wrong in being dependent. The activity caring concept has the potential to demean disabled people. This is such an important issue it deserves more extensive discussion and we will move on to that, after summarising my approach.

A good example of what I have in mind is the L'Arche community in which those with a range of abilities live. A study by Pamela Cushing and Tanya Lewis found many stories of mutually beneficial relationships in these communities.[54] All members of the community were open to learn from and grow with each other. To the community it is not a case of a set of 'carers' looking after 'those in need', but a community learning from, and helping, one another. To that community and to all good caring, the relationships are multi-directional. Those who might be labelled 'normal' gain as much from the community and give as much to it as those who would not be labelled 'normal'. Indeed it is only through abandoning the division between 'carer' and 'cared for' that the community thrives. What is revealing is that the power imbalances are recognised within the community, but are acknowledged and negotiated by the members. This provides a dramatic opposition to the normally negative portrayal of those with intellectual disabilities. The authors comment: 'In a healthy environment they can also reveal myriad, idiosyncratic gifts and talents that family or caregivers without intellectual disabilities can appreciate, foster, and learn from as they share their lives with them.'[55]

That is surely not news to those who live with, or are, people with learning or other disabilities. The 'mutuality of care' that was found in the L'Arche communities can be found in all caring relationships. The benefit of moving to a relational understanding of care is that care becomes an interrelationship and the 'dependent' person is not seen as an object which receives care, but a party to a relationship, giving and taking. Indeed studies of those in caring relationships show that these are often dynamic relationships with the precise quality of the relationship changing over time.[56]

This relational aspect is also important because it puts the activities within their context, a context which provides those acts with meaning.[57] The provision of care only makes sense and can be properly understood when placed in

---

[53] M Fine and C Glendinning, 'Dependence, Independence or Inter-Dependence? Revisiting the Concepts of Care and Dependency' (2005) 25 *Ageing and Society* 601.

[54] P Cushing and T Lewis, 'Negotiating Mutuality and Agency in Care-Giving Relationships with Women with Intellectual Disabilities' (2002) 17 *Hypatia* 173.

[55] Ibid.

[56] Eg L Skar and M Tamm, 'My Assistant and I: Disabled Children's and Adolescents' Roles and Relationships to their Assistants' (2001) 16 *Disability and Society* 917.

[57] M Daly and J Lewis, 'The Concept of Social Care and the Analysis of Contemporary Welfare' (2000) 51 *British Journal of Sociology* 281.

the context of the parties' relationships.[58] An act of caring for the parties can have a meaning well beyond the here and now. It may reflect a long-standing commitment or a mutual responsibility. The act may have overtones recalling aspects of the relationship many years ago. Consider the following comment from a woman about using her husband, Andy, as a 'carer':

> I prefer to have Andy's help as a caregiver as little as possible, simply because if your husband becomes your caregiver, then he isn't your husband any more. The relationship is blurred there. If I still want to be a person unto myself, then I don't want to include him in some parts of care, like a bowel treatment or a shower day.[59]

This quotation captures the fact that activities of care can take on different meanings, depending on the relationship between the parties. Here, because of their relationship, the most caring thing was for Andy not to undertake these tasks.

In saying that caring should be relational, I do not mean to imply it must necessarily be affectionate. In Clare Ungerson's analysis of emotion in caring relationships, she categorises them as cold, cool, warm and hot.[60] Interestingly in cold relationships, although the relationship was described as not emotional, in fact there were feelings of anger and resentment on both sides. Such relationships were easily brought to an end and were regarded as short-term relationships. Warm relationships were more common and characterised by 'acceptance and respect on both sides of the relationship'. The boundaries were clearly drawn and understood. Typically these involved cases where a carer had multiple clients. For warm relationships Ungerson notes:

> Such warmth often arose out of care relationships that had continued over a long period and the warmth itself meant that these relationships were not at risk of breaking down, at least in the short-term. Often the good feelings that people had for each other appeared to be a matter of serendipity and it is difficult therefore to relate the likelihood of warmth developing with a particular funding regime.[61]

Hot relationships were seen as established long-term relationships. They were volatile and not easy to exit. Typically, the carer was dependent on the person needing care for housing. Clare Ungerson comments:

> Given the core vulnerability of frail old age on the one hand, and illegal immigration on the other, combined with spatial proximity, very low wages, and twenty-four hour availability, it is not surprising that these relationships are full of feelings, not all of them healthy or likely to underwrite reasonable quality care.[62]

---

[58] S Schwarzenbach, 'On Civil Friendship' (1996) 107 *Ethics* 97, 102.

[59] K England and I Dyck, 'Managing the Body Work of Home Care' (2011) 33 *Sociology of Health & Illness* 206.

[60] C Ungerson, 'Care, Work and Feeling' (2005) 53 *The Sociological Review* 188.

[61] Ibid.

[62] Ibid.

Ungerson's discussion shows there are dangers with both emotionally 'hot' and emotionally 'cold' relationships in the context of care. It is hard to imagine a caring relationship which exhibits the characteristics in my model being cold.

It may be claimed that my discussion of relational care idealises the situation, especially with those with profound needs. While a baby can 'give back' to her mother in the relationship, as can a profoundly disabled person, it may be argued that to describe this as a relationship is to ignore the profound difference in the labour involved in the relationship and the distinction in the positions of power.[63] Diemut Bubeck argues that a key element of caring is that it:

> involves ... a one-sided dependency of the person in need of care on the prospective carer. Their relationship is not one between equals or of equal bargaining strength since the carer has the power to withhold care and the cared for's needs have to be met. This power differential is irreducible since the needs to be met cannot be met by those in need themselves.[64]

This raises an important concern about my approach. I would make three points in response.

First, it would be utterly wrong to assume that by saying care is relational, all relationships are good. That is why respect is such a key element of my understanding of care. An abusive relationship might contain elements of caring activities, but would not be caring if no respect was shown.

Second, the nature of power in a caring relationship is not straightforward. As Eva Feder Kittay argues, the disadvantage to one party flows to and impacts upon the other. Carers often report feeling powerless. It is simplistic, to see care as involving an exercise of power by the 'caregiver'.[65] A study of carers of patients with Alzheimer's found recipients of care resisting the attempts of others to provide care.[66] Some caregivers felt powerless in the situation. The pressures they face can mean they feel far from in charge in the relationship. There is a mutual powerlessness in the relationship. This is not, I repeat, not to say abuse cannot take place under the 'guise' of a relationship, but in a good caring relationship the issue of who has power over whom is a non-question.

Third, I fear some critics of the relational approach to care over-emphasise the rational and physical aspects of a relationship. A severely disabled patient might not readily be able to offer care in the traditional sense of offering services to the other. Objectively comprehensible communication may even be difficult. But relationships are made up of more than the doing of deeds

---

[63] E Feder Kittay, 'Dependency, Difference and the Global Ethic of Longterm Care' (2005) 13 *Journal of Political Philosophy* 433.

[64] D Bubeck, *Care, Gender and Justice* (Clarendon Press, 1995) 141.

[65] C Chorn Dunham and J Harms Cannon, '"They're Still in Control Enough to be in Control": Paradox of Power in Dementia Caregiving' (2008) 22 *Journal of Aging Studies* 45.

[66] Ibid.

and the saying of words. A touch, an expression, the slightest smile, can convey great warmth. Further, the care needs to be seen in the context of the whole relationship between the parties and while appearing more one-sided at this point in time, when looked at in the context of the whole relationship between the parties it will be viewed differently. As Wendy Holloway notes:

> But it is impossible to separate the practices of meeting needs from the psychological meanings, imported from many quarters, which even simple acts will carry .... [A]ny relationship carries with it the meanings that have built up through the life histories of both parties.[67]

The argument that those with serious disabilities cannot engage in a relationship suggests too narrow an understanding of how parties can relate to each other.

Finally, and this issue will be explored more in chapter three, the relational approach captures the merging of identities which can occur in care, where the boundaries between 'me and you' and 'my body and your body' become merged. Talk of one party having power over the other or an unequal contribution makes no sense, in the closest of caring relationships, where the two merge together as one. In a good caring relationship there is no competition for benefits.

v. Summary of My Approach

In short, my approach to defining care is centred on care as a relational activity. At its heart is doing that which meets the needs of the parties. I argue that caring involves an attitude of respect and acceptance of responsibility. It requires an awareness of the wishes of each party and due respect of that. It also involves a taking on of obligations to meet the care needs of each other. It does not require love or even affection. The exhausted disinterested nappy changer is caring, even if they don't exactly have that warm fuzzy feeling at the time![68] I would emphasise that my model of care is seeking to present care at its best. It not meant to set parameters so that behaviour which does not exhibit these characteristics is not necessarily uncaring.

Crucially, I argue that caring must be seen in the context of the relationship between the parties. As Eva Feder Kittay argues:

> There appear to be universal aspects of the meaning and experience of caring. In a paradigmatic sense, all caregiving involves a direct, intimate relationship between two or more people. All caregiving occurs in a psychological and social context that has

---

[67] W Hollway, 'Introducing the Capacity to Care' in W Hollway (ed), *The Capacity to Care: Gender and Ethical Subjectivity* (Routledge, 2006).

[68] A Mullin, 'Parents and Children: An Alternative to Selfless and Unconditional Love' (2006) 21 *Hypatia* 181.

shaped, and shapes the experiences of the participants in the caring practice. All caring, therefore, is at once intensely personal and inextricably social, symbolic, and meaningful. It is both deeply emotional and a rational, pragmatic, and practical endeavor. It is a practice that comprises certain fundamental moral virtues and human goods.[69]

There is a danger in the approach I advocate in that caring covers such a 'multitude of sins' that it loses all meaning! If we are all in mutually interdependent caring relationships, in what way can we provide legal intervention, support, or regulation for caring relationships? That, in part, is what I seek to set out in this book. For now it is enough to note that they may be particular circumstances in which some caring relationships will require or deserve support and/or legal regulations and others that don't. Similarly, there may be individuals in those relationships which due to their roles require particular forms of legal intervention. This is not to deny that there are many forms of caring relationship, it is rather to acknowledge that not all caring relationships require the same legal response.

It should also be acknowledged that there are grave dangers in presenting 'caring relationships' as an homogenous category. Of course they are not. The needs and interests of frail spouses looking after each other may be very different from those of neighbours keeping an eye out for each other or a child looking after a parent. Further, there may be particular issues facing carers on the grounds of their age,[70] gender, race or sexual orientation.[71] The nature of caring relationships involving mothering, nursing, old age, or friendship may all be very different and not readily susceptible to a single set of principles.[72] This is true, but it should not overlook the linking features of what it is to care. As suggested above, we can find similarities in care, without thinking that the legal and social response to all caring relationships should be the same.

III. The Disability Critique of Care

As already indicated, a strong attack on the notion of care has come from some writing from a disability perspective.[73] In order to fully appreciate this critique it is necessary to take a broader look at disability.[74]

---

[69] E Feder Kittay, 'Dependency, Difference and the Global Ethic of Longterm Care' (2005) 13 *Journal of Political Philosophy* 433.
[70] C Dearden and S Becker, *Young Carers in the UK: The 2004 Report* (Carers UK, 2004).
[71] J Manthorpe and E Price, 'Lesbian Carers: Personal Issues and Policy Responses' (2005) 5 *Social Policy & Society* 15.
[72] P Bowden, *Caring: Gender-Sensitive Ethics* (Routledge, 1997).
[73] For an excellent discussion see T Shakespeare, *Disability Rights and Wrongs* (Routledge, 2006).
[74] M Oliver, 'The Individual and Social Models of Disability' (1990) www.leeds.ac.uk/disability-studies/archiveuk/Oliver/in%20soc%20dis.pdf.

There has been considerable debate over whether disability should be seen on an individual or social model. For the individual model the problem with disability lies within the individual. The cause of any problems flowing from disability is the limited functional or psychological loss the individual is thought to suffer from. Janet Radcliffe Richards describes the individual model as the 'common sense' one, which generates a clear response:

> The common sense view of disability is the one according to which disability is a characteristic of the disabled person, and a straightforward misfortune. And, as with other misfortunes, moral questions arise about how much effort society as a whole ought to put into trying to prevent or alleviate them and what forms that effort should take .... The question of what form the attempts at remedy should take seems ... to have fairly clear answers. The first aim should be to eliminate the problem at its roots by trying to eliminate disability, either by preventing the existence of disabled people in the first place, or by using our increasing skills to cure their disabilities. To the extent that we cannot do that, we should supply devices (including human and animal helpers) that provide substitutes for the missing ability. And finally, for the disabled whom we cannot enable properly by any of these means, we should minimize the impact of disability as far as practicable by adapting the environment, by making a range of special concessions, and by improving interactions between able and disabled people.[75]

The social model, by contrast, sees the problems flowing from disability as society's failure to provide the necessary services to ensure no difficulties flow from the difference in function or psychology. This model might point out that none of us would survive without a whole range of services to deal with the difficulties we would face alone: be it shops; transport; sewerage, etc. We all need social services to a greater or less extent. We all have a range of limitations and society is willing to meet some but not all of them. Those which society does not meet are labelled as disability. The defining characteristic of a disability on this model is not located within the individual, but rather the lack of provision within society. The 1976 Union of Physically Impaired Against Segregation (UPIAS), adopting the social model, defined disability in the following way:

> Disability is something imposed on top of our impairments by the way we are unnecessarily isolated and excluded from full participation in society. Disabled people are therefore an oppressed group in society. To understand this it is necessary to grasp the distinction between the physical impairment and the social situation, called 'disability,' of people with such impairment. Thus, we define impairment as lacking part of or all of a limb, or having a defective limb, organ or mechanism of the body; and disability as the disadvantage or restriction of activity caused by a contemporary social organization which takes no or little account of people who have physical impairments and thus excludes them from participation in the mainstream of social activities. Physical disability is therefore a particular form of social oppression.[76]

---

[75] J Radcliffe Richards, 'How Not to End Disability' (2002) 39 *San Diego Law Review* 693, 695.
[76] Union of Physically Impaired Against Segregation, *Fundamental Principles of Disability* (UPIAS, 1975).

Of course this debate between the social and individual models of disability is complex and has become intense.[77] This book is not the place to explore all the issues properly. I would argue in favour of some kind of middle route between the two schools of thought. While the effects of many 'disabilities' can be mitigated by the provision of social support, it is not possible to completely eradicate the impact of serious disabilities, whatever services are provided. As John Gardner and Timothy Macklem argue,[78] although a wheelchair can in some ways be as good as a pair of legs,

> the experience of walking is also independently valuable. We don't hike merely to get there. We don't stroll around the park just to reach the other side. Those in wheelchairs are excluded by that fact from the hiking and the strolling and the independent goodness of those activities.

The authors are quick to add that the opposite can be said that those 'who walk, miss out on the wheelchair user's special wheelchair-use abilities'. Despite this they argue it would be wrong simply to say the disabled are differently abled. They conclude:

> although we (Tim and John) can walk perfectly well either or both of us could still opt for life in a wheelchair. We have that luxury. The wheelchair-bound person does not have the option of walking, and it follows that the wheelchair, for him or her, is not a luxury.

While that may be true for that example, there are many other disabilities where it is not. I cannot experience the world as an autistic person does; or experience the soundlessness or soundfulness of the deaf. Further, we should recognise that we all have our vulnerabilities. We are all dependent on others and social provisions for a broad range of things that are important to our lives. We tend as a society to be proud of the 'accommodations' (such as wheelchair ramps) that we create to help 'disabled people', while ignoring all the many accommodations that are made for 'non-disabled people'. While, therefore, accepting the Gardner and Macklem point that some people's bodies mean that there are limitations on what they can do, we should recognise that that is true for all of us.[79]

For this book the more relevant debate is over the attitude towards care. As the social model supporters point out, there are dangers in assuming that a disability must be 'remedied' by care. Care involves interfering in the body

---

[77] J Swain and S French, 'Disability and Communication: Listening is Not Enough' in S Barrett, C Komarony, M Robb and A Rogers (eds), *Communication, Relationships and Care: A Reader* (Routledge, 2004). J Harris, 'One Principle and Three Fallacies of Disability Studies' (2001) 27 *Journal of Medical Ethics* 383.

[78] J Gardner and T Macklem, 'Human Disability', available at http://users.ox.ac.uk/~lawf0081/pdfs/humandisability.pdf.

[79] R Garland-Thomson, 'Integrating Disability, Transforming Feminist Theory' (2002) 14 *NWSA Journal* 1.

of the individual rather than changing societal provisions. It assumes the characteristics of a 'disabled person' are automatically undesirable or need to be regarded as a misfortune, generating a need for care. A comparison may be made to the disadvantages suffered by women in society. The answer is not to try and 'cure' women so they are more like men, but rather to change society so that disadvantages do not flow from being a woman. This leads supporters of the social model to be more sceptical about care or medical treatments designed to amend 'disabled bodies' or limit the impact of disability rather than seeking social means of overcoming the disadvantages flowing from disabilities.[80]

It is not just the broader political argument which concerns some writing from a disability perspective about care. Care can be experienced in a negative way. As one disabled person wrote:

> We are who we are as people with impairments, and might actually feel comfortable with our lives if it wasn't for all those interfering busybodies who feel that it is their responsibility to feel sorry for us, or to find cures for us, or to manage our lives for us, or to harry us in order to make us something we are not, i.e. 'normal'.[81]

Richard Woods[82] contends:

> Disabled people have never demanded or asked for care! We have sought independent living, which means being able to achieve maximum independence and control over our own lives. The concept of care seems to many disabled people a tool through which others are able to dominate and manage our lives.

As this last quote indicates, many disability rights activists emphasise independence.[83] Rather than being the objects of care, they argue, disabled people need to be able to exercise control over the help.[84] Care, therefore, should not be seen as something a 'carer' does to the other, but as a tool used by the disabled person to achieve independence.[85] The focus should be on empowerment, control and choice for those with disabilities, even if self-sufficiency is not possible.[86] Some disability rights activists have argued for the use of

---

[80] M Oliver, 'The Individual and Social Models of Disability' (1990) www.leeds.ac.uk/disability-studies/archiveuk/Oliver/in%20soc%20dis.pdf.

[81] Colin, quoted in S French and J Swain, 'Whose Tragedy? Towards a Personal Non-Tragedy View of Disability' in J Swain, S French, J Barnes and M Thomas (eds) *Disabling Barriers— Enabling Environments* (Sage, 2004) 54.

[82] Quoted in T Shakespeare, *Help* (Venture Press, 2000) 63.

[83] N Watson, L McKie, B Hughes, D Hopkins and S Gregory, '(Inter)Dependence, Needs and Care: The Potential for Disability and Feminist Theorists to Develop an Emancipatory Model' (2010) 38 *Sociology* 221.

[84] S Brisenden, *A Charter for Personal Care* (Disablement Income Group, 1989) 9–10.

[85] J Morris, 'Impairment and Disability: Constructing an Ethics of Care that Promotes Human Rights' (2001) 16 *Hypatia* 1.

[86] A Vernon and H Qureshi, 'Community Care and Independence: Self-Sufficiency or Empowerment?' (2000) 20 *Critical Social Policy* 255.

the term 'helper' or 'personal assistant'[87] rather than carer, in an attempt to remove any implication that the person needing care is suffering a particular misfortune, which needs attention, or is passive in the enterprise.[88] The helper is assisting the disabled person to achieve what they wish for.

Another way of analysing this issue is to recognise that power is a theme in caring relationships.[89] Zygmunt Bauman warns that 'the impulse to care for the other, when taken to its extreme, leads to the annihilation of the autonomy of the other, to domination and oppression'.[90] Julia Twigg's recent qualitative research on older people's experiences of being bathed highlights this quite clearly:

> One person, strong and able, stands above and over another who is frail and physically vulnerable, forced to rely on their strength and goodwill. Being naked in the face of someone who is not, contains a powerful dynamic of domination and vulnerability, and it is often used in situations of interrogation and torture as a means of subjugating the individual.[91]

This is a powerful critique of care.[92] The lack of perspective of those 'receiving care' in the care literature should be a cause of considerable embarrassment. Much is written in the care literature on the social isolation of carers; the personal and economic disadvantage of carers; and the lack of recognition that carers are given in society. This is all welcome and important, but in making such points those 'receiving' the care and the disadvantages they face have also been ignored. Further, there is the possibility that the abuse of care gets overlooked in the care literature.

This disablist critique leads me to prefer the relational model of care, explained above, and therefore to talk of caring relationships, rather than carers. The traditional division between the carer and person receiving care fails to capture the dynamic in caring relationships. It tends to emphasise the vulnerability of some, rather than recognising the vulnerability of all. It paints the 'cared for' as passive. By seeing caring relationships, we can recognise that we are all givers and receivers of care. Maybe in different ways and the kinds of care involved are different. The language of caring relationships can capture the dynamic nature of relationships. Caregiving relationships change over time so that pigeonholing the parties into categories of carer and care receiver become artificial.

---

[87] C Kelly, 'Making "Care" Accessible: Personal Assistance for Disabled People and the Politics of Language' (2011) 31 *Critical Social Policy* 562.

[88] B Hughes, L McKie, D Hopkins, N Watson, 'Love's Labours Lost? Feminism, the Disabled People's Movement and an Ethic of Care' (2005) 39 *Sociology* 259.

[89] T Shakespeare, *Help* (Venture Press, 2000); M Daly, 'Care as a Good for Social Policy' (2002) 31 *Journal of Social Policy* 251.

[90] Z Bauman, *Postmodern Ethics* (Blackwell, 1993) 11.

[91] J Twigg, 'Carework as a Form of Bodywork' (2000) 20 *Ageing and Society* 389.

[92] A Silvers, 'Reconciling Equality to Difference: Caring (f)or Justice for People with Disabilities' (1995) 10 *Hypatia* 30.

Janet Fink argues that the failure to include evidence of the lives of disabled people has had several effects:

> First, it has perpetuated the continuing tendency of discourses of care to consti-tute disabled people as an inevitable burden on their families, thereby setting up a dichotomy between 'normal' families and families with disabled members. This suggests that one set of relationships is benign and 'the other is problematic and pathological'. Second, it has elided the ways in which care relationships can be understood as being built around elements of reciprocity and interdependence, failing, thereby, to acknowledge that in some places and at some times, we have all experienced giving and receiving care.[93]

There is another important point here and that is the division of 'carer' is not only false because it imagines that one party to the relationship is the provider of the care, it also overlooks the point that the 'carer' may themselves be receiving care from others.[94] Notably 378,000 carers are themselves registered as perma-nently sick or disabled according to official statistics.[95] Thus, it is more accurate to acknowledge the networks of care that we live in, rather than dividing us up into providers of and recipients of care.[96] All of us fall into both categories.

There is yet further significance in focusing on relationships of care.[97] The discrimination against those seen as having a disability or infirmity can oper-ate as a disadvantage to those in a relationship with them. Negative attitudes about disability are reflected in negative attitudes about care. As Bill Hughes and his colleagues[98] put it:

> the parties involved in the caring relationship are perpetually invalidated because the value of care is measured against the autonomous adult male who neither requires nor delivers care. To be a carer or cared for—male or female, disabled or non-disabled in either role—is to be found wanting, to be other in relation to the masculine subject of modernity, to be reduced to 'the other of the same'. Those who give and receive care are marginalized, 'used and wasted' bodies, existing, by and large, on the margins of what counts as the truly human community.[99]

To conclude, the disability critique of care is powerful. It highlights the dangers in seeing care as an activity done by one person to another. However, I have argued that by considering caring relationships and acknowledging

---

[93] J Fink, *Care Personal Lives and Social Policy* (Policy Press, 2004) 14.

[94] N Watson, L McKie, B Hughes, D Hopkins and S Gregory, '(Inter)Dependence, Needs and Care: The Potential for Disability and Feminist Theorists to Develop an Emancipatory Model' (2010) 38 *Sociology* 221.

[95] Carers UK, *Facts About Carers* (Carers UK, 2009).

[96] C Beckett, 'Women, Disability, Care: Good Neighbours or Uneasy Bedfellows?' (2007) 27 *Critical Social Policy* 360.

[97] N Watson, L McKie, B Hughes, D Hopkins and S Gregory, '(Inter)Dependence, Needs and Care: The Potential for Disability and Feminist Theorists to Develop an Emancipatory Model' (2010) 38 *Sociology* 221.

[98] B Hughes, L McKie, D Hopkins and N Watson, 'Love's Labours Lost? Feminism, the Disabled People's Movement and an Ethic of Care' (2005) 39 *Sociology* 259.

[99] Ibid.

the vulnerability and care offered by all, we can move to a model which recognises that we all need different forms of care. We are all dependent on others; all recipients and givers of care, albeit in different ways and at different times.

IV. Paid and Unpaid Care

There is quite some debate over whether care should include both paid and unpaid care.[100] In fact, the distinction between the two is becoming increasingly blurred. As will be discussed later in chapter four, those needing care are often being given budgets which they can use to pay friends or relatives to care for them. This provides a route whereby some informal care can become paid. Under the benefits system the financial recognition of 'carers' includes direct payments and pensions credits.

The idea that 'paid carers' are professionals, while 'unpaid carers' are amateurs is not sustainable. Indeed some carers object to the term 'informal carer' being used to describe family carers precisely because it suggests their care is casual or unskilled, which is far from the truth.[101] Personal care can involve a high degree of skill and sensitivity.[102] Nevertheless, there are characteristics which are likely to flow from paid care and less likely to be associated with unpaid care. These would include:

(i)   Formalism. Care being seen as a set of tasks to be completed as part of a job, rather as part of a relationship.
(ii)   Regulation. A paid carer is likely to be subject to regulation, oversight and supervision. Typically unpaid carers operate outside external examination.
(iii) Emotion. A paid carer would not be expected to receive from the relationship, except through payment.

There are concerns that the nature of care will change if it becomes contractualised. Linda Pickard and Caroline Glendinning explain that caring 'is boundless: it is not contained within a specific timescale, but is virtually limitless, characterised by spontaneous, unexpected events or crises which could occur at any time, with demands being made during the night experienced as

---

[100] L Lloyd, 'Call us Carers: Limitations and Risks in Campaigning for Recognition and Exclusivity' (2006) 26 *Critical Social Policy* 945.

[101] Eg S Payne, P Smith and S Dean, 'Identifying the Needs of Informal Carers in Palliative Care' (1999) 13 *Palliative Medicine* 37.

[102] P Beresford, *What Future for Care?* (Joseph Rowntree Foundation, 2008).

particularly onerous.'[103] This nature may be lost if carework is fitted within a model used for employment. We shall return to this important issue in chapter four.

The charity Carers UK is keen for the term carer to only be used in relation to unpaid carers. The benefit of this would be that there would be no confusion when claims are made to improve the conditions of carers.[104] Liz Lloyd criticises this approach due to its differentiation from carers and those in need of care.[105] She does recognise the benefits of providing carers with an identity and ready access to services. However, sharply identifying a group identity carries the danger of over-simplifying what care involves[106] and excluding those who do not fit the classic mode of a carer.[107] Liz Lloyd asks, 'if caring is a normal activity, the effect of which is likely to be felt by all of us, what is the logic of establishing an exclusive grouping with a specific and separate identity?'

Another danger of separating paid and unpaid carers is that it is incorrect to assume that poverty or inequality is only found among unpaid carers.[108] Paid carers can suffer poverty and exclusion too. Liz Lloyd suggests

> A more productive approach would be to develop a collective political voice that highlights the shortcomings in community care services and the impact of these on all those who support, including disabled and older people as well as paid and unpaid carers.[109]

I find Lloyd's analysis compelling. However, it should be borne in mind that the rhetoric of carers has proved a powerful tool.

The Government definition (cited at page 13) suggests that a distinction can be drawn between a family member offering care and a friend, neighbour or others. This distinction is far from convincing. The quality and nature of the care must certainly be viewed within the context of the relationship. Yet the blood tie between the carer and the cared for plays no part in that. While many family members do care for each other, many do not. It is the care and the actual relationship between the parties, rather than the blood ties, which

---

[103] S Pickard and C Glendinning, 'Comparing and Contrasting the Role of Family Carers and Nurses in the Domestic Health Care of Frail Older People' (2002) 10 *Health and Social Care in the Community* 144.

[104] Carers UK, *A Manifesto for Carers* (Carers UK, 2005).

[105] L Lloyd, 'Call us Carers: Limitations and Risks in Campaigning for Recognition and Exclusivity' (2006) 26 *Critical Social Policy* 945.

[106] N Fraser, 'Rethinking Recognition: Overcoming Displacement and Reification in Cultural Politics' in B Hobson (ed), *Recognition Struggles and Social Movements: Contested Identities, Agency and Power* (Cambridge University Press, 2003).

[107] B Bytheway and J Johnson, 'The Social Construction of "Carers"' in A Symonds and A Kelly (eds), *The Social Construction of Community Care* (Macmillan, 1998); K Stalker, 'Carers: An Overview of Concepts, Developments and Debates' in K Stalker (ed), *Reconceptualising Work with Carers: New Directions for Policy and Practice* (Jessica Kingsley Press, 2002).

[108] J Nelson, 'Feminist Philosophies of Love and Work' (2002) 17 *Hypatia* 1.

[109] L Lloyd, 'Call us Carers: Limitations and Risks in Campaigning for Recognition and Exclusivity' (2006) 26 *Critical Social Policy* 945.

are crucial. Consider, for example, an adoptive parent and child: there is no reason to think that the relationship between an adoptive parent and child is any different from that between a biological parent and child. While a blood tie may impact on the sense of obligation, it is the quality of the day to day relationship of care which matters more than the blood tie between the parties.[110] So too for all in a caring relationship.

V. Gender and Caring

Central to understanding the treatment of care is its gendered nature. Throughout history care has been regarded as the work of 'slaves, servants, and women'.[111] Through the lowly treatment of care, the privileged position of men has been maintained.[112]

The statistics indicate that women undertake the majority of the carework.[113] Although an increasing number of men have been involved,[114] women still disproportionately bear the care burden.[115] The most accurate figures come from the 2001 Census. Then 11 per cent of women were someone's main carer, compared to 7 per cent of men. Five per cent of women were engaged in more than 20 hours per week in caring tasks, as opposed to 3 per cent of men.[116] In the 50–59 age group, 17 per cent of all men and 24 per cent of all women were carers.[117] Of the 4.3 million working age carers, 1.8 million were men and 2.4 million were women, although in terms of hours spent, women undertook a higher number, supplying around 70 per cent of all care hours.[118] However, in the later stages of life there appeared to be more male carers than female, with the 2001 Census indicating that there were 179,000 male carers over the

---

[110] Of course the extent to which the genetic tie should carry weight is hotly debated.

[111] J Tronto, *Moral Boundaries: A Political Argument for an Ethic of Care* (Routledge, 1983) 21.

[112] Ibid.

[113] F Bettio and J Platenga, 'Comparing Gender Regimes in Europe' (2004) 10 *Feminist Economics* 85; E Watson and J Mears, *Women, Work and Care of the Elderly* (Ashgate, 1999); E Feder Kittay, *Love's Labour: Essays on Women, Equality and Dependency* (Routledge, 1999); J Parks, *No Place Like Home? Feminist Ethics and Home Health Care* (Indiana University Press, 2003).

[114] C Ungerson, 'Thinking about the Production and Consumption of Long-Term Care in Britain: Does Gender still Matter?' (2000) 29 *Journal of Social Policy* 623.

[115] F Carmichael and S Charles, 'The Opportunity Costs of Informal Care: Does Gender Matter?' (2003) 22 *Journal of Health Economics* 781.

[116] L Dahlbert, S Demack and C Bambra, 'Age and Gender of Informal Carers: A Population-Based Study in the UK' (2007) 15 *Health and Social Care in the Community* 439.

[117] House of Commons Work and Pensions Committee, *Valuing and Supporting Carers* (The Stationery Office, 2008) para 17.

[118] House of Commons Work and Pensions Committee, *Valuing and Supporting Carers* (The Stationery Office, 2008) para 344.

age of 75 and 169,000 female carers.[119] The impact of care affects women more harshly than men in economic terms. The likelihood of a male carer giving up paid employment as a result of caring responsibilities was 12.9 per cent; whereas for females it was 27 per cent.[120]

The gendered division of care labour in marriage and intimate relation-ships is marked. On marriage or cohabitation, women's care work increased by 4.2 hours and men's decreased by 3.6 hours.[121] Women still undertook the majority of child care.[122] Even where both parents were working full time, women did 75 per cent of the child care.[123] This was so whether physical, moral or emotional care was considered.[124] Women were not just dispropor-tionately represented among those giving care. Sixty one per cent of people receiving care were women. In 33 per cent of cases, a carer looked after a spouse or partner, 13 per cent a disabled child and a friend in only 9 per cent of cases.[125] Whether you look at care in the home, or care outside the home to relatives, friends, neighbours and through voluntary groups to strangers, the bulk is done by women.[126] Even where women are in paid employment, their care responsibilities constitute a 'second shift'[127] or even 'third shift' where they take on responsibilities not only for family members but also for friends.[128] It is true that in the past decade or so we have seen that an increas-ing number of men have been involved.[129] The study which shows the highest proportion of men's care work is the European Panel Survey, which reported that women average 22 hours per week caring, as compared to 18 hours for men.[130] While some recent studies have suggested a dramatic increase in men's reported child care and housekeeping responsibilities,[131] it is unclear to what extent this reflects a real change or merely a change in what men feel they ought to do and so the studies may reflect over-reporting.[132]

---

[119] L Beesley, *Informal Care In England* (King's Fund, 2006).

[120] F Carmichael, S Charles, 'The Opportunity Costs Of Informal Care: Does Gender Matter?' (2003) 22 *Journal of Health Economics* 781.

[121] B Featherstone, *Contemporary Fathering* (Policy Press, 2009) 26.

[122] K Silbaugh, *'Turning Labor into Love: Housework and the Law'* (1996) 91 *Northwestern University Law Review* 1, 82–83.

[123] B Featherstone, *Contemporary Fathering* (Policy Press, 2009) 26.

[124] Whirlpool Corporation, *Report Card on the New Providers: Kids and Moms Speak* (Whirlpool, 1999).

[125] Information Centre, NHS, *Survey of Carers in Households* 2009/2010 (Information Centre, NHS, 2011).

[126] N Gerstel, 'The Third Shift: Gender and Care Work Outside the Home' (2000) 23 *Qualitative Sociology* 467.

[127] A Hochschild, *The Second Shift* (Avon, 1989).

[128] N Gerstel, 'The Third Shift: Gender and Care Work Outside the Home' (2000) 23 *Qualitative Sociology* 467.

[129] C Ungerson, 'Thinking about the Production and Consumption of Long-Term Care in Britain: Does Gender Still Matter?' (2000) 29 *Journal of Social Policy* 623.

[130] S Harper, *Families in Ageing Societies* (Oxford University Press, 2004) ch 6.

[131] R Neno, 'Male Carers: Myth or Reality?' (2004) *Nursing Older People* 14.

[132] J Press and E Townsley, 'Wives' and Husbands' Housework Reporting: Gender, Class, and Social Desirability' (1998) 12 *Gender & Society* 188.

A number of reasons have been put forward for why women do more care work than men. These include essentialist claims that women are biologically attuned to care more than men;[133] that differences in socialisation mean that the drive to care is stronger in women than men;[134] and that there are powerful social forces in legal structures and social expectations that push women into caring roles, specifically that family and employment structures restrict women into caring roles.[135] The essentialist claims hold little validity in biological terms.[136] The most popular view is that the answer lies within a combination of the latter two factors.

Caring has become tied up in society's expectations around womanhood. Hilary Graham[137] argues: 'Caring is "given" to women: it becomes the defining characteristic of their self-identity and their lifework. At the same time, caring is taken away from men: not caring becomes a defining characteristic of manhood.'

Caring has become tied up with the ideals of wife and mother. Diemut Bubeck argues:

> women's self-respect and feelings of self-worth do not necessarily depend so much on any of the public indicators of power such as success, powerful positions, or control of material resources, but often on their being needed by and being able to help others.[138]

Bubeck is certainly not claiming that women should feel like this or that this is a natural feeling. Rather it is the strong social expectation that makes women feel obliged to do this. She explains:

> Caring as an activity, disposition, and attitude forms a central part of probably all cultural conceptions of femininity and is virtually absent from, or even incompatible with, conceptions of masculinity. In these conceptions, woman the carer or nurturer is opposed to and contrasted with man the hunter or fighter. Caring is part of what it is, or even entirely what it is, to be a woman: caring supposedly comes naturally to women, hence the care for husband, children, parents, relatives, neighbours, and more generally the needy is supposed to be the ultimate fulfilment in women's lives. Men, by contrast, are supposed to be fighters. If they are not involved in physical fight or war and can express their masculinity in this way, they express it by being competitive and more generally by having, and being in, power.[139]

Of course, the nature of women's lives is changing. It has become easier for women to enter the professions and use hired staff to take on their care work. However, those hired staff are largely women. Ironically, this furthers social

---

[133] See discussion in E Maccoby, *The Two Sexes* (Belknap Press, 1998).

[134] C Gilligan, *In a Different Voice* (Harvard University Press, 1982).

[135] J Lorber, *Paradoxes of Gender* (Yale University Press, 1994).

[136] W Hollway, *The Capacity to Care: Gender and Ethical Subjectivity* (Routledge, 1996).

[137] H Graham, 'Caring: A Labour of Love' in J Finch and D Groves (eds), *A Labour of Love: Women, Work and Caring* (Routledge & Kegan Paul, 1983) 18.

[138] D Bubeck, *Care, Gender and Justice* (Clarendon Press, 1995) 148.

[139] Ibid 160.

inequality and is a real concern for feminism.[140] This is particularly true as hired staff can suffer low wages; sexual harassment; lack legal protection; all of which adds to the general devaluing of care work. As Audrey Macklin bluntly states,

> The grim truth is that some women's access to the high-paying, high-status professions is being facilitated through the revival of semi-indentured servitude. Put another way, one woman is exercising class and citizenship privilege to buy her way out of sex oppression.[141]

Dorothy Roberts suggests we are even witnessing a categorising between different kinds of care work:

> Domestic labor is divided into two aspects—the spiritual and the menial. Some work in the home is considered spiritual: it is valued highly because it is thought to be essential to the proper functioning of the household and the moral upbringing of children. Other domestic work is considered menial: it is devalued because it is strenuous and unpleasant and is thought to require little moral or intellectual skill. While the ideological opposition of home and work distinguishes men from women, the ideological distinction between spiritual and menial housework fosters inequality among women. Spiritual housework is associated with privileged white women; menial housework is associated with minority, immigrant, and working class women. Recent welfare reform laws, which require poor women to leave home to assume menial jobs, highlight the importance of identifying and shattering this dichotomy in women's domestic labor.[142]

There is, therefore, no getting away from the gendered significance of care work. However, the nature of care and its impact on the lives of women, also varies depending on race, class and sexuality.

VI. The Status of Carers

For a long time care work has not been acknowledged by the state or the law.[143] Susan Dodds states that carers have been undervalued, exploited and expected to offer unrealistic standards of care.[144] Care work was seen as a private matter of little public significance. However, as mentioned at the start of

---

[140] J Tronto, 'The "Nanny" Question in Feminism' (2002) 17 *Hypatia* 34.

[141] A Macklin, 'On the Outside Looking in: Foreign Domestic Workers in Canada' in W Giles and S Arat-Koç, *Maid in the Market: Women's Paid Domestic Labor* (Fernwood Publishing, 1994) 34.

[142] D Roberts, 'Spiritual and Menial Housework' (1997) 9 *Yale Journal of Law and Feminism* 51.

[143] HM Government, *Carers at the Heart of 21st-Century Families and Communities* (The Stationery Office, 2008).

[144] S Dodds, 'Depending on Care: Recognition of Vulnerability and the Social Contribution of Care Provisions' (2007) 21 *Bioethics* 500.

this chapter, that is changing. The role of carers is acknowledged.[145] In *Carers at the Heart of 21st-Century Families and Communities*, the Government purported to undertake a major re-examination of the relationship between carers and the state. That work is still ongoing. We will explore in chapter four the reasons for the increased recognition of the social value of care work.

The changing attitudes to care do not simply reflect concerns about the economic costs. They reflect broader social changes. Our attitude towards how we wish to be cared for in old age appears to be changing, or at least our expectations are changing.[146] One recent survey of middle-aged people thought it unlikely that their children could take on their care if they were to need it. More significantly, they did not think their children ought to, nor did they think their children should feel that they ought.[147] The expectation of family care may be weakening.

The Government has acknowledged these changing social attitudes towards care:

> Family life has changed over the last 50 or so years. The move to smaller nuclear families means that it is no longer as easy to share the caring role as widely as in the past. Society is more mobile and families are more geographically dispersed. More families rely on two incomes, or longer working hours, to maintain an adequate standard of living. Many families find it difficult to balance work with the care needs of friends and relatives without significantly impacting on their own standard of living, esteem and independence—the lifestyle to which the family has become accustomed.[148]

Other social changes have played an important role too. The increasing rates of paid employment among women; higher rates of family breakdown and increased levels of informal relationships have all played their role in impacting on the availability or perceived desirability of offering or receiving care.[149] Robert Goodwin and Diane Gibson[150] have written of the 'decasualisation' of care. In the past, they suggest, care of dependents was casual, not in the sense of being unloving or unthoughtful, but rather that it was simply integrated into normal everyday life. A person would not see themselves as specifically spending some time caring or undertaking a care task. Doing so would

---

[145] The Princess Royal Trust for Carers, *Eight Hours a Day and Taken for Granted* (PRTC, 1998); P Smith, 'Elder Care, Gender, and Work: The Work-Family Issue of the 21st Century' (2004) 25 *Berkeley Journal of Employment and Labour Law* 351.

[146] R Levenson, M Jeyasingham, and N Joule, *Looking Forward to Care in Old Age Expectations of the Next Generation* (King's Fund, 2005).

[147] Ibid 27.

[148] HM Government, *Carers at the Heart of 21st-Century Families and Communities* (The Stationery Office, 2008) para 1.61.

[149] F Williams, *Care, Values and Future of Welfare* (University of Leeds, 2004).

[150] R Goodwin and D Gibson, 'The Decasualisation of Eldercare' in E Feder Kittay and E Feder (eds), *The Subject of Care: Feminist Perspectives on Dependency* (Lanham, 2003).

be a normal part of life. Nowadays care is often regarded as a designated task. This is most obviously captured, perhaps, in the idea of parents spending 'quality time' with their children.

VII. The Extent of Caring

In assessing the extent of caring, it is important to realise the statistics use a very narrow understanding of care, such as the official Government definition (see page 13 above). These statistics do not include, for example, parents caring for children, and are restricted to care of those with disabilities. They also rely on the kind of separation of the position of the 'carer' and 'cared for' rejected earlier in this chapter. The discussion that follows uses that terminology to provide some insight into the nature of caring.

The most reliable sources of statistics on carers are the 2001 Census, which suggested there were 5.67 million carers.[151] It found that 1,247, 291 million people provided more than 50 hours of care per week.[152] Sixty eight per cent of carers provided up to 19 hours a week, while 21 per cent cared for more than 50 hours. In a 2011 survey, 60 per cent of carers were found to be women,[153] 46 per cent were in paid employment, while 48 per cent cared for more than 20 hours a week.

The General Household Survey in 2000 estimated that there were over seven million carers.[154] In 2009 there were 417,800 people in receipt of Carers Allowance, although many carers failed to claim that allowance or were not eligible for it.[155] A survey in 2009/2010 found that 12 per cent of adults were giving special help to a sick, disabled or elderly adult.[156] Carers UK reported that of those aged between 45 and 59, 23 per cent of all women and 16 per cent of all men were providing a degree of care. That amounted to five million adults. Fifteen per cent of all households contained a carer. The 2001 Census found that more than a fifth of carers who were living with the care recipient provided care for 100 or more hours a week.[157] These figures may be underestimated as some carers did not perceive themselves as such and rather saw their care work as part of normal life. Carers UK have claimed that three in

[151] Carers UK, *Facts About Carers* (Carers UK, 2009), 1.
[152] National Statistics, *2001 Census Standard Tables* (The Stationery Office, 2003).
[153] Information Centre, NHS, *Survey of Carers in Households* 2009/2010 (NHS, 2011).
[154] Maher, J and Green, H, *Carers 2000* (The Stationery Office, 2001).
[155] The Standing Commission on Carers, *Carers at the Heart Of 21st-Century Families and Communities—Work In Progress* (Department of Health, 2009).
[156] Information Centre, NHS, *Survey of Carers in Households* 2009/2010 (NHS, 2011).
[157] L Beesley, *Informal Care in England* (King's Fund, 2006).

every five people will become a carer at some point in their lives.[158] By the age of 75 almost two thirds of women and close to a half of men will have spent some point in their lives providing at least 20 hours of care per week.[159]

Discussion of the statistics on carers tend to be used to portray a picture of an ever increasing number of people needing care, an ever reducing number of carers and ever greater pressures on them. Focus tends to be on the changing age demographic. It is easy to use statistics to project such a picture. In 1981 there were 0.6 million people over the age of 85 needing care. By 2006 there were 1.2 million, but it is estimated that by 2031 it will be three million.[160] The number of disabled people over the age of 65 will increase from 2.3 million in 2002 to four million in 2031. The ratio of working age people for those above the state pension age was 3.32 in 2006, but that will fall to 2.91 by 2031.[161] Projections suggest that although in 2002 0.6 million people received care from a spouse, by 2031 this will rise to 1.2 million and for those receiving care from adult children this will rise from 0.7 million in 2002 to 1.1 million in 2031.[162] It has been estimated that by 2041 there will be a 50 per cent increase in the number of adults with care needs.[163]

VIII. Caring Relationships and Disadvantage

There are plenty of surveys recording distress among those in caring relationships.[164] Care work carries with it significant economic, emotional and physical disadvantages.[165] Levels of employment among carers are lower than among the general population and this is particularly true of women.[166] Carers UK claim that 77 per cent of carers are financially less well off as a result of their care work.[167] Carers' health suffers too, with 21 per cent of carers who provide over 50 hours of care reporting that their health is

---

[158] Carers UK, *Facts About Carers* (Carers UK, 2009) 1.

[159] M Hirst, *Informal Care Over Time* (University of York, 2001).

[160] J Lloyd, *Living and Caring for All* (International Longevity Centre, 2008).

[161] Ibid.

[162] Ibid.

[163] HM Government, *Carers at the Heart of 21st-Century Families and Communities* (The Stationery Office, 2008).

[164] Carers Trust, *New Research Finds Unpaid Carers Struggle without Support* (Carers Trust, 2012); M Hirst, 'Carer Distress: A Prospective, Population-Based Study' (2005) 61 *Social Science & Medicine* 697.

[165] M Hirst, 'Carer Distress: A Prospective, Population-Based Study' (2005) 61 *Social Science & Medicine* 697.

[166] F Carmichael and S Charles, 'The Opportunity Costs of Informal Care: Does Gender Matter?' (2003) 22 *Journal of Health Economics* 781.

[167] House of Commons Work and Pensions Committee, *Valuing and Supporting Carers* (The Stationery Office, 2008) para 102.

not good.[168] Only 62 per cent of carers felt their own health was good.[169] Fifty two per cent said their health had been affected by the care, while 25 per cent reported feeling stressed.[170] One study found that nine out of 10 carers suffered stress, anxiety, depression or loss of sleep.[171] The burdens of those caring for mental health service users;[172] disabled children;[173] and those suffering dementia[174] can be particularly heavy. Carers find their responsibilities impact on their ability to access health services for themselves; holidays or day trips; and on their overall health.[175] In one survey, 42 per cent of carers said the care work had affected their personal relationships or their social life.[176] Caring can be isolating. A recent report by the Carers Trust found that 64 per cent of carers had not accessed support services, with many not realising that help was available.[177] Of course, the impact of care giving depends very much on the carer's own health, and socio-economic status.[178] A survey looking at carers found that satisfied carers tended to be male and in higher socioeconomic groups, with supportive family relationships.[179]

It is important to remember that the burdens of care can be unpredictable. Unexpected crises, requiring substantial periods of time, can arise at any time. Caring is far from being a nine to five job and in relationships of heavy care it can become difficult to organise other activities with confidence. This, it is important to say, can be equally true for the person providing the care and receiving it. The disabled person becomes dependent on their assistant turning up and plans can be ruined if the assistant becomes unwell or is stuck in traffic. A bleak picture of care is offered by Diemut Bubeck, although it fails to appreciate the feelings of the person receiving care:

A carer can easily feel exhausted by the seemingly or often actually never-ending demands of others and by the fact that her efforts are directed towards looking

---

[168] HM Government, *Carers at the Heart of 21st-Century Families and Communities* (The Stationery Office, 2008).

[169] Information Centre, NHS, *Survey of Carers in Households 2009/2010* (2011).

[170] Ibid.

[171] B Keeley and M Clarke, *Carers Speak Out Project* (Princess Royal Trust for Carers, 2002).

[172] V Yates, 'Ambivalence, Contradiction and Symbiosis: Carers' and Mental Health Users' Rights' (2007) *Law & Policy* 435; D Jones, *Myths, Madness and the Family: The Impact of Mental Illness on Families* (Palgrave, 2002).

[173] M Hirst, 'Carer Distress: A Prospective, Population-Based Study' (2005) 61 *Social Science & Medicine* 697.

[174] K Covinsky, R Newcomer, P Fox and J Wood, 'Patient and Caregiver Characteristics Associated with Depression in Caregivers of Patients with Dementia' (2003) 18 *Journal of General Internal Medicine* 1006.

[175] J Lloyd, *Living and Caring for All* (International Longevity Centre, 2008).

[176] Information Centre, NHS, *Survey of Carers in Households* 2009/2010 (2011).

[177] Carers Trust, *New Research Finds Unpaid Carers Struggle without Support* (Carers Trust, 2012).

[178] J Lloyd, *Living and Caring for All* (International Longevity Centre, 2008).

[179] Y Kartalova-O'Doherty and D Tedstone Doherty, 'Satisfied Carers of Persons with Enduring Mental Illness: Who and Why?' (2009) 55 *International Journal of Social Psychiatry* 257.

after others' well-being. Worse than this, she may even feel used by those she cares for, like cheap labour or even like a servant or slave, neither of whose lives are their own. She may feel this way because, in fact, she does not have a life of her own, because her life is filled with caring for others. She may feel completely out of control and powerless because as a carer she is at the constant beck and call of others. These feelings may be seen to be linked to the fact that, as a carer, a person will be extremely vulnerable to others' demands because of the peculiar skills and virtues of receptivity and responsiveness that caring involves. They are, moreover, linked to the fact that care *is* asymmetrical in that, unless it is paid, it implies benefiting others and burdening oneself.[180]

These feelings will be exacerbated if the 'carer' feels compelled to care due to the lack of or inadequacy of alternative forms of care.[181]

This picture emerges of ever increasing care needs, ever decreasing levels of care and ever burdened carers. However, it would be dangerous if that were the only picture to emerge from caring. It should not be forgotten that caring provides considerable pleasure and value.[182] In a major survey published in 2011, 80 per cent of carers described their quality of life as good.[183] Further, there is a danger that a recitation of statistics of the kind just provided can perpetuate the image of a 'noble self-sacrificing carer',[184] rather than care being an essential part of life for which we need to give support.

Laura Kessler has emphasised the way that caring can be transgressive. While for many it can be a route into social isolation and a loss of prestige and position, for others it can be a mark of political resistance. This is especially true for those ordinarily regarded not as family or not having an official status. They can claim the label carer, even though they cannot claim marriage or family. Laura Kessler reminds us:

> Caregiving is not one single thing, but a complex practice in dynamic relationship with other social practices and institutions. A woman who does significantly more housework and child care than her husband is likely to view caregiving work differently than an unmarried welfare recipient who wishes to gain an exception to her state's workfare program in order to spend more time with her infant child or a lesbian choosing to bring a child into her family through alternative insemination.[185]

Kessler, discussing black women, argues that their caregiving can be understood as a resistance to the exploitation and control of their work by men and the state. It provides a space for meaning and value, outside other spheres of

---

[180] D Bubeck, *Care, Gender and Justice* (Clarendon Press, 1995) 149–50.

[181] E Nakano Glenn, *Forced to Care* (Harvard University Press, 2010).

[182] H Al-Janabi, J Coast, T Flynn, 'What do people value when they provide unpaid care for an older person? A meta-ethnography with interview follow-up' (2007) 61 *Journal of Epidemiology and Community Health* 1.

[183] Information Centre, NHS, *Survey of Carers in Households* 2009/2010 (NHS, 2011).

[184] V Yates, 'Ambivalence, Contradiction and Symbiosis: Carers' and Mental Health Users' Rights' (2007) *Law & Policy* 435.

[185] L Kessler, 'Transgressive Caregiving' (2005) 33 *Florida State University Law Review* 1.

life, such as employment, where racism and sexism may impede self-expression. She also argues that for gay men and lesbians, care practices likewise can be seen as a form of politics. Gay caring life is a testament to difference. Within the negative portrayal of not really family, a radical identity through caring, performing family to perfection, can be seen as a radical act.

The overall statistics can hide variations between carers. Ethnic background can have a significant impact on care support.[186] Ethnic minority carers can face particular difficulties in accessing housing and other services. Members of ethnic minority groups can find accessing caring assistance complex and/or stigmatic.[187] There have even been claims of institutional racism revealed in the low levels of service for carers of disabled children.[188] This may especially be where cultural assumptions about care conflict with those of the majority culture.[189]

Gay and lesbian couples also face exclusion. There is a danger of assuming that care takes place in a heterosexual context.[190] The Alzheimer's Society launched a major campaign on this issue claiming that between 35,000 and 70,000 lesbian, gay and bisexual people care for someone with dementia, but when seeking to access services they can be faced with prejudice and ignorance.[191]

A group that has attracted particular concern are young carers. In the literature young carers are typically defined as those undertaking care work under the age of 18.[192] The 2001 Census suggested that at that time there were 175,000 young carers, with 13,000 working more than 50 hours a week, their average age being 12.[193] Young carers may care for siblings, parents, grandparents or friends.[194] More than half of young carers live in a one parent family.[195] Even these figures may be on the low side with one survey suggesting there could be 700,000 young carers in the UK.[196] The survey suggested that one in 12 schoolchildren had caring roles such as helping

---

[186] Eg J Merrell, F Kinsella, F Murphy and S Philpin, 'Support Needs of Carers of Dependent Adults from a Bangladeshi Community' (2005) 51 *Journal of Advanced Nursing* 549.

[187] G Mir and P Tovey, 'Asian Carers Experience of Medical and Social Care' (2003) 33 *British Journal of Social Work* 465.

[188] P Bywaters, Z Ali, Q Fazil, L Wallace and G Sing, 'Attitudes Toward Disability Among Pakistani and Bangladeshi Parents of Disabled Children in the UK' (2003) 11 *Health as Social Care in the Community* 502.

[189] J Anderson and W Turner, 'When Caregivers are in Need of Care: African-American Caregivers' Preferences for their Own Later Life Care' (2010) 24 *Journal of Aging Studies* 65.

[190] J Conaghan and E Grabham, 'Sexuality and the Citizen Carer' (2007) 58 *Northern Ireland Legal Quarterly* 351.

[191] The Alzheimer's Society, *Lesbian and Gay Carers* (Alzheimer's Society, 2010).

[192] B Gray and C Robinson, 'Hidden Children: Perspectives of Professionals on Young Carers of People with Mental Health Problems' (2009) 15 *Child Care in Practice* 95.

[193] Barnados, *Young Carers* (Barnados, 2012).

[194] B Gray and C Robinson, 'Hidden Children: Perspectives of Professionals on Young Carers of People with Mental Health Problems' (2009) 15 *Child Care in Practice* 95.

[195] Ibid.

[196] BBC News Online, 'UK's "Hidden Army" of Young Carers' 16 November 2010.

dressing, washing or bathing and 17,000 young people live with parents with enduring mental illness.[197]

Young carers have until relatively recently been a largely hidden group.[198] There is widespread concern at the lack of support for young carers. The Children's Commissioner for England has said:

> Young carers in the UK are too often caught in the middle of a well-meaning muddle, missing out on vital support and services that can help them .... For young carers who are still at school, poor or uncoordinated support from the statutory sector can result in them missing out on the opportunities enjoyed by other children, which can blight their life chances as adults.[199]

Being a young carer, it is said, can limit young people's education and social opportunities.[200] It can cause anger, exhaustion and a sense of isolation.[201]

Despite this negative portrayal of young carers, I suspect there is a danger of devaluing care. Is it clear that a young person's life spent caring for others is necessarily less desirable than a life of playing sports, hanging out with friends or partying? It should not be assumed that people performing care work are thereby being disadvantaged. As we will explore further in chapter three, being in a caring relationship should be seen as a natural activity and one which is essential to well-being. The negative portrayal of young carers in much of the literature is in danger of downgrading care and demeaning parents with disabilities.[202] The focus is on their disabilities and the burden children face in meeting their needs. However, we should recognise that all parent-child relationships involve give and take, with all children supporting their parents in some way.[203] The care offered by 'child carers' is no different in nature from the care given by all children to their parents. In saying that I do not mean to argue against support and help being given to child carers, but to suggest that being a child carer should not be seen as a blight. Many child carers report developing maturity, responsibility and closer relationships.[204] Indeed there is a danger that the discussion of young carers overlooks the

---

[197] S McAndrew, T Warne, D Fallon and P Moran, 'Young, Gifted, and Caring: A Project Narrative of Young Carers, their Mental Health, and Getting them Involved in Education, Research and Practice' (2012) 21 *International Journal of Mental Health Nursing* 12.

[198] B Gray and C Robinson, 'Hidden Children: Perspectives of Professionals on Young Carers of People with Mental Health Problems' (2009) 15 *Child Care in Practice* 95.

[199] BBC News Online, 'UK's "Hidden Army" of Young Carers' 16 November 2010.

[200] K Lloyd, 'Happiness and Well-Being of Young Carers: Extent, Nature and Correlates of Caring among 10 and 11 Year Old School Children' (2012) *Journal of Happiness Studies* forthcoming.

[201] H Rose and K Cohen, 'The Experiences of Young Carers: A Meta-Synthesis of Qualitative Findings' (2010) 13 *Journal of Youth Studies* 473.

[202] L Keith and J Morris, 'Easy Targets: A Disability Rights Perspective on the "Children as Carers" Debate' (1995) 15 *Critical Social Policy* 36.

[203] C Smyth, M Blaxland and B Cass, 'So that's how I found out I was a young carer and that I actually had been a carer most of my life. Identifying and supporting hidden young carers' (2010) 13 *Journal of Youth Studies* 1.

[204] G Schofield and J Walsh, 'Young Carers—or Children in Need of Care? Decision Making for Children of Parents with Mental Health Problems' (2010) *Child and Family Law Quarterly* 223.

importance of care in forming identity and being part of a good life. Indeed young carers report feeling pride and self-esteem from their caring identity. Surveys into their position complain more about a lack of support rather than complaints about their role.[205]

There are special issues that surround care in old age.[206] Carers UK state that at some point in their lives three in every five people will become a carer.[207] By the age of 75 almost two thirds of women and close to a half of men will have spent some point in their lives providing at least 20 hours of care per week.[208] Of course, these are not just carers of older people but include other adults needing care. In 2000, 16 per cent of those over 65 were providing some form of care, while 28 per cent of those providing 20 hours or more of care per week were over 65.[209] In the UK, 25 per cent of carers are over 60[210] and over 44, 000 carers are over the age of 85.[211] Age can have a particular impact on some communities. It appears that Bangladeshi, Pakistani and Indian groups are more likely to care than the average for the population.[212] Given the greater incidence of intergenerational households within such communities that is not surprising.

IX. Conclusion

This chapter has sought to explore the meanings and experience of caring. It is argued that caring carries four markers: the meeting of needs; respect; responsibility and rationality. The importance of seeing care in a relational way, rather than being a uni-directional activity has been emphasised. Otherwise, as the powerful disability critique of care has pointed out, there is a danger of care becoming the exercise of power over a passive individual. Further the uni-directional model is in danger of overlooking the extensive networks of care within which we all live. Care is not a strange activity which is undertaken by a few brave souls, but is ingrained into the existence of every person. As we shall explore in the next chapter, this requires a radical rethinking of our legal and ethical tools which have traditionally built on an individualistic model.

---

[205] H Rose and K Cohen, 'The Experiences of Young Carers: A Meta-Synthesis of Qualitative Findings' (2010) 13 *Journal of Youth Studies* 473.
[206] A Ross, J Lloyd, M Weinhardt and H Cheshire, *Living and Caring? An Investigation of the Experiences of Older Carers* (International Longevity Centre, 2008).
[207] Carers UK, *Facts About Carers* (Carers UK, 2005) 1.
[208] M Hirst, *Informal Care over Time* (University of York, 2001).
[209] L Beesley, *Informal Care in England* (King's Fund, 2006).
[210] G Hopkins, 'Duty, Love and Sacrifice' (2006) 16 *Community Care* 47.
[211] House of Commons Work and Pensions Committee, *Valuing and Supporting Carers* (The Stationery Office, 2008) para 344.
[212] L Beesley, *Informal Care in England* (King's Fund, 2006).

3

Ethic of Care

I. Introduction

Many commentators reflecting on the ethical and legal responses to caring relationships have been drawn to an ethic of care.[1] This approach provides a challenge to the way legal rights and responsibilities are commonly understood. Much of the law is based on the assumption that we are competent, detached, independent people who are entitled to have our rights of self-determination and autonomy fiercely protected.[2] Legal rights and rules operate to draw boundaries around ourselves and protect us from interference from others. However, the reality is that we are ignorant, vulnerable, interdependent individuals, whose strength and reality is not in our autonomy, but our relationships with others.[3] An approach based on an ethic of care seeks to use these facts as a starting point to the law's response. It starts with a norm of interlocking mutually dependent relationships, rather than an individualised vision of rights.[4] Rights and interests are not designed to protect individuals

---

[1] Leading works on ethic of care include: C Gilligan, 'Moral Orientation and Moral Development' in E Feder Kittay and D Meyers (eds), *Women and Moral Theory* (Rowman and Littlefield, 1987); M Mayeroff, *On Caring* (William Morrow, 1990); M Friedman, *Liberating Care* (Cornell University Press, 1993); J Tronto, *Moral Boundaries* (Routledge, 1993); D Bubeck, *Care, Gender and Justice* (Oxford University Press, 1996); S Sevenhuijsen, *Citizenship and the Ethics of Care* (Routledge, 1998); N Noddings, *Educating Moral People* (Teachers College Press, 2002); N Noddings, *Starting at Home: Caring and Social Policy* (Berkeley: University of California Press, 2002); E Feder Kittay, *Love's Labour: Essays on Women, Equality and Dependency* (Routledge, 1999); R Groenhout, *Connected Lives: Human Nature and an Ethics of Care* (Rowman and Littlefield, 2004); V Held, *The Ethics of Care* (Oxford University Press, 2006); M Slote, *The Ethics of Care and Empathy* (Routledge, 2007); D Engster, *The Heart of Justice. Care Ethics and Political Theory* (Oxford University Press, 2007); J Bridgeman, *Parental Responsibility, Young Children and Healthcare Law* (Cambridge University Press, 2009).

[2] L Lloyd, 'Mortality and Morality: Ageing and the Ethics of Care' (2004) 24 *Ageing and Society* 235.

[3] C Meyer, 'Cruel Choices: Autonomy and Critical Care Decision-Making' (2004) 18 *Bioethics* 104.

[4] R West. *Caring for Justice* (New York University Press, 1997) 356.

per se, so much as upholding and maintaining networks of relationships. This is not downgrading the value of people, because it is in their relationships that people will find value and meaning in their lives.

An ethic of care requires a rethinking of the understanding of the role of law and the nature of rights. As Tove Petersen explains, at the heart of most ethical theory is a core value: 'deontology accentuates rights; the theories of justice emphasize justice; and the utilitarian tradition values the society's overall well-being'.[5] For ethics of care the central value is care.

II. The Origins of an Ethic of Care

It is widely agreed that contemporary understandings of an ethic of care arise from the work of Carol Gilligan, although no doubt its origins can be traced much further back than that.[6] Carol Gilligan's *In a Different Voice*[7] emerged from a critique of Lawrence Kohlberg's suggestion that women, on average, had a lower moral development than men. He reached this conclusion based on an assumption that there was a journey of moral development. He argued that moral maturity involved a progression from a 'pre-conventional level', where there was simply a desire to please authority figures; through to a conventional level where there was an attempt to conform to the rules and standards of the group; and finally through to a post-conventional level in which the individual evaluates and tests conventional rules by abstract universal principles. He observed that generally women were less developed on the basis of his approach because when faced with a problem they reverted to the conventional approach. In particular he argued that they became overly concerned with their conflicting responsibilities to particular people, rather than viewing their position in abstract terms.

Gilligan's response was not to challenge whether men and women thought in these different ways, but rather to re-examine Kohlberg's assumptions about what moral maturity meant and in particular to challenge his assumption that the use of universal abstract principles was a sign of moral sophistication. She suggested that the women's approach was not inferior, but rather that women were speaking with a 'different voice': women's approach was emotional and more concerned with personal connections and nurturing, whereas men's were focused on rational argument. While men were concerned with universal

---

[5] T Pettersen, 'The Ethic of Care: Normative Structures and Empirical Implications' (2011) 54 *Health Care Analysis* 51.

[6] R Groenhout, *Connected Lives: Human Nature and an Ethics of Care* (Rowman and Littlefield, 2004), for example, draws on the writing of Augustine.

[7] C Gilligan, *In a Different Voice* (Harvard University Press, 1982).

abstract principles and competing rights; women focused more on the importance of preserving ongoing relationships and balancing conflicting responsibilities. The moral relationships between the self and others was marked by the obligations that flow from relationship and the dependency of the other person; rather than an assertion of one's rights, or generalised rules of justice. Her central claim was that the women's approach was not less mature, simply different.

Since the publication of Gilligan's book, much has been written in an attempt to develop her approach. The significance of her work, in retrospect, lies not in the specific claims about the ways men and women might think, indeed that has been questioned by many. Rather, the significance of her work lies in the hope it offered of a new approach to ethical analysis, described by Maria Drakopoulou as embracing

> a vision of human relationships and of society grounded upon the primacy of human connectedness, wherein care and compassion are seen as fundamental and where emotions, peaceful co-operation, empathy, friendship and responsibility are aspired to rather than universal, abstract, rational principles (autonomy, freedom, justice, equality and rights).[8]

These points will be developed shortly.

Carol Gilligan was writing from the perspective of a developmental psychologist, but writing on the ethic of care has been enriched by a range of other perspectives. An early prominent advocate was Nel Noddings,[9] who argued that there was a primary injunction to meet others in a caring way. Noddings's emphasis was that an ethic of care required an individual to be responsive to the particular details of the situation she was in. This involved a sensitive response to the surroundings, rather than a detached or objective approach based on generalised rules. She also emphasised that care was not just a practice but an attitude, an important part of which was that the person cared for did not feel they were being cared for out of duty. As we shall see later, this point feeds into a broader debate among care ethicists about the meaning of care.

Ethics of care has taken off and been developed with considerable sophistication by philosophers, and practical applications have been produced in a wide range of situations. In more recent times, the writings of political scientists Joan Tronto[10] and Selma Sevenhuijsen[11] and philosopher Virginia Held[12] have been particularly influential. These have moved care ethics

---

[8] M Drakopoulou, 'The Ethic of Care, Female Subjectivity and Feminist Legal Scholarship' (2000) 8 *Feminist Legal Studies* 199.

[9] N Noddings, *Caring: A Feminine Approach to Ethics and Moral Education* (University of California Press, 1984).

[10] J Tronto, *Moral Boundaries, a Political Argument for an Ethic of Care* (Routledge, 1983).

[11] S Sevenhuijsen, *Citizenship and The Ethics of Care* (Routledge, 1998).

[12] V Held, *The Ethics of Care* (Oxford University Press, 2006).

beyond its application to caring relationships to provide political and social doctrines based on care.[13] Hence, Joan Tronto[14] sees an ethic of care as:

> ... a set of moral sensibilities, issues and practices that arise from taking seriously the fact that care is a central aspect of human existence ... a species activity that includes everything that we do to maintain, continue and repair our 'world' so that we can live in it as well as possible. That world includes our bodies, ourselves and our environment, all of which we seek to interweave in a complex, life-sustaining web.

In this it has departed from Gilligan's attempt to provide an alternative voice to be heard alongside traditional moral approaches, to become a fully-fledged ethical approach in its own right.

III. Central Themes in an Ethic of Care Approach

Of course, there is no complete agreement over what an ethic of care means. The following, I suggest, are the central principles underpinning it. These will be set out next, before I highlight some of the issues of disagreement among care ethicists and consider some of the objections to care ethics.

A. Care is Part of Being Human

A starting point of an ethic of care is that we all have needs and that caring for others in meeting these needs is a universal experience.[15] Dependency and care are an inevitable part of being human.[16] Caring relationships are the very stuff of life.[17] Wendy Holloway argues that 'care is the psychological equivalent to our need to breathe unpolluted air'.[18]

Although, in a person's lifespan, the extent of caring may vary during different ages, there is probably no point in our lives at which we are neither cared by nor caring for another,[19] and often both at the same time.[20] In failing

---

[13] R Eisler, *The Real Wealth of Nations* (Berrett-Koehler Publishers, 2008).

[14] J Tronto, *Moral Boundaries, a Political Argument for an Ethic of Care* (Routledge, 1983).

[15] V Held, *The Ethics of Care* (Oxford University Press, 2006).

[16] M Fineman, *The Autonomy Myth* (New Press, 2004) xvii; T Levy, 'The Relational Self and the Right to Give Care' (2007) 28 *New Political Science* 547.

[17] F Williams, 'The Presence of Feminism in the Future of Welfare' (2002) 31 *Economy and Society* 502.

[18] W Hollway, 'Introducing the Capacity to Care' in W Hollway (ed), *The Capacity to Care: Gender and Ethical Subjectivity* (Routledge, 2006).

[19] S Sevenhuijsen, 'The Place of Care. The Relevance of the Feminist Ethic of Care for Social Policy' (2003) 4 *Feminist Theory* 179.

[20] J Bridgeman, 'Book Review' (2006) 14 *Feminist Legal Studies,* 407. See also J Herring and P-L Chau, 'My Body, Your Body, Our Bodies' (2007) 15 *Medical Law Review* 34.

to acknowledge care work properly, the law is missing a critical aspect of life. Eva Feder Kittay writes:

My point is that this interdependence begins with dependence. It begins with the dependency of an infant, and often ends with the dependency of a very ill or frail person close to dying. The infant may develop into a person who can reciprocate, an individual upon whom another can be dependent and whose continuing needs make her interdependent with others. The frail elderly person . . . may herself have been involved in a series of interdependent relations. But at some point there is a dependency that is not yet, nor longer an interdependency. By excluding *this* dependency from social and political concerns, we have been able to fashion the pretence that we are *independent*—that the cooperation between persons that some insist is *inter*dependence is simply the mutual (often voluntary) cooperation between essentially independent persons.[21]

Quite how ethics of care understands vulnerability is complex, but I would argue as follows. The law typically identifies groups of people as vulnerable and in need of particular protection: children; those lacking mental capacity; those with physical disabilities. This however, disguises the vulnerability all of us face. As Lévinas states: 'The I, from head to foot and to the bone-marrow, is vulnerability.'[22] Even if we seek to deny our own vulnerabilities, the vulnerabilities of those we are in a relationship with become our own vulnerabilities.[23] We might like to emphasise our independence, capacity for rational thought and autonomy. However, we puff ourselves up with such talk.

Martha Fineman has argued that looking at a typical lifespan there will be times of different capacity and strengths. The typical 'adult liberal subject' focuses on just one part of that lifespan and essentialises that as the norm for all people. We could take other sections of the typical lifespan and have a very different ideal around which to base a legal system. As Martha Fineman argues:

The vulnerability approach recognizes that individuals are anchored at each end of their lives by dependency and the absence of capacity. Of course, between these ends, loss of capacity and dependence may also occur, temporarily for many and permanently for some as a result of disability or illness. Constant and variable throughout life, individual vulnerability encompasses not only damage that has been done in the past and speculative harms of the distant future, but also the possibility of immediate harm. We are beings who live with the ever-present possibility that our needs and circumstances will change. On an individual level, the concept of vulnerability (unlike that of liberal autonomy) captures this present potential

---

[21] E Feder Kittay, *Love's Labour: Essays on Women, Equality and Dependency* (Routledge, 1999) xii.

[22] E Lévinas, *Humanismo Del Otro Hombre* (Edit Siglo Veintiuno Editores, 1993) 123.

[23] M Shildrick, *Embodying the Monster: Encounters with the Vulnerable Self* (Routledge, 2002); A Beckett, *Citizenship and Vulnerability* (Palgrave, 2006); J Herring, 'Vulnerability, Children and the Law' in M Freeman (ed), *Law and Childhood Studies* (Oxford University Press, 2012).

for each of us to become dependent based upon our persistent susceptibility to misfortune and catastrophe.[24]

I would go further and question whether even in our so-called prime we do have the kind of autonomy and capacity traditional liberalism claims for adults. My point is that we are *all* vulnerable.[25] We are all profoundly dependent on others for our physical and psychological well-being. Part of our vulnerability leads from our embodiment.[26] We like to present our bodies as self-contained and secure structures. In fact our bodies are leaky and in a constant change of flux.[27] Our bodies are insecure and vulnerable. Our society has built up a wide range of structures and forms of assistance which disguise our vulnerability. Indeed we are forced by a wide range of societal pressures to disguise or mitigate our vulnerability so that we can behave in an acceptable way in the public realm. In a powerful article, Kate Lindemann contrasts the emphasis that is paid to the accommodations for disabled people so as to minimise the impact of their disability, with the lack of appreciation of the similar accommodations for the able bodied:

> Colleagues, professional staff members, and other adults are unconscious of the numerous accommodations that society provides to make their work and life style possible. ATM's, extended hours in banks, shopping centres and medical offices, EZpass, newspaper kiosks, and elevators are all accommodations that make contemporary working life possible. There are entire industries devoted to accommodating the needs of adult working people. Fast food, office lunch delivery, day time child care, respite care, car washing, personal care attendants, interpreters, house cleaning, and yard and lawn services are all occupations that provide services that make it possible for adults to hold full time jobs.[28]

We thus highlight the facilities used to deal with the vulnerabilities of others, while overlooking the accommodations 'we' need to deal with our vulnerabilities. Further, we readily class those who need care from others as vulnerable, without seeing the vulnerability that caring creates for the carer.[29]

---

[24] M Fineman, 'The Vulnerable Subject: Anchoring Equality in the Human Condition' in M Fineman (ed), *Transcending the Boundaries of Law: Generations of Feminism and Legal Theory* (Routledge, 2011) 168.

[25] M Fineman, 'Responsibility, Family and the Limits of Equality: An American Perspective' in C Lind, H Keating and J Bridgeman (eds), *Taking Responsibility, Law and the Changing Family* (Routledge, 2011).

[26] R Groenhout, *Connected Lives: Human Nature and an Ethics of Care* (Rowman and Littlefield, 2004).

[27] J Herring and P-L Chau, 'My Body, Your Body, Our Bodies' (2007) 15 *Medical Law Review* 54.

[28] K Lindemann, 'The Ethics of Receiving' (2003) 24 *Theoretical Medicine and Bioethics* 501.

[29] B Hughes, L McKie, D Hopkins, and N Watson, 'Love's Labours Lost? Feminism, the Disabled People's Movement and an Ethic of Care' (2005) 39 *Sociology* 259.

We could, and should, present a rather different legal system, which starts with an acknowledgement of everyone's vulnerability.[30] This is what is offered by an ethic of care perspective. Law degrees would have the law on mental health, child law, carer law, elder law and undue influence at its heart. This would produce a rather different way of looking at the world. Gone would be the special 'concessions' involved in protecting especially disadvantaged groups such as the disabled or children. Rather they would be regarded as the norm and the focus would be on the special privileges that are given to the able bodied or some adults.[31]

Many other ethical theories sideline care or see it as of marginal interest in ethical analysis. Yet as Daniel Engster argues, care of dependency should be seen as being of central significance:

> There would be no individual liberty or equality, community values or good life without the caring practices necessary to sustain and foster human life and society. As such the aims and virtues of caring may be said to precede and underlie all other theories of justice.[32]

As Engster notes, under a classically Rawlsian model, equality and autonomy come together to form a political society in a hypothetical social contract. However, under care ethics, we start with individuals in their 'natural' state: as embedded in relationships and dependent upon each other for survival and development. Obligations flow from these interdependencies, not from being chosen by an individual autonomous person.

The fact of our shared vulnerability means we must acknowledge the importance of care.[33] In a society of the vulnerable, mutual care is essential.[34] As Joan Tronto writes:

> Care is not a parochial concern of women, a type of secondary moral question, or the work of the least well off in society. Care is a central concern of human life. It is time we began to change our political and social institutions to reflect this truth.[35]

Susan Dodds also argues that we need a legal and social system which is not premised on individualistic conceptions of autonomy but an acceptance of our vulnerability:

> A vulnerability-centered view of the self and of persons is better able to capture many of our moral motivations and intuitions than can be captured by an autonomy-focused approach. We are all vulnerable to the exigencies of our embodied,

---

[30] P Blaikie, T Cannon, I Davis, and B Wisner, *At Risk: Natural Hazards, People's Vulnerability, and Disasters* (Routledge, 2003).

[31] M Fineman, 'The Vulnerable Subject: Anchoring Equality in the Human Condition' (2008) 20 *Yale Journal of Law and Feminism* 1.

[32] D Engster, *The Heart of Justice* (Oxford University Press, 2007) 5.

[33] M Fineman, *The Autonomy Myth* (New York, 2004) xvii; S Levy, 'The Relational Self and the Right to Give Care' (2006) 28 *New Political Science* 547, 548.

[34] R Groenhout, *Connected Lives: Human Nature and an Ethics of Care* (Rowman and Littlefield, 2004).

[35] J Tronto, *Moral Boundaries: A Political Argument for an Ethic of Care* (Routledge, 1993) 180.

social and relational existence and, in recognizing this inherent human vulnerability, we can see the ways in which a range of social institutions and structures protect us against some vulnerabilities, while others expose us to risk. We do not have to view our obligations towards those who lack the capacity to develop or retain autonomy as having a different source from our obligations towards those whose autonomy is made vulnerable due to a degree of dependency. It may be easier to recognize the social value of provision of care if it is viewed as something on which we all have been dependent and on which we are all likely to be dependent at different points in our lives, rather than altruistic behaviour extended to those who lack 'full personhood.'[36]

The significance of the failure to acknowledge our common vulnerability is that, as Martha Fineman argues, we lose sight of the power and privilege that is used by some to disguise theirs:

When we only study the poor, the rich remain hidden and their advantages remain relatively unexamined, nestled in secure and private spaces, where there is no need for them or the state to justify or explain why they deserve the privilege of state protection. We need to excavate these privileged lives. While sometimes this will be a difficult and complex undertaking, there are certainly abundant records and instruments of privilege all around us that can be accessed relatively easily. These archives are located in corporate boardrooms and in the rules setting up or limiting state and national regulatory regimes. They can be gleaned from tax and probate codes, history books, literature, political theories, and of course, from the language and logic of the law.[37]

In summary, ethics of care criticises other general approaches to ethics as 'modelled on the experience of men in public life and in the marketplace'[38] and not appropriate for the lives of those caring. While the marketplace model is based on assumptions of our independence and need to peruse our own goals, an ethics of care has at its heart an acknowledgement of our vulnerability from which flows an acknowledgement of the importance of interdependency and care. The law and society should above all be seeking to uphold and maintain caring relationships. It is because we are, have been, and will be, dependent on others, that caring is so important.[39]

---

[36] S Dodds, 'Depending on Care: Recognition of Vulnerability and the Social Contribution of Care Provision' (2007) 21 *Bioethics* 500, 507.

[37] M Fineman, 'Equality: Still Illusive After All These Years' in J Grossman and L McClain (eds), *Social Citizenship and Gender* (Cambridge University Press, 2010).

[38] V Held, *The Ethics of Care* (Oxford University Press, 2006) 23–24.

[39] D Engster, *The Heart of Justice. Care Ethics and Political Theory* (Oxford University Press, 2007) 40.

B. Care is a Good Part of Life

Not only is care an inevitable part of life; it is a good part of life. Care should be treasured and valued. As Robin West puts it:

> Caregiving labor (and its fruits) is the central adventure of a lifetime; it is what gives life its point, provides it with meaning, and returns to those who give it some measure of security and emotional sustenance. For even more of us, whether or not we like it and regardless of how we regard it, caregiving labor, for children and the aged, is the work we will do that creates the relationships, families, and communities within which our lives are made pleasurable and connected to something larger than ourselves.[40]

Care is the manifestation of that most basic moral value: love. It involves meeting the needs of others, which is a primary good.[41]

Care not only meets needs, it provides great satisfaction. Daniel Engster argues:

> Caring is not only morally obligatory but also one key to a happy life. Individuals regularly point to their caring relationships with others as the most fulfilling aspects of their lives. Caring for others is not all drudgery and toil but often a joyous and deeply meaningful experience. Caring institutions and policies not only make the experience of personal caring more available to all human being, but also expand this experience to our relations with all other human beings. In this way, they make possible a more satisfying and moral existence for all human being in both our private and public lives.[42]

The value of care is not, of course, simply for the individuals themselves. Without caring relationships, the burden that would fall onto society would be impossible to bear.[43] As Mona Harrington explains:

> The key idea for a new politics of family care ... is to add care to the pantheon of national social values. That is, to assure good care to all members of the society should become a primary principle of our common life, along with the assurance of liberty, equality and justice.

> We need to elevate care to this level of importance for the basic reason that it is essential to human health and balanced development. It is also crucial to developing human moral potential, to instilling and reinforcing in an individual a sense of positive connection to others. And it is this sense of connection that makes possible

---

[40] R West, 'The Right to Care' in E Feder Kittay and E Feder (eds), *The Subject of Care: Feminist Perspectives on Dependency* (Lanham: Rowman & Littlefield, 2002) 89.

[41] S Clark Miller, 'Need, Care and Obligation' (2005) 57 *Royal Institute of Philosophy Supplement* 137.

[42] D Engster, *The Heart of Justice. Care Ethics and Political Theory* (Oxford University Press, 2007) 18–19.

[43] L McClain, 'Care as a Public Value: Linking Responsibility, Resources, and Republicanism' (2001) 76 *Chicago-Kent Law Review* 1673; M Daly, 'Care as a Good for Social Policy' (2002) 31 *Journal of Social Policy* 251.

the whole range of mutual responsibilities that allow the people of a society to respect and work toward common goals.[44]

The goodness of care does depend on one's understanding of care. It raises the issue discussed in chapter two of whether care is a feeling or a practice.[45] If it is just a feeling then its general benefit to others is harder to find. The goodness of care also depends on the extent to which there is a judgement about the nature of care: does care mean good care or is any care, care?[46] In chapter two I proposed a definition of care which had four key markers: it met needs, was relational, involved responsibilities and was respectful. If that is accepted, then the goodness of care becomes inherent within the notion of care.

There is, however, a danger here, and this is an important theme in this book; if we see care as a good because it meets needs, it might be assumed that having needs is bad. There is no doubt that dependency and vulnerability are commonly assumed to be bad things. David Archard, writing on childhood, has stated:

> There may be features of childhood but not of adulthood which are valuable, such as innocence, wonder and trust. There may, correspondingly be features of adulthood but not childhood which are valuable, such as experience and independence. It is also evident that there may be features of childhood but not of adulthood which are not valuable, such as dependence and vulnerability.[47]

This dislike of dependence and vulnerability is not restricted to philosophers. John Moore, a former Secretary of State for Social Security, commented:

> A climate of dependence can in time corrupt the human spirit. Everyone knows the sullen apathy of dependence and can compare it with the sheer delight of personal achievement.[48]

I think both of these views are profoundly mistaken. Vulnerability and dependence are not only inevitable parts of humanity, as argued above, they are to be greatly welcomed. They are virtues, not vices.

Self-reliance has become a dominant theme in social policy.[49] Be it lone parents or care in the community, autonomy and independence have become key policy goals. But this ignores the fact that as humans we are interdependent.[50]

---

[44] M Harrington, *Care and Equality: Inventing a New Family Politics* (Routledge, 2000) 48–49.

[45] J Tronto, 'Care Ethics: Moving Forward' (1999) 14 *Hypatia* 112.

[46] L Campbell-Brown, 'The Ethic of Care' (1997) 4 *UCL Jurisprudence Review* 272.

[47] D Archard, 'Philosophical Perspectives on Childhood' in J Fiona (ed), *Legal Concepts of Childhood* (Hart, 2001) 52.

[48] J Moore, UK, 1987, quoted in M Fine and C Glendinning, 'Dependence, Independence or Interdependence? Revisiting the Concepts of 'Care' and 'Dependency'' (2005) *Ageing and Society* 601, 601.

[49] K Halvorsen, 'Symbolic Purposes and Factual Consequences of the Concepts 'Self-Reliance' and 'Dependency' in Contemporary Discourses on Welfare' (1998) 7 *Scandinavian Journal of Social Welfare* 56.

[50] S Dodds, 'Gender, Ageing, and Injustice: Social and Political Contexts of Bioethics' (2005) 31 *Journal of Medical Ethics* 295.

Any personal achievements of the kind referred to by Moore are in reality the product of many people's efforts.[51] No one can be truly independent. Hence, the Government's aspiration in its latest document on care is utterly misguided: 'Our vision is one that promotes people's independence and wellbeing by enabling them to prevent or postpone the need for care and support.'[52]

The anti-vulnerability narrative tends to promote disablist approaches to the issue. As many writers from disability studies have written, there is great pressure to be perceived as being independent and lacking vulnerability. As the quote just given implies, success for a person with a disability is measured by the extent to which they may be able to be (or present themselves as being) independent and autonomous. In short, to be 'normal'.[53]

Being vulnerable is an aspect of many of the things people value most in their lives. Relationships; intimacy; care; all of these things in their nature render us vulnerable.[54] It is only by properly appreciating our vulnerable nature that the importance of human rights is appreciated.[55] Similarly, dependency should not be something to be afraid of or ashamed of. Something has gone very wrong with our care of vulnerable older people when 'not being a burden' is reported as the main goal of their lives by patients living in nursing homes.[56] Dependency on others is an aspect of our humanity.

Recognition of the practice of care as a basic ethical good and a central social good is, therefore, central to an ethic of care. Contrast the view of the male imagination that care is 'waste',[57] because it deals with the mess of human bodies, and failing to be economically productive. Rather care, with all its messiness, is at the heart of well-being.[58]

C. Emotions are Ethically Significant

Much of the law emphasises the importance of rationality and intellect. The concepts of mental capacity; informed consent; compliance with standards expected by a responsible body of opinion all privilege in legal discourse logical thought and sound judgement. There is nothing wrong in that, but the emotional side of humanity is lost. The love which goes on caring and caring;

---

[51] M Fine and C Glendinning, 'Dependence, Independence or Interdependence? Revisiting the Concepts of "Care" and "Dependency"' (2005) *Ageing and Society* 601.

[52] HM Government, *Caring for Our Future* (The Stationery Office, 2012) 18.

[53] T Shakespeare, *Help* (Venture, 2000).

[54] GW Harris, *Dignity and Vulnerability* (University of California Press, 1997).

[55] B Turner, *Vulnerability and Human Rights* (Pennsylvania State University Press, 2006) ch 2.

[56] S Pleschberge, 'Dignity and the Challenge of Dying in Nursing Homes: The Residents' View' (2007) 36 *Age and Ageing* 197.

[57] B Hughes, L McKie, D Hopkins, and N Watson, 'Love's Labours Lost? Feminism, the Disabled People's Movement and an Ethic of Care' (2005) 39 *Sociology* 259.

[58] C Foster and J Herring, 'Welfare Means Relationality, Virtue and Altruism' (2012) 32 *Legal Studies* 480.

the grief, disappointment, frustration, anger and despair, which are all part of life, find no place.[59] The exclusion of emotion means the voice of carers talking about how their cared for one should be looked after finds no ready legal mouthpiece. The law often struggles to respond to issues which are not readily reducible to an economic value nor expressed in terms of individualised rights. That can be seen, for example, in the law of tort where damages for an economic loss are readily recoverable, whereas loss for distress, unwanted pregnancy or bereavement finds the courts struggling to produce a coherent response. An ethic of care seeks to acknowledge the role that both emotion and rationality plays in relationships. We do not live by rational thoughts alone.[60]

The reason why emotions are a source of moral insight for care ethicists is that emotions are central to good care. Trust, sympathy, empathy, sensitivity; such things are essential. If the response to a dilemma undermines these emotions it will undermine the care. However, the law tends to be suspicious of emotion. Too much emotion can lead one to being found to lack capacity and one's views discounted.[61]

The elevation of rational thought to an exclusive place is in its most extreme in our attitude towards children and those with mental disorders.[62] Children are seen as *potential* citizens, and as regarded as having 'the right to a free future'.[63] Children are not there yet, but are on their way. The views and wishes of those who lack mental capacity are downplayed because they are not the product of rational thinking.[64] Eva Feder Kittay[65] has written movingly of the attitudes displayed towards her severely disabled daughter, Sesha:

> Sesha's life is a human life, but a tragic one because her situation is such that she can never achieve functioning of all the capabilities to some satisfactory degree. I believe that were Sesha capable of replying, she would remind us that people with disabilities have worked hard to insist that life with impairments, even serious impairments need not be 'tragic'. What is tragic is the failure of the larger society to include people with variant bodies and modes of functioning. Yes, when Sesha was born I had envisioned a different future for her. Yes, when I learned of her very significant impairments I saw a human tragedy. But I have since learned—from her,

---

[59] Occasionally it peeps through (see the refusal of the medical team who had done so much work to care for the patient in *Re B (Adult: Refusal of Medical Treatment)* [2002] All ER 449 that they felt unable to switch off her life support machine as the Court ultimately ordered).

[60] A Gibbard, *Wise Choices, Apt Feelings* (Harvard University Press, 1990); and S Blackburn, *Ruling Passions* (Clarendon Press, 1998).

[61] See eg *Re MB* [1997] EWCA 1361.

[62] Eg P Singer, 'Speciesism and Moral Status' (2009) 40 *Metaphilosophy* 56.

[63] C Mills, 'The Child's Right to an Open Future?' (2003) 34 *Journal of Social Philosophy* 499.

[64] J Herring, 'Losing it? Losing what? The Law and Dementia' (2009) 21 *Child and Family Law Quarterly* 3.

[65] E Feder Kittay, 'Equality, Dignity and Disability' in M Lyons and F Waldron (eds), *Perspectives on Equality* (Liffey Press, 2005) 95.

from the disability community and from my own observations—that she is capable of having a very good life, one full of joy, of love, of laughter: a life that includes the appreciation of some of the best of human culture, great music and fine food, and the delights of nature, water, the scent of flowers, the singing of birds. No, she cannot participate in political life, she cannot marry and have children, she cannot read a book or engage in moral reasoning, but her life is richly human and full of dignity. We need to work hard to see that her life is not tragic ...

In this passage, Feder Kittay shows how the disabled can be branded and defined by their lack of abilities in accordance with the norm. If we value in humanity not, or not only, a certain kind of rational thought, but the capacity for wonder, for unconditional loving, intense feeling, then many children and those with mental disability can have these to a greater extent than many adults.

Feder Kittay concludes her discussion of dignity with a central point:

I urge that we not look for the basis of dignity in attributions we have as individuals, but in the relationships we bear to one another. Relationships of caring serve as conduits of worth—the worth of the caregiver is conferred on the one to whom she devotes herself.

Although I would want to add to this analysis that, as explained in chapter two, in relationships of care it is hard to separate out who is the cared for and who is carer.[66] There is often an interdependency and interchange which means the obvious categories of care and cared for break down.

Emotions are, therefore, significant. Some have criticised care ethics as being an anti-intellectual kind of ethics, by valuing feeling over thought[67] and therefore inferior to, for example, Kantian ethics, which emphasise rationality and universal principles, rather than emotions. The attraction of the abstract principles is that it makes for easy decision making: the rules must be followed.[68] But in turn that can lead to an anti-ethical tendency. Thinking and acting in a way which makes 'emotional' sense is as important, if not more so, than doing so in a way which makes rational sense.[69] We need then, in our legal and ethical assessment, to place as much weight on what a person is thinking as on what they are feeling.[70] We need to focus on actual experience which is centred around emotion, rather than hypothetical people driven by rational thought alone.

---

[66] J Herring, 'Caregivers in Medical Law and Ethics' (2008) 25 *Journal of Contemporary Health Law and Policy* 1.

[67] E Loewy, 'Care Ethics: A Concept in Search of a Framework' (1995) *Cambridge Quarterly* 59.

[68] M Gray, 'Moral Sources and Emergent Ethical Theories in Social Work' (2010) 40 *British Journal of Social Work* 1794.

[69] For a discussion of emotion and autonomy, see M Friedman, *Autonomy, Gender, Politics* (Oxford University Press, 2006).

[70] R Pettersen, *Comprehending Care* (Lexington Books, 2008).

D. Intermingled Interests

An ethic of care is based on the belief that people are relational. They do not seek to promote only their own interests, not because they are 'selfless' but because their interests are tied up with the interests of others. They cannot seek to promote their own interests with no attention paid to others. It is the improvement of the relationship they seek. If good things happen to those they are in a positive relationship with then that is good for them. And the same is true for bad things.

An ethic of care, therefore, takes a particular view of the nature of the self,[71] one that is constructed through and finds its meanings in relation to others.[72] Supporters of an ethic of care do not need to entirely reject the notion of an individual self, but simply recognise that its identity and nature can only be appreciated through relation to others.[73] As Catriona Mackenzie writes: 'To be a person is to be a temporally extended embodied subject whose identity is constituted in and through one's lived bodily engagement with the world and others.'[74] Judith Butler, for example, has written of the 'negotiation of potential selves' that take place within intimate relationships, leading to co-creating mutual identities.[75] This can produce complex psychological tensions, as explained by Polona Curk:

> Intimacy constitutes the self as a dynamic entity, constructing its meanings (including the meaning of oneself) in close relationships with others. This immediately evokes vulnerability at the foundation of such meaning-making, based in the dynamics that includes both dependency and power relationship with the intimate other. These are held in mind in a shaky balance, with a constant defensive tendency to repudiate and hide one's own needy and vulnerable parts. Yet the desire to relate to another continually re-opens issues of attachments and mutual dependencies.[76]

The traditional approaches of law and ethics both fall into the trap of isolating the interests of each party. Family lawyers are familiar with the requirement under the Children Act 1989 to ascertain what order will promote the welfare of

---

[71] S Sherwin, 'A Relational Approach to Autonomy in Health Care' in S Sherwin (ed), *The Politics of Women's Health* (Temple University Press, 1998) 19.

[72] C Crittenden, 'The Principles of Care' (2001) 22 *Women & Politics* 81; S Andersen and S Chen, 'The Relational Self: An Interpersonal Social-Cognitive Theory' (2002) 109 *Psychological Review* 619–645; J Brown, *The Self* (McGraw-Hill, 1998).

[73] J Downie and J Llewellyn, *Being Relational* (UBC Press, 2011).

[74] C Mackenzie, 'Personal Identity, Narrative Integration and Embodiment' in S Campbell and L Meynell and S Sherwin (eds), *Embodiment and Agency* (Pennsylvania State University Press, 2009); P Curk, 'Passions, Dependencies, Selves: A Theoretical Psychoanalytic Account of Relational Responsibility' in C Lind, H Keating and J Bridgeman (eds), *Taking Responsibility, Law and the Changing Family* (Routledge, 2011).

[75] J Butler, *Antigone's Claim: Kinship between Life and Death* (Columbia University Press, 2000).

[76] P Curk, 'Passions, Dependencies, Selves: A Theoretical Psychoanalytic Account of Relational Responsibility' in C Lind, H Keating and J Bridgeman (eds), *Taking Responsibility, Law and the Changing Family* (Routledge, 2011); M Friedman, 'Feminist and Modern Friendship' in C Sustein (ed), *Feminism and Political Theory* (University of Chicago Press, 1990).

the child, considering only the interest of the child and not those of the parents.[77] As if we could separate the interests of a child from those of the parents! The Mental Capacity Act 2005 requires decisions to be made in the best interests of the person lacking capacity. Again, that appears to assume we can separate their interests and the interests of those in caring relationships with them. Typically, human rights pit the rights of one person against another and seek to balance them. Again this falsely assumes that we can separate out the rights of individuals. We will return to these issues in chapters five and six.

In relationships of caring and dependency, interests become intermingled.[78] We do not break down into 'me' and 'you'. To harm one person in a caring relationship is to harm the other. There should be no talk of balancing the interests of 'the carer' and the person 'cared for', rather the question should be emphasising the responsibilities they owe to each other in the context of a mutually supporting relationship.[79] This provides another reason why, as argued in chapter two, we should move away from the language of 'carer' and 'cared for'.

In summary, a recognition that our interests are intermingled causes problems for some of the mainstays of the law: individualised conceptions of best interests and of rights. Approaches based on an ethic of care require the development of legal tools which recognise that separating interests into individual rights is impossible and undesirable. Instead we can focus on assessing the impact of decisions on and in the context of caring relationships.

E. The Importance of Responsibilities

Ethics of care emphasise the importance of responsibilities within caring relationships. While not necessarily opposed to the idea of legal rights, they are wary of their dominance in the legal discourse, and the dangers that rights are used in an individualistic way. Supporters of ethics of care argue that rather than the primary focus of the legal or ethical enquiry being whether 'is my right to do X?', the question should be 'what is my proper obligation within the context of this relationship?'[80] Rather than the law promoting people's freedom from responsibility, the focus should be on how the law can enable people to fulfil their responsibilities. Rights primarily exist to enable people to carry out their responsibilities.[81]

---

[77] J Herring, 'The Welfare Principle and the Rights of Parents' in A Bainham, S Day Sclater and M Richards (eds), *What is a Parent?* (Hart, 1999).

[78] T Shakespeare, *Help* (Venture, 2000).

[79] G Clement, *Care, Autonomy and Justice: Feminism and the Ethic of Care* (Westview, 1996) 11.

[80] V Held, *The Ethics of Care* (Oxford University Press, 2006) 15.

[81] F Williams, 'The Presence of Feminism in the Future of Welfare' (2002) 31 *Economy and Society* 502.

In emphasising responsibilities, care ethicists do mean to imagine responsibilities in a rigid way, as simply the corollary of rights. Selma Sevenhuijsen explains:

> While the moral subject in the discourse of individual rights looks at moral dilemmas from the stance of the 'highest moral principles' and takes rights and responsibilities as a means of establishing relationships, the moral subject in the discourse of care already lives in a network of relation and (inter)dependence, in which he/she has to find balances between different forms of care: for the self, for others and for the relations between these.[82]

As this quote recognises, there is a danger that emphasising responsibilities can lead to an abusive result. This issue will be examined further when we look at the controversial relationship between care and justice shortly.

Care ethics take a very different approach to our understanding of how responsibilities arise. The classic liberal perspective is that one is 'born free' and that any responsibilities one takes must be in some sense voluntarily assumed.[83] However, for an ethic of care approach, with its starting point being that people are relational, then the supposition is that there will be responsibilities for others. We are born into relationships which carry responsibilities with them. So the response to a person in need is not an assessment of the extent you might owe them an obligation to assist, but rather an assessment of how one can meet that need, giving other caring responsibilities.[84] This approach is captured by Noddings:

> … an ethic of caring implies a limit on our [moral] obligation. Our obligation is limited and delimited by relation. We are never free, in the human domain, to abandon our preparedness to care; but, practically, if we are meeting those in our inner circles adequately as ones-caring and receiving those linked to our inner circles by formal chains of relation, we shall limit the calls upon our obligation quite naturally. We are not obliged to summon the 'I must' if there is no possibility of completion in the other. I am not obliged to care for starving children in Africa, because there is no way for this caring to be completed in the other unless I abandon the caring to which I am obligated.[85]

Therefore, the question is not 'is there a good reason to restrict my freedom?', but rather 'is it possible to have some freedom, given the responsibilities of those I am connected to?' This might, to some, seem shocking. Surely, they say, we should start with a presumption of freedom, rather than responsibility. However, I suggest two reasons why we should not. First, that reflects the

---

[82] S Sevenhuijsen, 'A Third Way? Moralities, Ethics and Families' in A Carling, S Duncan and R Edwards (eds), *Analysing Families* (Routledge, 2002) 131.

[83] V Davion, 'Autonomy, Integrity, and Care' (1993) *Social Theory and Practice* 161.

[84] S Sevenhuisen, 'Caring in the Third Way: The Relation between Obligation, Responsibility and Care in *Third Way* Discourse' (2000) 20 *Critical Social Policy* 5.

[85] N Noddings, *Caring: A Feminine Approach to Ethics and Moral Education* (University of California Press, 1984) 86.

reality of life for most people. Our lives are not marked by freedom, but by our responsibilities to others. Second, it is in our responsibilities that relationships flourish and in our relationships that we flourish. As Polona Curk puts it, 'We take responsibility for each other because we continue to need each other and because we establish meaningful relationships through taking responsibility for each other.'[86]

F. The Importance of Non-Abstraction

One of the key aspects of care ethics is the rejection of abstract moral rules. Instead we should start with the context and concrete reality of the particular situations and the individuals and their relationships and characteristics. What might work for one group of people in one situation, will not work in another. Hence it is that those taking an ethics of care approach will often say in the face of an ethical dilemma, 'well it all depends on the circumstances of the case'. That is because it does.

Nel Noddings writes: 'Since so much depends on the subjective experience of those involved in ethical encounters, conditions are rarely "sufficiently similar" for me to declare that you must do what I must do.'[87]

She explains:

> To act as one-caring, then, is to act with special regard for the particular person in a concrete situation ... she acts in a non-rule-bound fashion in behalf of the cared-for ... [An ethic of care] does not attempt to reduce the need for human judgment with a series of 'Thou shalts' and 'Thou shalt nots'. Rather, it recognizes and calls forth human judgment across a wide range of fact and feeling, and it allows for situations and conditions in which judgment (in the impersonal, logical sense) may properly be put aside in favor of faith and commitment.[88]

This is, in part, a corollary of the nature of care. Care seeks out the needs of the particular individual in their particular context. What meets one particular individual's needs is inevitably personalised and not susceptible to generalised rules. Similarly, the extent to which a person may be expected to provide care involves an assessment of their particular circumstances.

Some of the writing on an ethic of care on this issue exaggerates the distinction between abstract and individualised principles.[89] There can be very few if, any, ethicists who seek to apply abstract principles to a problem, with

---

[86] P Curk, 'Passions, Dependencies, Selves: A Theoretical Psychoanalytic Account of Relational Responsibility' in C Lind, H Keating and J Bridgeman (eds), *Taking Responsibility, Law and the Changing Family* (Routledge, 2011).

[87] N Noddings, *Caring: A Feminine Approach to Ethics and Moral Education* (University of California Press, 1984) 5.

[88] Ibid 24–25.

[89] O O'Dowd, 'Care and Abstract Principles' (2012) 27 *Hypatia* 407.

no understanding of context.[90] Even the principle 'thou shalt not kill' is typically then hedged around with conditions which take into account the circumstances of the individual case. Similarly, an ethics of care approach is not without principle, not least the principle of promotion of care. Further, in considering the context, there must be some principles limiting what factors are relevant and which constitute the context that should be considered.[91]

The debate is therefore better understood as striking the balance between principle and context. Presenting the debate in extremes is unhelpful. I would emphasise that an ethic of care is a particularly sensitive context in four particular ways.

First, it looks at the history of the relationships. It is only in understanding where the relationship has travelled that we can understand what responsibilities might have arisen as a result.

Second, it looks forward to what is likely to be undertaken during the course of the relationship in the future and asks why a decision now will (a) be a fair aspect of the relationship and (b) provide the best foundation of an ongoing caring relationship.

Third, it will be attuned to the individuals' other caring responsibilities and relationships. As already mentioned, it may be that caring responsibilities in one relationship mean that a person cannot meet their caring responsibilities in another.

Fourth, it means people and their relationships should be reduced to a general principle or presumption. To give one example, in family law we should not place significant weight on a presumption that a child should have contact with both parents after divorce, when looking at a particular case. That may be generally true, but we must consider what is best for this child in the context of their relationships, rather than placing weight on generalisations. As Jo Bridgeman powerfully argues:

> unless consideration is given to the individual child, to the person they are, their personality, character, feelings of pleasure and pain, and relational interests (relationships with those upon whom they depend), determination about the best interests of the child are reached according to current ideas about the child and according to adult memories of childhood.[92]

A fine example of the importance of context in practice is the decision of the Supreme Court in *R (McDonald) v Royal Borough of Kensington & Chelsea*.[93] This case will be discussed properly in chapter four. For now it is enough to note in the case concerned whether it was lawful for the local authority to withdraw finance for a carer who would assist Ms McDonald in

---

[90] J Grimshaw, *Philosophy and Feminist Thinking* (University of Minnesota Press, 1986) 205.

[91] H Kuhse, *Caring* (Blackwell, 1997) 120–121.

[92] J Bridgeman, *Parents, Young Children and Healthcare Law* (Cambridge University Press, 2007) 9.

[93] [2011] UKSC 33.

using the bathroom at night and, instead, require her to wear incontinence pads. The judgments of the majority focused on applying the legal principles from previous case law. For Baroness Hale in the minority the focus was on the practical impact of the decision on Ms McDonald. Her speech led Lord Walker to write: 'I find it rather regrettable that Lady Hale's judgment makes so many references to defecation.'[94] Yet Lady Hale's emphasis on the practical realities, rather than the abstract principles, is one of the things that make her judgment so compelling, and so appropriate from the perspective of a supporter of an ethic of care.[95]

IV. Disputed Issues Surrounding an Ethic of Care

Having set out some of the main themes of an ethic of care, we shall now further explore some of the issues of particular difficulty or dispute within an ethic of care.

A. What is Care?

This important issue is discussed in chapter two. There I considered arguments about whether care was a feeling or an action; whether caring should be restricted to meeting basic needs; and the relevance of relationships in care. I argued that care should be seen as carrying the markers of meeting needs; being respectful; acknowledging responsibilities and being relational.

B. Justice and Care

In her writing, Carol Gilligan contrasted an ethic of care with an ethic of justice.[96] This was seen by some to imply that justice had no part to play in an ethic of care, although a close reading of Gilligan suggests that in drawing the distinction she was not arguing that an ethic of care should abandon concepts of justice altogether. This distinction between care and justice has proved both problematic and fruitful for care ethicists.

---

[94] Ibid, para 32.

[95] Many fine examples can be found in the book, R Hunter, C McGlynn and E Rackley (eds), *Feminist Judgments* (Hart, 2010), where leading cases are considered and a feminist judgement offered. In many of these, the impact of the decisions on the real lives of those involved, so often sidelined in the legal analysis, is brought to the fore.

[96] N Noddings, *Caring: A Feminine Approach to Ethics and Moral Education* (University of California Press, 1984).

There is a dilemma for care ethicists. Without justice, an ethic of care might be seen to support harmful or manipulative activities.[97] Without a concept of justice is it possible to restrict the obligations of care or to acknowledge the unfairness of the distribution of care? However, if we focus on justice without care insufficient weight is placed on the value of care.

The issue of the relationship between care and justice has proved controversial but most contemporary care ethicists agree there needs to be some kind of 'meshing of care and justice'.[98] We must have some process of evaluating the goodness of the relationship and that requires values independent of care itself.[99] Otherwise there is a danger that the parties will become objectified.[100] Quite how this is expressed may differ. For some justice plays a primary role within which care ethics can operate; for others care ethics must be the starting point and justice mitigates its application.

I find the writing of Virginia Held particularly persuasive on this issue. She wants to keep the distinction between an ethics of care and an ethic of justice:

> An ethic of justice focuses on questions of fairness, equality, individual rights, abstract principles, and the consistent application of them. An ethic of care focuses on attentiveness, trust, responsiveness to need, narrative nuance, and cultivating caring relations. Whereas an ethic of justice seeks a fair solution between competing individual interests and rights, an ethic of care sees the interest of carers and cared-for as importantly intertwined rather than as simply competing.[101]

Held makes it clear that an ethic of care includes justice:

> There can be care without justice. There has historically been little justice in the family, but care and life have gone on without it. There can be no justice without care, however, for without care no child would survive and there would be no persons to respect.[102]

With those observations we can start to see how care and justice actually need to work together.[103] We cannot understand justice, without appreciating care. As Selma Sevenhuijsen explains:

> ...Justice should be based on values such as reconciliation, reciprocity, diversity and responsibility, and on the willingness and ability of citizens to accept responsibility for each other's well-being. Justice, thus conceived, explicitly opens up discursive

---

[97] P Meyers, 'The "Ethic of Care"' and the Problem of Power' (1998) 8 *Journal of Political Philosophy* 142; D Koehn, *Rethinking Feminist Ethics: Care, Trust and Empathy* (Routledge, 1998).

[98] V Held, *The Ethics of Care* (Oxford University Press, 2006) 128; R West, *Caring for Justice* (New York University Press, 1999).

[99] V Davion, 'Autonomy, Integrity, and Care' (1993) *Social Theory and Practice* 161.

[100] W Hollway, 'Introducing the Capacity to Care' in W Hollway, *The Capacity to Care: Gender and Ethical Subjectivity. Women and Psychology* (Routledge, 2006).

[101] V Held, *The Ethics of Care* (Oxford University Press, 2006) 15.

[102] Ibid 17.

[103] A Mol, *The Logic of Care: Health and the Problem of Patient Choice* (Routledge, 2008) 75.

space for deliberating about what constitutes injustice or, in other words, for continuous reflection on which 'social evils' we need to address.[104]

Justice, so understood, supports care. Just to be clear, we are talking here not about the 'ethic of justice' Gilligan was talking about, but a justice that operates to promote caring relationships. The relationship between the two can be clarified in the following points.

First, a relationship marked by injustice, where there is no due respect for each party, where there is no relational aspect, will fall outside the definition of a caring relationship which I set out in chapter two. As explained there, elements of justice are central to the understanding of care. This must be an essential point for care ethics. John Eekelaar has powerfully warned of the dangers of emphasising the importance of communal values over the individual.[105] As he emphasises, within communities individuals can suffer serious oppression. However, this should not lead us to abandon relational values but rather ensure they operate justly.

Eekelaar's concerns may to some extent be met by Robert Leckey's helpful distinction between what he calls a relational approach and a communitarian one. He argues:

> Relational theory distinguishes itself from communitarianism in its commitment to the capacity for individuals, especially women, to revise their life plans and choose ways of living other than those presented to them by the social contexts in which they are embedded and by which they are constituted. It is awareness of the oppression of unchosen attachments that prevents relational theory from rejecting core elements of liberalism, such as the priority of individuals.[106]

While a communitarian approach might place the interests of the community above the individual, an ethic of care would not. True, it would promote caring relationships, rather than pursuing individual rights, but it would do so it would not be undermining the value of the individual. Rather, it would claim that it is within these relationships that individuals find their value and meaning. It promotes relationships and in so doing will promote the interests of individuals. So, an ethic of care escapes the danger which troubles Eekelaar, that the rights of individuals may be downtrodden in the name of promoting the community good; because it take the interests of the individual seriously. However, unlike the traditional individualistic model, it identifies the interests of the individual within their relationships.

Second, justice must be understood within the context of care. An incident viewed in isolation may appear to be unjust, an unreasonable demand; but when viewed in the context of the relationship is a reasonable sharing of the

---

[104] S Sevenhuijsen, *Citizenship and the Ethics of Care: Feminist Considerations on Justice, Morality, and Politics* (Routledge, 1998) 145.
[105] J Eekelaar, 'Law, Family and Community' in G Douglas and N Lowe (eds), *The Continuing Evolution of Family Law* (Jordans, 2009).
[106] R Leckey, *Contextual Subjects* (University of Toronto Press, 2008) 10.

burdens. We can only produce a coherent model of justice if we start with a norm of people existing in interlocking relationships, because that is the reality for people's lives. If we seek to produce a model of justice which is not premised on care then we will be building a model of justice on a false basis.

Third, justice plays a crucial role in care ethics, because it means that it seeks not just the promotion of caring relationships, but also a fair sharing of the burdens of care at a national and international level.[107] Given the limited resources of individuals, to meet peoples' needs the burdens of care need to be shared out fairly, supplying, where necessary, the means for people to do that. A caring society likewise will ensure that the burdens of caring relationships are shared appropriately and fairly between people and that where a caring relationship causes disadvantage, society does what it can to restrict that disadvantage.[108] You could reach a very similar conclusion from a justice perspective. As Martha Nussbaum writes:

> A just society ... would not stigmatize these children and stunt their development; it would support their health, education, and full participation in social and even, where possible, political life. A just society, we might think, would also look at the other side of the problem, the burdens on people who provide care for dependents.[109]

Fourth, attempting to consider justice, without prioritising care, will fail. As Virginia Held explains:

> I now think that caring relations should form the wider moral framework into which justice should be fitted. Care seems the most basic moral value ... Without care ... there would be no persons to respect and no families to improve ... Within a network of caring, we can and should demand justice, but justice should not push care to the margins, imagining justice's political embodiment as the model of morality, which is what has been done.[110]

Care is the most primary value as it is essential to meet people's most basic survival needs, without that talk of justice would be meaningless.[111] We need to support and enable care, so that justice can be considered. To be blunt we could survive in a society which was not just, but we could not survive in a society in which there was no care.

There are some ethics of care writers who are worried that if too much is claimed for an ethics of care it will lose its distinctive edge. Daniel Engster argues that care theory should not be 'a repository for all feminist and other

---

[107] T Pettersen, 'The Ethics of Care: Normative Structures and Empirical Implications' (2011) 19 *Health Care Analysis* 51.

[108] B Rodríguez Ruiz, 'Caring Discourse: The Care/Justice Debate Revisited' (2005) 31 *Philosophy and Social Criticism* 773.

[109] M Nussbaum, 'Capabilities as Fundamental Entitlements: Sen and Social Justice' (2003) 9 *Feminist Economics* 33.

[110] V Held, *The Ethics of Care* (Oxford University Press, 2006) 71–72.

[111] P Meyers, 'The "Ethic of Care" and the Problem of Power' (1998) 8 *Journal of Political Philosophy* 142.

social justice concerns'.[112] There is no doubt that ambitious attempts have been used to utilise ethics of care to deal with a huge range of problems, from environmental concerns to regulation of markets to international relations. Indeed one of the things demonstrated by these writings is how many different facets of life do impact on caring.

To conclude, care and justice should go hand in hand. As Grace Clements writes, 'Care and justice should not be seen as competitors, but as allies which are indispensable to one another.'[113] Unless there is caring there is no possibility for justice, yet we need justice so that we can care. Without justice care can become abuse and without care justice loses its heart. There is, therefore, no conflict, it is a matter of reimaging what we mean by care to ensure there is justice and justice to ensure that it enables care.

C. Care of Self

Does an ethic of care have room for a care of the self? Certainly there is writing that seems to suggests not, or at least that caring is about putting one's own interests last. Nel Noddings claims: 'even in situations when I find it difficult to engage in caring action, I am under an obligation to do so if I want to be moral, that is, to maintain myself as one-caring'.[114]

However, I argue that part of care, is care of self. A simple point is that a degree of care for the self is required if one is to care. As Robin West argues:

> Relationships of care, untempered by the demands of justice, resulting in the creation of injured, harmed, exhausted, compromised, and self-loathing 'giving selves,' rather than in genuinely compassionate and giving individuals, are ubiquitous in this society, and it is far more often women than men who are injured by them.[115]

Further, if one does not meet one's own needs, then these may well become the responsibility of someone else to fulfil. In some cases that may be the appropriate balancing of caring responsibilities between the individuals themselves. However, it may also mean that making oneself a burden for others is not an appropriate allocation of the burdens of caring relationships.

Diemut Bubeck is highly critical of Nel Nodding's description of an ethic of care, which appears to call for the carer to be utterly altruistic. She argues that this leads to an 'oppressive ideology' and 'a catalyst for exploitation by preventing those who endorse it from taking seriously or even realizing

---

[112] D Engster, *The Heart of Justice* (Oxford University Press, 2007) 14.

[113] G Clements, *Care, Autonomy, and Justice* (Westview, 1996) 109.

[114] N Noddings, *Caring: A Feminine Approach to Ethics and Moral Education* (University of California Press, 1984) 82.

[115] R West, *Caring for Justice* (New York University Press, 1997) 81.

the fact that they are being exploited'.[116] However, these concerns should not lead us to abandon an ethic of care. By asking whether this is a caring relationship, exhibiting justice of the kind just mentioned, we can escape that danger and give self-care its proper place.

D. Gender and Ethic of Care

There are two issues here. The first is an empirical claim that was made in Carol Gilligan's writing that women are more likely to reason using ethic of care than men.[117] Gilligan portrays women as nurturers, who define themselves by their relationships and contextualise their moral reasoning, while men are seen as defining themselves by individual achievement and abstract thinking. Noddings argues that an ethic of care is feminine and can be contrasted with the 'masculine ethics of universal love and justice'. Men, she argued, are fundamentally separate selves, while women (due to such experiences as pregnancy, intercourse, and breast-feeding) are 'essentially connected' to others.[118] Such a claim in more recent times has been played down.[119] More recent studies have questions whether differences in moral reasoning are simply reflecting cultural or societal norms, rather than neurobiological differences between men and women.[120] Indeed Gilligan herself made it clear she was not claiming there was a biological cause of the 'different voice' for women. Any difference, therefore, in the care capabilities between men and women is culturally produced, rather than biologically essential.[121]

More interesting, is the debate over whether it is useful to see an ethic of care as necessarily feminist. There can be no doubt that anyone asking 'the women's question' should be concerned about care.[122] Women undertake the vast majority of care work and therefore suffer, particularly from the inadequate weight placed on care in society's allocation of resources. In Becker's words:

Traditionally, women have been—and women continue to be—caretakers of dependents, the young, the old, and others unable to care for themselves. Women have done this work for no pay, in their own families, or for low pay, when caring for dependents in other women's families .... Workers with significant caretaking

---

[116] D Bubeck, *Care, Gender and Justice* (Oxford University Press, 1996) 177.

[117] C Gilligan, *In a Different Voice* (Harvard University Press, 1982).

[118] R West, *Caring for Justice* (New York University Press, 1997) 3.

[119] S Edwards, 'Three Versions of an Ethics of Care' (2009) 10 *Nursing Philosophy* 231.

[120] Eg S Juujarvi, 'Care and Justice in Real-Life Moral Reasoning'(2005) 12 *Journal of Adult Development* 199.

[121] S Bowlby, L McKie, S Gregory and I Macpherson, *Interdependency and Care over the Lifecourse* (Routledge, 2010).

[122] P Bowden, *Caring: Gender Sensitive Ethics* (Routledge, 1997).

responsibilities are at a disadvantage in the wage-labor market, in politics, sports, and other 'public' areas of human endeavor .... [U]ntil we place greater value on caretaking and provide support for caretakers of dependents, women will continue to be unequal.[123]

In a similar vein, Robin West[124] claims that

women as a women, as a group, have been *subordinated* in this culture, rather than simply 'discriminated against' by the state. One (but not the only) consequence of that subordination, is that *all* women's work, distinctive attributes, experiences, perspectives and sensibilities have been undervalued: such attributes, experiences, perspectives, and sensibilities must be, in order to sustain the moral justification for women's lesser status and lesser lives.[125]

While that does, I argue, make an ethic of care particularly appealing for feminists and, when seen in the broader feminist context, can provide a further argument in favour of adopting an ethic of care approach, there is no reason why a non-feminist could not also be attracted to an ethic of care approach.

It certainly is possible to develop an ethic of care which is not 'feminist'. Michael Slote,[126] for example, grounds ethic of care in terms of virtue ethics, and in particular the virtue of empathy. There is nothing particularly gendered about his presentation of it, although he thinks more women than men have the virtue. Daniel Engster[127] promotes what he describes as a 'minimally feminist theory of care', wanting to emphasise that many other feminist concerns fall outside an ethic of care.

The ethic of care approach ties in most neatly with those writers espousing feminism of difference. This accepts that (for whatever reason) men and women undertake different roles in society but insists that we must ensure that they are not disadvantaged by the performance of those roles. This, crudely, can be differentiated from feminism of equality which promotes a society in which women and men have equal access to the same goals.

While many feminists of difference would promote an ethic of care, they need not. As Joan Williams points out, a feminist of difference might seek to 'stress women's intuition, their sexual power, and their alliance with deep forces of irrationality';[128] rather than their caring. Such feminists of difference might be concerned that an ethic of care too easily slips into caricaturing women as emotional and irrational and not capable of abstract thought. Indeed Gilligan's talk of 'women's voice' carries with it dangers of sidelining women for whom the care talk does not resonate.

---

[123] M Becker, 'Care and Feminists' (2002) 17 *Wisconsin Women's Law Journal* 57, 58.
[124] R West, *Caring for Justice* (New York University Press, 1997).
[125] Ibid 7–8.
[126] M Slote, *The Ethics of Care and Empathy* (Routledge, 2007) 172–73.
[127] D Engster, *The Heart of Justice* (Oxford University Press, 2007) 5.
[128] J Williams, 'Deconstructing Gender' (1989) 87 *Michigan Law Review* 797.

To conclude on this issue, an ethic of care is especially attractive to feminist writers, especially those who espouse feminism of difference. It can be a powerful tool to explore the subordination of women's work and values. Promoting values of care can have a direct impact on the lives of women. However, I suggest, it is possible to adopt an ethic of care from a non-feminist perspective.

E. Autonomy and Care

One of the central rights in the liberal legal world is the right to autonomy. This section will consider how an ethic of care interacts with this powerful concept. Joseph Raz defines it in this way:

> The ruling idea behind the ideal of personal autonomy is that people should make their own lives. The autonomous person is a (part) author of his own life. The ideal of personal autonomy is the vision of people controlling, to some degree, their own destiny, fashioning it through successive decisions throughout their lives.[129]

Such an understanding of autonomy is central to a liberal conception of the self. As Helen Reece puts it:

> within liberalism, what is arguably most essential to the individual's identity is the individual's capacity to choose his or her own roles and identities, and to rethink those choices.[130]

This individualist conception of autonomy is linked to a whole set of other ideas: self-sufficiency, self-sovereignty, moral independence, self-government, pluralism and liberty.[131]

Autonomy is commonly presented in an individualistic way. Jeremy Waldron explains:

> Talk of personal autonomy evokes the image of a person in charge of his life, not just following his desires but choosing which of his desires to follow. It is not an immoral idea, but it has relatively little to do with morality. Those who value it do not value it as part of the moral enterprise of reconciling one person's interest with another's; instead they see it as a particular way of understanding what each person's interest consists in.[132]

Individual autonomy is an idea that is generally understood to refer to the capacity to be one's own person, to live one's life according to reasons and motives that are taken as one's own and not the product of manipulative

---

[129] J Raz, *The Morality of Freedom* (Oxford University Press, 1986) 369.

[130] H Reece, *Divorcing Responsibly* (Hart, 2003) 13.

[131] M Fineman, *The Autonomy Myth* (New Press, 2004) 263.

[132] J Waldron, 'Moral Autonomy and Personal Autonomy' in J Christman (ed), *Autonomy and the New Challenges to Liberalism* (Cambridge University Press, 2005).

or distorting external forces.[133] Supporters of the traditional approach will quickly add that the definition of autonomy does not tell people how to behave. People might exercise their autonomy to build up deep and caring relationships. Indeed we might hope they do. There is nothing, they would emphasise, that discourages or prevents people being relational. It is therefore perfectly consistent with an ethic of care. That suggestion is, I suggest, unconvincing and I will seek to explain why.

The precise link between autonomy and an ethic of care is somewhat troubled. One approach is to abandon the concept of autonomy as being of no relevance in a relational setting. However, the other is seeking to develop a new relational approach to autonomy. It is this which I would promote.

There are close links between an ethic of care and relational autonomy.[134] Relational autonomy grew out of a perception that many forms of liberal autonomy were overly individualistic and thereby failed to accord sufficient weight to the fact that decisions are taken within the context of relationships.[135] It requires that people's decisions are understood in the context of the relationships they live in and that the obligations that flow from those relationships are given due weight.

Lorraine Code[136] argues that for supporters of individualised autonomy:

> Autonomous man is—and should be—self-sufficient, independent, and self-reliant, a self-realizing individual who directs his efforts towards maximizing his personal gains. His independence is under constant threat from other (equally self-serving) individuals: hence he devises rules to protect himself from intrusion. Talk of right, rational self-interest, expedience, and efficiency permeates his moral, social, and political discourse. In short, there has been a gradual alignment of autonomy with individualism.

It might be thought that this argument is criticising the way some people exercise their autonomy, rather than criticising the principle of autonomy itself. However, the concept of autonomy, as traditionally understood, is based on the idea that we are and should be free to live our lives as we wish. Yet, what supporters of an ethic of care would emphasis is that talk of 'our lives' is mistaken.[137] At the heart of relational autonomy is a 'shared conviction ... that persons are socially embedded and that agents' identities are formed

---

[133] J Christman, 'Autonomy in Moral and Political Philosophy', available at http://plato.stanford.edu/entries/autonomy-moral/.

[134] M Verker, 'The Care Perspective and Autonomy' (2001) 4 *Medicine, Health Care and Philosophy* 289.

[135] J Nedelsky, *Law's Relations* (Oxford University Press, 2011).

[136] L Code, 'Second Persons' in L Code (ed), *What Can She Know? Feminist Theory and the Construction of Knowledge* (Cornell University Press, 1991) 78.

[137] C Mackenzie and N Stoljar, 'Autonomy Refigured' in C Mackenzie and N Stoljar (eds), *Relational Autonomy* (Oxford University Press, 2000) 4.

within the context of social relationships and shaped by a complex of intersecting social determinants, such as race, class, gender, and ethnicity'.[138]

A relational autonomy model argues that the image of the self-controlled, bounded, independent man at the heart of autonomy misconceives how people understand their lives, especially when in close emotional relationships. We are not constantly clashing rights with those we live with; rather our interests are intertwined. People in close relationships seek a compromise which is good for 'us' and do not see it as a matter of weighing up competing interests.

The intertwining of identities and interests means that to discuss 'my decision' is simply a fiction. Our decisions are constrained by the responsibilities and realities of our lives and the relationships within which we are embedded.[139]

So the starting point for relational autonomy is not the free unencumbered self, but rather a person who is integrated into a network of relationships. These relationships and the obligations and restriction on choice that flow from them are constitutive of autonomy, rather than being seen as restrictive of it.

A supporter of traditional autonomy may be left wondering what room is left for autonomy in this model. The autonomy is there. People have freedom in their caring functions and these relationships, but these are bounded by them and subject to restrictions flowing from them. So it is the goal of relational autonomy to build up relationships that enhance our lives, rather than seeking to maximise freedom and thereby enhancing our lives.[140]

Some autonomy supporters might see dangers in this explanation of relational autonomy. In particular, a person within an oppressive set of relationships may have their personal autonomy too readily overridden.[141] However, there are good reasons to doubt this concern. First, taking an ethic of care will require a careful evaluation of the context of the relationship. If it is one which does not promote a caring relationship or is not showing due respect, then an ethic of care approach will bring this out better than any other. Second, an ethic of care will acknowledge that a person may leave one relationship to find a more caring relationship. Indeed where that is an appropriate response to differing caring responsibilities that may be required. The victim of an oppressive relationship does not need splendid isolation but a new, more caring relationship.[142]

---

[138] Ibid 4.

[139] J Nedelsky, 'Reconceiving Autonomy: Sources, Thoughts and Possibilities' (1989) 1 *Yale Journal of Law and Feminism* 7.

[140] M Verker, 'The Care Perspective and Autonomy' (2001) 4 *Medicine, Health Care and Philosophy* 289.

[141] J Christman, *The Politics of Persons* (Cambridge University Press, 2009).

[142] V Held, *The Ethics of Care* (Oxford University Press, 1996).

F. For Whom Should We Care?

One area of keen debate in care ethics is to whom the obligation of care is owed.[143] There are two main questions here. The first concerns particularism: does the caring relationship create particular obligations between the two parties over and above obligations to others? Second, on what principles should a person determine to whom they owe a duty of care?

On the first question, imagine there is a fire in a house. Does a mother have a greater obligation to rescue her child than another child in the house? For Nel Noddings, the care relationship imposes restrictions on the obligation on the carer. This is because, she argues, care involves 'engrossment and motivational displacement'.[144] The motivational displacement is important because to Noddings this means that the goals of the cared for person must become the goals of the carer in a caring relationship. Hence the greater call of the cared for over and above any other seeking claims against the carer.

That may not, at first, seem controversial. At least, it is an answer that can be provided from a range of ethical perspectives. But, a telling and controversial example has been presented by Noddings. She discusses a woman who knows a black man who is facing racist abuse. Should she fight against the racists with him, even if some of the abusers are the woman's family? To some commentators siding with the family would be clearly immoral.[145] Noddings finds the issue less straightforward because of the woman's commitments of care to her family. Even though many care ethicists would not share Nodding's difficulty in deciding the appropriate course of action, this leads some to criticise an ethic of care as leading to a conclusion that preference to preserving family relationships fails to attach sufficient moral weight on the interests of others.

In contrast to the Noddings approach, Peter Singer has argued in favour of a principle of equal consideration of interests such that 'we give equal weight in our moral deliberations to the like interests of all those affected by our actions'.[146] Virginia Held[147] disagrees, arguing that the 'universal, impartial, liberal principles of justice and right' should not always have priority over the 'concerns of caring relationships, which include considerations of trust, friendship, and loyalty'.

One of the reasons in favour of partiality is that care is personal. Robin West explains, 'When we nurture, we nurture particular persons, not groups,

---

[143] L Campbell-Brown, 'The Ethic of Care' (1997) 4 *UCL Jurisprudence Review* 272.

[144] N Noddings, *Caring: A Feminine Approach to Ethics and Moral Education* (University of California Press, 1984) 15–20, 33–34.

[145] V Davion, 'Autonomy, Integrity, and Care' (1993) *Social Theory and Practice* 161, 171.

[146] P Singer, *Practical Ethics* (Oxford University Press, 1993) 21. For further discussion see M Baron, 'Impartiality and Friendship' (1991) 101 *Ethics* 836; and B Barry, *Justice as Impartiality* (Oxford University Press, 1995) ch 10.

[147] V Held, *The Ethics of Care* (Oxford University Press, 2006).

nations, or species, and when we nurture a particular person, we seek to make that person as fulfilled as possible.'[148]

As argued in chapter two, a central aspect of care is responsibility. In caring relationships the parties take on responsibilities to meet the needs of another, so far as is compatible with other caring responsibilities. Responsibilities are key. Because of our vulnerabilities we need to be able to rely on others to meet our needs. The parent's knowledge of the best way to deal with the over-excited autistic child or the carer's knowledge of how to calm the distressed dementia sufferer is only acquired through lengthy time together. That requires a priority given to those with whom we are in a caring relationship over other claims.

There is another important point here. It may be that the most caring thing to do in some cases is not to offer care. A person who is attentive to the needs of those around them and responsive to them, may determine that a particular set of needs are best met by someone else, or that the individual with needs does not want those needs met. This will narrow down the appropriate needs to seek to meet, so the burdens of an ethic of care do not become overwhelming.

The second issue is to ask where the obligation to care falls. The argument might be made that care ethics is either too broad or too narrow. If the claim is that we are to care only for those we are associated with, that restricts the significance of care ethics. It covers simply our obligations towards those we know. However, if it is said we owe obligations to the world at large then other principles must be relied upon to explain how the obligation is to be restricted.

Olivia Little suggests that although an ethic of care is directed to enabling concrete relations between individuals and the meeting of individual needs, it can also be used to develop broader social policies that enable care to happen.[149] Seeking a social and international approach based on caring relationships is something any caring person should want. Notably this is slightly different from requiring a society to promote compassion[150] or empathy.[151] This is because an ethic of care would require the promotion of acts of caring. Virginia Held argues that a world adopting an ethic of care would create caring non-governmental organisations seeking to improve the rights of others. She writes:

> The small societies of family and friendship embedded in larger societies are formed by caring relations ... A globalization of caring relations would help enable people of different states and cultures to live in peace, to respect each others' rights, to care together for their environments, and to improve the lives of their children.[152]

---

[148] R West, *Caring for Justice* (New York University Press, 1997) 69.

[149] O Little, 'Care: Theory to Orientation' (1998) 23 *Journal of Medicine and Philosophy* 190, 204.

[150] C Frakes, 'When Strangers Call: A Consideration of Care, Justice, and Compassion' (2010) 25 *Hypatia* 79.

[151] M Slote, *The Ethics of Care and Empathy* (Routledge, 2007).

[152] V Held, *The Ethics of Care* (Oxford University Press, 2006) 168.

An ethic of care, therefore, does not just require individuals to meet their caring responsibilities; it requires states and the international community to promote care too.

G. Care Ethics and Virtue Ethic

One major issue is the relationship between care ethics and virtue ethics.[153] Is it best to understand care ethics as simply an application of care ethics?[154] Raja Halwani has argued exactly that. She suggests we should see care as simply one virtue, a particularly important one, but only one among others that constitute a flourishing life. I will argue that despite the similarities between care ethics and virtue ethics, there are some important differences.

First, care ethicists focus on care as the central issue, rather that placing it alongside other virtues. They will do this because it is care that meets the central needs people have and so has priority over other activities. Indeed Virginia Held suggests it is the virtue from which all other virtues flow.[155]

Michael Slote contends that care ethics is based on the virtue of empathy.[156] He prefers empathy to care, because it opens the concept up to a broad range of people. We might have empathy with those suffering far away, we cannot care for them. Empathy, he argues, provides a principle of broader application than care. However that is a minority view. More common is Held's view: 'Virtue ethics focuses especially on the state of character of individuals, whereas the ethics of care concerns itself especially with caring relations. Caring relations have primary value.'[157] As suggested earlier, Slote's application of an ethic of care may be too narrow. Once we take into account the responsibilities and ethic of care would place on local, national and international organisations, the breadth of its application can be appreciated.

Second, and more significantly, care ethicists will emphasise the practical and pragmatic side of care. Care is valuable not because it makes you a virtuous person but it helps meet the needs of another.[158] This is where the most marked difference appears from most presentations of virtue ethics and care ethics. To deal with this point, Linda Zagzebski adopts a definition of virtue that involves motives and ends: '[virtue is] a deep and enduring acquired

---

[153] P Benner, 'A Dialogue between Virtue Ethics and Care Ethics' (1997) 18 *Theoretical Medicine and Bioethics* 1.

[154] R Halwani, 'Care Ethics and Virtue Ethics' (2003) 18 *Hypatia* 161.

[155] V Held, *The Ethics of Care* (Oxford University Press, 2006) ch 1.

[156] M Slote, *The Ethics of Care and Empathy* (Routledge, 2007) 172–73.

[157] V Held, *The Ethics of Care* (Oxford University Press, 1996).

[158] M Sander-Staudt, 'The Unhappy Marriage of Care Ethics and Virtue Ethics' (2006) 21 *Hypatia* 12.

excellence of a person, involving a characteristic motivation to produce a certain desired end and reliable success in bringing about that end'.[159]

It is not clear how many virtue theorists would be willing to include success in bringing about the result as significant in virtue ethics. In any event, what is of particular value to most care ethicists in caring is the meeting of needs, not the virtue that produces it.

Third, restricting caring to a virtue gives it a more limited political role, one more akin to personal morality, than the grander aims for an ethic of care. Care ethics wish to challenge the unjust division of care work and to challenge the idea that care work marginalises people, as well as recognising its moral worth. The goal of care ethics is not just to promote a virtuous life but to achieve a caring society and the promotion of caring relationships around the world.

Ultimately, therefore, there is some common ground between care ethics and virtue ethics. Both are likely to value caring attitudes and the practice of care, but the two are not synonymous and rather different in scope. It may be, and we will return to this later, that the distinction between the two is particularly relevant when developing a legal response to these issues.

V. Criticisms of an Ethic of Care

We now turn to criticisms that have been made of an ethic of care.

A. Importance of Self

As argued earlier, one of the themes of an ethic of care is that our identity is found in relationship with others. It is through relationships of care that we are who we are and the boundaries between us and others become blurred. However, that view has raised concerns. Robert Goodin argues that

> the trouble with subsuming individuals into relationships of 'we'ness is precisely that we then risk losing track of the 'separateness of people. Within a full ... relationship of 'we'ness, we are a single entity, a single personality. Then any can speak for all. That, in turn, makes it easy for everyone to impose upon (to exploit, if not strictly dominate) any or indeed every other.[160]

---

[159] L Zagzebski, *Virtues of the Mind: An Inquiry into the Nature of Virtue and the Ethical Foundations of Knowledge* (Cambridge University Press, 1996).

[160] R Goodin, 'Structures of Political Order: The Relational Feminist Alternative' (1996) 38 *Political Order: NOMOS* 498, 507.

This is similar to the argument we have already encountered from John Eekelaar that in focusing on relationships we lose sight of the importance of individuals.[161]

John Christman[162] argues:

Just as conceiving of persons as denuded of social relations denies the importance of such relations to the self-understandings of many of us at various times in our lives, to define persons as necessarily related in particular ways similarly denies the reality of change over time, variability in self-conception, and multiplicities of identity characteristic of modern populations.

These arguments are important and are the best arguments against an ethic of care approach. The answers have been trailed in the discussion to date and they explore some very deep questions about the nature of our identity. Is our identity found in our relationship with others? Or is our identity found in ourselves and therefore it is from our sense of self that our identity needs to be developed? My view is that the relational sense of self is a better way to approach the issue.

I would emphasise that from our earliest biological beginnings, during pregnancy and then birth, our selves are found in relationship with others. The relationship between the child and the adults caring for her will profoundly affect her sense of self and self-worth. True, as the child grows she may depart from some of her parents' beliefs, but this is likely to be as a result of new attachments and relationships. For most adults their sense of self is constructed through relations with other: be that through biological relationships, religious beliefs, political affiliation, book clubs, sports teams and so on. The chestnut at a party 'so what do you do?', whether answered seriously or frivolously, is unlikely to be answered in a way that is not relational. As Elizabeth Frazer and Nicola Lacey[163] argue:

The notion of the relational self, in contrast to both atomistic and inter-subjective selves, nicely captures our empirical and logical interdependence and the centrality to our identity of our relations with others and with practices and institutions, whilst retaining an idea of human uniqueness and discreteness as central to our sense of ourselves. It entails the collapse of any self/other or individual/community dichotomy without abandoning the idea of genuine agency and subjectivity.

Nevertheless, in adopting this as an ideal there must be concerns over the danger of misuse of ethic of care. Sasha Roseniel argues:

[M]any feminists have expressed reservations about the whole-hearted embracing of an ethics of care, regarding it as over-reliant on a model of care developed from thinking about the fundamentally gendered care practices of mothers for their

---

[161] V Davion, 'Autonomy, Integrity, and Care' (1993) *Social Theory and Practice* 161, 175.

[162] J Christman, 'Relational Autonomy, Liberal Individualism, and the Social Constitution of Selves' (2004) 117 *Philosophical Studies* 143.

[163] E Frazer and N Lacey, *The Politics of Community* (Harvester Wheatsheaf, 1993) 178.

children, and fearing that it brings with it a diminution of concern about the ethics of justice and social equality. ... We should be wary that advocating an ethics of care might involve endorsing a model of self which is so fundamentally relational that any sense of individuality, separateness, and capacity to act autonomously is negated.[164]

As with all good ideas, there is a danger of it being open to appalling misuse. Under the label of an ethic of care women's interests could be seriously set back. However, that could only be under a misunderstanding and misappropriation of an ethic of care. As argued earlier, it is essential that justice is part of care. A caring approach will demand a fair share of the burdens of caring across society.

B. Gender Roles

A second danger with an ethic of care, one already mentioned in this chapter, is that an ethic of care can be used against the interests of women.[165] By talking up the importance of care and being seen to valourise the caring role, the danger is that current gender division in caring will be emphasised and that women will become the 'eternal nursemaid'.[166]

It is easy in a discussion of an ethic of care to glamorise care. No one should overlook the sheer exhaustion and exasperation that caring brings.[167] Caring can be mucky, nasty, and frustrating.[168] Care is hard work; extremely hard work.[169] Carers can often feel trapped: their life goals come to an end and they must adopt the role of carer while the rest of their life is put on hold.[170] Caring can become abusive for both the carer and cared for.

Catherine MacKinnon argues that men value women for providing care.[171] By emphasising the value and importance of caring, supporters of an ethic of care may be unintentionally promoting patriarchy by ignoring the fact that many women are forced into care. This is particular dangerous with those writings from within an ethic of care which regards care as a

---

[164] S Roseneil, 'Why We Should Care About Friends: An Argument for Queering the Care Imaginary' (2004) 3 *Social Policy Social Policy and Society* 409, 414.

[165] J Keller, 'Autonomy, Relationality and Feminist Ethics' (1997) 12 *Hypatia* 152.

[166] T Hassan, An Ethic of Care Critique, available at http://dspace.sunyconnect.suny.edu/bitstream/handle/1951/43954/An_Ethic_of_Care_Critique.pdf.

[167] M Goldsteen, T Abma, B Oeseburg, 'What Is It to Be a Daughter? Identities under Pressure in Dementia Care' (2007) 21 *Bioethics* 1.

[168] K Abrams, 'The Second Coming of Care' (2001) 76 *Chicago-Kent Law Review* 1605; J Oliver and A Briggs, *Caring Experiences of Looking after Disabled Relatives* (Routledge, 1985).

[169] A Hubbard, 'The Myth of Independence and the Major Life Activity of Caring' (2004) 8 *Journal of Gender, Race and Justice* 327; C Ungerson, 'Social Politics and the Commodification of Care' (1997) 4 *Social Policy* 362.

[170] Department of Health, *Caring about Carers* (London, Department of Health, 1999) para 69.

[171] W Friedman et al, 'Sex Differences in Moral Judgments? A Test of Gilligan's Theory' (1987) 11 *Psychology of Women Quarterly* 37.

particularly feminine activity. Robin West complains that girls are taught to be self-sacrificial and develop domestic skills.[172] These are the characteristics girls are rewarded for by parents and society. She also argues that practice and fear of sexual violence means that women 'give themselves' in marriage and caring obligations that flow from that as a form of protection.[173]

Mary Becker agrees, but also notes that there are pressures on women to be economically successful and not to be mothers.[174] She argues there is a double bind: if a woman chooses not to be a mother, then she is not 'a real women'; if she chooses to be a mother, then she is restricted to just being a mother. A telling exchange between Carol Gilligan and Catherine Mackinnon is revealing. When Carol Gilligan argued that she was seeking to assimilate women's voices into mainstream discussion, Mackinnon responded that women's voices could not be heard because men's feet were 'on her throat'.[175] The argument being that seeking to respect care because that is what women want to do, is very dangerous if you believe that women only want to care because men force them to.

One response is that there is no avoiding care; it is not going to go away. Ethic of care at least offers a way of ensuring that care is valued in ethical terms and provides a tool for achieving economic and political recognition of an ethic of care. But all ethic of care supporters should be wary of the dangers of the rhetoric of an ethic of care being hijacked without resulting in any political changes. To Mackinnon's argument we might say that in seeking to value care you are at least doing a little to improve the position of women who care and do a little to reduce the pressure on the throat. And that an ethic of care with its emphasis on responsibilities can make a powerful case for a fairer sharing of care work between men and women.

Diemut Bubeck,[176] writing from a feminist perspective, has provided a powerful critique of the standard presentation of an ethic of care. She argues, focusing on the writing of Nel Noddings, that in fact an ethic of care 'renders carers vulnerable to exploitation because they do not have the "moral resources" within their caring perspective to deal with this problem.'[177] By rejecting ideas such as the need for equal respect and justice, ethic of care leaves individuals, and particularly women, open to exploitation. Indeed she sees that a just society seeking to ensure there is no exploitation will ensure there is the 'systematic social provision of care' or (her preference) an obligation on all citizens to contribute a 'caring service' during their lifetime. That will liberate women from their 'slavist relationship' to care.

---

[172] R West, *Caring for Justice* (New York University Press, 1997) 81.
[173] Ibid 82.
[174] M Becker, 'Care and Feminists' (2002) 17 *Wisconsin Women's Law Journal* 57.
[175] L Kessler, 'Transgressive Caregiving' (2005) 33 *Florida State University Law Review* 1.
[176] D Bubeck, *Care, Gender and Justice* (Oxford University Press, 1996).
[177] Ibid 140.

Again these are important points, but fail to appreciate the scope of an ethic of care as developed by writers since Nel Noddings. In a society which is seeking to promote relationships of care which are respectful of both parties, recognise the caring responsibilities of all and are fair in relational terms, we would be concerned about the allocation of burdens of care and exploitation of individuals. It would ensure jobs were structured around employees who had caring responsibilities. A relationship which is exploitative would not fall under the definition of a caring relationship explained in chapter two, and so would not be promoted by an ethic of care.

C. The Dangers of Regulation

One of the aims of an ethic of care is to bring caring practices to the centre of ethical, social and legal analysis. Yet that brings dangers with it. The more the public good of caring is emphasised, the more the danger that it becomes subject to legal and social regulation, inspection and supervision.[178] Caring relationships in their nature should be spontaneous, free and individualised. These values will all be challenged by the kind of regime which could be attached to caring if the arguments of the public importance of care are recognised.

This is a serious and important point, which will be explored further in chapter four. For now, I would make two responses. The first is to point out that currently the deregulation of care enables significant levels of abuse to take place within the caring relationship. There is nothing in an ethic of care which would seek to support that, indeed much of which would wish to challenge it. So, legal intervention in intimate relationships being necessary to ensure protection from abuse must be welcomed from an ethic of care perspective. That will be explored in chapter seven.

As to more general concerns about regulation, this is happening already.[179] Significant levels of state paid for care is already occurring and that is set to increase. There is much debate over the nature of regulation of that care. I suggest that ethic of care has within it the best tools to ensure the regulation is of an appropriate extent. In short, for reasons explored in chapters four and seven, regulation is inevitable and to some extent desirable, but ethic of care is well placed to ensure that the regulation will promote, not hinder, caring relationships.

---

[178] K Franke, 'Taking Care' (2001) 76 *Chicago-Kent Law Review* 1541.
[179] C Benoit and H Hallgrimsdottir, 'Conceptualising Care Work' in C Benoit and H Hallgrimsdottir, *Valuing Carework* (University of Toronto Press, 2011).

D. Non-Traditional Care

There is certainly a legitimate concern that an ethic of care draws its understanding of care too narrowly. Mary Ann Case argues:

> [P]art of what needs to be questioned ... may be the traditional and limited way
> care obligations and family relationships have been defined [by legal maternalists]...
> [T]he parents of young children are not the only ones with family responsibilities.
> I am the legal guardian of a mentally incapacitated mother, but no part of the out-
> of-pocket expenses of caring for my mother ... is covered in anything comparable to
> the way that ... my current employer covers certain out-of-pocket expenses associated
> with childrearing.[180]

If the definition of care is drawn too narrowly, then there is a danger of reinforcing stereotypes of approved care and failing to recognise the diversity of caring
relationships. This is of particular concern to writers such as Sara Ruddick, who
use the maternal-child relationship as the central example of care. Case's point
that it would be wrong to necessarily privilege the parent-child relationship over
other caring relationships is well made. On the other hand, as emphasised in
chapter two and explored further in chapter four, where caring relationships
meet basic needs there is a particularly strong case for offering state support,
because otherwise meeting that need would fall on the state. There is, therefore,
a case for distinguishing between caring which meets basic needs and caring
which does not. As will be argued in chapter five, an ethic of care enables us, for
example, to move beyond a set formal definition of the kinds of relationships
that will be recognised and approved, to reward all relationships of care.[181]

There is a danger too of treating all care relationships in the same way.
The additional impact of disadvantage or advantage and broader social
forces will mean that issues of race, age, sexual orientation and religion can
all impact on the nature of the caring relationship. An ethic of care, with its
focus on the quality of the relationship and a recognition of the broader caring responsibilities an individual faces means it is particularly well equipped
to respond to the nuances of these relationships.

E. Disability

A major critique of an ethic of care is found in disability studies.[182] This issue
has been largely addressed in chapter two. There it was acknowledged that
many writers on care have presented the issue from the carers perspective,

---

[180] M Case, 'How High the Apple Pie? A Few Troubling Questions about Where, Why, and How
the Burden of Care for Children should be Shifted' (2001) 76 *Chicago-Kent Law Review* 1753, 1758.

[181] S Roseneil, 'Why We Should Care About Friends: An Argument for Queering the Care
Imaginary' (2004) 3 *Social Policy Social Policy and Society* 409.

[182] B Hughes, L McKie, D Hopkins and N Watson, 'Love's Labours Lost? Feminism, the Disabled
People's Movement and an Ethic of Care' in M O' Donnell (ed), *Structure and Agency* (Sage, 2010).

such as the calls for 'carers' rights'. Care has been presented as a uni-directional activity. In chapter two I argued in favour of promoting caring relationships in which the contributions of both parties would be recognised. Seeking to promote caring relationships, rather than carers, involves recognising the importance of viewing the relationship from both sides.

F. Choice

A common argument used against giving care a special place is that undertaking care work is simply a lifestyle choice people make. When people choose to undertake care work they do so aware of the low economic and social standing attached to it. They have, therefore, no grounds of complaint of the economic and social consequences that flow. Indeed if they are unhappy with those they should do something else. We should treat those disadvantaged by care in the same way as those who choose to be an impoverished artist. They make the choice aware of the low economic results, and we should respect their assessment that the economic disadvantages are outweighed by the benefits that result.

There are a number of ways of challenging this line of thought. One is to question whether the choice is one that is informed. A person agreeing to care for a vulnerable adult, while agreeing to undertake the care, may not be aware of the social and economic consequences. Someone choosing to be a parent may not be aware of the impact that will have on their social and economic circumstances.

Second, a question must be raised to the extent to which there is a choice. If your parent falls seriously ill, to what extent is it a choice to care for them? It often does not feel like a choice. Indeed in such a case to spend time nicely weighing up the competing options and determining what is the best choice to make seems heartless. The imperative to care is such that talk of choice is somewhat fictitious. In part the difficulty here is that the talk of choice overlooks the notion of responsibility that parents feel towards their children.[183] As Eichner puts it:

> Engaging in parenting responsibilities is... different from one's choice of chocolate ice cream over vanilla; the latter is a choice based on taste, the former is a moral imperative based on one's understanding of one's self (conceived of in terms of one's relationships), which stands independent of individual preferences.[184]

---

[183] N Buonocore Porter, 'Why Care about Caregivers? Using Communitarian Theory to Justify Protection of 'Real' Workers' (2010) 58 *University of Kansas Law Review* 355.
[184] M Eichner, 'Square Peg in a Round Hole: Parenting Policies and Liberal Theory' (1998) 59 *Ohio State Law Journal* 133, 172.

Third, and more importantly, the choice approach closes off the question of whether society should be structured so that care work involves disadvantage. Even if people do choose to care, that does not provide a justification for allowing those who undertake heavy care work to be seriously disadvantaged. Why should those who are caring suffer deleterious consequences as a result? That is the question to ask, not should we respect the choices of those who care and suffer the attended disadvantages.

VI. Ethic of Care and Law

While an ethic of care might be attractive to a philosopher, sociologist or professional seeking ethical guidance, is it helpful for lawyers? The argument that it might not would go as follows. Law operates when people are in disagreement. Spouses only need lawyers when their relationship breaks down. People only go to court when their relational tools cannot provide a solution. Is not an approach based on promoting caring relations particularly inappropriate in a legal system which is trying to resolve disputes between people whose relationship has broken down?

This kind of concern has even been recognised by Virginia Held[185] who suggests the analogy of

> friends engaged in a competitive game. When they play tennis, each tires above all to win, limited only by what the fair rules of the game require. If this approach were generalized to the whole of their relation, they would no longer be genuine friends, though it is suitable for limited interactions. Analogously, persons should be tied together as caring members of the same society, yet can agree to treat their limited legal interactions in ways that give priority to justice. When justice should then prevail in certain contexts, it need not oppose or cancel the care in which legal systems should be built.[186]

This seems to suggest that while an ethic of care can operate when relationships are working well, there needs to be a more abstract 'ethic of justice' to provide for rules to apply when the couple cannot agree.

I do not agree with Held's analysis on this issue. This entire book is an attempt to explain how the law can powerfully utilise an ethic of care in a whole range of areas, but I will make some more general points now.

The first is that law can have an influence far beyond the cases that come to court. To take a trivial example, the law on illegal parking impacts on a far larger range of people than simply those who receive parking fines. To take

---

[185] V Held, 'Can the Ethics of Care Handle Violence?' (2010) 4 *Ethics and Social Welfare* 115.
[186] V Held, 'Can the Ethics of Care Handle Violence?' (2010) 4 *Ethics and Social Welfare* 115, 117.

a more serious issue, the law on who can marry sends powerful messages to society about what kinds of relationships are approved of and why. Hence the intense debate over same-sex marriage. Legal regulations and the messages from them force or nudge people in various ways. They provide generalised guidance as to how people arrange their interactions. Court cases are but a small part of how the law operates. Law can therefore be used powerfully to encourage people to act in a way which will promote caring relationships. A particularly good example might be the law dealing with how those lacking mental capacity will be treated. Another example would be contract law. It is rare that people come to court following a breach of contract. But it is, in part, a testament to the effectiveness of contract law. Contract law provides a mechanism for people to enter contractual relationships and to give weight to the obligations created as a result. A legal, political and social system structured around an ethic of care would hope to see few cases reaching court.

The second is that the law can operate to control or require state intervention to enable (or indeed discourage) caring relationships. In chapter four we will look at the range of state financial and social support which can be offered to caring relationships. We can design our state support mechanisms in a way following an ethic of care. As we shall see in chapter four, an ethic of care has much to say about that area of the law.

The third is that it is wrong to assume that all people coming to court have relationships that have come to an end. Many cases involve people in ongoing relationships, such as family cases involving children and separated parents. Even if that is not so, the legal remedies that are sought in many cases are designed to move people on from where they are to find new caring relationships.

VII. Conclusion

It is one of the aims of the book to seek to give some practical applications of an ethic of care for the law. In this section I will conclude by highlighting some of the significant consequences of adopting an ethic of care.

Under an ethic of care the practice of caring would be highly valued within society. It would be recognised that in meeting people's key needs, caring was a central activity. Caregivers would, far from being hidden, come to represent a norm. Social structures and attitudes would need to be set up to encourage and enable caring relationships. A broad range of social policies promoting care would be required.[187] This would require adequate remuneration of

---

[187] O Hakivsky, *Social Policy and the Ethic of Care* (University of British Columbia Press, 2004).

caregivers: not the payment of benefits of the kind paid to those 'unable to work'; but payment acknowledging the key role they play.[188] Employment law and practices would need to be reworked around a model of the carer worker.

Our legal structure would not be based on individualist models prioritising autonomy and independence. Susan Dodds argues that we need a legal and social system which accepts our vulnerability and the resulting need for care:[189]

> A vulnerability-centered view of the self and of persons is better able to capture many of our moral motivations and intuitions than can be captured by an autonomy-focused approach. We are all vulnerable to the exigencies of our embodied, social and relational existence and, in recognizing this inherent human vulnerability, we can see the ways in which a range of social institutions and structures protect us against some vulnerabilities, while others expose us to risk. We do not have to view our obligations towards those who lack the capacity to develop or retain autonomy as having a different source from our obligations towards those whose autonomy is made vulnerable due to a degree of dependency. It may be easier to recognize the social value of provision of care if it is viewed as something on which we all have been dependent and on which we are all likely to be dependent at different points in our lives, rather than altruistic behaviour extended to those who lack 'full personhood'.[190]

When assessing the rights of any individual or the medical needs of an individual, such a person would have to be considered in a situational context. Never should it be a matter of assessing a person in isolation. Rather each person's needs and rights would have to be considered in the context of their relationships.

A central consequence of valuing caring would be that it would help combat gender discrimination. As Eva Feder Kittay argues:

> The call for sexual equality has been with us for a long time. But until relatively recently, the demands of even the most farsighted women have assumed very traditional and gendered arrangements of dependency work. Radical visions in which dependency work is taken out of the family have left many women cold—largely, I suggest, because they have failed to respect the importance of the dependency relationship. A view of society as consisting of nested dependencies, so constituted as to provide all with the means to achieve functioning that respects the freedom and relatedness of all citizens, is a view that can only emerge now, as women taste the fruits of an equality fashioned by men—and find it wanting. This equality has not left room for love's labors and love's laborers. It is time to shape a new vision by creating new theories and by forging the requisite political will. We need to revise

---

[188] The payment of carers has been said to carry dangers of causing the 'marketisation of intimacy and the commodification of care': C Ungerson, 'Cash in Care' in M Harrington Meyer (eds), *Care Work: Gender Class and the Welfare State* (Routledge, 2000) 69.

[189] S Dodds, 'Depending on Care: Recognition of Vulnerability and the Social Contribution of Care Provision' (2007) 21 *Bioethics* 500.

[190] Ibid 510.

our social and political commitment to ourselves as dependents and as dependency workers. Only through these efforts may we come to see what it means for men and women to share the world in equality.[191]

Work would need to be done to ensure that the burden of caring did not fall on the few, but was shared across the community. On a broader scale internationally a caring world would be one in which the essential needs of citizens around the world would be met. We should be seeking not only caring individuals, but caring institutions and governments.[192] Virginia Held calls for international practices of 'cultivating relations of trust, listening to the concerns of others, fostering international cooperation, and valuing interdependence'.[193] Fiona Robinson has developed an approach to international security on a global scale based around an ethic of care.[194] From a small scale study of the moral values of a small group of school girls, ethic of care has come a long way.

---

[191] E Feder Kittay, *Love's Labor: Essays on Women, Equality, and Dependency* (Routledge, 1999) 188.

[192] J Tronto, 'Creating Caring Institutions: Politics, Plurality, and Purpose' (2010) 4 *Ethics and Social Welfare* 158.

[193] V Held, *The Ethics of Care* (Oxford University Press, 2006) 48.

[194] F Robinson, *The Ethics of Care A Feminist Approach to Human Security* (Temple University Press, 2011).

4

State Support of Care

I. Introduction

Historically care was regarded as a private matter. It was none of the state's business. The state's role was to regulate the public areas of life: commercial dealings; crime and disorder on the street; protection of property; and the like. Behind the closed doors of the house or private institution, the Government was not to go. In part this was because care was seen as simply not important enough for the state to waste its energies and resources on. Economic production and state security were the state's primary concerns. It was also because it was intrusive for the state to intervene in the intimate lives of individuals. Traditionally the *pater familias*, the 'father figure' was the person who controlled that area and the state should not undermine his proper role by seeking to interfere in his dominion.[1] Further, women's care work was an expression of love and commitment and so not appropriate for state regulation.[2] Dorothy Roberts has written of the 'spiritualisation of housework' which saw it as a product of love and not as labour,[3] and therefore unsuitable for state intervention or social recognition. It was feared that state intervention would be treading on the hallowed ground of 'love work'.

Of course, this public-private divide has been much debated and few commentators would support the straightforward presentation of it just given.[4] Indeed many have questioned its very existence.[5] Even if the divide is recognised, the notion of non-intervention in the private sphere is highly

---

[1] S Fredman, *Women and the Law* (Oxford University Press, 1998).
[2] K Abrams, 'Cross-Dressing in the Master's Clothes' (2000) *Yale Law Journal* 745.
[3] D Roberts, 'Spiritual and Menial Housework' (1997) 9 *Yale Journal of Law and Feminism* 51, 51.
[4] See eg S Okin, *Justice Gender and the Family* (Basic Books, 1991).
[5] See the discussion in R Gavison, 'Feminism and the Public Private Distinction' (1992) 45 *Stanford Law* 1.

problematic.[6] The precise way the state arranges welfare, tax and educational policies can all encourage or discourage certain 'private' caring practices. It is impossible for the state to take a neutral stance towards forms of caring.

The state's involvement in care issues has become one of the great issues of our age.[7] Around the world countries are struggling to provide an appropriate response to the need for care.[8] While the value of care is recognised, the appropriate way to support, provide and enable it is much debated. Also, as we shall see in this chapter, the distinction between public and private forms of caring and between professional and non-professional caring, is being worn down, although it still carries significance. A doctor giving care and providing medical treatment is a well-paid, highly respected professional; a carer doing possibly exactly the same thing lacks either the pay or the respect.[9] Care within the family is too often taken for granted, an assumed given. The state only seems interested when the care is not provided.[10] As Martha Fineman[11] argues:

> The family in the United States has primary responsibility for the dependency of its members. Families that are unable to provide adequately for themselves are deemed deviant in that they do not conform to imposed aspiration and expectation of independence and self-sufficiency.

This, however, is changing. As we shall in this chapter the state is beginning to find a range of ways of responding to the needs of those in caring relationships.

It is also interesting to note that what is characterised as 'domestic work' has changed over time. For example, the production of clothing used to be regarded as primarily a domestic labour, but now it is generally regarded as economic production. Possibly we are seeing, at least for some families, a similar change in the production of food.[12] The rapid growth in child care, cleaning, prepared food and 'housekeeping' services is likewise challenging the traditional assumptions about what is economic behaviour and what is

---

[6] F Olsen, 'Feminist Critiques of the Public/Private Distinction' (1993) 10 *Constitutional Commentary* 319.

[7] M Fine, *A Caring Society? Care and the Dilemmas of Human Service in the 21st Century* (Palgrave, 2007); C Glendinning and D Bell, *Rethinking Social Care and Support: What Can England Learn from the Experiences of Other Countries?* (Joseph Rowntree, 2008).

[8] C Glendinning, and N Moran, *Reforming Long-term Care: Recent Lessons from Other Countries* (Social Policy Research Unit, 2009).

[9] M Daly and J Lewis, 'The Concept of Social Care and the Analysis of Contemporary Welfare' (2000) 51 *British Journal of Sociology* 51.

[10] L Kessler, 'The Politics of Care' (2008) 23 *Wisconsin Journal of Law, Gender and Society* 169.

[11] M Fineman, 'Responsibility, Family, and the Limits of Equality: An American Perspective' in C Lind, H Keating and J Bridgeman (eds), *Taking Responsibility, Law and the Changing Family* (Ashgate, 2011).

[12] J Williams, 'From Difference to Dominance to Domesticity: Care as Work, Gender as Tradition' (2001) 76 *Chicago-Kent Law Review* 1441.

domestic unpaid work. Another challenge can be found with the increasing numbers of employers allowing staff to work from home.[13]

II. The Political Background

While at one time it was plausible to speak of carers being unknown and unseen, ignored by the political elite and unmentioned in public debates,[14] such a claim could no longer be made today. There is now a widespread acceptance that care work is of immense social value. It matters very much to our society how, where and when it is done. The Government estimates that eight out of 10 people aged 65 will need care and support at some later point. Five million people care for friends or relatives.[15] In the current climate a major theme in public discourse is the reduction of state costs. We are seeing significant cuts in social care services offered by local authorities. Even so it is stated that there will be a funding gap of over a billion pounds by 2014.[16] Although in 2012 the spending on social care remained the same as 2011, this was in effect a 4.5 per cent cut once increased costs were taken into account.[17] In part this means a reduction in the number of people receiving local authority funded care. Carers UK note the number has fallen from 489,000 in 2004 to 299,000 in 2009/2010.[18]

Pressure on the care system due to a falling birth rate; increased participation of women in paid employment; the impact of divorce; and increased geographical mobility have all impacted on the extent to which care from family members can be expected.[19]

In the 1990s, Annie Bibbings wrote:

Usually the presence of a carer in a household is the signal for service providers to breathe a sigh of relief and think that this is one problem they can ignore, 'Is there a daughter?' being one of the first questions to cross the lips of many a consultant,

---

[13] Ibid.

[14] J Herring, 'Where are the Carers in Healthcare Law and Ethics?' (2008) 27 *Legal Studies* 51.

[15] HM Government, *Caring for Our Future: Reforming Care and Support* (The Stationery Office, 2012).

[16] Kings Fund.

[17] BBC News Online, 'Elderly Suffer as Social Care Spending Cut' 20 January 2012.

[18] Carers UK (December 2011) Health Select Committee, *Social Care Inquiry* (Carers UK, 2011).

[19] J Keefe, C Glendinning and P Fancey, 'Financial Payments for Family Carers: Policy Approaches and Debates' in A Martin-Matthews and J Philips (eds), *Ageing at the Intersection of Work and Home Life: Blurring the Boundaries* (Lawrence Eribaum, 2008).

doctor or social worker when faced with the problem of needing to organize community care for a patient or client.[20]

That attitude is nowadays rarely prevalent. Even if there is a daughter, there can be no assumption that she is in a position to care, or is willing to do so. Further, even if there is someone willing to offer care, she can expect a degree of support from the state.[21]

The change in approach to care has to be seen in the context of some broader political and social movements. First, there has been a move away from state provided care. Most prominent is the move towards 'community care'.[22] In part this move is motivated by the recognition of the unsatisfactory nature of institutional care, with concerns about abuse in large scale institutional settings, still very much present today.[23] It is also motivated by a desire to promote the well-being of those needing care.[24] An institutional setting was seen as doing nothing to promote independence and a reintegration into society. Acknowledging and enabling those who need intense levels of care to be full citizens will not be achieved if they are excluded from society. A more cynical view will see community care as an attempt to shift the financial burden of care from the state to family members. To the cynics the state was abandoning vulnerable people in the community, rather than ensuring their care.[25] When those individuals in the community who care for others do not receive adequate support or recognition, the complaints of the cynics carry much force. There are a sufficient number of reports of horrific abuse of those in the community to raise concerns.[26]

A second issue has been the rise of feminism and a widespread acceptance, even among those who do not buy into the whole feminist agenda, that we should remove sources of disadvantage for women. The lack of pay or recognition for much care is now generally recognised as a significant source of disadvantage for women.[27] This was discussed in chapter three, but provides an important argument in favour of state support for care.

A third issue has been the move to increase economic productivity among all members of society. In recent years governments have attacked 'the dependency culture'. No one is entitled to rely on state support. Everyone is

---

[20] A Bibbings, 'Carers and Professionals—the Carer's Viewpoint' in A Allott and M Robb (eds), *Understanding Health and Social Care an Introductory Reader* (Sage, 1998) 172.

[21] Department of Health, *Guidance on Eligibility Criteria for Adult Social Care* (Department of Health, 2010) 7.

[22] M Daly and J Lewis, 'The Concept of Social Care and the Analysis of Contemporary Welfare' (2000) 51 *British Journal of Sociology* 51.

[23] See ch 8.

[24] Care and Support Bill 2012, cl 1.

[25] M Daly and J Lewis, 'The Concept of Social Care and the Analysis of Contemporary Welfare' (2000) 51 *British Journal of Sociology* 51.

[26] Eg Mencap, *Pair Jailed for Murder of Vulnerable Man* (Mencap, 2010).

[27] M Daly and J Lewis, 'The Concept of Social Care and the Analysis of Contemporary Welfare' (2000) 51 *British Journal of Sociology* 51.

expected to at least attempt to become economically self-sufficient. This kind of thinking was well captured by James Purnell, then Secretary of State for Work and Pensions, introducing the 2009 Welfare Reform Bill:

> The Bill is intended to renew the partnership between the state and the individual by ensuring that everyone on benefits is preparing for work, so that support is matched with responsibility. We will support people, but in return they must support themselves.[28]

Or more rhetorically from the Prime Minister, David Cameron:

> We've got to recognise that in the end, the only thing that really beats poverty, long-term, is work. We cannot emphasise this enough. Compassion isn't measured out in benefit cheques—it's in the chances you give people ... the chance to get a job, to get on, to get that sense of achievement that only comes from doing a hard day's work for a proper day's pay.[29]

This thinking has led to attempts to encourage parents, the disabled and those with caring responsibilities, to all be involved in economic work, if possible. Interestingly, in the context of parents, that has meant the state has been willing to assist in the cost of child care in order to enable parents to work.[30] Of course, promoting employment as the way out of poverty for disadvantaged groups can be seen as a way for the Government to avoid its responsibilities in seeking to tackle social inequality.

Fourth, within political debates the concept of social exclusion has become a major one.[31] The EU Employment and Social Affairs Directorate defines social exclusion as 'The development of capacity and opportunity to play a full role, not only in economic terms, but also in social, psychological and political terms.'[32]

The precise definition of the term is debated and it has somewhat fallen out of political favour,[33] but it captures the idea that groups of people may not only suffer poverty, but also lack the opportunity to access social, psychological and political benefits. Caring can certainly bring with it social exclusion. Interestingly, the Coalition Government talks of 'problem families' more than social exclusion.[34] This identifies the problem as located within the private sphere of the family, rather than being a broader social problem.

---

[28] HC Deb, 27 January 2009, c181.

[29] David Cameron, Speech at Bluewater, Kent, 25 June 2012 at www.telegraph.co.uk/news/politics/david-cameron/9354163/David-Camerons-welfare-speech-in-full.html.

[30] M Daly and J Lewis, 'The Concept of Social Care and the Analysis of Contemporary Welfare' (2000) 51 *British Journal of Sociology* 51.

[31] L Kessler, 'Getting Class' (2008) 56 *Buffalo Law Review* 91.

[32] EU Employment and Social Affairs Directorate, *Social Exclusion* (European Union, 2012).

[33] R Levitas, C Pantazis, E Fahmy, D Gordon, E Lloyd and D Patsios, *The Multi-Dimensional Analysis of Social Exclusion* (University of Bristol, 2007).

[34] 'David Cameron Unveils £448m Plan to Help "Problem Families"' *The Guardian* (available at www.guardian.co.uk/politics/2011/dec/15/david-cameron-plan-problem-families).

Fifth, the major political focus on 'austerity' and 'deficit cutting' clearly impact on responses to care, but not in a straightforward way. In so far as support for carers can prevent people whose care might otherwise fall fully on the state; or prevent carers giving up on care, expenditure on support for care may be seen as a long term gain. Yet for local authorities seeking to cut budgets, the care budget is a natural target. In the longer term, the increasing role of women in paid work and changing demographics mean the larger economic issues surrounding care are going to be of increasing significance.[35]

As will be seen from this discussion, the increase in political interest in caring comes from a range of sources. For some, the Government's newfound celebration of care needs to be greeted with some cynicism. Gillian Parker and Harriet Clarke[36] refer to an unholy trio of deinstitutionalisation; keeping the costs of care for the state low; and encouraging individual and family responsibilities, combining to pass the cost of care away from the state and onto individual carers. Even if there is truth in this, the current move to provide great support for carers is undoubtedly providing benefit to some in caring relationships.

III. Why Care Matters to the State

In chapter two we explored the work of carers. While the benefits of caring are huge, so too is its toll. Unsurprisingly, this has led to calls for care work to be recognised and valued through the support of the state.[37] In this section I will examine the reasons why the state should support caring relationships. I will explore the range of arguments that have been adopted, although I do not find all of these arguments equally convincing.

A. Economic Concerns

Assuming it is unacceptable for individuals to be left in great need without any help, care must be performed. The question then arises who is to meet the costs associated with that care. Currently that largely falls on individuals within those relationships. But if people stop caring, through choice or economic need, that burden would fall on the state. If the state, through a

---

[35] M Daly and J Lewis, 'The Concept of Social Care and the Analysis of Contemporary Welfare' (2000) 51 *British Journal of Sociology* 51.

[36] G Parker and H Clarke, 'Making the Ends Meet: Do Carers and Disabled People have a Common Agenda?' (2002) 30 *Policy and Politics* 347.

[37] Carers UK, *Shaping the Future of Care Together* (Carers UK, 2010).

relatively low level of payment, can ensure carers keep caring and/or that people are not deterred from caring, then the payments can be said to make much economic sense.[38] By supplying sufficient economic and support services to maintain care levels, the Government would in fact be saving significant sums of money.[39]

Carers UK argues that the work of informal carers would cost £119 billion if the state had to perform it, a sum that exceeds the £98.8 billion spent on the NHS.[40] This is set to increase. Carers UK claims the number of carers that will be needed will rise from six million currently to nine million by 2037.[41] By 2050, it is predicted the UK could be forced to spend 21.6 per cent of GDP on long-term care, pensions and health services to cope with the rise in elderly people requiring state assistance.[42] A further cost that some also refer to is the paid work that carers would be able to undertake if appropriate support were offered, with its resulting tax revenue.[43] Carers UK suggest that carers who give up work to care give up income of £1.3 billion annually.[44]

While the argument to support caring based on economics might have much to be said in favour of it in terms of political campaigning, it carries with it dangers, including the following:

(i)   It assesses care work in financial terms, rather its value in itself. There is more to care than saving the Government money! In particular, the argument does nothing to challenge the value system that undermined care in the first place. It is the over-emphasis on economic productivity which has caused us to undervalue care. It is, therefore, somewhat ironic to rely on economic valuing as a reason for emphasising care.

(ii) Care will be undervalued if it is put in economic terms. As Susan Himmelweit argues: 'Care is the development of a relationship, not the production of a product that is separable from the person delivering it.'[45] So attempts to assess care in terms of output per hour are not possible. The output is caring and this means that it is hard to increase its productivity: it would be like telling an orchestra to increase productivity by playing a symphony faster! Fast and 'efficient' care is usually bad care.

---

[38] L Lloyd, 'Call Us Carers: Limitations and Risks in Campaigning for Recognition and Exclusivity' (2006) 26 *Critical Social Policy* 945.

[39] S Himmelweit and H Land, *Reducing Gender Inequalities to Create a Sustainable Care* (Joseph Rowntree Foundation, 2008).

[40] Carers UK, *Valuing Carers* (Carers UK, 2011).

[41] Carers UK, *Tipping Point for Carers* (Carers UK, 2010).

[42] 'OECD, Huge Elderly Care Bill Threatens Family Ties' *The Telegraph* (available at www.telegraph.co.uk/news/politics/8501333/OECD-huge-elderly-care-bill-threatens-family-ties.html).

[43] Carers UK, *Growing the Care Market* (Carers UK, 2012).

[44] Ibid.

[45] S Himmelweit, *Can we Afford (not) to Care: Prospects and Policy* (Open University, 2005).

(iii) Seeing care as simply an economic commodity would justify the state in regulating and supervising the care. It opens up an argument that it would in fact be cheaper not to have a person cared for at home, but rather cared for by the state. Or if not that then an argument that the state is justified in ensuring that the state gets value for money. Opening up caring relationships to such intervention may be counterproductive.

(iv) In political terms, there is a danger in emphasising the economic costs of caring. That is the issue which will be seen as so big and the costs of becoming involved so large, that politicians will be scared away from dealing with the central issue. Indeed, there is a widespread perception that politicians have shied away from dealing with the consequences of the changing age demographic, simply because it is too big a question.[46] It is an issue requiring long-term solutions, for which our short-term political systems are ill suited. There may be political merit in putting the argument forward in terms of justice and fairness rather than economic efficiency.

(v) The economic approach if used as the sole basis for intervention will require a distinction between care which saves the Government money, which will be supported, and care which does not, which will not. That is likely to depend upon the extent to which if the caring were to stop, a person would become an economic cost to the state. This is a controversial issue which we will need to address later.

B. Social Fairness

If it is accepted that our society has care needs and these are needs that our society wants to have met, then it is important to ensure that the distribution of the costs of meeting those needs are met fairly.[47] The argument is not the argument we have just seen that carers are saving the Government money, but rather that carers are undertaking a job on behalf of society that is a core obligation of a decent society. If so, it is only fair that their work be recognised. Martha Fineman argues that there is a social duty to compensate carers as a result of their social contribution:

> If infants or ill persons are not cared for, nurtured, nourished, and perhaps loved, they will perish. We can say, therefore, that they owe an individual debt to their individual caretakers. But the obligation is not theirs alone—nor is their obligation

---

[46] See for example the response to the Dilnot Commission, discussed later in this chapter.

[47] S Himmelweit, *Can we Afford (not) to Care: Prospects and Policy* (Open University, 2005); A Deacon, 'Civic Labour or Doulia? Care, Reciprocity and Welfare' (2007) 6 *Social Policy & Society* 481.

confined only to their own caretakers. A sense of social justice demands a broader sense of obligation. Without aggregate caretaking, there could be no society, so we might say that it is caretaking labour that produces and reproduces society. Caretaking labour provides the citizens, the workers, the voters, the consumers, the students, and others who populate society and its institutions. The uncompensated labour of caretakers is an unrecognized subsidy, not only to individuals who directly receive it, but more significantly, to the entire society.[48]

Martha Fineman suggests that it is best seen not as 'payment for care' but as a payment for debt. Nicole Busby puts it this way:

> In the current context, legal intervention intended to provide an adequate response to the unpaid care/paid employment conflict can be manifested as a right, based on our shared humanity, to the equal distribution of resources on the basis of an individual's contribution in labour market terms and in respect of the unpaid provision of care.[49]

Such arguments are seeking to move away from the perception that payments to carers are a special treatment. It is sometimes said that care is a choice people make and it is not for the state to subsidise people's lifestyle choice. However, caring should not be regarded as just 'a lifestyle choice' because it is work that carries considerable social value;[50] meets society's obligations to those in need[51] and fulfils a justified moral obligation.[52] Carers deserve financial recognition not as a token to thank them for their contribution, but to recognise that what they are doing is of fundamental importance to society.

Eva Feder Kittay, relying on what she calls the principle of doulia, suggests that in meeting the needs of a dependant, a carer is as a result less able to attend to her own needs and become dependent herself. This dependency creates an obligation on the community.[53] This is a more modest way of putting the argument. It could be phrased as a right to care without undue impoverishment.[54] This is an interesting way of seeing the claim: in terms of the dependency of the carer, rather than as recognition of the value of the work done. Such an argument might justify providing state support for those undertaking care work, even if without it the state would not incur an economic burden.

---

[48] M Fineman, 'Cracking the Foundational Myths: Independence, Autonomy and Self-Sufficiency' (2000) 8 *American University Journal of Gender, Social Policy and Law* 12.

[49] N Busby, *A Right to Care?* (Oxford University Press, 2011).

[50] N Porter, 'Why Care about Caregivers? Using Communitarian Theory to Justify Protection of 'Real' Workers' (2010) 58 *University of Kansas Law Review* 355.

[51] Ibid.

[52] M Eichner, 'Square Peg in a Round Hole: Parenting Policies and Liberal Theory' (1998) 59 *Ohio State Law Journal* 133, 150.

[53] A Deacon, 'Civic Labour or Doulia? Care, Reciprocity and Eelfare' (2007) 6 *Social Policy & Society* 481.

[54] H Arskey and M Morée, 'Supporting Working Carers: Do Policies in England and The Netherlands Reflect "Doulia Rights"?' (2008) 16 *Health and Social Care in the Community* 649.

C. Gender Equality

The state clearly has an interest in promoting gender equality.[55] As we saw in chapter two, the majority of care work is undertaken by women. In particular, the economic costs of care are largely borne by women. The state, therefore, has an interest in ensuring that the costs of care are fairly shared. As Susan Himmelweit and Hilary Land argue:

> The level of public expenditure on care is therefore a gender issue, since women have greater care needs than men and fewer resources to meet them. Inadequate funding also affects women in the paid care workforce and, when paid care is not forthcoming, as those more likely to end up providing unpaid care. Thus, inadequate spending on care is effectively a transfer of resources (unpaid labour) from women to relieve taxpayers, disproportionately men, of their responsibilities to provide for the most vulnerable citizens.[56]

It is not just in economic terms that the issue is important for women. Joan Williams argues that the treatment of care as 'domestic' has significant impact on women's live more broadly:

> That gender system, inherited from the nineteenth century, divides daily life neatly into the mutually exclusive realms of public life and domestic life. Separate spheres imputes specific, and different, biological and psychological characteristics to men and women. Women are deemed too good for the nasty and brutish world of commerce in which men—so the story goes—thrive. From this story stems a set of interlocking assumptions: that it is natural for women to take sole responsibility for child care, that doing so fulfils women's deepest nature and so makes them happy, that men are competitive and ambitious and thus naturally suited to employment but not to caregiving, and that homemakers' economic vulnerability in breadwinner-homemaker households is no big deal.[57]

The attitude towards care therefore reflects and reinforces what society regards as of value and worth. In so far as these downplay the significance of what women do, it works against their interests.

More needs to be said about the nature of the gender gap. There are three aspects to it. First, there is a gap in the performance of care work. Women perform significantly more care work then men. Second, women's place in the workplace is markedly lower than men.[58] Women are paid on average 14.9 per cent lower than men; are far more likely to undertake part time and

---

[55] MA Case, 'Feminist Fundamentalism at the Intersection of Government and Familial Responsibility for Children' in C Lind, H Keating and J Bridgeman (eds), *Taking Responsibility, Law and the Changing Family* (Ashgate, 2011).

[56] S Himmelweit and H Land, *Reducing Gender Inequalities to Create a Sustainable Care* (Joseph Rowntree Foundation, 2008).

[57] J Williams, *Reshaping the Work-Family Debate: Why Men and Class Matter* (Harvard University Press, 2010) 4.

[58] The Fawcett Society, *Equal Pay* (Fawcett Society, 2012).

other low paid jobs. Third, women are significantly more likely to need care than men. Caroline Glendinning, Frits Tjadens, Hilary Arksey, Marjolein Morée, Nicola Moran and Henk Nies explain:

> Caring is gender-based; women take the brunt of caring and are also the majority of care receivers. This gender bias is even more marked when physically intimate and/or emotionally more demanding tasks are involved. The proportion of men caring is smaller; they care for fewer hours per week; and the tasks they undertake are less onerous and stressful. Broadly speaking, the pattern is very similar to that found in relation to housework and childcare; women are more likely to organise paid work around care, while men tend to organise care around work.[59]

Before moving on to discuss how to address the gender issue, one argument against being concerned by it needs to be addressed. That is that if women choose to undertake the paid work and their choice should be respected just as much as a priest, musician or artist who chooses to follow their vocation and receive less income than they might otherwise have earned.[60] This argument may be challenged in several ways.

First, there are a series of arguments about the extent to which the decision to care should be seen as a choice. Some feminists, such as Martha Fineman,[61] have argued that preferences are structured through social forces and are the product of long-standing cultural and social arrangements and ideologies. For example, concepts of the ideal mother or father have powerful influences over people's choices. We must, therefore, be wary of assuming that the choice people make is genuinely their choice. You do not even need to buy into the more radical feminist versions of this argument to agree with Katherine Baker: 'Accepting low-status work and subordination can seem like a perfectly rational choice when the alternative seems so radical, so potentially damaging to those one loves, and so unknown.'[62]

So even if it is a choice, it is hardly a free one when made in face of the suffering of a loved one.

A second argument might accept it is a choice, but emphasise that the work done has huge social significance. Care, unlike, say, a bonsai tree growing, has considerable public benefit and in fact satisfies the obligations that the state would otherwise be obliged to meet. Alternatively, it is argued that caring meets a moral obligation flowing from a relationship. In a legal system seeking to

---

[59] C Glendinning, F Tjadens, H Arksey, M Morée, N Moran and H Nies, *Care Provision within Families and its Socio-Economic Impact on Care Providers* (University of York, 2009).

[60] D Roberts, 'Welfare Reform and Economic Freedom: Low-Income Mothers' Decisions about Work at Home and in the Market' (2004) 44 *Santa Clara Law Review* 1029.

[61] M Fineman, *The Autonomy Myth* (New Press, 2005).

[62] K Baker, 'The Problem with Unpaid Work' (2007) 4 *University of St Thomas Law Journal* 599.

follow an ethic of care complying with the obligations of relationship should be seen as a norm to be supported, not a choice to be responsible for.[63]

A third line of argument suggests that even if someone does choose care over employment, that does not mean that they are choosing to accept the current conditions of employment and lack of social support. We could structure society to offer a far wider range of options of combining work and care, and a better set of support systems for caring relationships, than is currently the case. Simply because a choice was between two options was made does not mean society was right to restrict a person those options. A person may choose to care even though it is undervalued, but that is no reason for not valuing care.

If, therefore, it is accepted that the gender gap does need tackling, there are three key fronts to address:

— The state should accept that women currently do more care work than men, but seek to ensure that the choices that are made do not disadvantage women. The focus should therefore be in providing benefits and support to carers to limit the disadvantage suffered.

— The state should challenge the current division of labour by seeking to encourage an equal undertaking of care work by men and women. Here policies can be used to encourage an equal sharing. An example could be the policies adopted in some Scandinavian countries which give an increased amount of parental leave to those couples who share their parental leave allowance. By improving the provision for carers, the state can make caring more attractive to men and thereby encourage them to undertake a greater share of the care work.[64]

— The state should challenge the current division of labour by seeking to encourage an equal undertaking of paid employment by men and women. This would involve seeking to disincentivise care work and encourage ways of non-familial care for those needing help.

The argument between these approaches depends in large part on the approach one takes to care. For those who see it as responsible for significantly disadvantaging women and a way of disempowering women by depriving them access to economic wealth and power, simply supporting caring will reinforce the care gender divide and not challenge, or even increase, the number of women undertaking care.[65]

It is, perhaps, unsurprising that most western countries adopt some kind of balance between these approaches. At the same time the states can be seen

---

[63] J Williams, 'Gender Wars: Selfless Women in the Republic of Choice' (1991) 66 *New York University Law Review* 1559.

[64] S Himmelweit and H Land, *Reducing Gender Inequalities to Create a Sustainable Care* (Joseph Rowntree Foundation, 2008).

[65] K Morgan and K Zippel, 'Paid to Care' (2003) 10 *Social Politics* 245.

to provide for carers, while also supporting carers who seek to work and promote a more equal sharing of care tasks.[66] There seems in many European countries no clear vision of how the state would like to see the division of care between family members and state care.[67]

This may be appropriate. It is not for the state necessarily to dictate precisely how individuals should balance their caring and other responsibilities. Janet Gornick and Macia Meyers argue for a range of solutions to deal with the problems:

> The role for public policy would be to encourage the dissolution of gender divisions in the home through the use of parental leave; to transform the workplace from its current androcentrism to reduce working hours and become more flexible to allow for better work/care balance; and to protect parents' rights for time to care and children's rights for quality care through provision of high-quality childcare provided by well-trained and well-paid care workers.[68]

As well as gender, class, race and culture all play a crucial role impacting on care. In Joan Williams's writing she has distinguished between working class women who are 'one sick child away from being fired' and professional women who have status in the workplace and more ready access to child care.[69] As she points out, the kinds of issues facing women juggling work and care may well depend on their socio-economic circumstances. Simply reducing the issue to one of gender, while a highly significant factor, is likely to over-simplify the issue. This means attempts to encourage greater levels of female employment or male care work are unlikely to succeed if a monolithic approach, one that is not sensitive to these issues, is adopted.[70] Similarly, concepts of masculinity will vary greatly across cultures. For some men the desire to appear manly will deter them from care work.[71] There is, for example, evidence that men are less willing than women to use family care as a reason for absence from work.[72] However, others talk of 'new men', embracing care work. A recent *Newsweek* article claimed 'To survive in a hostile world, guys

---

[66] T Warren, G Pascall, and E Fox, 'Gender Equality in Time: Low-Paid Mothers' Paid and Unpaid Work in the UK' (2010) 16 *Feminist Economics* 193.

[67] R Mahon, 'Child Care: Towards What Kind of Social Europe' (2002) 9 *Social Politics* 343.

[68] J Gornick and M Meyers, *Families That Work: Policies for Reconciling Parenthood and Employment* (Russell Sage Foundation, 2003).

[69] J Williams, *Unbending Gender: Why Family and Work Conflict and What To Do About It* (Oxford University Press, 2000).

[70] A McGinley, 'Work, Caregiving, and Masculinities' (2011) 34 *Seattle University Law Review* 703.

[71] J Williams, 'From Difference to Dominance to Domesticity: Care as Work, Gender as Tradition' (2001) 76 *Chicago-Kent Law Review* 1441.

[72] K Silbaugh, 'Deliverable Male' (2011) 34 *Seattle University Law Review* 733.

need to embrace girly jobs and dirty diapers.'[73] The truth of such claims, again, will depend greatly on class and cultural context.

Mark Selmi[74] believes that much of the writing has been too kind to men.[75] He argues, 'if men were to take more leave—if men were to share more of the responsibilities related to housework and child care—it would likely negate some of the penalty employers currently impose on female leave takers.'[76]

Referring to several empirical studies, he rejects the arguments that men face bigger penalties for taking care leave than women. He also notes that even where women do earn more than men, more women take the leave. He points out that men could use vacation or sick leave to undertake care work, but they don't. He is, therefore, sceptical about claims that a long hours culture is impacting on men's ability to care. He refers to a study suggesting that people have more leisure time today than they did 20 or 30 years ago.[77] Yet, he notes that women still do twice as much child care and housework than men.[78] While he accepts that this is a narrower gap than was in the past, the decreasing gap between men and women's housework does not reflect that men are undertaking more care work, but rather that women are doing less, with more work being outsourced (eg to cleaners, readymade meals). He concludes:

> Men still do much of their house-related work outside, or while playing with their children, and the time they spend on more mundane inside work such as cleaning, cooking or doing laundry has not increased appreciably over the last three decades.[79]

D. Moral Claim

Many of the claims made so far can be brought together in a central moral claim that caring itself should be seen as a central value and practice for any

---

[73] 'To Survive in a Hostile World, Guys Need to Embrace Girly Jobs and Dirty Diapers' *Newsweek* 20 September 2010.

[74] M Selmi, 'The Work-Family Conflict: An Essay on Employers, Men and Responsibility' (2007) *University of Saint Thomas Law Journal* 573.

[75] See also P Kersaw, 'Care*fair*: Choice, Duty, and the Distribution of Care' (2006) 13 *Social Politics* 341.

[76] M Selmi, 'The Work-Family Conflict: An essay on Employers, Men and Responsibility' (2007) *University of Saint Thomas Law Journal* 573.

[77] Suzanne M Bianchi, John P Robinson and Melissa A Milkie, *Changing Rhythms of American Family Life* (Russell Sage, 2006) 124.

[78] M Selmi, 'The Work-Family Conflict: An essay on Employers, Men and Responsibility' (2007) *University of Saint Thomas Law Journal* 573, 664.

[79] Suzanne M Bianchi et al, 'Is Anyone Doing the Housework? Trends in the Gender Division of Household Labor' (2000) 79 *Social Forces* 191; S Bianchi, J Robinson and M Milkie, *Changing Rhythms of American Family Life* (Russell Sage, 2006) 124.

state. Selma Sevenhuijsen argues: 'It is argued that care should be seen as a democratic practice, and that democratic citizenship supposes that everybody would be guaranteed equal access to the giving and receiving of care.'[80]

Seeing caring as a central aspect of citizenship and an essential part of a democracy is very helpful. Sevenhuijsen goes on to explain how this radically changes the approach the state take to responsibilities:

> An ethics of care implies a radically different argument on the relationship between morality and politics, and thus about responsibility and obligation. Because it starts from a relational ontology, it focuses primarily on the question of what politics could mean for the safeguarding of responsibility and relationship in human interactions. A relational approach would start from the idea that policy-making needs elaborated insights into the way individuals frame their responsibilities in the context of actual social practices and how they handle the moral dilemmas that go with the conflicting responsibilities of care for self, others, and the relationship between them.[81]

The fact, however, that care is valuable to the state does not mean that the state necessarily needs to support it. There are plenty of activities that the state does not support, despite their social value. Susan Himmelweit gives some powerful reasons why the state should not simply leave care alone:

> Without intervention people may be less willing and able to fulfil caring norms, which may thereby be eroded. Those who assume caring responsibilities despite such pressures will pay a higher price for doing so and may have less influence on policy than those conforming more to increasingly less caring dominant norms. Not to adopt a generous strategy for caring now will shift power away from those who continue to care, erode caring norms, and make it more difficult to adopt a more caring strategy in the future. Without such a strategy, standards and availability of care will fall with high cost to society as a whole and fall particularly heavily on those who continue to care.[82]

One of the great benefits of this approach is that it moves away from the idea that care work is some kind of optional extra that especially good people undertake. Rather it sees care as a central aspect of citizenship. It is not performing care work that is seen as surprising. If care work is a taken for granted responsibility for citizens then all aspects of society need to be reworked around that responsibility to ensure it can be done.

---

[80] S Sevenhuijsen, 'Caring in the Third Way: The Relation between Obligation, Responsibility and Care in *Third Way* Discourse' (2000) 20 *Critical Social Policy* 5.

[81] Ibid.

[82] S Himmelweit, *Can We Afford (not) to Care: Prospects and Policy* (Open University, 2005). See also D Bubeck, *Care, Gender and Justice* (Oxford University Press, 1995) 243–44.

IV. The Basis of the Support

Moving on from a discussion of why the state should support caring, we need to focus on the aim of the intervention. Inevitably, one's view on why caring should be supported will impact on its purpose.

For those for whom the primary goal of state intervention in the area of care is to ensure that the burden of care does not fall on the state, then the response of the state will be to provide the minimum support necessary to ensure that families keep on caring. Indeed that support may be targeted not at those who are most in need of it, but rather those who are most likely to pass the burden onto the state.[83] For those, like me, who think there is a much stronger argument to be made than simply a reduction of government expenditure in supporting care, such a level of support would be inadequate.

An alternative approach would seek to increase economic productivity. This approach would seek to ensure that care work is not performed at the expense of economic production.[84] This could lead to the state response to those in caring relationships being primarily to encourage economic self-sufficiency through participation in the labour market. There might be some cases where the person caring would not be economically productive but for the care, in which case there would be no particular reason for state intervention. Again such an approach does not appeal to me.

The argument I advocated earlier regards care work as important in society and that support should be put in place to ensure care work is done.[85] Virginia Held concludes:

> We should, then, recognize the enormous value of caring work—in expressing social connectedness, in contributing to children's development and family satisfaction, and in enabling social cohesion and well-being (the list could go on and on). And we should demand of society that such work, in all its various forms, be compensated in ways more in line than at present with its evaluated worth, noting that its exchange or market value is one of the least appropriate ways in which to think of its value.[86]

The state support needs to do more than ensure that the care work takes place. It needs to ensure that carers have at least a minimally decent quality

---

[83] S Himmelweit and H Land, *Reducing Gender Inequalities to Create a Sustainable Care* (Joseph Rowntree Foundation, 2008).

[84] H Arksey and C Glendinning, 'Combining Work and Care: Carers' Decision-Making in the Context of Competing Policy Pressures' (2008) 42 *Social Policy and Administration* 1.

[85] S Himmelweit and H Land, *Reducing Gender Inequalities to Create a Sustainable Care* (Joseph Rowntree Foundation, 2008).

[86] V Held, 'Care and the Extension of Markets' (2002) 17 *Hypatia* 22.

of life. More broadly it needs to ensure a fair sharing of the disadvantages that care work can bring.

If support should be given to carers, the next question is where the money should come from to pay for this support. It is often assumed that it will be the state, but there are alternatives.

Mary Anne Case,[87] for example, writing about support for parents, has argued that rather than seeking the state or employers to subsidise child care, fathers should step in. They had chosen to produce a child. Putting the cost of care of children on to other taxpayers is not fair on those who have decided not to have children. The state should only step in when support cannot be obtained from the father. Although Case does not make this argument, one might argue that someone caring for an infirm parent should receive some support from a wealthy sibling and that the state should be called upon only where family support cannot be found.

Behind Case's argument is a concern that if the state is seen as the primary payer of the costs of care for a child, this has two undesirable consequences. First, it involves the state subsidising an unfair distribution of the burden of care between the parents. In the example of child care, the state provides the money to prop up a relationship in which the father is failing to play his role. Second, it involves a preferencing of some forms of care work over others or other socially valuable activities. Should a carer of an elderly neighbour or a leader of a cub scout troop, receiving no support from the state, have to subsidise a parent caring for a child?

The second point is well made, but easily dealt with. We can implement a system of care support which recognises all forms of care of dependants. So the carer of the elderly neighbour should be included in any system of carer support. As for the cub scout leader, valuable as their work is, as they are not meeting the essential needs of a person otherwise dependent on the state, their claim for state support is weaker.

The first point is harder to deal with. One response is that Case's argument does not give enough attention to the fact that there are institutional difficulties in the structure of employment, making it difficult for a couple to share responsibilities. Our society is structured so as to encourage female caregiving. While the state has an important responsibility to respond to that, it also has a duty to ensure that women and children do not suffer unduly as a result of it. The recent difficulties in collecting child support are relevant. While the state should collect child support from non-resident parents where possible, where this is not forthcoming the child should not suffer unduly as a result.

[87] M Case 'How High the Apple Pie? A Few Troubling Questions about Where, Why, and How the Burden of Care for Children should be Shifted,' (2001) 76 *Chicago-Kent Law Review* 1753.

V. The Nature of the Support

The state has a range of ways of seeking to achieve the aim of supporting carers:[88]

— *Financial.* These can include direct cash payments to those providing care, through the benefits system or otherwise. For those carers in employment, the payments could be made by means of tax credits. This might be seen as desirable, if the policy is aimed at encouraging carers to combine care work and employment.
— *Services.* This will include practical help such as help with laundry, food, or care. It might also include respite care.
— *Incentives to employment or assistance to find employment.* This might include the use of tax or benefits provisions to assist someone who is providing care work.
— *Employment protection.* These will aim to secure the position of a person in paid work who has untaken care work. This could include, for example, leave, career breaks, rights to flexible working or reduced hours.

We will be exploring these further in this chapter, but they reflect the range of alternatives a state has on offer. How these are used and/or combined reflects an understanding of the basis for the state's intervention, as well as broader social and economic policies.

Central to debates over the nature of state support is the question of whether the focus of any state intervention is a means of supporting the dependant person or a means of supporting the carer. Is the primary aim of the state to meet the needs of the person with needs, and providing for the carer is a way of doing that? Or are carers entitled to support in their own right? Mary Daly and Jane Lewis explain:

> The choice has potentially deep ramifications because in the first instance—making the payment to the person requiring care—welfare states are in effect distancing themselves from how the care needs are actually satisfied, whereas making the payment to the carer is a trend in the opposite direction—drawing more people within the direct embrace of the welfare state. To the extent that welfare states follow the first model, we could be seeing the emergence of a new type of welfare citizenship. In this regard cash benefits and services have to be analysed closely together.[89]

---

[88] F Williams, *Claiming and Framing in the Making of Care Policies. The Recognition and Redistribution of Care* (United Nations, 2010).

[89] M Daly and J Lewis, 'The Concept of Social Care and the Analysis of Contemporary Welfare' (2000) 51 *British Journal of Sociology* 51.

Applying these in a practical context could lead to a number of ways of channelling benefits.[90] These could range from[91] providing the individual needing care with a budget they could use to employ carers;[92] to giving the carer an allowance to spend on providing the care; to giving the carer a direct payment for support.

A key issue on the level of payments is whether these are to be regarded as compensation for loss of pay[93] or providing the carer with a sufficient sum to live on.[94] The issues are not straightforward. As Janice Keefe, Caroline Glendinning and Pamela Fancey put it:

> On the one hand, cash payments for family carers do recognize and attempt to ameliorate the direct and opportunity costs associated with caregiving and provide some formal recognition of the caregiving role. On the other hand, these programs can entrap women into caregiving roles by offering financial support in place of other care options.[95]

Maxine Eichner argues that the correct sum for carers should be as follows:[96]

> At a minimum, the supportive state should arrange institutions in such a way that family members can, through exercising diligent but not Herculean efforts, meet the basic physical, mental, and emotional needs of children and other dependents and promote human development while avoiding impoverishment or immiseration. Translated into concrete government policies, this means that the welfare system must be structured in a way that those at the bottom of the economic ladder with dependents receive enough financial assistance so that they can provide them with decent environments that promote basic capabilities. Insofar as they are required by the state's welfare policies to work outside the home, they must also have realistic access to good-quality, affordable day care. Further, the state must regulate the workplace to ensure parents enough time with their children so that they are well parented and supervised, and not so pressed for time or frazzled by time pressures that it interferes with adequate caretaking. In this view, the state shirks its responsibility when it forces parents to choose between working to put food in their children's mouths and ensuring that their children receive adequate caretaking.[97]

---

[90] B Da Roit and B Le Bihan, 'Similar and Yet So Different: Cash-for-Care in Six European Countries' Long-Term Care Policies' (2010) 88 *Millbank Quarterly* 286.

[91] J Keefe, C Glendinning and P Fancey, 'Financial Payments for Family Carers: Policy Approaches and Debates' in A Martin-Matthews and J Philips (eds), *Ageing at the Intersection Of Work And Home Life: Blurring The Boundaries* (New York, Lawrence Eribaum, 2008).

[92] Ibid.

[93] J Lewis, 'Gender and Welfare Regimes: Further Thoughts' (1997) 4 *Social Policy* 160.

[94] J Keefe, C Glendinning and P Fancey, 'Financial Payments for Family Carers: Policy Approaches and Debates' in A Martin-Matthews and J Philips (eds), *Ageing at the Intersection Of Work And Home Life: Blurring The Boundaries* (New York, Lawrence Eribaum, 2008).

[95] Ibid.

[96] M Eichner, *The Supportive State* (Oxford University Press, 2010) 79.

[97] Ibid 78–79.

Daniel Engster sets out six principles which should govern the state's response to those in caring relationships:

(1)　To help individuals to meet their basic needs for nourishment, sanitary water, clothes, shelter, basic medical care, a clean environment, rest, and protection from physical harm when they cannot reasonably meet these needs on their own.

(2)　To help individuals to develop and sustain their basic capability for sensation, mobility, emotion, imagination, reason, communication, affiliation, literacy and numeracy when they cannot reasonably achieve these goals on their own.

(3)　To help individuals to avoid and alleviate unnecessary pain and suffering when they need help in meeting this goal.

(4)　When governments organize or fund programs to care directly for individual or support caring relationships, they should aim to involve the potential care recipients as much as possible in formulating and running these programs. In this way, they can better ensure that the programs will be tailored to recipients' actual needs and utilize their talents.

(5)　Governments should shift the delivery of care as much as possible to the personal and local level, facilitating the care of individuals primarily by providing support for parents, families, caregivers, and local organizations who can care for individuals in context-specific and particular ways.

(6)　Government should endeavour to make everyone aware of the programs that exist to support and accommodate caring, and should make access to these programs as easy as possible for all eligible individuals.[98]

These, I suggest, are an absolute minimum, but are certainly financially achievable.

Looking at the issue more broadly, Caroline Glendinning and Hilary Arksey[99] have suggested four approaches that public bodies could take to carers. These are:

— Carers as resource: carers are supported in order to maintain their caregiving role.
— Carers as co-workers: carers are regarded as working with social services in order to provide services to those in need.
— Carers as co-clients: carers are recognised as having needs in their own right and to be in need of services to maintain their well-being.
— Superseded carer: services should be offered to the service-user to enable them to be independent and no longer need a carer.

---

[98] D Engster, *The Heart of Justice: Care Ethics of Political Theory* (Oxford University Press, 2009) 37ff.

[99] C Glendinning and H Arksey, 'Informal Care' in P Alcock, M May and K Rowlingson (eds), *The Student's Companion to Social Policy* (Oxford, Blackwell, 2008) 219–25.

In the authors' view, the Government has tended to regard carers as a resource and that this has led to a failure to adequately protect the interests of carers as people in their own right. Contrast, however, the rhetoric behind the *National Strategy for Carers* which set several principles, which see the carers as the focus of state attention:

— carers will be treated with dignity and respect as expert care partners;
— carers will have access to the services they need to support them in their caring role;
— carers will be able to have a life of their own;
— carers will not be forced into financial hardship by their caring role;
— carers will be supported to stay mentally and physically well; and
— children and young people will be protected from inappropriate caring roles.[100]

I would argue that this kind of approach which focuses solely on carers is unhelpful. First, as a strategy towards care, it completely sidelines those 'receiving care'. This is the kind of approach that the critique from the perspective of disability studies seems particularly appropriate.[101] We explored this in chapter two.[102] The danger of focusing on the interests of carers is that it overlooks the power that is exercised in care. The language of care itself implies vulnerability and reinforces the social construction of disability.[103] It also portrays care as a uni-directional activity, which is an inaccurate portrayal of most caring relationships.

As already argued in chapter two, the better approach is to focus on the promotion of a caring relationship. A central aspect of a caring relationship is that it is responsive to the needs of both parties. Where the person receiving care wants a dispassionate kind of care, the caring relationship will be more dispassionate. The challenge then is to move away from seeing one party as being vulnerable and receiving care into recognising our mutual vulnerability. As Susan Dodds puts it:

> We are all vulnerable to the exigencies of our embodied, social and relational existence and, in recognising this inherent human vulnerability, we can see the ways in which a range of social institutions and structures protect us against

---

[100] Department of Health, *The National Strategy for Carers* (Department of Health, 2008).

[101] C Beckett, 'Women, Disability, Care: Good Neighbours or Uneasy Bedfellows' (2007) 27 *Critical Social Policy* 360; T Kroger, 'Care Research and Disability Studies: Nothing in Common?' (2009) 29 *Critical Social Policy* 398.

[102] See also L Scully, *Disability Bioethics: Moral Bodies, Moral Difference* (Rowman and Littlefield, 2008).

[103] There is much dispute over the preferable terminology here. I will use 'disabled person' as it is the most commonly used in England. For some 'people with disabilities' is preferred to a disabled person because it emphasises that the individual is a person first and foremost and not defined by their disability. However, the terminology 'disabled person' captures the social model of disability, namely that a person has been disadvantaged by social structures and facilities rather than being innately disabled. Another piece of terminology used is 'differability', emphasising that a person may be differently abled, but that does not necessarily indicate they are disadvantaged.

some vulnerabilities, while others expose us to risk. We do not have to view our obligations towards those who lack the capacity to develop or retain autonomy as having a different source from our obligations towards those whose autonomy is made vulnerable due to a degree of dependency. It may be easier to recognise the social value of provision of care if it is viewed as something on which we all have been dependent and on which we are all likely to be dependent at different points in our lives, rather than altruistic behaviour extended to those who lack 'full personhood'.[104]

This may all sound a little too 'up in the air', but there are many shared interests between the 'carer' and the 'cared for'. Having a safe work environment is essential for all, as is a good standard of housing and provision of equipment. A carer who is exhausted or dispirited is of little benefit to the person needing care.[105]

The lack of services might impact on both parties, but the claims to support an effective relationship for both should be the focus.[106] A good example of the tension that can arise between focusing on the needs of 'carers' and of the 'cared for' is evidence from social care practitioners that when local authorities were required to provide carers' grants for services to carers, cash-strapped local authorities used money that would otherwise have been provided for those receiving care. For example 'day care services' were recast as respite centres for carers.[107]

Just to be clear I am not arguing that 'carers' should not be entitled to be benefits in their own right as individuals. However, any benefits or services provided in respect of care should be aimed at the caring relationship, with a consideration of both parties and of what will assist the care. The correct approach is to consider what services this relationship requires. A service to one will be a service to the other.[108] To seek to separate out services to the 'cared for' and services to the 'carer' is likely to lead to contradictory results and a lack of joined up provision.

There is another issue concerning the relationship between state support and those in a caring relationship. If the state is supporting caring relationships, it might be argued that as care requires considerable skill then the normal consequences of skilled work should apply: training, supervision and regulation. It may be noted that with increasingly sophisticated technologies, the skill in caring for a disabled person is considerable.[109] The more the

---

[104] S Dodds, 'Depending on Care: Recognition of Vulnerability and the Social Contribution of Care Provision' (2007) 21 *Bioethics* 500.

[105] L Lloyd, 'Call us Carers: Limitations and Risks in Campaigning for Recognition and Exclusivity' (2006) 26 *Critical Social Policy* 945.

[106] J Lewis, 'Gender and Welfare Regimes: Further Thoughts' (1997) 4 *Social Policy* 160.

[107] L Lloyd, 'Call us Carers: Limitations and Risks in Campaigning for Recognition and Exclusivity' (2006) 26 *Critical Social Policy* 945.

[108] Ibid.

[109] J Keefe, C Glendinning and P Fancey, 'Financial Payments for Family Carers: Policy Approaches and Debates' in A Martin-Matthews and J Philips (eds), *Ageing at the Intersection Of Work And Home Life: Blurring The Boundaries* (New York, Lawrence Eribaum, 2008).

emotional side of care is emphasised, the benefits of psychological training become apparent. Indeed more generally the state could take the view that if caring becomes a trained profession then the professional carer is better placed to undertake the work than a family member or friend.[110] Helen Reece has warned about the danger of calling for greater state support for carers: 'Financial dependence on the State brings State and citizen into a relationship that the State will continue to exploit.'[111]

The response to these points is to emphasise the importance of the relationship in care. Sex is better with a lover than a trained professional,[112] precisely because the relationship is an essential element to it. So too with care, although technique may be a part of the work, the relationship is central. The skills acquired in a relationship are those that are personal to the relationship and cannot be taught or supervised, because they are unique to the two parties. I agree that we can set minimum levels of care and no doubt there are carers in some cases who cannot provide the required standard, but it must be recognised that the skill of the carer is often highly personalised. They know how the person is receiving care and the care is given in the context of their relationship.

If the state is willing to view care in this way, Reece's concerns may not materialise. Selma Sevenhuijsen[113] argues that many states now play the role of 'régisseur'[114] and supervisor. This requires the state to ensure there is collective attentiveness to the caring process. The state uses a combination of public and private services to ensure there is a coverage and that it meets standards of accessibility, social justice and expediency. It needs to ensure, for example, that there is access to employment and flexibility for those caring, but also good alternative care. This is the ideal the state should strive for.

VI. Defamilisation

For some commentators a central theme in relation to support for care is defamilisation. This is a claim that we are witnessing the transformation of care from being a private, familial practice into being a public one. That is

---

[110] Reece 'Review: The Autonomy Myth: A Theory of Dependency' [2008] *Child and Family Law Quarterly* 109.

[111] Ibid 114.

[112] I'm guessing!

[113] S Sevenhuijsen, 'The Relevance of the Feminist Ethic of Care for Social Policy' (2003) 4 *Feminist Theory* 179.

[114] Meaning 'manager'.

not necessarily to say it does not involve family members, but their role is to act on behalf of society, rather than as family members.[115]

A good example of defamilisation in practice, could be said to be the increased child care provision, so that at least mothers have the option to use state provided or subsidised child care.[116] Child care is increasingly regarded as much a responsibility of the state as for the family. Ensuring there is adequate non-familial child care provision has become taken on as a role for Government in a way it never would have been a couple of decades ago. In the past it might have been seen as primarily the job of the mother to care for the child, or failing that to make her own arrangements for child care. The provision of child care has become the responsibility of the state. Indeed it seems the expectation now is that the mother will use child care and seek employment.[117]

Indeed, we are even seeing a shift of the question about whether parents should work or undertake child care being seen as a decision in which the state has an interest, with the benefit system and government rhetoric encouraging mothers to work. The Department for Work and Pensions' policy document on lone parents states:

> Increasing the employment rate of parents is a key element in combating child poverty and we know that work is the best route out of poverty.

> It is important that people who can take up paid employment are given help and encouragement to do so and we believe it is reasonable to expect lone parents to take up paid work once their children are in full-time education.

> Lone parents who are capable of work can claim Income Support solely as a lone parent until their youngest child reaches age five. They will then ordinarily need to claim Jobseeker's Allowance and seek work.[118]

Further, through increased regulation of family life, through parenting orders and classes and increased political discussion of 'problem families', the public nature of child care has increased. We can see this with the growth in the role schools are expected to play in citizenship, sex education and diet.

Mary Daly sees these themes emerging across Europe:

— Encouraging if not compelling employment, for benefit claimants, 'workless households' and mothers in the home;
— Expanding services for the education and/or care of young children;

---

[115] G Esping-Anderson, *The Social Foundations of Postindustrial Economies* (Oxford University Press, 1999); J Lewis, 'Gender and Welfare Regimes: Further Thoughts' (1997) 4 *Social Policy* 160.

[116] A Leira, 'Caring as Social Right: Cash for Child Care and Daddy Leave' (1998) 5 *Social Politics* 362.

[117] See www.telegraph.co.uk/news/politics/david-cameron/9354163/David-Camerons-welfare-speech-in-full.html.

[118] Department for Work and Pensions, *Lone Parents* (DWP, 2012) 1.

— Balancing work and family life;
— Targeting men's behavior as fathers;
— Providing financial assistance for families with care tasks and obligations.[119]

She argues that there is a general acceptance by governments that societies should adopt an 'adult worker model', based on the assumption that all adults will work or are potentially able to work. That may be only part-time work, but the Government is clearly seeking to promote the expectation that all adults will work. Government policies towards carers, and indeed all those out of paid employment, have been to encourage them to undertake paid work.[120] The New Deal, tax credits and the National Minimum Wage were all part of a general drive to make work more attractive. Encouraging employment is seen as a way of promoting financial independence; helping with the costs of caring; providing satisfaction and increasing self-esteem.[121]

Certainly we seem to be moving to a model where the Government expects work and care to be combined.[122] Childcare subsidies and the national child care strategy have been developed to enable parents to do this.[123] The welfare system and the Government encourage lone parents in particular to undertake paid work, using child care if necessary. All of this means the state has a strong interest in providing support to care or alternatives to care so that carers can enter the labour market. For the Government, the self-financing carer is an ideal solution to the care crisis. The problem is that employment law and labour markets are yet to provide the flexibility to enable an effective combining of care and work.

Some feminists will welcome defamilisation, with its shifting of the responsibilities of care away from women, or at least moving away from an assumption that women should undertake care work. There are three reasons why I suggest that defamilisation is not welcome in a straightforward way.

First, as already noted in chapter two, I would support the feminist approach which seeks to value care. We should not regard care as an undesirable burden to be shifted, but important work to be recognised and valued.

Second, care can be a liberating practice, one that resists discriminatory practices elsewhere in society. Ethnic and racial minorities; gay and lesbian people might, for example, find in the practice of care, a way of living their

---

[119] M Daly, 'What Adult Worker Model? A Critical Look at Recent Social Policy Reform in Europe from a Gender and Family Perspective' (2011) *Social Policy* 1.

[120] H Arksey, 'Combining Work and Care: The Reality of Policy Tensions for Carers' (2007) 15 *Benefits* 137.

[121] Department of Health, *Caring about Carers: A National Strategy for Carers* (Department of Health, 1999).

[122] See eg Welfare Reform Act 2009.

[123] S Himmelweit and H Land, *Reducing Gender Inequalities to Create a Sustainable Care* (Joseph Rowntree Foundation, 2008).

lives which is free from oppressive practices elsewhere.[124] Through a caring relationship they may find a community in which the broader negative societal pressures cannot permeate. Again it should not be assumed that people want to be 'freed' to take up employment.

Third, as explained in chapter two, central to care is the notion of relationship. High quality care involves knowing a person really well and having a mutual relationship. While such relationships could be found within state care, they are unlikely to be. State alternative care, at least currently, is marked by high turnover of staff and low pay.[125] The implication in defamilisation that alternative care offered to enable carers to enter the labour market will be as good as the family care must be questioned.

It is easy to be cynical about the Government's attempts for carers to be self-financing. The double shift work pays taxes and meets the state's obligation. A less cynical approach might be that suggested by Maxine Eichner, who supports the model of the 'supportive state', a midway model. She explains, focusing on the example of children:

> It conceives of the state as serving an integral role in supporting families, not simply after they break down, but in the ordinary course of events. In this conception, the state possesses a duty to structure institutions to support children's welfare and development, a duty that exists simultaneously with parents' own responsibility for children. Yet the state's role is a limited one, which provides the institutional scaffolding to support caretaking, while also expecting family members to meet caretaking needs.[126]

She sees this as requiring the state 'to arrange societal institutions in such a way that family members can meet the basic physical, mental, and emotional needs of dependents without impoverishing or exhausting themselves or their financial resources'.[127]

Alison Diduck has argued:[128]

> New deal or other family-friendly work practices, not to mention providing so-called equal opportunities for carers to enter work or training programmes, present parents and carers as partners with the state and with the market in new ways. In this new partnership, private self reliance becomes one's social responsibility and founds one's claims to citizenship, and economic dependence becomes an individual failing that demands individualised solutions rather than social or structural ones. The new private partners also have the responsibility of 'ensuring that their children behave responsibly and are sufficiently informed and educated to become citizen works themselves'.

---

[124] L Kessler, 'The Politics of Care' (2008) 23 *Wisconsin Journal of Law, Gender and Society* 169.
[125] This is acknowledged in HM Government, *Caring for our Future* (The Stationery Office, 2012).
[126] M Eichner, *The Supportive State* (Oxford University Press, 2010) 70–72.
[127] Ibid 72.
[128] A Diduck, 'Shifting Familiarity' (2005) 58 *Current Legal Problems* 235, 252.

She notes that

> ... While it is framed in gender neutral terms, this new partnership ... frequently and profoundly affects women and the children in their care because structural conditions and the norms of family living encourage their continued and mutual economic dependencies.

Many have linked defamilisation with the concept of individualisation.[129] Commentators have claimed that individualisation is a major force in our society and this has impacted on the perception of care and government policy towards it. Individualisation is seen as involving an increased emphasis on independence, autonomy and self-sufficiency and a downplaying of family bonds and an increase in diversity of relationships. A common example is said to be the decreasing use of marriage, with its legal and social bonds, and the increase in cohabitation with less formality and few legal commitments.[130] Gone are the days, if ever there were such, when a pre-given life trajectory was followed: birth, engagement, marriage, children, death! Individuals increasingly create their own life stories and own relationships. This means that it cannot be assumed people will feel they must care for family members who are in need.

Mary Daly and Kirsten Scheiwe suggest that individualisation is better seen as a rejection of the institutional basis of obligations. They argue:

> We conceptualise individualisation as a process of continuing separation of an individual from traditional and familial dependencies, whereby the links to status groups or communities lose importance for determining one's decisions, status, and life chances. As part of this process, personal dependencies come to be replaced by dependencies on the market—a process that affects and changes family cohesion. Individualisation processes can be theorised also with regard to family law institutions (especially marriage and the linked concept of legitimacy) as affecting personal, family, and generational relationships.[131]

It is easy to exaggerate this trend.[132] It has been argued that individualisation has happened within social bonds, rather than away from them.[133] It is not that people no longer feel obligations to family members, but rather our understanding of who counts as family and how those obligations are weighed has changed. In particular there is a shift towards placing weight on the actual

---

[129] M Daly and K Scheiwe, 'Individualisation and Personal Obligations—Social Policy, Family Policy, and Law Reform in Germany and the UK' (2010) 24 *International Journal of Law Policy and the Family* 177.

[130] U Beck and E Beck-Gernsheim, *Individualization: Institutionalized Individualism and Its Social and Political Consequences* (Sage, 2002).

[131] M Daly and K Scheiwe, 'Individualisation and Personal Obligations—Social Policy, Family Policy, and Law Reform in Germany and the UK' (2010) 24 *International Journal of Law Policy and the Family* 177.

[132] G Therborn, *Between Sex and Power: Family in the World 1900–2000* (Routledge, 2004).

[133] F Williams, *Rethinking Families* (Calouste Gulbenkian Foundation, 2004).

personal relationships, as opposed to formal blood ties.[134] So, there may be greater obligation to an aunt, with whom one is close, than a sister whom one never sees. While there may have been a move away from more formal commitment, such as marriage, this does not mean there is no commitment within close relationships. Obligations are negotiated within the relationship itself, rather than arising from a status.[135] One must balance the commitments to family members with commitments to one's career or other projects. It is difficult to know the extent to which this kind of individualistic thinking has infiltrated society and it no doubt depends significantly on ethnic, religious and class factors.

Fiona Williams rejects the argument that an increased involvement of women in the work place can be put down to simply selfishness or consumerism. She argues:

> how mothers with young children make decisions around work and care: working mothers' investment in employment is based upon their own and their networks' moral reasoning about what is right and proper for their children. They do not act as individualist 'rational economic actors' where financial costs and benefits determine decisions. Money does matter of course to working mothers, but decisions about working are also taken in the context of being able to provide the quality of care they think is best for their children.[136]

Williams's quote indicates the pressures that women, in particular, feel over the competing pressures they face. These are most manifest in the work-life balance debate, which we consider next.

VII. Work-Life Balance

One of the great themes of school-gate chat and mums' internet chat sites is the work-life balance.[137] Is it possible to strike the balance between obligations to family, while maintaining obligations to an employer? Many feel a constant struggle to find a balance between work and family life, with family life suffering due to the demands of work, or career progression delayed when someone decides to focus on family time. Women balancing work and care face the danger of only just surviving at both. They manage just to keep their

---

[134] C Smart, *Personal Life* (Polity, 2007).

[135] F Williams, 'Good-Enough Life: Developing the Grounds for a Political Ethic of Care' (2005) 30 *Soundings* 17.

[136] Ibid.

[137] J Lewis, *Work-Family Balance, Gender and Policy* (Edward Elgar, 2009); B Hobson and S Fahlen, 'Parents' Work-Life Balance' in J Bridgeman, H Keating and C Lind (eds), *Taking Responsibility, Law and the Changing Family* (Ashgate, 2011).

jobs, while struggling to put in the expected hours and being overlooked for promotion due to their other commitments; while also feeling that the care provided to their children is only just good enough.[138] These issues are made all the harder for the 'sandwich generation', a term used to refer to those who are caring for their children and parents at the same time.[139] It is not just a case of balancing work and care, it can be about balancing work and care and more care. With increasing hours of employment expected; a precarious job market; and an intensification of what is expected of parents,[140] it is no wonder people find the balance impossible.

It should not be assumed that the problem necessarily lies in increased levels of employment among women. A major survey of the current data found that 'the dual-earner regimes, combining high levels of support for paid parenting leaves and public child care, are strongly associated with low levels of child poverty and child mortality.'[141] One survey of American working mothers found that work brought them benefits: increased income; increased self-esteem; feelings of independence; increased social integration and being a good example for their children.[142]

Vicky Schultz has argued in favour of work. For her it is a site for human flourishing:

> As individuals, our work provides us with a forum to realize at least some of our aspirations, to form bonds with others, to serve society, and to project ourselves into the larger world beyond our own families and friends. It also provides us with the wherewithal to sustain ourselves, economically and socially, so that we may enter into intimate relationships with the security that permits us to love (and leave) freely, without need of recompense. This world of equal citizenship, stable community, and a strong, secure selfhood for everyone is the world I believe feminism was born to bring into being.[143]

She explains:

> Work is a site of deep self-formation that offers rich opportunities for human flourishing (or devastation). To a large extent, it is through our work—how it is defined, distributed, characterized, and controlled—that we develop into the 'men' and 'women' we see ourselves and others see us as being. Because law's domain includes work and its connection to other spheres of existence, the prospect of who

---

[138] K Backett-Milburn, L Airey, L McKie and G Hogg, 'Family Comes First or Open all Hours?: How Low Paid Women Working in Food Retailing Manage Webs of Obligation at Home and Work' (2008) 56 *The Sociological Review* 474.

[139] E Grundy and J Henretta, 'Between Elderly Parents and Adult Children: A New Look at the Intergenerational Care Provided by the 'Sandwich Generation' (2006) 26 *Ageing and Society* 707.

[140] S Hays, *The Cultural Contradictions of Motherhood* (Yale University Press, 2011).

[141] D Engster and H Olofsdotter Stensöta, 'Do Family Policy Regimes Matter for Children's Well-Being?' (2011) 18 *Social Politics* 82.

[142] A London, E Scott, K Edin and V Hunter, 'Welfare Reform, Work-Family Trade Offs, and Child Well-Being' (2003) 54 *Family Relations* 148.

[143] V Schultz, 'Life's Work' (2000) 100 *Columbia Law Review* 1881.

we become as a society, and as individuals, is shaped profoundly by the laws that create and control the institutions that govern our experiences as workers. I believe that it is only by recognizing the formative power of such forces that we can imagine and invent ourselves as full human agents.[144]

Certainly this is picked up by the language used by governments arguing that work is the way out of social exclusion; a responsibility of a citizen; a way of establishing self-sufficiency and independence; the route out of poverty and providing a good role model to children.[145]

However, such rhetoric disguises the reality. Much of the discussion of this issue is conducted around a middle class discourse. For the wealthiest, combing a career and acceptable level of child care is difficult, but not unduly so. It is rarely the case, as it is with those of lower economic income, that child care issues threaten unemployment and that there is no real choice between working or not. Media images when discussing the work/life balance typically portray a woman in a smart business suit, dropping off a child at child care. This if far from the norm. More common are low-paid, low quality jobs[146] where pay is largely taken up paying for child care.[147] The difficulty is that part-time workers earn 64 per cent of full time male wage rates.[148]

There are tools available to assist those struggling with balancing these pressures.[149] The use of tax credits[150] has improved the position of those in low paid jobs slightly, making them a little more financially worthwhile. Another option might be to create flexible working hours, greater part-time work, cheaper child care, and working from home. These might make it easier for someone to combine employment and care. The Working Time Directive goes some way towards tackling the long hours culture in employment.[151]

The problem is that high quality care and employment are hard to combine. A central part of care is being there when needed. Parents of teenagers note that there are long periods of time where the role is to 'keep out', but suddenly, unexpectedly, the teenager needs support and attention. Such times cannot be 'booked in' or predicted. Generally being around is required. This point is no doubt true of many caring relationships. Further, care is not measured in hours, because it is often about getting to know the individual. Knowing

---

[144] Ibid 1884–85.

[145] F Williams, 'In and Beyond New Labour: Towards a New Political Ethics of Care' (2001) 21 *Critical Social Policy* 467.

[146] M Selmi, 'Women in the Workplace: Which Women, Which Agenda?' (2006) 13 *Duke Journal of Constitutional Law & Public Policy* 7.

[147] Pascal Barth, *Social Exclusion of Family Carers in Different Welfare State Regimes. A Comparison Between Germany And Sweden* (Grin, 2012).

[148] S Himmelweit and H Land, *Reducing Gender Inequalities to Create a Sustainable Care* (Joseph Rowntree Foundation, 2008).

[149] J Heymann, 'Can Working Families Ever Win?' *Boston Review* February 2002.

[150] J Wiggan, 'Managing Time: The Integration of Caring and Paid Work by Low-Income Families and the Role of the UK's Tax Credit System' (2010) 36 *Policy Studies* 631.

[151] [1993] OJ L307/18, and see the discussion in M Travis, 'What a Difference a Day Makes, or Does It? Work/Family Balance and the Four-Day Work Week' (2010) 42 *Connecticut Law Review* 1223.

the right words to comfort a crying 12-year-old; the right way to comfort an autistic teenager; the right touch for a distressed dementia patient requires knowing them, knowing them well. That takes time and energy.

There is no ready response to the work-life balance debate. Fiona Williams provides a useful set of tools to start thinking about the key themes:[152]

> Rather than care needs being fitted in to the traditional requirements of work, we can map people's work/life needs within three different but connected areas of their lives. First, there is *personal time and space*: what do we need for the care of self and maintenance of body, mind and soul (e.g. mobility/relationships/relaxation/life-long learning/ spirituality)? Second, *care time and space*: what do we need to care properly for others? This would include, for example, child care and adult care provision; home care services; cleaning, laundry and food services; domiciliary services; kite marking for services; raising standards and reward for paid carers; direct payments for people receiving care/support; carer credits to protect pensions; state support for residential care costs. These would be underpinned by principles of accessibility, affordability, variety, choice, quality, flexibility and user control; they would be complemented by the removal of disabling barriers around space, time, organisations and the environment and a commitment to a caring, enabling environment—e.g. safe and accessible public spaces; safe, accessible, affordable transport. Third, there is *work time and space*: what do we need to enable us to gain economic self-sufficiency and balance these other areas? Included here are paid maternity and paternity leave; paid carers' leave for women and men; job-sharing; annualised hours/lifetime hours; work-based nurseries/breakfast clubs/holiday clubs; sabbaticals; part-time/flexible hours; shorter full-time hours; decent universal pensions with added protection for poorer and older pensioners.

For all too many at the moment, it is the third category that takes up the energy.[153] We need a lot of work on our current structures of employment practice to put her proposals into practice. We will return to this issue in chapter seven.

VIII. Commodification

A major contemporary theme surrounding care is commodification.[154] We have seen an increase in the use of paid care, be that in the form of formal state care or state payment to those who might otherwise have performed the care

---

[152] F Williams, 'In and Beyond New Labour: Towards a New Political Ethics of Care' (2001) 21 *Critical Social Policy* 467.

[153] M Daly, 'What Adult Worker Model? A Critical Look at Recent Social Policy Reform in Europe from a Gender and Family Perspective' (2011) *Social Policy* 1.

[154] C Ungerson, 'Social Politics and the Commodification of Care' (1997) 4 *Social Politics* 362; C Ungerson, 'Care, Work and Feeling' (2005) 53 *Sociological Review* 288; C Ungerson, 'Cash in Care' in M Harrington Meyer (ed), *Care Work: Gender, Labor and the Welfare State* (Routledge, 2006); R Claasen, 'The Commodification of Care' (2011) 26 *Hypatia* 43.

without payment. More broadly, there appears to be a relocation of care from the private to the public, from collective services to commercial ones.[155]

The impact of this commodification on the care relationship is controversial.[156] Some argue that once payment is involved, 'the carer' will perceive their freedom to be restricted. While the care is offered informally it can be withdrawn or limited. Once it is 'paid for' or otherwise formally acknowledged by the state, the sense of obligation can increase. In one study[157] it was suggested that contracts helped carers structure their relationship. It drew a clear line between what was required and what was an act of affection.

Not everyone accepts this. The argument may place insufficient weight on the enormous sense of responsibility that those in caring relationships have for each other. These emotional and moral ties are likely to be far stronger than any created by a contract of employment.

Another concern surrounds the valuing of care. On the one hand commodification of care through payment could be seen in a positive light in that it recognises the value of care.[158] There are several dangers with this argument. To some the sums paid are so low that in fact they reflect a demeaning of care. However, not everything that has market value becomes understood in monetary terms only. A wedding ring might be bought and sold but its value to the parties is not purely financial.[159] So too with work, it may have a monetary value attached to it and yet have significant other value. It may, therefore, be better to see the sums paid as enabling care, rather than valuing it.

Perhaps the major concern with payment for care is that they will infect the practice of care with market values.[160] Virginia Held writes, 'The ideal of the market teaches that everyone is always motivated by self-interest, that firms seek to maximize profits, that economic value is the only kind of value that matters.'[161] As Held suggests, the language of the market and the goals of efficiency and productivity do not map into caring relationships.[162] However, plenty of people combine pay with care effectively. There is no evidence that payment of nursery workers or nurses negatively impacts on the level of care.[163]

---

[155] S Sevenhuijsen, 'The Place of Care: The Relevance of the Feminist Ethic of Care for Social Policy' (2003) 4 *Feminist Theory* 179.

[156] E Grootegoed, T Knijn and B da Roit, 'Relatives as Paid Care-Givers: How Family Carers Experience Payments for Care' (2010) 30 *Ageing and Society* 467.

[157] V Held, 'Care and the Extension of Markets' (2002) 17 *Hypatia* 19.

[158] M Fineman, 'Contract and Care' (2001) 76 *Chicago-Kent Law Review* 1403; M Daly and J Lewis, 'The Concept of Social Care and the Analysis of Contemporary Welfare' (2000) 51 *British Journal of Sociology* 51.

[159] S Himmelweit, 'Caring Labor' (1999) 561 *Annals of the American Academy of Political and Social Science* 27.

[160] C Ungerson, 'Social Politics and the Commodification of Care' (1997) 4 *Social Politics* 362; J Tronto, 'Creating Caring Institutions: Politics, Plurality, and Purpose' (2010) 4 *Ethics and Social Welfare* 158.

[161] V Held, 'Care and the Extensions of Markets' (2009) 17 *Hypatia* 19.

[162] Ibid 19.

[163] Ibid.

IX. Current Law

Here I will set out, briefly, the primary benefits offered to those offering care. While criticised in chapter two, the language of carer and cared for dominates the approach of the state benefits system and so will be used here.

A. Benefits and Caring Relationships

There is a range of state benefits available to carers. The regulations governing these are complex and they will only be explained in outline here.[164] As the Law Commission has acknowledged, the current legal framework for carers' assessments and provision is fragmented and multi-layered.[165]

i. Carers' Allowance

The main benefit for carers is Carers' Allowance. This is available to anyone who is providing at least 35 hours of unpaid care to a person receiving a relevant disability benefit. It is not available to those earning over £100 per week. There are currently 470,000 carers receiving it.

The benefit has received much criticism. It is the lowest of all income replacement benefits. It currently stands at £58.45 per week.[166] As a representative of the National Autistic Society put it to the House of Common Select Committee:

> Just to demonstrate how inadequate Carer's Allowance is, even if you did the minimum caring hours of 35 hours a week, that is equivalent to £1.44 an hour compared to a minimum wage of £5.52, which really demonstrates how we value that role. So the rate is inadequate, it sends a message to carers about how we value their role.[167]

Noticeably the Government's 2008 carers' strategy contains no commitment to reform benefits, at least in the short term. The Government explained that the Carer's Allowance is not intended as a carer's wage and so any analogy with the minimum wage is unfair.[168] Rather it is an 'income-maintenance' benefit, similar to Maternity Allowance or Incapacity Benefit, for those unable to participate in the labour market. Whether the appropriate analogy is with

---

[164] For a detailed analysis see L Clements, *Carers and Their Rights* (London, Carers UK, 2011).
[165] The Law Commission, *Adult Social Care. Report 326* (Law Commission, 2011) para 7.2.
[166] As at 1 June 2012.
[167] House of Commons, *Supporting Carers to Care* (2009) para 121.
[168] HM Government, *Carers at the Heart of 21st-Century Families and Communities* (London, The Stationery Office, 2008).

those suffering incapacity is open to debate. It could be argued that as carers are doing a job which otherwise would fall on the state, carers are saving the state substantial sums and therefore entitled to higher levels of benefit. One complaint of Carers UK is that the £100 income limit means that it can act as a disincentive to finding work.[169] Indeed it can operate so that a person is worse off by taking employment. Recent changes to the Working Tax Credit for those claiming Carer's Allowance should avoid this in some cases.

A further difficulty is the relatively low take-up rate, with just an estimated 65 per cent of those entitled taking it up.[170] The Health and Social Care Information Centre[171] report that only six per cent of carers claimed to be offered a carer's assessment and only four per cent had had an assessment. Only one per cent offered a review. Of those assessed, 67 per cent had received some kind of service. 11 per cent of all carers reported receiving Carer's Allowance and 27 per cent received Disability Living Allowance/Attendance Allowance. This rose to 23 per cent of carers who cared for 35 hours or more per week receiving Carer's Allowance and 50 per cent receiving Disability Living Allowance/Attendance Allowance.[172] Carers UK suggests over 300,000 have failed to claim their entitlements.[173] It found that 81 per cent of carers had been caring for over a year before getting financial support. Before receiving benefits, just under half of these had not received any support for five years. A recent poll for Macmillan Cancer support found that 49 per cent of carers of someone with cancer had no support and only five per cent had undergone a carers' assessment.[174] It seems two main factors are behind the failure to claim. One is simply ignorance of the availability of benefits. The other is fear over the degree of intrusion into private life that may occur if an application is made.[175]

ii. Carers' Benefit

The Carers' Benefit is only payable if the person cared for is entitled to a 'relevant benefit', such as Incapacity Benefit. The rules on Incapacity Benefit have been recently tightened up and this could adversely affect carers.[176] The Carers' Benefit has also proved complex, especially in the way it interacts with other

[169] Carers UK, *Consultation Response 21st Century Welfare* (Carers UK, 2010).

[170] R Berthoud, *The Take-Up of Carer's Allowance: A Feasibility Study* (Department for Work and Pensions, 2010).

[171] Health and Social Care Information Centre, *Support and Services for Carers* (NHSIC, 2010).

[172] Information Centre, NHS, *Survey of Carers in Households 2009/2010* (NHS, 2011).

[173] Carers UK, *Carers Missing Millions* (Carers UK, 2011).

[174] MacMillan Cancer, *Carers 'Missing out on Support'* (Macmillan Cancer, 2010).

[175] R Winder, S Richards, K Wyatt and J Campbell, 'Receiving Specialist Welfare Benefit Advice within Social Services: A Qualitative Interview Study of Older People and their Carers' (2008) 26 *Research, Policy and Planning 33*.

[176] L Clements, *Carers and their Rights* (London, Carers UK, 2011) para 123.

benefits.[177] This may explain why an estimated £740 million a year in Carers' Benefit goes unclaimed every year.[178] The House of Commons Select Committee were critical of the lack of access to support and information services to assist carers navigating the complex procedures governing access to help.[179]

iii. Carers' Credit

Another benefit which carers can claim is the Carers' Credit which can be used for pension purposes. It is available to those caring for 20 hours a week or more for a person who is severely disabled. It mitigates the negative impact on a person's pension provision if they give up work to care for children.[180]

iv. Other Benefits

There is also a Carers' Grant which can be used to allow carers to take breaks and a reduction in Council Tax can be claimed. There are additional special benefits that may be available for those caring for disabled children. These include Child Tax Credit and Disabled Child Premium in addition to the standard benefits.

v. Disability Living Allowance and Attendance Allowance

Disability Living Allowance (DLA) is for those who can demonstrate a physical or mental disability which requires someone to need help. DLA is not means-tested, and is available to those aged 65 or under. The DLA contains two parts. The care component seeks to cover care needs and a mobility component reflects needs due to mobility problems. The Attendance Allowance is similar but for those over the age of 65. It is not means-tested and contains the two elements.

B. Services for Carers

In the *National Carers Strategy*,[181] published in 1999, the Government accepted the need to create a coherent approach to offering support, both financial and practical, to carers. Four pieces of legislation provide the framework for this: Carers (Recognition and Services) Act 1995, Carers and

---

[177] Ibid para 121.
[178] Ibid para 92.
[179] Ibid para 93.
[180] See, for further discussion, J Herring, *Older People in Law and Society* (Oxford, Oxford University Press, 2009) ch 6.
[181] Department of Health, *National Carers Strategy* (Department of Health, 1999).

Disabled Children Act 2000 (the 2000 Act); Carers (Equal Opportunities) Act 2004 (the 2004 Act) and Work and Families Act 2006. In 2010 the Government attempted to produce national standards through the Fair Access to Care Services.[182] We shall later discuss the Care and Support Bill 2012 which will reform this area of law completely if enacted.

The focus in this section will be on services offered to carers by this legislation. The 2004 Act gives special rights to carers who provide a substantial amount of care on a regular basis.[183] 'Substantial amount' is not defined in the legislation and social services authorities will have to use their discretion to determine its meaning.[184] Whether or not the amount of care is substantial can involve considering the impact of the care on the well-being of the carer.[185] The substantial care must be given regularly, but this does not mean it must be given frequently.[186]

Sometimes a local authority will not be able to determine whether a carer is undertaking a substantial amount of care work without undertaking an assessment, in which case an assessment should be made.[187] The 2000 Act gives carers the right to be assessed by local authorities for their needs in their own right.[188] In other words, the local authority will determine what services they need for themselves as a carer; not just what services might help the person being cared for. Indeed the assessment of the carer can take place even if the person being cared for is not assessed.[189] The assessment should consider anything that could 'help the carer care for the person cared for' and can include an assessment of not just physical needs, but mental and emotional ones too. The 2004 Act requires specific attention in such an assessment to be paid to the carer's wish for employment, learning or training opportunities and leisure.[190] Luke Clements comments:

> The 2004 Act marks a major cultural shift in the way carers are viewed: a shift in seeing carers not so much as unpaid providers of care services for disabled people, but as people in their own right: people with the right to work, like everyone else: people

---

[182] Department of Health, *Prioritising Need in the Context of Putting People First: A Whole System Approach To Eligibility For Social Care Guidance On Eligibility Criteria For Adult Social Care, England* (Department of Health, 2010).

[183] An assessment can be made of a person intending to be a carer: Carers (Recognition and Services) Act 1995, LAC (96)7, para 16.

[184] There can be more than one person providing a substantial amount of care: Department of Health, *Combined Policy Guidance on the Carers and Disabled Children Act 2000 and Carers (Equal Opportunities) Act 2004* (London, Department of Health) para 46.

[185] Ibid.

[186] The Community Care Directions 2004 Guidance LAC (2004) 24.

[187] L Clements, *Carers and their Rights* (London, Carers UK, 2011) para 3.27.

[188] The local authority has the power, but not the duty, to assess a carer who is not providing a substantial amount of care.

[189] Carers (Equal Opportunities) Act 2004, s 1.

[190] Ibid, s 2.

who have too often been socially excluded and (like the disabled people for whom they care) often denied the life chances that are available to other people.[191]

Although carers have a right to be assessed, this arises only if they ask for it. The duty on the local authority is only to inform carers of their right to request an assessment.[192]

When an assessment is made, the local authority must respect the autonomy of the carer. Government guidance recognises 'the carer's freedom to choose the nature of the tasks they will perform and how much time they will give to their caring role'.[193] It should not be forgotten that at the end of the day the carer is entitled to walk away from the situation. The assessment should not, however, assume that the carer will provide care they do not wish to provide.

Following an assessment, the local authority must decide what additional services to offer the carer. The local authority can provide any service that could 'help the carer care for the person cared for'.[194] The guidance mentions such things as laundry, gardening help with housework, driving lessons, trips, or a computer.[195] The assessment should identify the carer's ability to provide care and to continue to do so.[196]

Respite care or short break care is a common form of assistance that is offered to a carer.[197] Technically, respite care services are community care, rather than services under the carers legislation. This means that there should be a legal obligation on local authorities to provide this.[198] However, the person needing care could be liable to pay for the service.[199] Carers UK has complained that the implementation of pledges to allocate £150 million for breaks has not been met.[200] A systematic review of respite care found that although there was some evidence of it having a positive effect on carers, the evidence was limited and weak.[201] However, other surveys have found strong evidence.[202]

---

[191] L Clements, *Carers and their Rights* (London, Carers UK, 2011).

[192] Carers (Equal Opportunities) Act 2004, s 1.

[193] Department of Health, *Combined Policy Guidance on the Carers and Disabled Children Act 2000 and Carers (Equal Opportunities) Act 2004* (London, Department of Health) para 69.

[194] Carers and Disabled Children Act 2000, s 2(2)(b).

[195] L Clements, *Carers and their Rights* (London, Carers UK, 2011) para 5.25.

[196] Carers (Recognition and Services) Act 1995, s 1(1), (2).

[197] This is a community care service, not a service provided under the Carers and Disabled Children Act 2000.

[198] Carers and Disabled Children Act 2000 s 1(1) and (2).

[199] See L Clements, *Carers and their Rights* (London, Carers UK, 2011) para 5.10–12 for discussion of cases where courts and the Ombudsman have criticised local authorities for failing to provide respite care. See also *R v Islington LBC ex p Rixon* (1996)1 CCLR 119.

[200] Carers UK, *Breaks Allocations for Primary Care Trusts* (Carers UK, 2010).

[201] C Shaw, R McNamara, K Abrams, R Cannings-John, K Hood, M Longo, S Myles, S O'Mahony, B Roe and K Williams, 'Systematic Review of Respite Care in the Frail Elderly' (2009) *Health Technology Assessment* 1.

[202] J Robertson, C Hatton, E Wells, M Collins, S Langer, V Welch and E Emerson, *The Impacts of Short Break Provision on Families with a Disabled Child: An International Literature Review* (Department for Children, Schools and Families, 2010); C Jardim and K Pakenham, 'Carers of Adults with Mental Illness: Comparison of Respite Care Users and Non-Users' (2010) 45 *Australian Psychologist* 50.

Section 2 of the 2000 Act makes it absolutely clear that there is a power on the local authority to provide support services for a carer, but it does not impose a duty to do so. Although there is no legal right, as such, to any services, this does not mean that legal proceedings cannot be used if access to services is denied.

The 2000 Carers and Disabled Children Act specifically states that social service authorities should consider how to support carers to remain or return to work. The Carers (Equal Opportunities) Act 2004 acknowledges, when assessing willingness and ability to care, carers' wishes regarding employment, education, training and leisure.[203]

A decision by a local authority not to provide services to a carer would be amenable to judicial review.[204] So a blanket policy on carer services (eg not to provide any carer services; or only carer services up to a certain maximum amount for any individual) would be illegal.[205] That would be regarded as an improper fetter of their discretion, although a local authority could develop general guidelines to assist in the exercise of their discretion. Similarly, if it could be shown that in exercising their discretion on whether to award carer services the local authority failed to take into account a relevant factor or took into account an irrelevant one, a judicial review application may succeed.[206]

Another remedy is to apply under the Human Rights Act. Under section 6, a local authority is required to respect carers' convention rights. If it fails to do so an order can be made under section 7 or 8 which can include an award for damages.[207] Such an action would only be likely to succeed if the impact on the carer's quality of life of the refusal to offer services was very severe. Even then the court may be persuaded that the local authority had to provide services to many people who were in great need and that the needs of others justified not providing the service to the claimant. Apart from court proceedings, complaints could be made to the Local Government Ombudsman or under the local authority's own complaints procedure.[208]

The existence of the legislative powers could be used to put pressure on a local authority to provide services. But with plenty of legal duties on a cash-strapped local authority, requests to exercise powers are always going to have second call on any funds. The Department of Health Practice Guidance encourages a radical shift in local authority practice in the provision of

---

[203] H Arksey, 'Combining Work and Care: The Reality of Policy Tensions for Carers' (2007) 15 *Benefits* 139.

[204] *R (HP) v London Borough of Islington* [2004] EWHC 7 (Admin).

[205] *R (on the application of Stephenson) v Stockton-on-Tees Borough Council* [2005] EWCA Civ 960, [2005] 3 FCR 248.

[206] Ibid.

[207] *R (Hughes) v Liverpool City Council* [2005] EWHC 428 (Admin).

[208] Local Authority (Complaints Procedure) Order 1990.

services to carers.[209] But the reality is shown in a recent survey of the operation of carers' assessments, which found the budgetary constraints mean that these were often not carried out effectively by local authorities and very limited funds were available.[210] In 2007 Carers UK claim there were only about half a million assessments a year. As Carers UK put it, 'only a tiny minority of carers go near social services'.[211] In another survey, following an assessment, only 37 per cent of carers questioned saw an improvement in the services they were receiving.[212] No doubt the comments reported of one carer (Bernard) are far from atypical: 'You get all these statements of intent to help, have these meetings, fill in dozens of multi-page forms, and then nothing happens. Except more talk, more forms, and endless waiting.'[213]

There is, therefore, a concern that the legislation creates a system of assessment which is costly to run and time-consuming for the carers to complete, and yet produces no tangible benefit to anyone.

Even where the local authority offers services to the carer, these can be charged for, subject to means testing.[214] It is not surprising that groups supporting carers claim that carers make enough financial sacrifices undertaking the burden of care, without being expected to finance their own support.[215] Indeed there is evidence that the extra charges are causing serious financial hardship to carers.[216] Carers UK has also objected to inconsistency in the amounts charged by local authorities.[217]

Despite the general welcome that the carers' assessment has received, I would question whether it is possible to separate out the interests of the carer and the person cared for. Inevitably their interests are intermingled. The emotional well-being of the carer will affect the person cared for and vice versa.[218] Indeed it can be difficult in some relationships to determine who is the carer and who is cared for. In most cases the parties will be caring for each other, albeit in different ways. It is often only the gratitude and willingness of the 'cared for' to receive the care that enables the 'carer' to continue. The relationship is rarely

---

[209] Department of Health, *Carers and Disabled Children Act 2000 and Carers (Equal Opportunities) Act 2004 Combined Policy Guidance* (London, Stationery Office, 2005).

[210] D Seddon, C Robinson, C Reeves, Y Tommis, B Woods, and I Russel, 'In their Own Right: Translating the Policy of Carer Assessment into Practice' (2007) 37 *British Journal of Social Work* 1335.

[211] House of Commons Work and Pensions Committee, *Valuing and Supporting Carers* (London, The Stationery Office, 2008) para 39.

[212] Carers UK, *Missed Opportunities: The Impact of New Rights For Carers* (London, Carers UK, 2005).

[213] E Nicholas, 'An Outcomes Focus in Carers Assessment and Reviews: Value Challenge' (2003) 33 *British Journal of Social Work* 31.

[214] Health and Social Services and Social Security Adjudications Act 1983, s 17.

[215] Carers UK, *Caring on the Breadline* (Carers UK, 2000).

[216] Ibid.

[217] Ibid.

[218] J Herring, 'Where are the Carers in Healthcare Law and Ethics?' (2008) 27 *Legal Studies* 51.

all one way. This means separating the interests of the carer and the cared for may be impossible.

There is no doubt that some carers feel the lack of support keenly. In evidence presented by the Care and Support Alliance,[219] carers were quoted as saying:

Dementia means—NO support whatsoever—no respite, no day care—NOTHING. My father was told by Social Services that he doesn't exist [he was present with mum at all times], he needs help for disabilities, he needs somewhere to go out to socialise. We are all prisoners in our own home. I do not have help from anyone—most friends have gone, relatives and neighbours pretend we do not exist.

The people that I see are not trained in autism or fibromyalgia. Autistic adults are referred to mental health teams, who have no idea about autism. But sadly, those with autism are not accepted by their learning disability teams/social services team.

We were assessed as needing at least 8 hours extra care due to my having had two full knee replacements and my husband having a pin inserted into one of his toes. I am 67 years old with multiple health issues and my husband is 71. Now due to the cuts the extra 8 hours has been refused.

Of those responding to a Care and Support Alliance survey, 68 per cent of carers felt they needed more support and 22.6 per cent reported a reduction in their support.[220] The Government has recently acknowledged the inadequacies of the current system:

The 5 million adults with caring responsibilities in England are too often forgotten or neglected. Assessments for carers are limited under current law, so their needs are often not identified. Even when carers' needs are identified, they are often ignored by local authorities and the NHS because there is no clear entitlement to carers' support.

We know that this is preventing carers from accessing the support they need to look after their own health and wellbeing. Carers make a vital contribution to promoting the wellbeing and independence of the people they care for, and it is crucial to support them to care effectively and to have a life of their own alongside caring.[221]

C. Social Care Services

While a person is receiving NHS care social care services are free of charge, however for a person in the community these services are the responsibility of the social service authorities and can be charged for. In determining

---

[219] Care and Support Alliance. *Evidence to the Commission on the Funding of Care and Support* (Care and Support Alliance, 2010).

[220] Ibid.

[221] HM Government, *Caring for Our Future* (The Stationery Office, 2012) 15.

charging for a disabled person only the disabled person's finances should be considered, and not those of the carer. This is true even where the carer and disabled person are married or civil partners. As the Combined Policy Guidance under the 2000 and 2004 Acts states:[222]

> Carers cannot be charged for community care services provided to the people they care for (including the community care services provided to enable carers to take a break from caring) unless those services are provided as the result of a carer's assessment under the 2000 Act.

Statutory Guidance has been issued,[223] which requires the care assessment to be based on an individual's need and involves consideration of a person's aspirations and support needs. Interestingly the Guidance provides:

> during assessment, no assumptions should be made about the level or quality of support available from carers. Inappropriate assumptions about how much support carers are willing or able to provide can lead to an underestimation of potentially eligible needs. An individual might be supported by a carer but still be eligible for community care services because of the nature of their needs and the level of support that both the individual and the carer require to maintain their independence and well-being.[224]

There is widespread dissatisfaction with the current provision of social care.[225] The Commission for Social Care Inspection (CSCI)[226] found little consistency between councils as to who was eligible for services and indeed quite a degree of inconsistency within councils.[227] One of its reports stated, 'Progress in modernising social care is being hampered by financial pressures in the social care and health system, an underdeveloped care market, continuing recruitment and retention problems, and organizational turbulence.'[228]

---

[222] Department of Health, *Combined Policy Guidance on the Carers and Disabled Children Act 2000 and Carers (Equal Opportunities) Act 2004* (London, Department of Health) para 62.

[223] Department of Health, *Prioritising Need In The Context Of Putting People First: A Whole System Approach To Eligibility For Social Care Guidance on Eligibility Criteria for Adult Social Care, England 2010* (London, Department of Health, 2010).

[224] Department of Health, *Prioritising Need In The Context Of Putting People First: A Whole System Approach To Eligibility For Social Care Guidance on Eligibility Criteria for Adult Social Care, England 2010* (Department of Health, 2010) para 95.

[225] House of Commons Work and Pensions Committee, *Valuing and Supporting Carers* (London, The Stationery Office, 2008).

[226] Commission for Social Care Inspection, *The State of Social Care in England 2006–07* (London, CSCI, 2008).

[227] See also King's Fund, *The Business of Caring* (London, King's Fund, 2005).

[228] Commission for Social Care Inspection, *The State of Social Care in England 2006–07* (London, CSCI, 2008).

The Law Commission described the legislative framework for adult social care as 'inadequate, often incomprehensible and outdated'. The Government White Paper has acknowledged that all is not well with the current system.[229] The following highlights the major problems with it:

— Too often the system only reacts to a crisis.
— Society is not making the most of the skills and talents in communities.
— People do not have access to good information and advice.
— Access to care varies across the country and is confusing.
— Carers have no clear entitlements to support.
— Not all care is good. The quality of care is variable and inconsistent.
— People often feel 'bounced around' and have to fight the system to have the joined-up health, care and support they need.

We shall shortly look at the proposals for reform the Government has offered.

Where people have to fund services themselves, there are real problems in finding good quality care. The difficulties in obtaining these services have been summarised thus by Carers UK:

> There is no quality advice and information and guidance to help people pick the right care. The care market is under stimulated. There is not enough quality and quantity out there if you want to purchase it. If we really are going to help people who wish to work return to work, we have to get the care system sorted.[230]

A report by the Commission for Social Care Inspection found that 35 per cent of carers in England said the person they were supporting did not have the benefit of any formal services. Sixty per cent of carers said there were services they would like to use but were not able to. Another report suggests that 80 per cent of those who had stopped using care services blamed costs as a reason for doing so.[231]

The Joseph Rowntree Foundation found that the social care funding was failing to meet basic needs. The lack of funding has not only meant many are denied support, but where it is paid for the staff are poorly paid, and therefore poorly trained and have a high turnover. There has been a particular problem in providing services that are accessible and appropriate for people from black and ethnic minority groups.[232]

---

[229] Department of Health, *Prioritising Need In The Context Of Putting People First: A Whole System Approach To Eligibility For Social Care Guidance on Eligibility Criteria for Adult Social Care, England 2010* (Department of Health, 2010); Breaks for Carers of Disabled Children Regulations 2011 (SI 2011 No707).

[230] House of Commons Work and Pensions Committee, *Valuing and Supporting Carers* (London, The Stationery Office, 2008) para 222.

[231] Coalition on Charging, *Charging into Poverty* (London, NCIL, 2008).

[232] Commission for Social Care Inspection, *Putting People First: Equality and Diversity Matters* (London, CSCI, 2007).

D. Section 29 National Assistance Act 1948

By section 29(1) of the National Assistance Act 1948, a local authority is obliged to make arrangements for promoting the welfare of adults ordinarily resident in their area who are substantially and permanently handicapped by illness, injury, or congenital deformity or by other prescribed disabilities. This duty is extended by section 2 of the Chronically Sick and Disabled Persons Act 1970 to provide services to promote aspects of their well-being. Crucial to the effectiveness of these provisions is section 47(1) of the National Health Service and Community Care Act 1990, which requires the local authority to assess the needs of those for whom they may provide services. In the light of that assessment they must provide such services to meet those needs.

E. Individual Budgets

A major aspect of the Government's approach towards caregiving is in the use of individual budgets.[233] Since 2003 local authorities have a duty to make direct payments if the individual consents and is able to manage these budgets without assistance. The provider of that service is selected by the individual who is to use it, although the local authority may assist a person in selecting the provider.[234] The individual needing care can use the budget to purchase services from the local authority; private care providers; or from relatives and friends, as long as they do not live in the same household.[235] The reasoning behind this, presumably, is that the care from a co-resident is likely to be provided whether paid for or not; and so there would be no added benefit by the payment for those services. Direct payments can also be made to a carer to provide carer support, but that involves a separate application. The Government wants individual budgets to become the main vehicle to discharge social care obligations.[236]

The Community Care, Services for Carers and Children's Services (Direct Payments) (England) Regulations 2009 (SI 2009 No 1887) requires the local authority to provide a budget if a person's need for the relevant service can

---

[233] Department of Health, *Putting People First* (London, Department of Health 2007); L Clements, 'Individual Budgets and Irrational Exuberance' (2008) 11 *Community Care Law Review* 413; T Poole, *Direct Payments and Older People* (London, King's Fund, 2007).

[234] M Henwood and B Hudson, *Here to Stay? Self-Directed Support: Aspiration and Implementation* (Melanie Henwood Associates, 2007).

[235] In exceptional cases direct payments can be used to pay for care from a person who lives with the care recipient, but the local authority needs to agree it is the only satisfactory way of providing the care.

[236] Ibid.

be met by a direct payment, as long as the person consents. If the Care and Support Bill 2012 is enacted it will give people the right to a personal budget.

Personal budgets have been the subject of considerable debate. Their supporters claim that personal budgets promote personalisation. They give the individual in need of care control and choice over the services.[237] As *Putting People First* puts it, 'The time has now come to build on best practice and replace *paternalistic, reactive care of variable quality* with a mainstream system focused on prevention, early intervention, enablement and high quality personally tailored services.'[238]

In the Government White Paper, the Government promises to extend the use of personal budgets saying:

> We will transform people's experience of care and support, putting them in control and ensuring that services respond to what they want. We will ensure that people have control over their budget and their care and support plan, and will empower them to choose and to shape the options that best enable them to meet their goals and aspirations.[239]

Personal budgets have received judicial support. In the Supreme Court in *R (KM) v Cambridgeshire*[240] Lord Wilson said of the scheme, 'The admirable idea is to empower him with control over his own budget.'[241] Interestingly the Welsh Assembly has preferred the term 'self-directed support' rather than personalisation.[242] That might suggest slightly less control over how the money is spent.

The central aim of the scheme is to allow someone to choose the services they seek, rather than have someone else make that decision for them. The flexibility provided by personal budgets could mean that a person may choose to spend their money on tickets to a football match, rather than time at a day care centre.[243] It has been said to open up a new vision of citizenship.[244] Those needing care are equipped to become citizens with autonomy, inclusion and choice. They become operators in the market and take control of their life. It does something to remedy the power inequalities between the carer and cared for. These budgets are, then, in part a response to the critique of care offered

[237] P Beresford, *What Future for Care?* (York, Joseph Rowntree Foundation, 2008).

[238] HM Government, *Putting People First* (HM Government, 2007) 2.

[239] HM Government, *Caring for our Future* (The Stationery Office, 2012) 19.

[240] [2012] UKSC 23.

[241] Ibid, para 23.

[242] Welsh Assembly Government, *Sustainable Social Services for Wales* (2011) paras 3.16 and 3.17.

[243] C Glendinning, 'Increasing Choice and Control for Older and Disabled People: A Critical Review of New Developments in England' (2008) 42 *Social Policy & Administration* 451.

[244] C Leadbeater, *Personalisation through Participation: A New Script for Public Services* (Demos, 2004) 19–20.

by the disability groups that we discussed in chapter two. As Fiona Williams comments:

> I would suggest that, in so far as this move to direct payments has also been, in part, and in some places, the consequence of demands from the disability movement, then it indicates not simply a 'distancing', but also a challenge to the assumed, all-encompassing dependency of the 'cared-for' in care relations and practices.[245]

A survey for Carers UK[246] found that only nine per cent of those questioned had a negative experience of direct payments, and 38 per cent had mixed feelings, particularly concerning the increased payment. Fifty seven per cent would recommend the scheme to friends. Seventy three per cent said the purchased care was better at meeting their need, but only 49 per cent said the staff were better. The comments of one carer were interesting:

> Much as I love him, I have no interest in my husband's hobbies—now I don't have to be involved in them as his workers are. It gives him something to tell me about or if he wants can keep it private, something he hasn't had for a long time. Direct payments suit us perfectly.

Not everyone's experience was positive and there is evidence that occasionally people are forced to use budgets against their wishes. Five per cent of those surveyed said they had been pressurised into accepting direct payments.[247] There were also concerns about a lack of information and that there were administrative burdens in its management.[248]

Another alleged benefit of personal budgets is flexibility. Individual budgets can be topped up by an individual's own resources or from friends or charities. The range of services could be broader than conventional services and there are generally of higher levels of satisfaction.[249] It is hoped that their availability will open up a wider range of markets of care provision. The expectation is that through competition, costs will be reduced and the quality of services improved.

A further benefit of personal budgets is that it does mean that some informal carers, especially those not living with the individual, can receive pay for their care work when they would not otherwise receive that pay. Clare Ungerson has argued:

> by allowing for the payment of relatives who previously have been 'classic' unpaid and formally unrecognised informal carers, [these schemes] actually provide a means whereby the work of care-givers is recognised and recompensed, such that they become more and more like care-workers.[250]

---

[245] F Williams, 'In and Beyond New Labour: Towards a New Political Ethics of Care' (2001) 21 *Critical Social Policy* 467.

[246] Carers UK, *Choice or Chore?* (Carers UK, 2011).

[247] Ibid.

[248] C Glendinning, 'Increasing Choice and Control for Older and Disabled People: A Critical Review of New Developments in England' (2008) 42 *Social Policy & Administration* 451.

[249] P Bresford, *What Future for Care?* (York, Joseph Rowntree Foundation, 2008).

[250] C Ungerson, 'Whose Empowerment and Independence?' (2004) 29 *Ageing and Society* 189.

Luke Clements summarises the apparent benefits of direct payments:

> They appear to require no additional expenditure on social care (indeed they promise 'savings'); they have the potential to dismantle the remaining apparatus of public provision and also to return primary responsibility for social care back to disabled people and their families. To this enticing cocktail, can be added the passionate espousal of [individual budgets] by leading members of the disability rights movement.[251]

The picture, however, is not all rosy. A cynic might suggest that the use of personal budgets means that the local authority can wash its hands of the responsibilities of care.[252] If an individual is not receiving appropriate care or the services are inadequate, the local authority cannot be blamed.[253] The person has simply misused their budget. It reinforces the perception that primary responsibility for care lies not with the state but with individuals, families and charities. It chimes with the themes privatisation, commoditisation and individualism.[254]

Nor should it be assumed that everyone wants to be in control of their budgets. They may lack the skills to find and negotiate care or simply find it stressful to do so.[255] Of course there will be plenty of others who are simply unable to manage their budgets, particularly those lacking mental capacity.[256] Those needing care may find they lack bargaining power to negotiate a good deal with their budget, especially if there are only a limited number of providers on offer. Care recipients who are most vocal and in the strongest position to get the best care will flourish, while the most vulnerable people will miss out. [257]

The toll of commissioning services should not be underestimated. Ann Stewart, an academic, in a powerful personal account,[258] tells of the difficulties she faced in obtaining services for her parents. Despite having a good grasp of the legal and practical issues, the commissioning and supervision of services was burdensome. As she points out, others will be in a much

---

[251] L Clements, 'Individual Budgets and Irrational Exuberance' (2008) 11 *Community Care Law Review* 413.

[252] H Spandler, 'Friend or Foe? Towards a Critical Assessment of Direct Payments' (2004) 24 *Critical Social Policy* 187.

[253] I Ferguson, 'Increasing User Choice or Privatizing Risk? The Antinomies of Personalization' (2007) 37 *British Journal of Social Work* 387.

[254] On these themes see A Pollock, *NHS PLC: The Privatization of Our Health Care* (Verso, 2005).

[255] C Glendinning, 'Increasing Choice and Control for Older and Disabled People' (2007) 37 *British Journal of Social Work* 1335.

[256] K Boxall, 'Selling Individual Budgets, Choice and Control: Local and Global Influences on UK Social Care Policy for People with Learning Difficulties' (2009) 37 *Policy and Politics* 499.

[257] L Clements, 'Winners and Losers' (2005) 32 *Journal of Law and Society* 34; C Needham, *Citizen-Consumers: New Labour's Marketplace Democracy* (Catalyst, 2003); C Needham, *The Reform of Public Services under New Labour: Narratives of Consumerism* (Palgrave Macmillan, 2007).

[258] A Stewart, 'Choosing Care: Dilemmas of a Social Market' (2005) 27 *Journal of Social Welfare and Family Law* 299.

weaker position than she was. The burden of managing the budget will in some cases fall on the carer and may become a further source of work and stress for them.[259] Indeed one survey reported that individual budgets had led to carers taking on extra responsibilities.[260] Where a person is unable to manage their own budget then family members can, through a trust, oversee use of the money, although there is one reported case of alleged misuse of such a fund.[261]

There are further difficult issues here. What is to be done with a person who wants to use their budget in a way the local authority decides fails to meet their care needs? The homely example of the person who would rather visit football matches than be taken to a day centre is perhaps unproblematic, but what if they wished to be taken to a strip club? Or if they left their podiatry needs unattended to visit the cinema? Indeed they may not select the services they genuinely need through embarrassment or lack of understanding.[262]

One issue yet to be fully explored is when there is a clash between the interests of the 'carer' and the 'cared for'.[263] A carer might, for example, have been relieved of some of the burden of care through provision of social service assistance. If these are withdrawn and replaced by a budget, which is not spent on directly meeting the needs, then the carer may end up having to meet those needs. The day in the day centre replaced by a morning fishing may well better meet the needs of the cared for but lead to an increase in the burden for the primary carer.

There is relatively little evidence about what direct payments money is used for. One survey[264] found that in Hampshire it was used to pay care assistants, but that 80 per cent of the care assistants employed were known by the person needing care.[265] This suggests that it should not be assumed that direct payments will expand the use of the private sector. That also raises the question of whether the payments are made for services which would have been given for free otherwise. Of course, that is not necessarily a bad thing. It may be appropriate that carers receive proper recompense for their work, but it means direct payments do not improve the care received.

---

[259] Carers UK, *Choice or Chore?* (Carers UK, 2011).

[260] C Glendinning, H Arksey, K Jones, N Moran, A Netten, P Rabiee, *The Individual Budgets Pilot Projects: Impact and Outcomes for Carers* (University of York, 2009).

[261] *R (G & H) v North Somerset Council* [2011] EWHC 2232 (Admin).

[262] H Arksey and C Glendinning, 'Choice in the Context of Informal Care-Giving' (2007) 15 *Health and Social Care in the Community* 165.

[263] K Keywood, 'Gatekeepers, Proxies, Advocates? The Evolving Role of Carers under Mental Health and Mental Incapacity Law Reforms' (2003) 25 *Journal of Social Welfare and Family Law* 355.

[264] C Ungerson, 'Whose Empowerment and Independence?' (2004) 29 *Ageing and Society* 189.

[265] T Poole, *Direct Payments and Older People* (King's Fund, 2007).

A further issue is that as care will be arranged by individuals, there is likely to be an increase in transaction costs, as compared with a local authority arranging care services for a collection of clients. As Morris argues:

> People who use direct payments consistently report difficulties in recruiting personal assistants. Poor rates of pay create situations where disabled people are forced to take on personal assistants who cannot provide them with a good service. If support needs are not properly funded, personal assistance service users find they cannot provide good working conditions for their workers.[266]

There is a particular concern that clients who are particularly demanding or require complex care may find it difficult to commission services, and care providers will be keen to be employed by 'easy clients'. Further, there needs to be a safety net of provision if the privately arranged provision breaks down.[267] All these points indicate that there can be hidden costs for local authorities in the introduction of these personal budgets. Although so far the limited research suggests the budgets are proving cost effective for local authorities.[268]

To conclude, while there undoubtedly can be benefits for use of personal budgets, there are dangers. An accurate picture on the ground is still awaiting more detailed research, but what is likely to emerge is that there will be some for whom the personal budgets provide independence and control to provide a service which best fits their needs. There may, however, be others who do not want or cannot control their budgets, who will be exploited or neglected by the market. The Government's White Paper, quoted earlier, indicates that they wish 'to ensure that everyone can take control of their care and support by giving them an entitlement to a personal budget'.[269] It should not, however, be assumed that personal budgets are appropriate for everyone. The White Paper does set out a system for support for those people who might struggle arranging their budgets, but there will be many who are not capable of using their budgets or who will misuse them.

F. Payment for Care

Central to understanding the current system on the provision of care is the distinction drawn between health care and social care. It is widely acknowledged that this division is unsatisfactory.[270] In short health care needs are

---

[266] J Morris, *Barriers to Independent Living* (University of Leeds) 1.

[267] Carers UK, *Choice or Chore?* (Carers UK, 2011).

[268] C Glendinning, H Arksey, K Jones, N Moran, A Netten, P Rabiee, *The Individual Budgets Pilot Projects: Impact and Outcomes for Carers* (University of York, 2009).

[269] HM Government, *Caring for Our Future* (The Stationery Office, 2012) 11.

[270] J Dreaper, 'Care for Elderly "Let Down by Fragmented System"' BBC News Online, 8 February 2012.

met by the NHS and are provided free of charge, while care needs are met by local authorities and are subject to means testing and restrictions. The Government has acknowledged that 'urgent reform of the care and support system is needed'. The King's Fund think tank estimates that 890,000 people are not receiving the care services they need.[271] Carers too are not provided services. The Commission for Social Care Inspection report on *The State of Social Care in England* produced in January 2008 'found approximately a half of councils have yet to address carers' needs effectively.[272]

In the opening paragraph of its report on *Adult Social Care*, the Law Commission explains:

> It is of little surprise that not only does the law perplex service users and social workers, but also the judiciary. Adult social care law, including how it relates to other legislation, has been described at various times by judges as 'piecemeal ... numerous', 'exceptionally tortuous', 'labyrinthine' and as including some of the 'worst drafted' subordinate legislation ever encountered.[273]

The outdated nature of the legislation is well demonstrated by the definition of disability contained in section 29 of the National Assistance Act 1948, which refers to 'welfare arrangements for blind, deaf, dumb and crippled persons'. The outdated and even offensive nature of the language used is a powerful symbol of the failure to grapple properly with these issues.

The NHS Act 2006 defines the central purpose of health services in England and Wales as securing improvement in physical and mental health, and in the prevention, diagnosis and treatment of illness. There is no definition in law of social care. Social care has increasingly taken on a broader understanding, moving beyond meals, care homes, and equipment to include non-traditional services such as emotional support and gym membership. The difficulties with this distinction are complex and many. As our understanding of health and the importance of looking at the well-being of an individual as a whole has improved, so too have our expectations of what a decent set of social services one might look for. The current law has two central flaws.

First, it can lead to a lack of 'joined up' thinking. Often care and health needs mingle. Having different bodies dealing with health and care needs can lead to people being 'passed like a parcel' between services.[274] This is especially because the different funding means that the distinction is highlighted, with organisations seeking to protect their budgets, trying to persuade other organisations to accept responsibilities for costly individuals. Too often, while it is clear the state should be providing care for an individual, the

---

[271] Ibid.

[272] Commission of Social Care Inspection, *The State of Social Care in England 2006/7* (CSCI, 2008) 14.

[273] The Law Commission, *Adult Social Care. Report 326* (Law Commission, 2011) para 1.1.

[274] J Dreaper, 'Care for Elderly "Let Down by Fragmented System"' BBC News Online, 8 February 2012.

different state bodies have argued over who should provide the care, leaving the individual to suffer and often, ironically, leading to increased costs for the state. The best known example of this is 'bed blocking'. Individuals who are in hospital and could be released to the community are not because social care departments are unable to provide care in the community (or seek to avoid the costs of doing so). The cost of hospital care is considerable and the impact on waiting lists has a knock-on effect on other patients. The Health and Social Care Act 2012 which creates health and well-being boards is designed to tackle this issue, but it is too early to know how effective they will be.

Second, the confusing system means that people are required to pay for services when they should not.[275] Some claim that there has been a gradual redrawing of the line between the two kinds of service.[276] If an official in a local authority tells you that you are expected to pay for this service as it is not a health need, it is difficult to challenge that decision unless you are particularly determined and well-informed.

The Law Commission Report on *Adult Social Care*[277] was not able to produce a definition of social care. It suggested the current definition was 'Adult social care means the care and support provided by local social services authorities pursuant to their responsibilities towards adults who need extra support.'[278]

The Law Commission accepted that definition was unhelpful, but they could not provide an alternative. The best they could do was to explain that the services should be designed to promote the well-being of individuals.

The very fact the Law Commission was unable to provide a definition to assist in the distinction between health and social care needs is revealing. The distinction is one which is of huge significance to some of the most vulnerable people in our society and has a huge impact on their lives. The House Of Commons Health Committee, in light of the Law Commission's efforts, has recommended abandoning the distinction:

> The Law Commission's attempt to define social care underlines the central problem. The overarching aim of social care as defined by them, to 'promote or contribute to the well-being of the individual', could just as easily be applied to health care or housing services. The conclusion we draw from this is that attempts to draw a distinction between these services and social care will fail because such distinctions are artificial and unhelpful, and because they directly contradict the policy objective. This objective is the same whether it is seen from the point of view of service user preference, objective outcome measurement or cost efficiency. It is to deliver a joined-up,

---

[275] BBC News, 'Vulnerable Elderly "Forced to Pay for Medical Care"' BBC News Online, 28 September 2010.
[276] The Law Commission, *Adult Social Care. Report 326* (Law Commission, 2011).
[277] Ibid.
[278] Ibid para 1.5.

integrated service that aims to deliver the best outcomes for the patient and in the most efficient manner possible. If that is the objective—and the Committee found that it is an objective shared between users, staff and policy makers—it seems perverse to attempt to build integrated service delivery on a fragmented commissioning system.[279]

This is a powerful argument. The difficulty is that simply offering all social services free of charge, as health services are, would, of course, greatly increase the cost to the state. However desirable that might be, there will be debates over the economic feasibility of doing it. I think the case for doing so is overwhelming. But, if that is not seen as feasible, a line has to be drawn somewhere and it will be artificial wherever it is drawn. We shall return to this issue shortly when looking at the proposal on funding for care.

X. Government Reforms on Support for Carers

In 2008 the Government undertook a major review of its policies towards carers and produced a new strategy: *Carers at the Heart of 21st-Century Families and Communities*.[280] In 2010 this was reviewed and updated with the report *Recognised, Valued and Supported: Next Steps for the Carers Strategy*.[281] The reports are rather stronger in rhetoric than in detailed proposals.

The Government's 2008 strategy set out a strategic vision that by 2018, carers should be universally recognised and valued as being fundamental to strong families and stable communities. Support should be tailored to meet individual carer's needs; enabling carers to maintain a balance between their caring responsibilities and a life outside caring, whilst enabling the person they support to be a full and equal citizen. It produced five intended outcomes:

(1)   Carers will be respected as expert care partners and will have access to the integrated and personalised services they need to support them in their caring role.

(2)   Carers will be able to have a life of their own alongside their caring role.

(3)   Carers will be supported so that they are not forced into financial hardship by their caring role.

---

[279] House of Commons Health Select Committee, *Social Care* (Hansard, 2012) para 17.

[280] Department of Health, *Carers at the Heart of 21st-Century Families and Communities* (The Stationery Office, 2008).

[281] HM Government, *Recognised, Valued and Supported: Next Steps for the Carers Strategy* (The Stationery Office, 2010).

(4) Carers will be supported to stay mentally and physically well and treated with dignity.
(5) Children and young people will be protected from inappropriate caring and have the support they need to learn, develop and thrive, to enjoy positive childhoods and to achieve against all the Every Child Matters outcomes.

The document, while recognising the importance of care, was strong on rhetoric and high ideals, with little practical or financial support to effect any reforms. In 2010 the Government sought to move the programme of support for carers along in its paper *Recognised, Valued and Supported: Next Steps for the Carers Strategy.*[282] It identified these four priorities:

(1) Supporting those with caring responsibilities to identify themselves as carers at an early stage, recognising the value of their contribution and involving them from the outset both in designing local care provision and in planning individual care packages.
(2) Enabling those with caring responsibilities to fulfil their educational and employment potential.
(3) Personalised support both for carers and those they support, enabling them to have a family and community life.
(4) Supporting carers to remain mentally and physically well.

The main thrust of the policy was to increase information and advice to carers and to increase employment opportunities, rather than to increase the level of funding. The main problem facing carers was seen to be the difficulty in accessing the financial and other support available, rather than the level of support itself. There is to be a new information helpline and an 'expert carers' training programme[283] and improved provision of breaks for carers and a greater level of support from the NHS. The Government further seeks to provide more support so that carers are able to combine employment and care.

In 2012 the Government produced a draft Care and Support Bill which is designed to reform the law on the provision of support and care.[284] At the time of writing it is up for consultation and it is far from clear which provisions will be retained in any final legislation. The White Paper started with a blunt assessment of the current law:

> Our system of care and support, developed in a piecemeal fashion over more than six decades, is broken and in desperate need for reform ... The care and support system in England today is not fit for the 21st century. It does not support people to

---

[282] Ibid.
[283] HM Government, *Carers at the Heart of 21st-Century Families and Communities* (The Stationery Office, 2008).
[284] HM Government, *Caring for Our Future* (The Stationery Office, 2012).

stay as independent as possible, or empower them to take control of their lives. And because the system is not fit for purpose, it cannot respond effectively to increasing pressures over the coming years from a growing and ageing population. It is in everyone's interests to make changes.[285]

It identifies the following as the key problems with the current law:

— too often the system only reacts to a crisis;
— society is not making the most of the skills and talents that communities have to offer;
— people do not have access to good information and advice;
— access to care varies across the country and is confusing;
— carers have no clear entitlement to support;
— not all care is good. The quality of care is variable and inconsistent;
— people often feel 'bounced around' and have to fight the system to have the joined-up health, care and support they need; and
— our growing and ageing population is only going to increase the pressures on the current system.

The White Paper has two principles at its heart:

The first is that we should do everything we can—as individuals, as communities and as a Government—to prevent, postpone and minimise people's need for formal care and support. The system should be built around the simple notion of promoting people's independence and wellbeing.

The second principle is that people should be in control of their own care and support. Things like personal budgets and direct payments, backed by clear, comparable information and advice, will empower individuals and their carers to make the choices that are right for them.[286]

The following are the key elements of the proposed reforms:

— Stimulating the development of initiatives that help people share their time, talents and skills with others in their community.
— Developing and implementing, in a number of trailblazer areas, new ways of investing in supporting people to stay active and independent, such as Social Impact Bonds.
— Establishing a new capital fund, worth £200 million over five years, to support the development of specialised housing for older and disabled people.
— Establishing a new national information website, to provide a clear and reliable source of information on care and support, and investing £32.5 million in better local online services.

---

[285] HM Government, *Caring for Our Future* (The Stationery Office, 2012).
[286] Page 3.

— Introducing a national minimum eligibility threshold to ensure greater national consistency in access to care and support, and ensuring that no one's care is interrupted if they move.
— Extending the right to an assessment to more carers, and introducing a clear entitlement to support to help them maintain their own health and well-being.
— Working with a range of organisations to develop comparison websites that make it easy for people to give feedback and compare the quality of care providers.
— Ruling out crude 'contracting by the minute', which can undermine dignity and choice for those who use care and support.
— Consulting on further steps to ensure service continuity for people using care and support, should a provider go out of business.
— Placing dignity and respect at the heart of a new code of conduct and minimum training standards for care workers.
— Training more care workers to deliver high quality care, including an ambition to double the number of care apprenticeships to 100,000 by 2017.
— Appointing a Chief Social Worker by the end of 2012.
— Legislating to give people an entitlement to a personal budget.
— Improving access to independent advice to help people eligible for financial support from their local authority to develop their care and support plan.
— Developing, in a small number of areas, the use of direct payments for people who have chosen to live in residential care, to test the costs and benefits.
— Investing a further £100 million in 2013/14 and £200 million in 2014/15 in joint funding between the NHS and social care to support better integrated care and support.[287]

There is to be a legal duty on local authorities to promote an adult's well-being in carrying out its functions under the Bill.[288] Clause 1(2) sets out what well-being means:

(2)   'Well-being', in relation to an adult, means that adult's well-being so far as relating to any of the following—
   (a)   physical and mental health and emotional well-being;
   (b)   protection from abuse and neglect;
   (c)   control by the adult over day-to-day life (including over the care and support provided to the adult and the way in which it is provided);
   (d)   participation in work, education, training or recreation;

---

[287] Page 8.
[288] Cl 1.

(e)   social and economic well-being;
(f)   domestic, family and personal relationships;
(g)   the adult's contribution to society.

The Bill goes on in clause 1(3) to set out factors which are to be taken into account by the local authority:

(a)   the importance of beginning with the assumption that the adult is best placed to judge the adult's well-being;
(b)   the adult's views, wishes and feelings;
(c)   the need to ensure that decisions about the adult are made having regard to all the adult's circumstances (and are not based only on the adult's age or appearance or any condition of the adult's or aspect of the adult's behaviour which might lead others to make unjustified assumptions about the adult's well-being);
(d)   the importance of the adult participating as fully as possible in decisions relating to the exercise of the function concerned and being provided with the information and support necessary to enable the adult to participate;
(e)   the importance of achieving a balance between the adult's well-being and that of any friends or relatives who are involved in caring for the adult;
(f)   the need to protect people from abuse and neglect;
(g)   the need to ensure that any restriction on the adult's rights or freedom of action that is involved in the exercise of the function is kept to the minimum necessary for achieving the purpose for which the function is being exercised.

It is hard to disagree with any of the factors on this list. The difficulty is in the balancing of them. The views of the adult (b) may conflict with the need to protect them from abuse and neglect (f). This is an issue which will be examined further in chapter eight. Similarly, there may be clashes between the views of the adult (b) and finding a fair balance between the well-being of the adult and those caring for her (e). Much will depend on the understanding of well-being, an issue addressed in chapter five.

Local authorities will also be under a duty to 'establish and maintain a service for providing people with information and advice relating to care and support for adults and carers'.[289] There is to be an amendment to the law on assessment so that any carer can be assessed, even if they are not providing regular and substantial care. Also, carers will be automatically assessed and there will be no need for a carer to request the assessment.[290] This will be most

---

[289]   Cl 2.
[290]   Cls 9 and 10.

welcome, although it only applies to adult dependants. Parents of disabled children will still need to request an assessment, as must young carers.[291]

Clause 7 of the Bill requires local authorities to take steps to prevent or the development of needs for care and support. The aim of this clause is to ensure that local authorities do not restrict their interventions to cases where a crisis has arisen. While that is a welcome policy, it will be difficult to define this in terms of an enforceable statutory duty.

The Bill contains more detailed provisions about assessments and the range of services offered. Notably it will put personal budgets on a statutory footing. As discussed earlier it will create a right to personal budgets where sought.

The White Paper, published along with the draft Bill, states there will be new national minimum eligibility criteria. These, it is said, will end the 'postcode' lottery of the extent of care being provided depending on where you live. There will also be duties on local authorities to develop a care market. This is key if personal budgets are to succeed.

There is much to be welcomed in these proposals, although at the end of the day it will be the levels of funding which are key, rather than legislative structure. The White Paper contains some specific funding promises including: a new care and support housing fund, worth £200 million over five years; new online information about local care and support options, with start-up funding of £32.5 million from the Government; £100 million in 2013/14 and £200 million in 2014/15 in joint funding between the NHS and social care to support better integrated care and support; and £400 million investment in breaks for carers, funded by the NHS.[292]

XI. Future Funding of Care

If care is not to be provided by the state there is no getting away from some kind of self funding. The central difficulty here is that care needs are unpredictable. You might drop dead in the street with no care needs or linger on for many years needing intensive care. This makes it difficult to expect people to plan for such costs. As the Dilnot Report[293] notes in cases of this kind, of potentially high unpredictable losses, insurance products are typically used. Car insurance is used, for example, to protect against very high claims that

---

[291] Carers UK, *Draft Care and Support Bill* (Carers UK, 2012).

[292] HM Government, *Caring for Our Future: Reforming Care and Support* (The Stationery Office, 2012).

[293] Department of Health, *Commission on Funding of Care and Support* (Department of Health, 2011).

might arise in connection with a car accident. Many drivers will make no claim, but their premiums will help pay for the losses of those with considerable claims. The system depends on many people not claiming and their premiums being used to pay for those who do. In effect it is a way of pooling or sharing the loss.

The Dilnot Report notes the difficulties with such a model in this context. One is that the costs may simply be too great. Unlike, say, car insurance, most people will have some costs to pay. To expect insurance to cover all care costs would mean that any insurance scheme would have very high premiums. That would make the costs of such a scheme too expensive for many to afford.

Hence the proposal from the Dilnot Report that the potential burden of care an individual is required to meet be capped, with exceptional care cases over the cap being covered by the state. In this way most people would be required to meet a low level of costs. Only where the costs exceed a fixed sum would insurance come in. This would make the cost of insurance more reasonable and it would be a more attractive market for insurance companies. However, this system would work best if an effective market of products became available.[294]

The key proposals of the Dilnot Report are as follows:

— Individuals' lifetime contributions towards their social care costs— which are currently potentially unlimited—should be capped. After the cap is reached, individuals would be eligible for full state support. This cap should be between £25,000 and £50,000. We consider that £35,000 is the most appropriate and fair figure.
— The means-tested threshold, above which people are liable for their full care costs, should be increased from £23,250 to £100,000.
— National eligibility criteria and portable assessments should be introduced to ensure greater consistency.
— All those who enter adulthood with a care and support need should be eligible for free state support immediately rather than being subjected to a means test.

The Dilnot Commission also sought a scheme whereby people in care homes could defer payment, meaning that they would not be required to sell their homes to pay for care. However, it may well be that on death their home would need to be sold to pay for the costs. The Commission estimates that its proposals— based on a cap of £35,000—would cost the state around £1.7 billion.[295]

The Dilnot Commission was clearly influenced by the political reality that an expensive scheme was unlikely to be supported by the Government. The cost of £1.7 billion, while considerable, was a feasible sum of money to

---

[294] Carers UK, *Caring For Our Future: Social Care and Carers* (Carers UK, 2012).
[295] See www.dilnotcommission.dh.gov.uk/our-report/.

deal with a major issue. The Government took a long time to respond.[296] It supported what it regarded as the two key principles behind the Dilnot Report:

— the Government should put a cap on the lifetime care costs that people face, and raise the threshold at which people lose means-tested support; and
— there should be universal access to deferred payments for people in residential care.

These the Government accepted should be the 'right basis' for any new funding model. However the Government explained:

> it is our intention to base a new funding model on them if a way to pay for it can be found, there remain a number of important questions and trade-offs to be considered about how those principles could be applied to any reformed system. Given the size of the structural deficit and the economic situation we face, we are unable to commit to introducing the new system at this stage. The Government will work with stakeholders and the Official Opposition to consider the various options for what shape a reformed system, based on the principles of the Commission's model, could take before coming to a final view in the next Spending Review. Taking a decision in the Spending Review will allow the Government to take a broad view of all priorities and spending pressures.[297]

The Government indicates that thought would need to be given to how high the cap would be. This suggests that it may well be higher than the £35,000 proposed by the Dilnot Report. Also, surprisingly, it moots the possibility that this will be in an 'opt-in scheme' where people who opt for it will finance the reform. Whether it can succeed on an opt-in basis and how those who do not opt in will be treated remains to be seen.

The failure of the Government to provide a clear response to the proposals of the Dilnot Report is deeply disappointing. There seems to be widespread acknowledgement that a scheme along the lines outlined in the Report is needed and yet the financial concerns are preventing progress.

It would be wrong, however, to exaggerate the claims for expenditure in the Dilnot Report. It should be remembered that the Dilnot Report is addressing only the difficulties for those whose wealth is over the minimum threshold (£14,250). Also, as the Dilnot Report acknowledges, a major motivation for reform is the distress at the possibility of someone having to sell their house to fund their care. A cynic might suggest that the Dilnot Report is focusing on the concerns of the middle classes. Indeed that might make it surprising that the Government has not sought to implement the Report. This is not to suggest that the proposals in the Dilnot Report should not be funded, but to suggest that the

---

[296] HM Government, *Caring For Our Future: Progress Report On Funding Reform* (The Stationery Office, 2012).
[297] Ibid 3.

claims of those seeking to protect the social care services for the poorest, which are currently often woefully inadequate, have a stronger claim.

XII. The Role of the Courts

Courts have become increasingly involved in social care cases. As cuts have had more dramatic impact on people's lives, applications to courts have risen. It is not possible to consider all the issues raised. However, a number of key themes emerge from the case law.

A. The Resources Argument

The courts have been very reluctant to intervene in a decision reached by a local authority which has been made on the basis of allocation of resources. However, the courts are willing to review the procedural aspects of a decision reached. This approach will be familiar to public lawyers as it is adopted in many areas of public law.

Cases where there has been success in the allocation of resources are those where there were procedural errors in the way the decision had been reached. In *R(W) v Birmingham CC*[298] Walker J had to consider the way a council had altered its eligibility threshold for adult social care from 'substantial' to 'critical'. He accepted that it was not the role of the court to get involved in the 'minute scrutiny of a mass of detail'. Nevertheless in this case there were failures in the way the decision had been reached. In particular the Disability Discrimination Act, section 49A equality duty[299] required the court to assess the practical impact on those whose needs were substantial but not critical. The Council had failed to consider this. Notably this simply requires the local authority to give due consideration to the impact of a decision on disabled people. In *JG v Lancashire CC*[300] the Council had considered the impact on disabled people and appreciated they would be adversely affected by cuts to provision. The challenge to the decision based on the equalities duty failed.[301] The Council, as required, had considered the impact of the cuts but decided to go through with them anyway.

---

[298] [2011] EWHC 1147 (Admin) 176.
[299] Now found in the Equality Act 2010.
[300] [2011] EWHC 2295 (Admin).
[301] *R (D) v Manchester CC* [2012] EWCH 17 (Admin); *R (Rajput) v Waltham Forest LBC* [2011] EWCA Civ 1577.

Perhaps the best argument in favour of focusing on procedural aspects is that it promotes transparency. It enables a political and public assessment of the decision. Keith Syrett, writing in the area of medical rationing, has argued that courts lack the democratic legitimacy to determine who should receive which medical resources.[302] However, he suggests, the courts play an important role in enabling the political debate to take place by requiring open and transparent reasoning. It is then for the press, activists and politicians to challenge the decisions through the political process.

This argument is attractive if, and it's a big if, there is effective political challenge to these kinds of decisions. If there is not, the approach of the courts means that there is no effective recourse for those who are denied basic access to funded care. Indeed there is a danger that local authorities can use the fact their decision cannot be judicially challenged as a way of justifying it. I would argue that the state must provide an effective way of ensuring that people have access to the basic level of services that their human rights require. If political pressures were effective, then the current procedural based approach of the courts could be supported. I do not see signs of the political pressures being effective and therefore the current approach of the courts needs to be more robust.

B. The Relationship between Needs and Resources

There has been considerable uncertainty over where the resources issue is relevant in the assessment of needs. Controversially, by a majority of three to two, it was decided by the House of Lords in *R v Gloucestershire County Council Ex p Barry*[303] that when a local authority considers the meaning of need within section 2(1) of the Chronically Sick and Disabled Persons Act 1970 that

> needs for services cannot sensibly be assessed without having some regard to the cost of providing them. A person's need for a particular type or level of service cannot be decided in a vacuum from which all considerations of cost have been expelled.[304]

That appears to suggest that resources can be relevant in deciding what needs a person has. That decision has come under intense challenge and it is doubtful it is still the law.

---

[302] K Syrett, *Law, Legitimacy and the Rationing of Healthcare: A Contextual and Comparative Perspective* (Cambridge University Press, 2007).
[303] [1997] AC 584.
[304] Ibid 604 (Lord Nicholls of Birkenhead).

A discussion on how a local authority should assess a person's needs under section 2(1) of the Chronically Sick and Disabled Persons Act 1970 is provided by the Supreme Court in *R (KM) v Cambridgeshire* CC.[305] It set out four questions:

(i)   What are the needs of the disabled person?
(ii) In order to meet the needs identified at (i), is it necessary for the authority to make arrangements for the provision of any of the listed services?
(iii) If the answer to question (ii) is affirmative, what are the nature and extent of the listed services for the provision of which it is necessary for the authority to make arrangements?[306]
(iv) What is the reasonable cost of securing provision of the services which have been identified at (iii) as being those for the provision of which it is necessary for the authority to make arrangements?[307]

The Court held that the resources issue is particularly relevant in the second, third and fourth questions, but not the first. Lord Wilson explained:

> The one matter is that it is always open to an authority to decide to meet a particular need by the provision of a cheaper service—so long as it duly meets it—rather than of a more expensive service; such is an elementary aspect of financial management and is better not even included within the debate about the relevance of constraints upon an authority's resources to the discharge of its duty under section 2 of the 1970 Act.[308]

But an assessment of the needs of a person always focuses on the individual and not the claims of others. That, however, was key in the later question:

> One important aspect of the question raised at the second stage is to ask whether the presenting needs of the disabled person can reasonably be met by family or friends (which I will describe as natural support) or by other organs of the state, such as the NHS, or by charities etc, or indeed out of the person's own resources. But it will by now be clear that the question at the second stage goes far further and, in particular, encompasses consideration of the relationship between the scale of the local authority's resources and the weight of other demands upon it, in other words the availability of its resources.[309]

As Lady Hale emphasised, there is a difference between the duty to meet needs and how that duty should be met:

> There is a clear distinction between need and what is done to meet it. We all need to eat and drink. Resources do not come into it. But there are various ways of meeting

---

[305] [2012] UKSC 23.
[306] Ibid, para 23.
[307] Ibid, para 29.
[308] Ibid, para 12.
[309] Ibid, para 19.

that need and it is perfectly sensible to choose the most efficient and economical way of meeting it.

Our nutritional needs can met by simple, wholesome food, rather than by giving us the expensive foods that we prefer.[310]

This is a fine example of requiring transparent reasoning. If care services are denied to a person on account of a rationing decision, the local authority should be explicit about that. Trying to disguise the decision by pretending it is in fact a finding that there are no needs, prevents the authority being held to account for the decision and is insulting to the individual concerned.

C. The Definition of Needs

What amounts to a need deserving of support? This question was highlighted in a major decision in this area. In *R(Macdonald) v Kensington and Chelsea*,[311] their lordships had to consider a former ballerina who suffered from a bladder condition, requiring her to urinate several times a night. Due to a stroke she had mobility problems, which prevented her getting to the commode. The care package offered by the local authority had been supplying a carer who could assist her to move during the night as needed. However, the cost of this was considerable and the council wished her to use incontinence pads or sheeting, which would mean there would be no need for there to be a carer.

For the majority the issue was clear: the authority was entitled to take into account resources in determining how to meet the needs of a person. In this case her needs were to deal with incontinence and the authority was entitled to determine that the use of pads was a more suitable way of meeting needs. Lord Wilson explained:

> The one matter is that it is always open to an authority to decide to meet a particular need by the provision of a cheaper service—so long as it duly meets it—rather than of a more expensive service; such is an elementary aspect of financial management and is better not even included within the debate about the relevance of constraints upon an authority's resources to the discharge of its duty under section 2 of the 1970 Act.[312]

However, as the speeches for the minority show, the definition of needs is not straightforward. For Lady Hale the need in this case was for a safe and hygienic place to urinate and defecate. The provision of incontinence pads and sheets did not meet her need. Notably, Lady Hale made it clear she was willing to accept an argument that the care sought was too expensive for the

---

[310] Ibid, para 71.
[311] [2011] UKSC 33.
[312] Ibid, para 12.

local authority, bearing in mind the other calls on its budget. She was not, however, willing to accept the argument the authority was making which was that the provision of pads and sheets met her needs. She went on to highlight the difficulties with the view of the majority:

> Furthermore, I am troubled by the implications of the contrary view. A person in her situation needs this help during the day as well as during the night and irrespective of whether she needs to urinate or to defecate. Logically, the decision of the majority in this case would entitle a local authority to withdraw this help even though the client needed to defecate during the night and thus might be left lying in her faeces until the carers came in the morning. This is not Ms McDonald's problem at the moment, but her evidence leaves one in no doubt that this is one of her fears. Indeed, the majority view would also entitle an authority to withdraw this help during the day. The only constraint would be how frequently (or rather how infrequently) it was deemed necessary to change the pads or sheets, consistently with the avoidance of infection and other hazards such as nappy rash.[313]

The majority denied this might be a consequence of its decision, although it is hard to see why not.

It might be thought that human rights claims would become relevant in cases where services were withdrawn from disabled people. In *R (Macdonald) v Kensington v Chelsea* it was argued that leaving Ms Macdonald in pads, rather than providing night time carers, infringed her article 8 rights. However, the majority dealt with this quickly. Even if she could claim, under Article 8, a right to the care,

> the clear and consistent jurisprudence of the Strasbourg Court establishes 'the wide margin of appreciation enjoyed by states' in striking 'the fair balance ... between the competing interests of the individual and of the community as a whole' and 'in determining the steps to be taken to ensure compliance with the Convention', and indeed that 'this margin of appreciation is even wider when ... the issues involve an assessment of the priorities in the context of the allocation of limited state resources'.[314]

This does not mean that a human rights argument can never succeed, but it will require a powerful argument to show the interference in rights caused by the failure to provide care is not justified by the need to spend the money on other claims.[315] This may require dramatic facts. In *R (Bernard) v Enfield London Borough Council*,[316] a couple had six children and the wife was in a wheelchair. Their housing was utterly inadequate and the council failed to provide them with alternative accommodation. The wife, who was incontinent, had to defecate and urinate on the living room floor and she could not play a

---

[313] Ibid, para 77.
[314] Ibid para 16.
[315] *Watts v UK* (2010) 51 EHRR SE5.
[316] [2002] EWHC 2282 (Admin).

role in caring for her children. The Court found the claim of interference of article 8 rights clearly made out and could not be justified.[317]

Colm O'Cinneide[318] argues that the McDonald decision 'serves to insulate almost all resource allocation decisions from being subject to review under the HRA'. This leads him to have concerns about 'limited reach of legal accountability' over challenges to austerity. So, 'existing legal accountability mechanisms can only provide remedies in very specific cases, where a resource allocation claim can be dressed up as a procedural violation or a violation of civil and political rights'.[319]

XIII. Conclusion

The relationship between the state and the provision of care is undergoing dramatic change. Bettina Cass and Sue Yeandle[320] list the following trends in the provision of care:

— a mixed economy of care, with independent sector providers giving public care provisions;
— a move to intensive packages of care focused on strict eligibility criteria;
— individualisation, with increased focus on choice for care users as consumers, through direct payments;
— attempts to better integrate health and social care systems; and
— greater attention to carers with better information and opportunities for respite.

Many of these have been touched on in this chapter. While now undeniably the provision of care is seen as a matter of public significance, there is still much dispute over how the care should be provided.

The key point is this. There is no getting away from the fact that the meeting of needs through care carries costs. Those costs must lie somewhere. At the moment those costs largely fall on individuals: carers who perform an enormous amount of care work which is not recognised or valued at an enormous personal loss; or individuals who have needs which are simply not met. When, therefore, it is said that it is 'too expensive' for the state to cover these costs, we are accepting they

---

[317] *Anufrijeva v Southwark London Borough Council* [2004] QB 1124 and *R (L) v Leeds CC* [2010] EWHC 3324 (Admin) shows this will be rare.

[318] C O'Cinneide, 'Legal Accountability and Social justice', available at SSRN: http://ssrn .com/abstract=2017027 or http://dx.doi.org/10.2139/ssrn.2017027.

[319] See further S Fredman, 'The Public Sector Equality Duty' (2011) 40 *Industrial Law Journal* 405.

[320] B Cass and S Yeandle, *Policies for Carers in Australia and the UK*, available at www.cccg .umontreal.ca/rc19/PDF/Cass-B_Rc192009.pdf.

should stay where they currently lie. It is not as if the costs are not there if the state does not meet them. The question must be where should the costs flowing from needs lie? At the moment they fall all too often on those in caring relationships. As argued above, this is unfair on those individuals and fails to meet society's obligations to meet the core needs of citizens.

At the heart of the issue is what we expect from our citizens. Much of the current rhetoric from the Government is that the primary duty of the citizen is to be self-sufficient, independent and self-financing. David Cameron in his 'Bluewater speech' asks what can be expected of those on benefits. For example, he asks of parents on benefits:

> now there is free childcare for all children from age three, that does prompt a question about how some of that time—15 hours a week, more than a thousand hours over a couple of years—should be used by parents on Income Support.[321]

Underlying the whole speech is an assumption that you need to have a good reason why you need to be on benefits and not in employment. Benefits should be a 'safety net' of last resort.

This employed self-supporting model has been challenged in this book. I have argued that undertaking caring responsibilities is a central role of a citizen and plays as full a role in the working of society as the person in employment. Our benefits system needs to support those who are contributing to the central role of society through caring. There are more ways of being a good citizen than making money.

A further difficulty with the self-supporting citizen model is that it fails to appreciate the many barriers that get in the way of those seeking to combine paid employment with care. Maxine Eichner argues that employers should be required to provide an improved package of employment rights, including:

> paid maternity leaves and job retention guarantees for women at childbirth, and parental leave rights and benefits during children's first few years to give workers time and opportunity for caregiving while allowing them to resume their jobs. They also include granting parents and other caretakers the rights to some further paid leave in order to deal with short-term needs for care that may arise.[322]

We will explore these issues further in chapter seven. Until there is an employment market that enables employees to combine care and employment, this is an unrealistic expectation. In any event, for some, caring responsibilities or health restrictions will mean employment is never possible.

---

[321] See www.telegraph.co.uk/news/politics/david-cameron/9354163/David-Camerons-welfare-speech-in-full.html.

[322] M Eichner, *The Supportive State* (Oxford University Press, 2010) 79.

5

Caring and Medical Law

I. Introduction

Medical law might be thought an obvious place to find legal recognition
and support for caring relationships. After all, medicine is about care. Yet,
medical law seems to place little weight on the interests of carers. Indeed
textbooks on medical law rarely, if ever, discuss them. 'Where are the carers
in healthcare law and ethics?'[1] I asked in a 1997 article, highlighting their
absence from legal and ethical discussions. They are 'ignored and invisible'.[2]
As we shall see later in this chapter there are a number of doctrines and
approaches which mean that the interests of caring relationships are sidelined
within the medico-legal literature. Before getting into the detail, some of the
general themes of this chapter will be summarised in this introduction.

First, medical law and ethics is dominated by individualism. The ethical
and legal literature is replete with arguments that *I* have the right to make
decisions about *my* medical treatment; and that *I* should receive the treatment that is appropriate for *me*.[3] The rights of patients have come to play a
major role in the law. Medicine is becoming increasingly personalised, with
the promotion of the health of an individual being emphasised rather than
the health of the community. Donna Dickenson has described this as the
growth of 'me medicine'.[4] The problem with the approach typically taken
is that, as Martha Minow points out, the question 'who is the patient?' goes
unasked.[5] Unasked because many people think the answer is obvious: it is

---

[1] J Herring, 'Where are the Carers in Healthcare Law and Ethics?' (2007) 27 *Legal Studies* 51.

[2] M Henwood, *Ignored and Invisible* (Carers' National Association, 2008).

[3] For a powerful polemic against the emphasis on autonomy see: C Foster, *Choosing Life,
Choosing Death: The Tyranny of Autonomy in Medical Ethics and Law* (Hart, 2009).

[4] D Dickenson, 'Me Medicine', available at www.project-syndicate.org/commentary/
me-medicine.

[5] M Minow, 'Who's the Patient?' (1994) 53 *Maryland Law Review* 1173.

the person sitting in front of the doctor. But that is to ignore those who are caring for the patient and who are cared for by them.

Second, and linked to the first point, autonomy has come to play a central role in medical law and the debates surrounding it. As often in legal thought, the focus is on the image of an autonomous, competent man who can enforce his rights,[6] rather than recognising how our plans are usually connected to other people.[7] A decision to refuse treatment, by the individual or the doctor, will have dramatic consequences on the individual's family, friends, and others, as well as the patient herself. This is hidden in orthodox presentation of the autonomy principle.

Third, accounts of medical law have emphasised the role of doctors, above other medical professionals and others. In part this is understandable: most legal cases constitute some kind of challenge to the decision made by a doctor. But, in many legal cases, the doctor is elevated to the expert, unquestioningly. Is it in the best interests of a child in a serious condition to have their life support withdrawn? Is it in the best interests of a child who is a Jehovah's Witness to receive a blood transfusion against her will? Should a woman with mild dementia be taken into a care home against her wishes? To resolve such questions courts typically turn to a learned consultant physician. Yet, while doctors and medical 'experts' have things to contribute to debates over such questions, there are other important ethical, social, political and personal issues, on which it cannot be assumed that a doctor has the expertise. Indeed on such issues, the views of the individual's family, carers, nurses, and others who have been in a similar position, could all usefully be brought into the equation. In many cases, seeing the issue as essentially a medical one cuts out core values.

Once the voice of carers are listened too, we gain the wisdom of a new expertise. This challenges the expertise of the medial professional which is the basis of their prestige, power and payment.[8] The individual patient and those in relationship with them can speak about the impact of medication on the particular patient; the values that matter to them; the pleasure they find in life; what they need or do not need their bodies to do; and the impact of their condition on the life they lead. This expertise can in many cases, be at least as valuable as that of the person with a medical degree.[9] No longer is the focus of medical attention on the patient in isolation, but rather in the network of relationships of care within which we all find ourselves.

---

[6] I use the male pronoun deliberately because the image of the isolated, rational-driven male patient is the image that dominates much of the writing.

[7] C Foster, *Choosing Life, Choosing Death, The Tyranny of Autonomy in Medical Ethics and Law* (Hart, 2009).

[8] L Prior, 'Belief, Knowledge and Expertise: The Emergence of the Lay Expert in Medical Sociology' (2003) 25 *Sociology of Health & Illness* 41.

[9] Ibid.

Fourth, even the very definition of illness can be seen as reflecting a 'medicalised model'. The fact that loneliness,[10] for example, is not a medical condition but depression is, reflects the individualised scientific understanding of the self. Such an understanding can sideline the relational aspects of our lives and thereby shut out the caring relationships we are in. Linked to this point, it may be argued that medical law has a very narrow view about what health care is about. Indeed, arguably, using the terminology 'medical law' rather than, say, 'health law' focuses on the diagnosis and treatment typically provided by a doctor, rather than the many other ways in which care meets the health care needs of an individual.

II. The Place of Carers in Medical Law

There are several ways that the interests of carers may be relevant in medical law cases. First, there may be claims based on carers' own interests. For example, a carer may claim that their interests need to be weighed alongside the interests of a person with whom they are in a caring relationship with, when a decision is made about them.

Second, the carer may claim a role not in respect of his or her own interests, but as a protector of the interests of another. In this regard, Kirsty Keywood[11] suggests three primary roles a carer may play as a protector of the interests of another. Writing with mental capacity legislation in mind, she suggests:

(1) Gatekeepers. They can seek access to and admission to specialist services.
(2) Proxies. They take actions which will be in the best interests of the person lacking capacity.
(3) Advocates. They represent to professionals or others, representing the best interests for a person lacking capacity.

A third approach, and this is the approach predominantly adopted in this chapter, is that the interests of carers should not be protected by virtue of their own interests per se, nor by virtue of their position as protectors of the interests of another. Rather, the point is that it is simply impossible to make an assessment of any individual's interests outside the context of their

---

[10] P Stanley, 'The Patient's Voice: A Cry in Solitude or a Call for Community' (2004) 23 *Literature and Medicine* 346.
[11] K Keywood, 'Gatekeepers, Proxies, Advocates? The Evolving Role of Carers under Mental Health and Mental Incapacity Proposals' (2003) 25 *Journal of Social Welfare and Family Law* 355.

relationships. Medical law should be based on dealing with the promotion of networks of relationships. Quite what this means will become clearer as the chapter progresses.

III. Mental Capacity and Carers

In this section two issues will be examined. The first is the assessment of capacity. This is commonly done by treating the patient in isolation. It should not be. A better approach, it will be argued, is to consider whether the patient within their relationships is able to make a decision. Second, it will be argued that the best interests assessment for those lacking capacity fails to attach sufficient weight to the significance of the relationships within which everyone lives.[12]

A. Assessment of Capacity

The definition of mental capacity is found in section 2(1) of the Mental Capacity Act 2005:

> a person lacks capacity in relation to a matter if at the material time he is unable to make a decision for himself in relation to the matter because of an impairment of, or a disturbance in the functioning of, the mind or brain.

Section 3(1) explains that:

> for the purposes of section 2, a person is unable to make a decision for himself if he is unable—
> (a) to understand the information relevant to the decision,
> (b) to retain that information,
> (c) to use or weigh that information as part of the process of making the decision, or
> (d) to communicate his decision (whether by talking, using sign language or any other means).

It is not possible here to go into a detailed analysis of this definition. It is fairly self-explanatory.[13] There are three points to highlight. First, there is a presumption in favour of a person having capacity.[14] Second, a person can

---

[12] J Manthorpe, J Rapaport and N Stanley, 'Expertise and Experience: People with Experiences of Using Services and Carers' Views of the Mental Capacity Act 2005' (2009) 39 *British Journal of Social Work* 884.

[13] See eg J Herring, *Medical Law and Ethics*, 4th edn (Oxford University Press, 2012) ch 4.

[14] Mental Capacity Act 2005, s 1(2).

be found to have capacity to make some decisions, but not others.[15] They might, for example, have capacity to decide they prefer strawberry ice cream to chocolate, but lack the capacity to make a will. Third, the wisdom of the decision should not affect the issue of competence.[16] As we can probably all testify: even competent people make foolish decisions! The Mental Capacity Act 2005 makes this explicit: 'A person is not to be treated as unable to make a decision merely because he makes an unwise decision.'[17] Of course, as the word 'merely' in the statute indicates, the fact that a decision is widely regarded as bizarre may indicate that a patient is incompetent, but further evidence is required before that conclusion can be reached.

There is much in these provisions to welcome. However, for the purposes of this book I wish to focus on the argument that the application of the approach to assessment is over-individualistic. Incompetent people are assessed and treated in isolation, and not seen as relational people, in mutually inter-de-pendant relationships. An assessment of capacity should be of an individual located within their network of family, friends and care-givers.[18] Instead, the assessment is made of the individual sitting alone in a doctor's office.

Traditional methods of competence assessment are based on internal, formal assessment by the individual.[19] The archetype might be the philosopher sitting alone in his study carefully thinking through his decision. Compare this with a model which is made socially, thinking it through with others and relying on their insights. The friends chatting through a topic with a cup of tea might be the archetype for this model. A study by Roy Gilbar,[20] unsurprisingly, found that nearly all patients in his sample of those with long-term health issues did wish to discuss their cases with their relatives and confirmed that they were helpful in making the decision.

Few of us, in fact, make important decisions on our own and without consultation and discussion with those around us. Regularly in relationships partners will divide up decision making between them or at least recognise the different expertise that each has. It is very common for a person to lack the capacity to make the decision alone, but to be able to do so in co-operation with others. At least part of the assessment of capacity should be the extent to which the person within their support group of family and/or friends is able to make choices. Of course, in making that assessment we would need

---

[15] *LBL v RYJ* [2010] EWHC 2665 (Fam).

[16] Mental Capacity Act 2005, s 1(3).

[17] Ibid.

[18] H Mun Chan, 'Sharing Death and Dying. Advance Directives Autonomy and the Family' (2004) 18 *Bioethics* 87.

[19] N Stoljar, 'Informed Consent and Relational Conceptions of Autonomy' (2011) 36 *Journal of Medicine and Philosophy* 375; T Breden and J Vollmann, 'The Cognitive Based Approach of Capacity Assessment in Psychiatry: A Philosophical Critique of the MacCAT-T' (2004) 12 *Health Care Analysis* 273.

[20] R Gilbar, 'Family Involvement, Independence, and Patient Autonomy in Practice' (2011) *Medical Law Review* 192.

to take care that the relationships were not abusive ones. Further, when decisions need to be made for a person of doubtful capacity, decisions should be made within the person's relational context.[21] The *Mental Capacity Act 2005: Code of Practice*, sees this role for families and friends:

> Family members and close friends may be able to provide valuable background information (for example, the person's past behaviour and abilities and the types of decisions they can currently make). But their personal views and wishes about what *they* would want for the person must not influence the assessment.[22]

While that is a fair point, it does not give sufficient weight to the way that others can enable the person lacking capacity to make a decision.[23] As Anita Ho argues:

> We are socially-embedded beings, such that autonomy often incorporates intrinsically relational or social content, and it is thus impossible to assess patient autonomy without critically evaluating how or whether the interconnected social, political, and health-care structural frameworks often foreclose certain opportunities or predetermine how individuals approach various health-care situations.[24]

Considering a person's relational context might, in some cases, mean that a person is found to lack capacity, rather than have it.[25] *A Local Authority v Mr and Mrs A*[26] shows that well. Mrs A was held to be so dominated by her husband that she was unable to make a decision for herself as to contraceptive treatment. For her, the Court held, capacity was to be found not in removing her from the relationship, but rather enabling the decision to be made with others (her social worker support team) that would better help her make her own mind up.

Narrative ethics can provide a useful perspective here. It sees decision making used through stories about where we have been and where we are going. As Roger Higgs argues:

> We also need some way of being able to understand whole lives, in order to assess the capabilities of those who live those lives. One possible way of doing this is to listen to the 'narrative' of those lives, the story that individuals are telling or struggling to tell about their own lives.[27]

That cannot be done outside the context of a relationship.

---

[21] S Horton-Deutsch, P Twigg and R Evans, 'Health Care Decision-Making of Persons with Dementia' (2007) 6 *Dementia* 105.

[22] Department for Constitutional Affairs, *Mental Capacity Act 2005: Code of Practice* (The Stationery Office, 2007) para 4.49.

[23] L Barclay, 'Autonomy and the Social Self' in C Mackenzie and N Stoljar (eds), *Relational Autonomy: Feminist Essays on Autonomy, Agency and the Social Self* (Oxford University Press, 2000).

[24] A Ho, 'The Individualist Model of Autonomy and the Challenge of Disability' (2008) 5 *Journal of Bioethical Inquiry* 193.

[25] Ibid.

[26] [2010] EWHC 1549 (Fam).

[27] R Higgs, 'The Contribution of Narrative Ethics to Issues of Capacity in Psychiatry' (2004) 12 *Health Care Analysis* 307.

We have no difficulty with accepting that a person can receive the information and advice from a professional, such as a doctor or lawyer, and as a result gain the knowledge they require to gain capacity to consent. An assessment of capacity will involve a careful consideration of what they were told and how by the doctor. Why is it any different if the decision involves, as it nearly always will, those the person is in a caring relationship with? Is not the information they can provide just as important, albeit more often of an emotional or relational significance, than technical information? We see here the use of 'expertise' as a way of privileging a certain kind of information and consultation over others.[28]

Helpfully, Natalie Stoljar provides a practical example of the approach that I suggest is needed:

> Consider a woman who is deciding whether to take hormone replacement therapy for menopausal symptoms. To secure informed consent to the use of hormone replacement therapy, it will be sufficient to provide the woman with complete and up to the minute medical evidence, for instance that the therapy is likely to reduce the risk of heart disease. Once in possession of the evidence, it will be open to the woman to 'do what she wants' and make her choice. However, the decision-making process will likely be influenced by factors in addition to a weighing up of the medical evidence that is presented to the woman, including her education, race, and class; her conception of herself and her unique experience of menopause; cultural norms such as that looking young is attractive and valued whereas looking old is unattractive and devalued; the attitude of family members to the symptoms of menopause; the support of family members for the woman's decision; and so on. The complexity of all these factors and the uncertainty experienced by the woman in weighing them up may lead to diminished self-trust... Self-trust is one of the 'subject-referring' attitudes that we described above, some of which are necessary for the exercise of autonomy. Informed consent, as an opportunity concept, is inadequate to ensure that agents *exercise* their preference formation with the required subject-referring attitudes. The process of preference formation that we call informed consent is therefore not sufficient for autonomy.[29]

I would argue, therefore, that assessments of capacity must take into account not just the mind of the individual in relationship to the particular question, but also the relationships in which the individual lived.[30] In some cases, involving family members and carers will enable an individual to have the

---

[28] A Ho "'They Just Don't Get It!'" When Family Disagrees with Expert Opinion' (2009) 35 *Journal of Medical Ethics* 497.

[29] N Stoljar, 'Informed Consent and Relational Conceptions of Autonomy' (2011) 36 *Journal of Medicine and Philosophy* 375, referencing C McLeod, *Self-Trust and Reproductive Autonomy* (MIT Press, 2002).

[30] S Moorman, 'Older Adults' Preferences for Independent or Delegated End-of-Life Medical Decision Making' (2011) 23 *Journal of Ageing and Health* 135.

capacity to make a decision they otherwise would not have.[31] In other cases, as in the examples above, an appreciation of the relational context of the decision might mean that in fact they therefore lack the capacity they may otherwise be thought to possess. Certainly external conditions can amount to oppression causing false consciousness ('a cognitive process of coming to believe in an ideology that oppresses oneself'[32]), or deformed desire ('the combined affective and cognitive process of value formation, in which the oppressed come to desire that which is oppressive to them').[33] These can only be appreciated when the individual is sited within the social context within which they are making a decision. Indeed it might even be argued that in order to be properly autonomous, certain external conditions are essential.[34]

So, rather than assessment of capacity being simply as assessment of rationality and understanding and ability to communicate,[35] we need an assessment of the individual within their relationships, considering the emotional, biographical and social aspects of the decision making.[36] Competence should not just be about reasoning, but being able to relate to the world[37] and appreciate the relational context of the decision.

B. The Best Interests Assessment

Where a person lacks capacity over a particular issue, a decision will be made on their behalf based on an assessment of what will be in that individual's best interests.[38] This involves a consideration of all the relevant issues to determine what will best promote their welfare. The *Mental Capacity Act 2005: Code of Practice* states:

> When working out what is in the best interests of the person who lacks capacity to make a decision or act for themselves, decision-makers must take into account all relevant factors that it would be reasonable to consider, not just those that they think are important. They must not act or make a decision based on what they would want to do if they were the person who lacked capacity.[39]

---

[31] R Sharma and S Dy, 'Cross-Cultural Communication and Use of the Family Meeting in Palliative Care' (2011) 28; A Ho, 'Relational Autonomy or Undue Pressure? Family's Role in Medical Decision-Making' (2008) 22 *Scandinavian Journal of Caring Sciences* 128.

[32] A Cudd, *Analyzing Oppression* (Oxford University Press, 2006) 176.

[33] Ibid 176.

[34] M Oshana, *Personal Autonomy in Society* (Ashgate, 2006).

[35] R Berghmans, D Dickenson and R Ter Meulen, 'Mental Capacity: In Search of Alternative Perspectives' (2004) 12 *Health Care Analysis* 251.

[36] T Breden and J Vollmann, 'The Cognitive Based Approach of Capacity Assessment in Psychiatry: A Philosophical Critique of the MacCAT-T' (2004) 12 *Health Care Analysis* 273.

[37] R Berghmans, D Dickenson and R Ter Meulen, 'Mental Capacity: In Search of Alternative Perspectives' (2004) 12 *Health Care Analysis* 251.

[38] Mental Capacity Act 2005, s 4.

[39] Department for Constitutional Affairs, *Mental Capacity Act 2005: Code of Practice* (The Stationery Office, 2007) para 5.7

Although a broad range of factors is to be taken into account, the focus must be on the best interests of the person lacking capacity (P) and the interests of others are not in themselves to be given any weight in the assessment.[40] Section 4 provides factors that for a person, or court, seeking to ascertain what is in a person's best interests. Of particular relevance to caring relationships is section 4(7) which states:

> He must take into account, if it is practical and appropriate to consult them, the views of—
>
> ...
>
> (b) anyone engaged in caring for the person or interested in his welfare
>
> ...
>
> as to what would be in the person's best interests ...

Although carers' views are to be taken into account, they are only relevant in so far as they reveal what is in the best interests of P. Carers' views as to what would assist them as carers is not a relevant consideration, unless it can be 'dressed' up as being about the benefit of the individual. So, if a carer says 'if my views on this issue are not followed, I will cease to care for this person, and that will cause them to suffer', then her views will be given weight. It would often not be in the best interests of the person lacking capacity to be left without a carer. However, if the carer were to say 'the burden of care will be greatly eased if my views are followed and doing so will not really harm the individual, but if my views are not followed, despite my disappointment I will make sure the individual does not suffer', then their views do not appear to be relevant. That is because they do not directly relate to the well-being of the person lacking capacity.

The decision of *Re Y (Mental Patient: Bone Marrow Donation)*[41] provides a revealing example of how the best interests test operates. A 25-year-old woman (Y) lacked capacity and lived in a community home, where she was regularly visited by her mother. Y's sister suffered from a bone disorder and her only prospect of recovery was if a bone marrow donor could be found. The only suitable donor who could be found was Y. The sister sought a declaration that the harvesting of Y's bone marrow be authorised. Connell J granted the declaration. The donation would be in Y's best interests. It was explained that Y's mother was very important to Y's welfare. Y was anxious due to the sister's illness. If the sister died this would have a severe impact on the mother's health and this would, in turn, impact on Y's welfare. It was, therefore, in Y's welfare to donate the marrow. The physical discomfort and invasion caused by the donation were outweighed by the emotion and

---

[40] Mental Capacity Act 2005, s 4. See further J Manthorpe, J Rapaport, and N Stanley, 'Who Decides Now? Protecting and Empowering Vulnerable Adults' (2007) 37 *British Journal of Social Work* 557.

[41] [1997] 2 FCR 172.

psychological benefits of her relationship with her mother. My argument will be not that the result reached was incorrect, but that the reasoning is weak. The same reasoning could be used if Y's sister needed cosmetic surgery and that using tissue from Y would help the surgery go well, if that gave the mother pleasure and therefore helped her care for Y. To exclude from the reasoning the fact that a life would be saved seems to ignore the elephant in the room.

Despite the initial appearance in 2005 that the best interests test precludes a consideration of the interests of carers in their own right, I will argue that the Act does in fact allow the interests of carers to be considered when decisions are made for those lacking capacity.[42] Four arguments will be relied upon.

i. The Past Wishes, Beliefs and Values of the Individual

First, section 4(6) requires the decision maker, when determining what is in the best interests of the individual lacking capacity (P) to consider:

(a) the person's past and present wishes and feelings (and, in particular, any relevant written statement made by him when he had capacity).
(b) the beliefs and values that would be likely to influence his decisions if he had capacity, and
(c) the other factors that he would be likely to consider if he were able to do so.

A consideration of these factors justifies taking the interests of carers into account. The decision maker must consider P's past wishes, feelings, beliefs and values.[43] Most people do not live utterly selfish lives and do take account of the interests of others in their decision making, and particularly those they are in close relationships with. Indeed the *Code of Practice* accepts this:

> Section 4(6)(c) of the Act requires decision-makers to consider any other factors the person who lacks capacity would consider if they were able to do so. This might include the effect of the decision on other people, obligations to dependants or the duties of a responsible citizen.[44]

In Ronald Dworkin's influential analysis he draws a much discussed distinction between experiential interests and critical interests.[45] Critical interests are those things which make a person an individual; the things that make a person's life worthwhile. Experiential interests may produce pleasure and fun

---

[42] J Herring, 'The Place of Carers' in M Freeman (ed), *Law and Bioethics* (Oxford University Press, 2008).

[43] *Re MB* [1997] 2 FLR 426, 439.

[44] Department of Constitutional Affairs, *Mental Capacity Act 2005. Code of Practice* (London, The Stationery Office, 2007) para 5.47.

[45] R Dworkin, *Life's Dominion* (Alfred A. Knopf, Inc., 1993) 224.

(eg doodling) but are not part of a person's life goals.[46] If this distinction is used,[47] I would argue that for many people their caring relationships will be part of their critical interests. Their partnership, marriage, sibling relationship, or friendship will have been a defining part of their lives. The individual's interest in promoting that relationship as give and take will be a part of their critical interest which should continue after losing capacity.

ii. Best Interests are not Inconsistent with Selfless Acts

Best interests are not defined in the Mental Capacity Act. They are not, however, an entirely materialistic concept.[48] In *Re MB*[49] it was made clear that best interests are not restricted to medical best interests. As Butler-Sloss P in *JS v An NHS Trust* stated, the Court should define best interests 'in the widest possible way'.[50] The *Code of Practice* states:

> The Act allows actions that benefit other people, as long as they are in the best interests of the person who lacks capacity to make the decision. For example, having considered all the circumstances of the particular case, a decision might be made to take a blood sample from a person who lacks capacity to consent, to check for a genetic link to cancer within the family, because this might benefit someone else in the family. But it might still be in the best interests of the person who lacks capacity. 'Best interests' goes beyond the person's medical interests.[51]

As the example with the blood sample indicates, a minor harm might be justified if seen as in the person's best interests, taking into account the obligations a person properly has towards another. Indeed the Mental Capacity Act itself recognises that people lacking capacity can be treated in a way which does not directly benefit them, when in Chapter 11 of the Act it permits an incompetent person to be involved in research.

Taking this point further, it might be said that it would not be in the best interests of a person lacking capacity to have every decision made about them considering only their needs. No one actually lives their lives only considering their own interests and placing no weight on the interests of others. Such

---

[46] Ibid.

[47] There are difficulties with it. See J Herring, 'Losing it? Losing what? The Law and Dementia' (2009) *Child and Family Law Quarterly* 3.

[48] For a detailed discussion of this argument see J Herring and C Foster, 'Welfare Means Rationality, Virtue and Altruism' (2012) 32 *Legal Studies* 480.

[49] [1997] 2 FLR 426.

[50] [2002] EWHC 2734 (Fam.) para 60.

[51] Department of Constitutional Affairs, *Mental Capacity Act 2005. Code of Practice* (London, The Stationery Office, 2007) para 5.48.

a way of life would be neither rewarding nor beneficial.[52] As Charles Foster and I put it:

> acting in a morally right way is a crucial part of human thriving. It is the job of best-interests-determining judges to facilitate human thriving. Indeed the only legitimate business of the law is to help citizens become more truly what they should be; to help them be humans; to humanise.[53]

No one would want to be cared for in a relationship in which one person's interests counted for nothing. The relationship of caring does, and should, involve give and take. It is not in either party's best interests to be in a relationship which was utterly oppressive of one.[54] It is, therefore, argued that when considering the best interests of an incompetent person such an assessment must consider their well-being in the context of their relationships. This might involve making decisions which in a narrow way do not explicitly promote P's welfare or even slightly harms it, if that is a fair aspect of a caring relationship which is a necessary part of P's well-being.

The point can be developed by further consideration of the notion of well-being. According to one view (hedonism), well-being is entirely tied to happiness.[55] The happier a person is the greater their well-being, the less happy they are the less their well-being. There must, however, be more to well-being that happiness. Imagine a case where a gay couple moves in next door to person A. Person A is a homophobe who is distressed by their presence. Are we to say that A's well-being has been diminished by their presence and that if the couple were removed that could increase A's well-being?

Further, few people do seek to live their lives entirely based on what will promote their happiness. Parents regularly make sacrifices for children; people comfort distressed friends, despite the inconvenience; money is given to charity. A better understanding is that virtue is an element of well-being.[56] Those who support the relevance of virtue argue that a good life is not just one that is full of pleasure, but one that is good.[57] The argument that a virtuous life is an aspect of well-being has a long pedigree going back to the writings of Socrates, Plato and especially Aristotle.[58]

---

[52] J Piliavin and H-W Charng, 'Altruism: A Review of Recent Literature and Research' (1990) 16 *Annual Review of Sociology* 27 discusses the nature of altruism.

[53] J Herring and C Foster, 'Welfare Means Relationality, Virtue and Altruism' (2012) 32 *Legal Studies* 12.

[54] For a development of this approach in relation to parents and children, see J Herring, 'The Human Rights Act and the Welfare Principle in Family Law—Conflicting or Complementary?' [1999] *Child and Family Law Quarterly* 223.

[55] F Feldman, *Pleasure and the Good Life* (Oxford University Press, 2004).

[56] N Badhwar, 'Self-Interest and Virtue' (1997) 14 *Social Philosophy and Policy* 226; R Hursthouse, *On Virtue Ethics* (Oxford University Press, 1999); M Slote, *Morals from Motives* (Oxford University Press, 2001), especially chs 6–7.

[57] L Sumner, 'Is Virtue its Own Reward?' (1998) 15 *Social Philosophy and Policy* 18.

[58] Aristotle (1984 [C4 BCE]) *The Complete Works of Aristotle,* J Barnes (ed) (Princeton University Press); Aristotle (2000 [C4 BCE]) *Nicomachean Ethics,* R Crisp (ed) (Cambridge University Press).

Susan Wolf[59] has argued that an essential part of the good life is that life has meaning. She explains, 'meaningful lives are lives of active engagement in projects of worth'.[60] She suggests as a helpful way of thinking about well-being that we consider the sorts of questions people ask about their lives on contemplation of death. A sense of pride and accomplishment in life is unlikely to be found, certainly not solely found, in making oneself happy. It is one's relationships, accomplishments and virtues in which value might be found.[61]

This might all sound too airy fairy to be of legal significance, but the argument has some support in the case law. In *Re G(T)*,[62] the Court had to consider the position of a woman who lacked capacity to make decisions for herself. One of her children was in great need. The question was whether some of the woman's money should be given to her. As the judge noted, at one level the question may appear clear because the giving of the money would not help Mrs G. However he disagreed with that conclusion:

> the word 'interests' in the phrase 'best interests' is not confined to matters of self-interest or, putting it another way, a court could conclude in an appropriate case that it is in the interests of P for P to act altruistically. It seems unlikely that the legislature thought that the power to make gifts should be confined to gifts which were not altruistic or where the gift would confer a benefit on P (or the donor of the lasting power of attorney) by reason of that person's emotional response to knowing of the gift.[63]

The judge noted that under section 4(6)(b) and (c) the Court was required to consider matters P would be likely to consider if she had capacity. These could include altruism.

This is a welcome acknowledgement that the legal understanding is not, indeed it should not, be limited to selfish interests entirely. Obligations, relationships and concern for fellow people can, quite properly, be taken into account under a rich account of what well-being involves.

iii. Human Rights Arguments

A rather different argument is that when the court interprets the meaning of best interests under the Mental Capacity Act 2005, it must do so bearing in mind the Human Rights Act 1998. These are not arguments that would be

---

[59] S Wolf, 'Happiness and Meaning: Two Aspects of the Good Life' (1997) *Social Philosophy and Policy* 207.
[60] Ibid 209.
[61] T Hope, A Slowther and J Eccles, 'Best Interests, Dementia and the Mental Capacity Act' (2005) 35 *Journal of Medical Ethics* 733.
[62] [2010] EWHC 3005 (COP).
[63] Ibid, para 35.

made from an ethic of care perspective, but could be used to support a result that would be consistent with it. The concept of best interests must be interpreted and given effect to in a way which respects the rights of the incapacitated individual and their carer under the European Convention on Human Rights. Under article 8 of the Convention, the right to respect for the private and family life of the incapacitated person and carer must be protected.[64] If the decision is going to severely impact the personal life of the carer then their article 8 rights will be engaged. Under article 8(2) the interests of the person lacking capacity can justify an interference in the carer's rights, but only if the interests are sufficiently strong to make the interference necessary and proportionate. The courts may therefore be required to take into account the human rights of carers when interpreting the best interests principle and this might mean that an order which only slightly benefits the incapacitated person, while greatly harming the carer could not be made.[65]

iv. Interconnection

It is not possible to consider P's well-being, without considering the well-being of those who are in a caring relationship with him or her. The interests of the two are intertwined. No carer could possibly undertake the task of caring if every decision which has to be made was solely on the basis of what is in the interests of the cared for person. As the US President's Council on Bioethics puts it:

> As a simple rule of thumb, caregivers should do the best they can do; they are never compelled to do what they cannot do, but they are obligated to see how much they can do without deforming or destroying their entire lives. But in practice, this rule of thumb rarely leads to any fixed rules, because every person faces different demands and has different capacities. And inevitably, we cannot do our best simultaneously in every area of our life: that is to say, we cannot do our best for everyone all the time; we cannot be there for everyone all the time; we cannot devote resources to everyone equally all the time. To be a caregiver is to confront not only the limitations of the person with dementia who relies upon us entirely, but our own limitations as human beings who are more than just caregivers or who are caregivers in multiple ways for multiple people.[66]

There is another important aspect of this issue. That is that emphasising interdependence and mutuality means that the division between carer and cared for dissolves.[67] In truth there is often give and take in the 'carer' and

---

[64] *Sheffield CC v S* [2002] EWHC 2278 (Fam).

[65] *B Borough Council v Mrs S, Mr S* [2006] EWHC 2584 (Fam) [2007] 1 FCR 574.

[66] President's Council on Bioethics, *Taking Care* (Washington, President's Council on Bioethics, 2004) 198.

[67] M Fine and C Glendinning, 'Dependence, Independence or Inter-Dependence? Revisiting the Concepts of Care and Dependency' (2005) 25 *Ageing and Society* 601, 619.

'cared for' relationship. Their relationship is marked by interdependency.[68] We have already explored this point in chapter three.

So can we be more precise about how the interests of carers should be taken into account? It is suggested that the key is to examine the decision at issue in the context of the relationship between two people. How does this decision fit in with the giving and taking involved in this relationship? This will mean that carers will not be treated 'as objects to be manipulated as part of patient care'.[69] There will be decisions that looked at in isolation be seen as favouring one party or another. However, if they are reasonable within the context of the caring relationship, they can be seen as an acceptable part of a relationship which is in the welfare of both parties. Of course, it is extremely difficult, if not impossible to imagine that a decision that severely harms either the carer or the dependant could be seen as justified in the context of a relationship.[70]

v. Conclusion

It may help to add what I am not saying.[71] I am not claiming that treating a person lacking capacity in a way which is not in their best interests, but promotes altruism, creates a moral good.[72] Altruism which is forced is probably not properly described as altruism. At least it does not exhibit the characteristics which we admire in altruism.[73] Nor am I saying that the procedure is justified because making decisions which benefit the caregiver can be shown to create benefits for the dependant person in the long run.[74] My claim also differs therefore from John Hardwig, who regards it as a matter of justice when families make sacrifices for an incapacitated patient.[75] His approach fails to place sufficient weight on the intermingling of the interests of the incapacitated person and his or her caregivers.

Rather my claim is that the incompetent person cannot be viewed in isolation. He or she must be viewed in the context of the relationships which he or she is in. This will be a fair and just assessment which promotes the rights

---

[68] D Gibson, *Aged Care: Old Policies, New Solutions* (Cambridge University Press, 2005).

[69] M Minow, 'Who's the Patient?' (1994) 53 *Maryland Law Review* 1173.

[70] For a different view see P Lewis, 'Procedures that are Against the Medical Interests of Incompetent Adults' (2002) 22 *Oxford Journal of Legal Studies* 575.

[71] Ibid.

[72] See J Lantos, 'Children as Organ Donors: An Argument for Involuntary Altruism' in G Burgio and J Lantos (eds), *Primum Non Nocere* (Elsevier, 1994).

[73] See J Seglow, 'Altruism and Freedom' (2002) 5 *Critical Review of International Social and Political Philosophy* 145.

[74] M Goodwin, 'My Sister's Keeper?: Law, Children, and Compelled Donation' (2007) 29 *Western New England Law Review* 357.

[75] J Hardwig, 'The Problem of Proxies with Interests of their Own: Toward a Better Theory of Proxy Decisions' (1993) 4 *Journal of Clinical Ethics* 20.

and interests of both parties. As with all healthy relationships, the care giving relationship will involve give and take. Under the orthodox analysis there will be some decisions which are in the interests of the person lacking capacity and some which are in the interests of the care giver. This is how it is in real life in a well working, caring relationship and this is how it should be in the law.

IV. Carers as Decision Makers

A person, foreseeing that they may lose capacity, may wish to make provision about how they will be treated if that happens. One option is to make an advance decision. Sections 24 to 26 of the Mental Capacity Act 2005 give effect to an advance decision to refuse treatment. The law on advance directives is complex and I will not go into it here.[76] For many individuals, however, there is such a variety of issues that could arise if capacity is lost, that rather than seeking to fix in advance what would happen in an advance directive, they prefer to appoint a respected friend to make decisions on their behalf. That is likely to be, although it need not be, someone they are in a caring relationship with. It is important that the law provides a mechanism to take into account the relationships a person is in, even when losing capacity.

Before exploring the legal mechanisms for appointing a substitute decision maker, it is worth remembering the position a carer will be in if nothing is done. Under the Mental Capacity Act 2005, section 5, a carer has the authorisation to act towards a person lacking capacity in accordance with their best interests. There is a general provision that protects anyone dealing with P. It means that acts which might otherwise be unlawful, are lawful. However, that only protects the position of the carer who has acted in a particular way towards P. It does not provide the carer with any authority or legal power to make decisions about how others may treat P. If the carer seeks that power then they need to apply for a more formal legal status. There are two options: lasting power of attorney or deputy.

A. Lasting Power of Attorney

Through a power of attorney a person with capacity can select a person to make decisions on their behalf if they were to lose capacity in the future.[77] The attorney can then make decisions on behalf of the individual only when

---

[76] J Herring, 'Losing it? Losing what? The Law and Dementia' (2009) *Child and Family Law Quarterly* 3.

[77] Mental Capacity Act 2005, s 9.

they lose capacity, assuming the appointment[78] has not been revoked. There are, however, restrictions on the attorney's decision-making power. They cannot make decisions about life-sustaining treatment unless the donor has stated they may.[79] Further, the holder of the lasting power of attorney must make decisions which are in P's best interests and must take into account the likelihood of P regaining capacity.[80]

Jo Samanta argues that these limitations are overly restrictive and do not enable P to exercise autonomous choice, by appointing a person whose views will be respected, even if they are not objectively in P's best interests.[81] Nor, quite possibly, do they enable the lasting power of attorney to find solutions that will work in the context of their relationships, even though the particular decision is harmful to P. They also open up the possibility that a medical professional who disagrees with the approach taken by an attorney will simply state they believe the decision not to be in P's interests and so the attorney's direction can be ignored.

Whether Samanta's concerns are realised will depend on two factors. The first is the extent to which the relationships P is in are taken into account. If a more relational approach to best interests, of the kind described above, is used, the court should attach weight to the importance of the relationship between P and the attorney. A second factor is the extent to which respect will be paid to P's exercise of autonomy in appointing the attorney. The courts may well determine that only where the attorney's decision is causing clear harm to P should the attorney's decision be open to challenge. If the courts adopt these two arguments then sufficient weight can be attached to the relationship between P and their attorney.

i. Deputies

If P has not made a power of attorney then a deputy can be appointed by the court. The court is likely to make such an order if there are a series of decisions which need to be made about P and it will be helpful to have a single person make them on P's behalf, rather than the decisions being made by the court. The court can restrict which decisions can be made by the deputy and can restrict the length of the appointment. The deputy, like the attorney, must act in accordance with the best interests of P. While the Act does not restrict who can be a deputy, it makes sense that it is someone who knows P well and

---

[78] The appointment of a lasting power of attorney must satisfy the formality requirements set out in the Mental Capacity Act 2005, sch 1.

[79] Ibid, s 11(8).

[80] Ibid, s 4.

[81] J Samanta, 'Lasting Powers of Attorney for Healthcare under the Mental Capacity Act 2005' (2009) 17 *Medical Law Review* 377.

is in a position to assess their best interests. That is likely to be someone with whom they are in a caring relationship. There are limitations on the powers of deputies: they cannot prohibit a person from having contact with P, nor direct who shall provide health care to a person. If necessary a court can make an order relating to those matters.[82]

The way the law has developed on this is interesting. On the one hand, the courts have recognised in *Re P*[83] that when deciding about who should be appointed as a deputy, the starting point should be to consider the family before state care:

> in a society structured as is ours, it is not the State, whether through the agency of an authority or the court, which is primarily responsible for individuals who are subjects or citizens of the State. It is for those who naturally have their care and wellbeing at heart, that is to say, members of the family, where they are willing and able to do so, to take first place in the care and upbringing, not only of children, but of those whose needs, because of disability, extend far into adulthood. It seems to me at least that the Act ought to be read subject to that overriding policy aim.[84]

From this flowed the principle that where family members offer themselves as deputies, the court should 'approach such an application with considerable openness and sympathy', unless there are family disputes or other evidence that queries their suitability.[85]

On the other hand, there is the recognition that appointing a deputy may not be necessary in many cases. *G and E v Manchester CC*[86] emphasises this:

> The Act and Code are therefore constructed on the basis that the vast majority of decisions concerning incapacitated adults are taken informally and collaboratively by individuals or groups of people consulting and working together. It is emphatically not part of the scheme underpinning the Act that there should be one individual who as a matter of course is given a special legal status to make decisions about incapacitated persons.[87]

The appropriateness of appointing a deputy may depend on the number of people in a close relationship with P. Where there is a single person, then appointing them as a deputy seems appropriate. Where, as in *G and E*, there are a number of individuals in relationship with P, the appointment of a deputy may not be appropriate and, as suggested in that case, it may be better to rely on a more informal collaborative approach.

---

[82] *G and E v Manchester and F* [2010] EWHC 2512(COP) (Fam), para 22.
[83] [2010] EWHC 1592 (Fam).
[84] Ibid, para 8.
[85] Ibid, para 9.
[86] [2010] EWHC 2512(COP) (Fam).
[87] Ibid, para 57.

V. Mental Health Act 1983 and Carers

The 'nearest relative' of a person detained under the Mental Health Act 1983 has a special place in the legislation to ensure the rights of detained people are respected. Their rights include, for example, that their nearest relative must be consulted before an application is made to admit a patient under section 3 of the Act to make an application for the patient's admission and detention in hospital under sections 2, 3 and 4, or for reception into guardianship under section 7 (although it is important to note that the Mental Health Act Code of Practice states that this role is normally better left to an approved mental health professional). The other roles of the nearest relative include:

(1) applying for detention in hospital if the mentally disordered person cannot be cared for in the community;
(2) being consulted when an approved social worker applies for detention;
(3) objecting to detention for treatment;
(4) directing the discharge of a detained patient who is not dangerous to self or others;
(5) applying to a Mental Health Review Tribunal if discharge is barred by the psychiatrist certifying that the patient is likely to be a danger to self or to others; and
(6) being kept informed if the patient is discharged from detention.

The definition of 'nearest relative' in section 26 of the Act is as follows:

(1) husband or wife or civil partner;
(2) son or daughter;
(3) father or mother;
(4) brother or sister;
(5) grandparent;
(6) grandchild;
(7) uncle or aunt;
(8) nephew or niece.

If none of these are available under section 26(7), a person who has been residing with the patient for at least five years prior to the admission to hospital may be consulted. The court also has the power to appoint someone else not on this list to be the 'nearest relative'.[88]

Carers, as carers, are not mentioned in the list. It is true that a person not included in the definition in section 26 could be appointed by the county

---

[88] Mental Health Act 1983, s 29.

court to act as the patient's nearest relative,[89] or be authorised to act as the nearest relative.[90] However, section 26(5) states that if the 'patient ordinarily resides with or is cared for by one or more of his relatives', then that relative will be the nearest relative unless there are others higher up the list who have undertaken a caring role or reside with the patient. Although this is a welcome recognition of the significance of care, it should be noted that this offers no status to a carer who is not also a relative. A direct contrast can be seen with the Mental Health (Scotland) Act 2003 which gives priority to carer status over family blood ties in deciding who can challenge detention. The preference for the blood relationship over the caring relationships is hard to justify. If the role of the 'next relative' is to preserve the interests and respect the wishes of the person detained, it is sensible for this to be the person who knows them best. This may well be a person who has a formal relationship with the person, but a blood tie is no guarantee that the person has the best interests of the other at heart or knows them well. A close caring relationship will demonstrate both of these things.

VI. Human Tissue Act 2004 and Carers

The Human Tissue Act 2004 was passed to regulate the storage and use of human material. Where that material is to be used for certain purposes then 'appropriate consent is required'. If the person whose material it is is alive and competent then their consent is required, but if the person has died or they are incompetent, then the Act produces a list of 'qualifying relationships':

(1) spouse or partner;
(2) parent or child;
(3) brother or sister;
(4) grandparent or grandchild;
(5) child of a person falling within paragraph (c);
(6) stepfather or stepmother;
(7) half-brother or half-sister;
(8) friend of longstanding.[91]

Notably this list does not include carers. The carer will have washed and cared for the body, and yet their role is unrecognised by the terms of the Act. The list is determined largely by virtue of marriage, civil partnership or blood ties. This means that a carer who is not a relative will not have a say

---

[89] Ibid.
[90] Mental Health (Hospital, Guardianship and Consent to Treatment) Regulations 1983 (SI 1983 No 2156), reg 14.
[91] Human Tissue Act 2004, s 3.

in how the body of the deceased is treated. This is so even if the relative has played a full role in the deceased's care. Nor is there any preference given to a relative who was a carer over another relative higher up the list who was not a carer. The views of the person who has washed, lifted or stroked the body of the deceased will count for nothing unless they are lucky enough to also be a relative.

VII. Autonomy

Earlier in this chapter I made the controversial claim that in making a decision about a person lacking capacity (P), a decision could be made which, on a superficial level, harmed P if that was a fair part of a caring relationship with someone else. I explained how a relational understanding of best interests, and a proper appreciation of what best interests included, could justify that decision. I wish now to make an even more controversial claim and that is that even an interference in the wishes of a person with capacity can be justified when the relational context is taken into account.

For those who possess legal capacity, the cardinal principle is the right of self-determination or autonomy.[92] Subject to the constraints of the law, people remain generally free to live their lives as they wish. In the context of medical law this is reflected in the right to bodily integrity—the right for our bodies not to be touched or interfered with without our consent. As Justice Cardozo famously declared: 'Every human being of adult years and sound mind has a right to determine what shall be done with his own body; and a surgeon who performs an operation without his patient's consent, commits an assault ...'[93]

As indicated at the start of this chapter, a consideration of caring relationships challenges the pre-eminence which is given to the principle of autonomy. As Pamela Scheininger put it:

> Because the law is conceived of in its application to the isolated individual rather than in its application to the individual's various associations and relationships, the law does not accurately reflect the reality of human existence. The legitimacy of the law is thus challenged. Individual persons do not operate as independent, separate entities, but as interdependent, connected parts of larger groups. In failing to deal with laws as they affect human relationships, lawmakers ignore a fundamental aspect of our humanity ...[94]

---

[92] D Beyleveld and R Brownsword, *Consent in the Law* (Hart, 2007) 1–35.
[93] *Schloendorff v Society of N.Y. Hosp* 105 N.E. 92, 93 (N.Y. 1914).
[94] P Scheininger 'Legal Separateness, Private Connectedness: An Impediment to Gender equality in the Family' (1998) 31 *Columbia Journal of Law and Social Problems* 283.

A recognition of the significance of caregiving relationships which are central to all our lives shifts the starting point away from the autonomous individual to a person sited in interdependent relationships, as discussed in chapters two and three.[95]

Once, then, we accept our inherent vulnerability and dependency on others, the image of the all-powerful rights bearer falls away. So seen, autonomy is not so much about rational choice but, rather, it is relational. Far then from needing what Justice Brandeis identified as the 'right to be let alone',[96] we need our relationships and corresponding responsibilities recognised and protected. Our sense of self is a mixture of interlocking and sometimes conflicting social identities.[97] This then challenges the very notion that there are medical decisions which are 'mine' in the sense of just affecting me. Indeed, as will be discussed later, even to say 'my body is mine' is to over-simplify the issue.[98] We need then to accept that decisions about medical treatment are not just the patients' decisions. Our bodies and lives in their interconnected states do not readily break down into individualised models, whereby the interests of one person automatically trump another.[99]

Take a hypothetical example. Imagine a wife has been caring for her husband for many years. He has an incontinence problem, which could be resolved by minor surgery. He, with capacity to do so, refuses to consent. She is very keen on him having it due to the unpleasantness of having to solve the issue. The straightforward legal analysis of this dilemma is that his right to bodily integrity and right of autonomy would mean that the operation could not be performed without his consent. An argument that the interests of the wife would justify performing the procedure without his consent would not get off the ground.[100] The analysis presented in this chapter would show that this is a far from straightforward case. The bodies here are connected: what happens to his body affects hers. Her bodily integrity is affected by his not having the operation, just as his will be if he does. Arguably, given the relationship between the two of them his having a minor procedure would be a reasonable sacrifice as part of that relationship and the responsibilities they owe to each other following it. An approach based on an ethic of care would encourage a dialogue between the patients and those around them to determine what ought to be done, rather than the use of a court order.

---

[95] S Dodds, 'Depending on Care: Recognition of Vulnerability and the Social Contribution of Care Provision' (2007) 21 *Bioethics* 500, 501.

[96] *Olmstead v United States* 277 U.S. 438, 478 (1928) (Brandeis J, dissenting).

[97] See A Donchin, 'Understanding Autonomy Relationally' (2001) 26 *Journal of Medicine and Philosophy* 365; J Nedelsky, 'Reconceiving Autonomy: Sources, Thoughts and Possibilities' (1989) 1 *Yale Journal of Law and Feminism* 7.

[98] See J Herring and P-L Chau, 'My Body, Your Body, Our Bodies' (2007) 15 *Medical Law Review* 34, 51–52.

[99] A Ho, 'The Individualist Model of Autonomy and the Challenge of Disability' (2008) 5 *Journal of Bioethical Inquiry* 193.

[100] *S v St George's NHS Trust* [1998] 3 WLR 936.

It would recognise that the decision needs to be made in the context of the inter-dependent relationships between all those involved. Depending on a more detailed analysis of the facts I could support the making of an order, although many ethic of care supporters would not, I suspect. What all ethic of care supporters would agree on is that such a case is not simply resolved by saying that it is his body and his right to autonomy which is the only argument that carries weight.

VIII. Bodies

One of the topics medical lawyers love to debate is whether a person owns their body. Although there is much discussion among lawyers and philosophers about whether bodies are property, and whether people can or should regard their bodies as their property. Most of those who have written on that issue can broadly be said to fall into one of two camps. There are those who argue that bodies should be regarded as property which can be owned by the individual. Others deny this but claim that rights of self-determination, privacy or autonomy can be used to ensure protection of a person's interests in their body. This is not the place to explore the arguments in that debate. I wish to challenge an assumption that underpins both of these assumptions. That is that our bodies are ours.

P-L Chau and I have argued that to say 'my body is mine' is to over-simplify the issue:

> First, our bodies are often in a state of dependency on other bodies. Second, our bodies are constantly interacting and reacting with the world around us. Third, our bodies are not immutable entities, but are constantly changing and recreating themselves. We need to move away from a vision of a society of bodies which are only of concern to ourselves and recognise that to a significant degree, our bodies depend on other bodies and the world around us for their meaning and survival.[101]

Our bodies are deeply interconnected with and interdependent upon other bodies. Our bodies are constantly interacting with the world around us and our bodies are not static organisms, but are constantly changing and mutating.[102] We have already seen that our bodies start in a relationship of connection through pregnancy. Many of the activities that give our life value and meaning involve bodily interchange: from breast feeding to sport; from sexual intercourse to shaking hands: it is the intermixing of bodies that give them meaning.

---

[101] See J Herring and P-L Chau, 'My Body, Your Body, Our Bodies' (2007) 15 *Medical Law Review* 34, 51–52.
[102] Ibid.

Caregiving too often involves bodily interaction. For example, not only is a child dependent on their carer, but the carer becomes dependent on the child. If the child suffers an infectious childhood illness and is required to remain indoors, in effect this quarantine is imposed on the body of the carer too. If the child will not sleep, nor, in reality, will the parent. Our bodies are 'leaky', to use the term coined by Margrit Shildrick.[103]

I argue that a key component of understanding our bodies is that they exist in relationship with other bodies, are interdependent with other bodies and are in a constant state of flux. These aspects are not caught by the approaches normally taken to the legal status of bodies based on property or rights to integrity or privacy.

IX. Rationing

There is now general acceptance that rationing has become a routine part of the provision of health care services in both the United States and United Kingdom.[104] In England rationing decisions are made quite openly with the National Institute for Health and Clinical Excellence (NICE[105]) determining which medicines are, or are not, to be made available on the NHS.[106] The rationing of medical treatment is not only a controversial and complex topic, but also one of great societal importance.[107] As George P Smith explains:

> Essentially, all efforts to achieve justice in the distribution of health care resources are utilitarian in character and definition. Since these resources are not infinite, they cannot be offered to or used by everyone. This, of necessity, then forces choices between those individuals and among groups seeking their use. Allowing improper distribution of these scarce resources is not only inefficient, it is wasteful.[108]

Not surprisingly, attempts have been made to produce a formula that will ensure that decisions are made which take on board, in an appropriate way, the benefits and costs of different treatments and enable them to be compared.

---

[103] M Shildrick, *Leaky Bodies and Boundaries. Feminism, Postmodernism and (Bio)ethics* (Routledge, 1997).

[104] GP Smith II, *Distributive Justice and the New Medicine* (Edward Elgar, 2008).

[105] To critics this acronym holds a degree of irony: J Harris, 'It's Not NICE to Discriminate' (2005) 31 *Journal of Medical Ethics* 373.

[106] K Syrett, *Law, Legitimacy and the Rationing of Health Care* (Cambridge University Press, 2009).

[107] J King, 'The Justiciability of Resource Allocation' (2007) 70 *Modern Law Review* 197; K Syrett, 'Nice Work? Rationing, Review and the "Legitimacy Problem" in the New NHS' (2002) 10 *Medical Law Review* 1.

[108] GP Smith II, *Distributive Justice and the New Medicine* (Edward Elgar, 2008) 1.

Additionally, such formulas are perhaps the smallest of fig leaves to hide behind in the face of a patient being denied treatment:[109] 'The computer says no.'

This is not the place to consider the general issues concerning health care rationing.[110] Here the focus will be on the extent to which the interests of carers are and should be taken into account when health care rationing decisions are made. Most rationing decisions are taken using an approach based on Quality Adjusted Life Years (QALY). This is the approach used by NICE.[111] This is probably the most popular way of analysing the cost-effectiveness of treatments and is widely used in decision making when rationing health care. QALY, as used in rationing decisions, requires an assessment of three factors:

— How many extra years of life will the treatment provide this patient?
— What will the quality of those extra years be?
— How expensive is the treatment?

A treatment that provides a year of perfect health scores as one; however, a year of less than perfect health will score less than one. Death is equivalent to 0. Under QALY, therefore, a treatment that provides a patient with an extra year of perfect health would be preferred to a treatment which provides a patient with an extra year, but a year of pain and low quality of life.[112] A treatment which offered a large number of QALYs for a small amount of money would be highly cost effective, while one that produced a low number of QALYs for a large amount of money would not be.[113] Someone required to ration health services can therefore examine a range of different services and consider how many QALYs for how much money is provided by particular treatments.[114] NICE indicates that if a treatment gives £20,000 per QALY it is likely to be approved, whereas if it is more than £30,000 there will need to be a strong justification before approval.[115] There are many ways in which one could argue that QALYs are problematic. For the current purposes my complaint will be with the way they are too often used which ignores the significance of caregivers.

---

[109] For discussion of needs in this context see A Hasman, T Hope, and L Østerdal, 'Health Care Need: Three Interpretations' (2006) 33 *Journal of Applied Philosophy* 145.

[110] See J Herring, *Medical Law and Ethics* (Oxford University Press, 2012) ch 2.

[111] See GP Smith II, *Distributive Justice and the New Medicine* (Edward Elgar, 2008) 2–3.

[112] M Adler, 'QALYs and Policy Evaluation: A New Perspective' (2006) 6 *Yale Journal of Health Policy Law and Ethics* 1, 1–2.

[113] Ibid 2.

[114] National Institute for Health and Clinical Excellence, *The Guidance Manual* (NICE, 2007) para 8.1.3; National Institute for Health and Clinical Excellence, *Social Value Judgements* (NICE, 2005) para 4.2.

[115] National Institute for Health and Clinical Excellence, *Social Value Judgements* (NICE, 2005) para 4.2.

QALY is normally used in a highly individualistic fashion, focusing just on the impact of the treatment on the particular patient. The improvement in the patient's quality of life alone is considered and the impact on their caregivers counts for nothing. Imagine, for example, a drug which prevents incontinence. It may be with a highly incapacitated patient receiving excellent care that the benefit of the drug will be very limited.[116] It might therefore score very low indeed on a QALY scale. The fact that the drug might have a dramatic impact on the quality of life for their caregiver would not be relevant under a traditional analysis of QALY, unless it can be shown that the impact on the caregiver is such as to affect the quality of care and thereby harm the patient.[117]

Even if the interests of caregivers are examined, they may be found to count for nothing. In 2006 NICE considered whether to approve a drug which could delay the impact of Alzheimer's disease. They considered whether to take into account the benefit of the treatment to caregivers, but concluded:

> The Committee considered that although at any point in time a carer may have a higher utility if they were caring for a person responding to drug treatment than if the person were not on the drug or not responding to the drug, the effect of the drug would be to delay progression of the condition, in which case the carer would still be faced at some time in the future with the same difficulties caused by disease progression. Exceptions could be if the person did not progress to later and more difficult stages of the disease within 5 years or because of death.[118]

This argument is, with respect, unconvincing. The claim appears to be that if someone is going to have the burdens of caring for a relative suffering from Alzheimer's disease at some point in their life, then it matters not whether that is now or at some future point in time. So medication which simply delays the inevitable onset of Alzheimer's disease does not benefit the caregiver. However, delaying the onset of the condition provides the benefit of the caregiver having a longer time with their loved one before the condition takes its toll. Maybe in purely financial terms the loss to the caregiver is no different, but in terms of quality of life there is certainly a loss.

The failure to consider the interests of caregivers when making rationing decisions means that the costs to national health systems or insurance companies' budgets are given weight, but the costs to caregivers count for nothing. Yet the costs to the individual caregiver are costs to real people whose lives bear the blight of caring. By contrast, any cost to the state or

---

[116] See J Herring, 'The Place of Carers' in M Freeman (ed), *Law and Bioethics* (Oxford University Press, 2008) for a discussion of this issue as it applied to the decision of NICE to limit access to drugs to treat Alzheimer's disease.

[117] National Institute for Health and Clinical Excellence, *Donepezil, Galantamine, Rivastigmine (Review) and Memantine for the Treatment of Alzheimer's Disease (Appraisal Consultation)* (NICE, 2006) para 4.2.6.

[118] Ibid para 4.3.10.2.

insurance company is spread widely. Politically, of course, the approach is understandable. Costs to the Government are in the public eye and impact on the sensitive issue of levels of taxation. Costs to caregivers go unnoticed in the public arena, although they are real enough to those who suffer them, and real enough in their effect on society as a whole.

It must not be thought, however, that including the costs to caregivers when making rationing decisions is without difficulty. There are potential dangers in that those cared for by a large number of caregivers or a more vulnerable caregiver will be regarded as having a greater call on health care resources than a person who is alone, with no family or caregivers.[119] In *R (Rogers) v Swindon Primary Care Trust*,[120] the Court of Appeal approved the use of social and personal characteristics for determining which patients should be given Herceptin[121] under the NHS. The Court held that it could be appropriate to 'make the difficult choice to fund treatment for a woman with, say, a disabled child and not for a woman in different personal circumstances'.[122]

Jo Bridgeman has rejected such an approach.[123] She has argued:

> The needs of a child with disabilities are no different whether they are met by her mother or another. The needs of a woman with breast cancer are no different, whether she is the carer of a child with disabilities or not.[124]

In some ways this is a surprising comment in the light of her comments in the same article which reflect many of the views expressed in this book,[125] namely that we should not view patients in isolation, but in the context of a network of dependencies. The problem with saying 'the needs of a woman with breast cancer are no different, whether she is the caregiver of a child with disabilities or not' is that it imagines we can assess the needs of a patient without looking at their network of relationships in which they find themselves.

However, this may be to misinterpret Bridgeman's point. Her argument is that we are all in a network of dependencies. So all women with breast cancer have people who are dependent on them and we should not be in the job of giving greater preference to some dependent relationships over others. Indeed, there is a danger that the woman's own identity becomes subsumed

---

[119] Although see D Shickle, 'Public Preference for Health Care' (1997) *Bioethics* 277 for some evidence that surveys of the general public suggest that the number of dependants should be a factor in rationing health care. Contrast P Anand and A Wailoo, 'Utility versus Rights to Publicly Provided Rights: Augments and Evidence from Health Care Rationing' (2000) 67 *Economica* 543.

[120] [2006] EWCA Civ 392.

[121] A drug for use in the treatment of cancer.

[122] *R (Rogers) v Swindon Primary Care Trust* [2006] EWCA Civ 392, para 77.

[123] J Bridgeman, '"Exceptional" Women, Healthcare Consumers and the Inevitability of Caring' (2007) 15 *Feminist Legal Studies* 235.

[124] Ibid 236.

[125] We would both agree that a society seeking to promote an ethic of care would ensure that such essential drugs were available.

within a 'caring role'. As Bridgeman notes, it is interesting that the primary care trust in *Rogers* regarded as an exceptional case for treatment for breast cancer, 'caring for a disabled child'; rather than, say, outstanding success in a career, or other criterion.[126]

So, we have seen in this discussion that the primary method of allocating health care resources, the QALY approach, fails appropriately to take into account the interests of caregivers. In the allocation of health resources, it has been argued, the benefits to those caring for and being cared by the patient should be taken into account, as well as the benefits to the patient themselves. Indeed it has been argued that there is no way of separating the benefits to the patient and those they are in caring relationships with. It has, however, been acknowledged this is not straight-forward. There is a lack of research into the benefits for caregivers of particular medication and, in particular, a lack of a theoretical model which gives appropriate weight to those benefits when rationing decisions are made. Further, there are the difficulties inherent in seeking to compare different sets of caring relationships. Despite these difficulties, it is argued that rationing decisions should not be restricted to considering the benefit to an individual patient, without recognition being given to the network of relationships within which they live.

X. Confidentiality

One of the central pillars of medical law is the principle of protection of confidential information. This principle is rarely challenged. It is justified by a combination of arguments, including an implied contract between the doctor and patient; the public interest in ensuring that patients can be completely open with their doctors; and a claim of ownership in the private information. There are many other arguments that are added and expounded to justify this important protection.[127]

The issue for this book is how confidentiality relates to the position of those in caring relationship with the individual.[128] In relation to patients with capacity, it seems clear that consent from the individual is required before disclosure can be made, unless exceptional circumstances can be shown, such

---

[126] J Bridgeman, '"Exceptional" Women, Healthcare Consumers and the Inevitability of Caring' (2007) 15 *Feminist Legal Studies* 235.

[127] See, for further discussion, J Herring, *Medical Law and Ethics* (Oxford University Press, 2012) ch 4.

[128] MD Pérez-Cárceles, JE Pereñiguez, E Osuna, A Luna, 'Balancing Confidentiality and the Information Provided to Families of Patients in Primary Care' (2005) 31 *Journal of Medical Ethics* 531.

as issues around child protection.[129] In relation to patients lacking consent, the General Medical Council states:

'You may need to share personal information with a patient's relatives, friends or carers to enable you to assess the patient's best interests. But that does not mean they have a general right of access to the patient's records or to have irrelevant information about, for example, the patient's past healthcare. You should also share relevant personal information with anyone who is authorised to make decisions on behalf of, or who is appointed to support and represent, a mentally incapacitated patient.[130]

This is a little bit vague as to what and when information can be disclosed. Notably the guidance suggests that early discussion should be had with patients about how their information is shared with friends or relatives.[131] Although the official guidance suggests that carers should be given the information they need, there is evidence that in practice they are not.[132]

There are practical reasons why in a caring relationship information should not be regarded as straightforwardly belonging to only one person. A carer needs to know relevant medical information to carry out their effective caring role.[133] The 1999 *Caring About Carers* Report acknowledged that:

Carers need good information on the health needs and treatment of the person they are caring for—especially on medication: when to take it, and recognising any side effects arising from it. They need information to allow them to deal with the symptoms of some illnesses and to recognise when they should urgently ask for professional help and where to get such help, especially when they are caring for someone with a mental health problem.[134]

Given the interaction between bodies in caring roles, in the case of infectious diseases there may be very good reasons for the disclosure of information. Unless caring is to be discouraged, openness about the health conditions of a person which pose a direct serious risk to a carer need to be revealed. There is strong evidence that carers may provide informational, functional and emotional support[135] and that patients do rely on those they are in caring relationships with to assist with making decisions. [136]

---

[129] Department of Health, *Confidentiality: NHS Code of Practice* (Department of Health, 2003).

[130] General Medical Council, *Confidentiality* (GMC, 2009).

[131] Ibid para 64.

[132] G Machlin, 'Carers and Confidentiality—Law and Good Practice', available at http://its-services.org.uk/silo/files/carers-and-confidentiality-law-and-good-practice.pdf.

[133] J Rapaport, S Bellringer, V Pinfold and P Huxley, 'Carers and Confidentiality in Mental Health Care: Considering the Role of the Carer's Assessment: A Study of Service Users', Carers' and Practitioners' Views' (2006) 14 *Health and Social Care in the Community* 357.

[134] Department of Health, *Caring About Carers* (Department of Health, 1999) para 15.

[135] R Gilbar, 'Family Involvement, Independence, and Patient Autonomy in Practice' (2011) *Medical Law Review* 192.

[136] C Charles et al. 'Shared Decision-Making in the Medical Encounter: What Does it Mean (or it Takes at Least Two to Tango)' (1997) 44 *Social Science and Medicine* 681.

This is not as radical a claim as may at first appear. As the NHS Code of Practice on confidentiality acknowledges:

Similarly, whilst patients may understand that information needs to be shared between members of care teams and between different organisations involved in healthcare provision, this may not be the case and the efforts made to inform them should reflect the breadth of the required disclosure. This is particularly important where disclosure extends to non-NHS bodies.[137]

Carers can legitimately be regarded as a part of the health care team providing care to a patient. The NHS Code of Practice acknowledges this:

Carers often provide valuable healthcare and, subject to complying with the best parental responsibility practice outlined, every effort should be made to support and facilitate their work. Only information essential to a patient's care should be disclosed and patients should be made aware that this is the case. However, the explicit consent of a competent patient is needed before disclosing information to a carer. The best interests of a patient who is not competent to consent may warrant disclosure.[138]

The position is, however, more complicated than is often presented. A key principle of confidentiality is that information about oneself should be kept confidential. However, that assumes that the notion of personal confidential information is a coherent one. From the perspective of this book it is not. In the life of a caring relationship, information is commonly shared. The information about one body is information that is relevant to another body. An illness affecting one person will affect the person they are in a caring relationship with. The health of one is intimately connected to the health of another.

Genetic information is, perhaps, the most obvious example of this.[139] The genetic information in one body can be highly revealing about the genetic information in a close relative. To describe the genetic information of one person as 'theirs' is a fiction in the sense that the information is not just about them, but others genetically related to them. That is a particularly powerful illustration of the interconnection between lives and bodies that blur the line between what information belongs to one person or another.[140]

More controversial and difficult is the issue of children's confidentiality. Plenty of commentators argue that the current law fails to adequately protect children's right to confidentiality.[141] While the law appears to have developed

---

[137] Department of Health, *Confidentiality: NHS Code of Practice* (Department of Health, 2003) para 12.

[138] Ibid 40.

[139] H Widdows and C Mullen (eds), *The Governance Of Genetic Information: Who Decides?* (Cambridge University Press, 2009).

[140] R Rhodes, 'Genetic Links, Family Ties, and Social Bonds: Rights and Responsibilities in the Face of Genetic Knowledge' (1998) 23 *Journal of Medicine and Philosophy* 10.

[141] J Loughrey, 'Can You Keep a Secret? Children, Human Rights, and the Law of Medical Confidentiality' [2008] *Child and Family Law Quarterly* 312.

so that clearly a competent child has a right to medical confidentiality,[142] the position of incompetent children is less clear. Joan Loughney argues that 'It should be recognised that violating a non-competent child's right to confidentiality, and betraying his trust, of itself harms his welfare.' Leaving aside for the moment the difficulty with the concept of betraying the trust of a person who lacks capacity, what is missing from this analysis is that breach of confidentiality is essential if the doctor is to act lawfully in a child's welfare. Let us imagine a parent takes a child to a doctor and the doctor diagnoses the child's condition for which an injection is required. Under the law only the parent can consent. How could the doctor obtain consent without 'breaching confidence'? A doctor must obtain consent. Loughney admits this, accepting, 'arguably the right to confidentiality of the very young will not be breached if disclosure is confined to what is required for the care and treatment of the child'. Where I agree with Loughney is that the right of access to the information should not be seen as a kind of parental right. However, the child-carer relationship is so close that information about the child becomes information about the carer. It is not possible to disentangle their lives or interests. The apparent injustice in relation to children is the inappropriate approach towards confidentiality in caring relationships generally.

To conclude, the current approach on confidentiality privileges an individualistic approach.[143] As Gilbar has argued about the current approach to confidentiality:[144]

Arguably, the roots of this legal position reflect a liberal-individualistic discourse. The legal approach to confidentiality is based on an individualistic perception of patient autonomy in that the patient is viewed as separate from others and free from social constraints when making informed choices, so long as he/she does not harm others. The unit of medical care, according to this legal position, consists of only one member—the individual patient.

We need to rethink confidentiality in relation to relationships of care. There will be some information which genuinely relates only to one person and has no relevance to the current relationship. But for those in interconnected caring relationships, health information is often mutual.

---

[142] R (Axon) v Secretary of State for Health (Family Planning Association Intervening) [2006] EWCA 37 (Admin).

[143] D Wulff, S St George and F Besthorn, 'Revisiting Confidentiality: Observations from Family Therapy Practice' (2011) 33 Journal of Family Therapy 199.

[144] R Gilbar, 'Medical Confidentiality within the Family: The Doctor's Duty Reconsidered' (2004) 18 International Journal of Law, Policy and the Family 195.

XI. Personhood

A central theme in some disputes over medical law and ethics is personhood. When personhood begins or ends can be key to an understanding of moral status, particularly in disputes over the beginning or end of life.

Typical of the pro-life position on abortion would be this comment:[145]

> The adult human being that is now you or me is the same being who, at an earlier stage, was an adolescent and, before that, a child, an infant, a fetus, and an embryo. Even in the embryonic stage, you and I were undeniably whole living members of the species Homo sapiens. We were then, as we are now, distinct and complete—though, in the beginning, developmentally immature—human organisms. We were not mere parts of other organisms.[146]

The argument is that as the fetus contains the entire genetic material of the adult it will become it has the hallmark of humanity and is a person.

By contrast there are those who deny the embryo has personhood from conception and argue that the features of personhood are factors such as those listed by Joseph Fletcher:[147]

(1) Minimal intelligence
(2) Self-awareness
(3) Self-control
(4) A sense of time
(5) A sense of futurity
(6) A sense of the past
(7) The capability to relate to others
(8) Concern for others
(9) Communication
(10) Control of existence
(11) Curiosity
(12) Balance of rationality/feeling
(13) Idiosyncrasy change/changeability
(14) Neo-cortical function.

As the fetus lacks such features, or only has them to a limited extent, it cannot claim the moral or legal status of personhood. There is little agreement as to when these characteristics are acquired. For some it will be in the later stages of pregnancy, although for others it is not until sometime after birth that these characteristics are displayed sufficiently to grant personhood.[148]

---

[145] R George, 'Embryo Ethics' (2008) 137 *Daedalus* 23, 23.
[146] R George, *Statement on the Cloning Report Issued by the President's Council on Bioethics* (2002).
[147] J Fletcher, *Humanhood: Essays in Biomedical Ethics* (Prometheus Books, 1979) 15.
[148] P Singer, *Practical Ethics* (Cambridge University Press, 1979).

An approach based on a relationship of care would argue that both these attempts to define personhood are flawed as they focus on status as the source of legal rights and obligations. Martha Nussbaum explains why she believes the individual should be the basic unit for political thought:

> It means, first of all, that liberalism responds sharply to the basic fact that each person has a course from birth to death that is not precisely the same as that of any other person; that each person is one and not more than one, that each feels pain in his or her own body, that the food given to A does not arrive in the stomach of B.[149]

It will be immediately apparent that what she says is not true of the fetus. The pain of the mother can affect the child and the food given to the mother will certainly arrive in the stomach of the fetus.

The argument of this book is that legal rights and duties should flow from relationship, not individual status. The fetus is in a particularly clear way a relational entity. The fetus and pregnant woman share fluids and space. There is no clear place where the body of the fetus ends and the body of the pregnant woman ends.[150] Pregnancy involves an extraordinary degree of corporeal intertwining. The status of the fetus must be understood in the context of the physical impact of the pregnancy: the profound biological changes that take place during it. The circumstances of the creation and nurturance of the fetus are sidelined by a focus on current fetal characteristics. The woman is not simply a fetal container.[151]

Our focus must be on the relationship between the pregnant woman and fetus. The question is not what rights we give the fetus, given its status. Rather, what is the appropriate legal response to the relationship between pregnant woman and fetus. They are both two and one. Any dealings with the fetus must be mediated by the woman; and some dealings with the woman will need to be mediated through the fetus. As Elvey[152] explains:

> ...the pregnant body ... calls into question these assumptions of separateness and sameness. When I am pregnant, 'my' body is both 'I' and 'not I', mine and not mine. The boundaries of the body shift as the pregnant body creates its own expanding space. While the skin stretches the boundary between the body and its outside is continually renegotiated, until in birth the inside enters the outside. The pregnant body is, moreover, two or more under the influence of a third, the placenta, through the agency of which self and other are interconnected.

Adopting a relational approach would mean that it would not be appropriate to consider questions based on observations about 'fetuses' in general. Instead we would need to consider the appropriate legal and moral response

---

[149] M Nussbaum, *Sex and Social Justice* (Oxford University Press, 1999) 62.

[150] J Herring and P-L Chau, 'My Body, Your Body, Our Bodies' (2007) 15 *Medical Law Review* 34.

[151] G Annas, 'Pregnant Women as Fetal Containers' (1986) 16 *Hastings Centre Report* 13.

[152] A Elvey, 'The Material Given: Bodies, Pregnant Bodies and Earth' (2003) 18 *Australian Feminist Studies* 199, 203.

to the relationships between fetus, pregnant woman, others in relationship with her and the wider society. It flows from this that, for example, the rights and responsibilities that a pregnant woman has would differ greatly in the case where pregnancy was desired and where the pregnancy was unwanted. They might also differ depending on social contexts or the set of personal relationships the pregnant woman was in. The nature of the relationship will affect what responsibilities may be imposed upon the community and those close to the woman. This has important implications for the provision of health care for pregnant woman and for social and financial support from the wider community and from the father.

I have used this approach to advocate a permissive abortion law, but one which is also protective of the relationship between the pregnant woman and the fetus when it is a wanted one. I will not develop that argument here.[153] Others could use the approach to argue for a more restrictive approach to abortion.

XII. Conclusion

This chapter has explored some of the issues that would arise if the law were to become centred around care and some of the deficiencies with the approach of the current law. There are plenty of other issues that could have been discussed. But what has been highlighted in this chapter is the way that medical law is built around highly individualised concepts of what are people, what are bodies and what our rights are. This chapter has promoted a relational approach to these questions. The aim of medicine should not be to treat the patient as an isolated individual, but seek to promote caring relationships and recognise the responsibilities and rights that arise from them.

---

[153] J Herring, 'The Loneliness of Status: The Legal and Moral Significance of Birth' in F Ebtehaj, J Herring, M Johnson and M Richards (eds), *Birth Rites and Rights* (Hart, 2011).

6

Family Law and Caring

I. Introduction

Care is at the centre of family life. Yet it is sexual relationships which have, for a long time, dominated family law and been regarded as the focus of the definition of a family and the marker for legal intervention. This chapter will argue in favour of a major refocusing in the area of family law around the notion of care. It will make four radical claims:

— That caring relationships rather than sexual relationships should be at the heart of family law.
— That parenthood is created by day-to-day care, rather than blood ties.
— That orders in relation to children must be made based on their relationships with others.
— That financial orders on separation are best justified as a way of ensuring that care work is undertaken and valued.

We have, I suggest, begun to see a shift in these directions over the past decade or two. This is to be welcomed and encouraged. It is to be hoped, that in future years we will see a more decisive move in the direction of these claims.

II. Care at the Heart of Family Law

Traditionally, family law has focused on sexual relationships. Marriage and cohabitation are still major themes in family law. Typically, textbooks on family law open with an explanation of the law of marriage, with an overly detailed analysis of the law on consummation. The authors explain that other relationships which are marriage-like (by which is meant sexual relationships) are protected in varying degrees. Moving on to parenthood, students are taught that parenthood is paradigmatically established by the biological link or through marriage. While textbooks on family law have extensive chapters on marriage; cohabitation and parenthood; little is written on, for example, the relationships between an adult child and her parent; a parent and an adult disabled child; a friend and someone with a disability; or the position of older people in families. Sex and blood ties are the meat and bones of family law.

Gillian Douglas notes that over the last 50 years parenthood has gradually replaced marriage as the 'the organizing principle and cornerstone of family law in England and Wales'.[1] However, marriage is still of considerable significance. Marriage still plays a major role in proof of parenthood. For example, a husband of a mother is automatically presumed to be the father, while an unmarried partner would need to establish his paternity through a parental agreement, court order or being registered as the father on the birth certificate.[2] As a result of the allocation of parenthood, married and unmarried fathers are treated differently for the purposes of allocation of parental responsibility. In the financial consequences of separation for parents, marriage still plays a major role. Carol Smart notes that the

> thinking behind the Children Act presumed that a distinction could be made between adult/adult relationships and adult/child relationships within a marriage (or cohabitation). Thus part of the argument resided in the idea that while divorce would foreclose on the spousal relationship, it need not affect the parents' relationship with the child. Thus two sets of relationships are envisaged which appear to be autonomous of one another and which can operate independently of one another.[3]

As Smart goes on to argue, the idea that we can treat the parents' relationship with the child separately from their relationship with each other has failed.

Writing in 2008, Lisa Glennon writes that:

> Marriage remains the central adult relationship to which obligations legitimately attach notwithstanding that these find expression, not during the relationship, but on divorce where strict property entitlements can be overridden, and maintenance obligations imposed at the court's discretion. Thus it is the ancillary relief system, which allocates capital and income on divorce, that is most expressive of the legal obligations created by marriage.[4]

---

[1] G Douglas, 'Marriage, Cohabitation, and Parenthood—from Contract to Status?' in S Katz, J Eekelaar and M Maclean (eds), *Cross Currents: Family Law and Policy in the US and England* (Oxford University Press, 2005) 211.

[2] See J Herring, *Family Law* (Pearson, 2011) ch 7 for the detail.

[3] C Smart, 'The "New" Parenthood: Fathers and Mothers after Divorce' in C Smart and E Silva (eds), *The New Family?* (Sage, 1999) 100.

[4] L Glennon, Obligations between Adult Partners: Moving from Form to Function?' (2008) 22 *International Journal of Law, Policy and the Family* 22.

Marriage is therefore still very much at the heart of family law. It is also, as we shall see, central to the law's approach to the definition of a family.

Some of the tensions in the correct focus of family law can be seen in *Fitzpatrick v Sterling Housing Association Ltd*,[5] where the House of Lords had to consider the meaning of 'family' for the purposes of the Rent Act 1977. The case involved a Mr Thompson and a Mr Fitzpatrick who had lived together in a flat for 18 years before the former's death. For Lord Slynn, writing in the majority, the hallmarks of family life were 'that there should be a degree of mutual inter-dependence, of the sharing of lives, of caring and love, or commitment and support'.[6] Nevertheless, Lord Nicholls stated that 'the paradigm family unit was, and still is, a husband and wife and their children'. Lord Clyde explained:

> It seems to me that essentially the bond must be one of love and affection, not of a casual or transitory nature, but in a relationship which is permanent or at least intended to be so. As a result of that personal attachment to each other other characteristics will follow, such as a readiness to support each other emotionally and financially, to care for and look after the other in times of need, and to provide a companionship in which mutual interests and activities can be shared and enjoyed together. It would be difficult to establish such a bond unless the couple were living together in the same house. It would also be difficult to establish it without an active sexual relationship between them or at least the potentiality of such a relationship.

As this diversity of views shows, it seems that the paradigm of marriage has a strong hold in definitions of marriage, although there is increasing willingness to include within the idea of a family relationship which is sufficiently similar to marriage. Craig Lind argues that the law still seeks 'to foster the marriage-based family as the ideal family of law', even though other relationships can be included within its ambit.[7] Interestingly, he suggests this may be why the law has been surprisingly progressive in recognising same-sex relationships. They can be seen as analogous to marriage and are allowed into the scope of family law.

The argument in this chapter will be that it should not be marriage or even cohabitation or friendship which is at the heart of the concern of family lawyers.[8] Rather we should focus on caring relationships as being at the centre of family law.[9]

---

[5] [2000] 1 FCR 21.

[6] Ibid, 32.

[7] C Lind, 'Power and the Taking of Responsibility: Shifting the Legal Family from Marriage to Friendship' in C Lind, H Keating and J Bridgman (eds), *Taking Responsibility: Law and the Changing Family* (Ashgate, 2010).

[8] L McClain, *The Place of Families* (Harvard University Press, 2006).

[9] J Masson, 'Caring for our Future Generations' in G Douglas, *The Continuing Evolution of Family Law* (Jordans, 2009).

A. The Function of Family Law

A popular starting point in deciding the nature of family law is to ask what the functions of family law are.[10] This is a dangerous approach to take. It is easy to assume there is agreement over the functions of family law and that typically involves assuming a particular image of the family. Nevertheless, it is helpful to identify what family law is trying to do, as long as one acknowledges that these are open to debate and are not givens. I would respectfully adopt John Eekelaar's[11] suggestion of three primary functions for family law:

(1)   Protective: to guard members of a family from physical, emotional or economic harm.
(2)   Adjustive: to help families which have broken down to adjust to new lives apart.
(3)   Supportive: to encourage and support family life.[12]

My claim will be that for each of these roles the existence of a sexual relationship between the parties is irrelevant. Rather, a caring relationship should be key.

i. Protective

One important role of family law is to tackle domestic abuse. That issue is discussed in chapter eight. For now it is sufficient to emphasise that a sexual element is not a prerequisite for domestic abuse. The violence, structural inequality or coercive control which can mark domestic abuse can occur in non-sexual as well as sexual relationships[13] as the writing on elder abuse shows.[14] It is the intimacy of the relationship, not its sexual nature, which is key to the wrong in domestic violence. Therefore this function of family law is correctly focused not on sexual relationships, but on intimate ones, typically marked by care. Restricting domestic violence to marriage-like relationships

---

[10]   See N Polikoff, *Beyond (Straight and Gay) Marriage* (Beacon Press, 2008).

[11]   J Eekelaar, *Family Law and Social Policy* (Weidenfeld & Nicholson, 1984) 24–26. For the difficulties and dangers of using a functionalist approach, see J Dewar, 'The Normal Chaos of Family Law' (1998) 61 *Modern Law Review* 467.

[12]   The extent to which family law should facilitate, rather than support family law, is open to considerable debate.

[13]   Although, of course, sexual relations might be one part of structural inequality in a particular relationship. Occasionally in England the court has been willing to grant parents non-molestation orders against their violent teenage children: *Re H* [2001] 1 FLR 641.

[14]   See eg J Herring, *Older People in Law and Society* (Oxford University Press, 2010).

has meant that some forms of abuse have gone without an effective remedy, such as elder abuse and abuse by teenagers of their parents.[15]

The other area of protection which is central to family is protection from financial exploitation. As we have seen in chapter two, care work is closely tied to financial inequality. In a relationship in which neither party has to dedicate significant amounts of time to care for others, it is unlikely there is any financial unfairness that requires a remedy. Sexual relationships do not themselves cause financial loss! Caring relationships typically do.[16] I shall develop that point later in this chapter. So those seeking to protect parties in relationships from abuse and economic disadvantage would be better targeting caring relationships, rather than sexual ones.

ii. Adjustive

As to the adjustive role, a primary function of family law is to ensure that at the end of a relationship, suitable arrangements are made for any child who has been living with the parties and to ensure a suitable distribution of the assets of the marriage. Again, both of these are required whether there is a sexual relationship between the parties or not. While there may be some debate over whether there is an appropriate difference in the way property is distributed between those who have formalised their relationships in marriage or some equivalent status and those who have not; the length of time the couple have lived together; the way they have structured their finances etc, the sexual nature of their relationships seems particularly irrelevant. It is care which causes the kind of relationship-based disadvantages which best justify the intervention of the law.

iii. Supportive

It is the supportive function of family law where there is likely to be most dispute. Craig Lind explains:

> In the first instance law protects the parameters of an appropriate family norm that those exercising power within a society have determined should be established and protected. It creates a status that will enjoy legal protection. The status is sometimes set pre-emptively. But sometimes some of its detail is established in the context of particular individual family disputes. In either instance the object is to create privileged relationships so that people can anticipate the way in which problems will be

---

[15] B Cottrell, *Parent Abuse: The Abuse of Parents by Their Teenage Children* (Family Violence Prevention Unit, Health Canada, 2001).

[16] See further eg L Glennon, 'Obligations between Adult Partners: Moving from Form to Function?' (2008) 22 *International Journal of Law, Policy and the Family* 22.

solved should the law be called upon to resolve them. Law frames the social world to create idealized or privileged family relationships.[17]

It is marriage which represents that ideal. That should be questioned. Are sexual relations between adults, or even particular kinds of sexual relationship of such significance that they deserve promotion through the law?[18] I would argue that what might make a relationship worthy of promotion by the state is care and mutual support, rather than sex. To be blunt, society does not really gain much from a couple having sex, however pleasurable it may be for the participants! However, the state does benefit from care, particularly where that is of a person whose needs would otherwise fall on the state. It is such relationships that should receive the support of the state. Whether the relationship has a sexual side is a red herring.

It might be argued that given the fluid nature of care, we can use sex as a proxy for care. However, that is a very weak argument. Nowadays sexual relationships often take place in the context of casual relationships. Any assumption that sex is a sign of commitment looks terribly old-fashioned. Certainly, care can certainly take place outside a sexual relationship.

The questionable significance of sex is well raised by *Burden v United Kingdom*.[19] In that case two elderly sisters claimed that their inability to marry or enter a civil partnership and claim the resultant tax exemptions meant that they were discriminated against. The Grand Chamber of the European Court of Human Rights rejected their complaint:

> The Grand Chamber commences by remarking that the relationship between siblings is qualitatively of a different nature to that between married couples and homosexual civil partners under the United Kingdom's CPA 2004. The very essence of the connection between siblings is consanguinity, whereas one of the defining characteristics of a marriage or CPA 2004 union is that it is forbidden to close family members (see para 17, above, and, generally, *B and L v UK* (App no 36536/02) (admissibility decision, 29 June 2004)). The fact that the applicants have chosen to live together all their adult lives, as do many married and CPA 2004 couples, does not alter this essential difference between the two types of relationship.[20]

The argument seems to be that there is 'essential difference' between the Burden sisters and those who are married or in civil partnerships, but there is no explanation of what that is. It is just assumed that anyone would agree. Judges Zupan and Borrego provided powerful dissenting judgments. They were not convinced that the majority had explained why consanguinity meant

---

[17] C Lind, 'Power and the Taking of Responsibility: Shifting the Legal Family from Marriage to Friendship' in C Lind, H Keating and J Bridgman (eds), *Taking Responsibility: Law and the Changing Family* (Ashgate, 2010) 76.

[18] L McClain, 'Love, Marriage, and the Baby Carriage: Revisiting the Channelling Function of Family Law' (2007) 28 *Cardozo Law Review* 2133.

[19] [2007] 1 FCR 69.

[20] Ibid, paras 62 and 63.

that the relationship was different from other couples. Indeed, Judge Zupan suggested that one could argue that the congruity means that the blood tie makes the relationship closer.

There seems much force in the dissenting judgments. It is hard to deny that the only distinguishing feature between the Burdens' relationship and civil partnership or marriage is the sexual element. If one were to try to find a distinction, one argument may be that there is a lack of an intimacy in their relationship, marked by the lack of a sexual element. However, this assumes that intimacy can only be found in sex. It is true that some couples living together without a sexual relationship may not have the degree of intimacy that civil partners or spouses would have, but there is no reason to think that sex is an essential element of intimacy nor indeed that sex necessarily marks intimacy.

And if sex is not a good marker of commitment or intimacy, why should it be of any legal significance?[21] The only answer seems to be that society has an interest in ensuring that sex takes place in order to produce a sufficient number of children. However, the vast majority of sexual encounters do not produce children. Further, at least currently in Western Europe, it is the care of children that poses far greater challenges than their production.[22] If the law or state is to promote certain kinds of relationship through family law, it should do so for caring relationships, rather than sexual ones. [23]

B. Centreing Care

An alternative vision for family law, focusing on relationships of care for dependants, rather than sexual relationships,[24] would produce a very different kind of family law. The focus of state support and legal confirmation would not be marriage-like sexual relationships, but rather those in which care is provided and received. This would make the primary focus of family law in some ways narrower (there might be some marriages in which there was insufficient caring of dependency to justify legal support) while there would be other relationships of care not currently covered (eg an adult caring for an older dependent relative) which would be covered. It would move closer

---

[21] This is not to say I think the Burdens should not pay inheritance tax. That is an issue which raises broader issues about inheritance taxation policy: J Herring, *Older People in Law and Society* (Oxford University Press, 2009) ch 9.

[22] L Kessler, 'Community Parenting' (2007) 24 *Washington University Journal of Law and Policy* 47.

[23] J Herring, 'Caregivers in Medical Law and Ethics' (2008) 25 *Journal of Contemporary Health Law and Policy* 1.

[24] M Fineman, *The Autonomy Myth* (New Press, 2004); L Murry and M Barnes, 'Have Families been Rethought? Ethic of Care, Family and "Whole Family" Approaches' (2010) 9 *Social Policy and Society* 533.

to adopting Iris Marion Young's[25] definition of a family: 'as people who live together and/or share resources necessary to the means for life and comfort; who are committed to caring for one another's physical and emotional needs to the best of their ability'.

I would see no requirement that the people live together. There would, however, need to be a significant amount of care and that would require considerable amounts of time spent together. I propose the following definition of the unit which would be the focus of family law: People providing each other with a substantial amount of care in a relationship marked by commitment. Note that this includes no need for a sexual element. Nor does it restrict a family to two people and certainly has no restrictions based on the gender of the people.

There are signs of this shift occurring in the understanding of family life.[26] England has shifted its support in the tax system away from marriage and towards those who raise children, by replacing married couple's tax allowance with child tax credits, but is still behind in failing to adequately support those who care for dependent adults.[27] To see caring as limited to the care of children would be unduly narrow.[28]

This last comment highlights two difficulties with my approach. First, how can we determine when the degree of care and commitment in a relationship is sufficient to justify state protection and legal recognition? I accept that the current family law legal system with its focus on marriage and civil partnership has an ease of use which would be lost by a focus on care and commitment. Nevertheless I believe that there are many relationships of care where there is a need for the adjustive, protective and supportive functions of the family law to used, but which fall outside the scope of the law. The plight of those whose care goes unrecognised and unrewarded justifies any increased bureaucratic difficulties. My proposed redefinition of marriage (below) would help in cases where people in a caring relationship wanted to formalise their relationship.

The temptation is to start to breakdown the category of caring relationships: parents, friends, partners.[29] But these categories tell us nothing about the disadvantages flowing from the caring. A friend may incur enormous sacrifices in a caring relationship with a friend and spouses may incur none.[30] Once we seek to separate out kinds of caring relationship, we are in danger

---

[25] I Young, *Intersecting Voices* (Princeton University Press, 1997) 106.

[26] But see The Conservative Party, *The Conservative Manifesto 2010: An Invitation to Join the Government of Britain* (Conservative Party, 2010) for a strong view in favour of marriage promotion.

[27] J Herring, 'Where are the Carers in Healthcare Law and Ethics?' (2007) 27 *Legal Studies* 51.

[28] J Bridgeman, 'Book Review' (2006) 14 *Feminist Legal Studies* 407, 408. See also J Herring and P-L Chau, 'My Body, Your body, Our Bodies' (2007) 15 *Medical Law Review* 34, 51.

[29] L Rosenbury, 'Friends with Benefits?' (2007) 106 *Michigan Law Review* 189.

[30] Ibid.

of privileging the contexts of the caring relationship, rather than the work within it.[31]

It would be preferable to stick with the definition of caring relations used above, but give it more clarity by listing some indicators of when a relationship would fall within my definition, including an indication of the amount of time expected; the kinds of activities which would be considered caring; and factors which would suggest commitment to the relationship.

A second response to my argument is that if we are to centre care we should abandon the terminology 'family law'.

This claim is likely to be made by those who think that there is something 'fundamentally natural'[32] about what a family is. It is difficult to respond to such an argument for those who see nothing 'natural' about a family. I can only note that family forms have varied enormously over the ages and that the notion of what a family is or what family life involves changes between generations and societies. Even if there is such a thing as a natural family form that does not tell us what the state should do about that. In any event the label is of little importance if we need to abandon the label of family law and replace it with relationship or caring law, we should do that.

There is a deeper concern that may be raised at this point. John Eekelaar notes if we attach legal obligations to selfless relationships then there is a danger that these relationships will become polluted with people using friendship for personal or material advantage.[33] One of the joys of intimate relationships is that they are 'law free'. It is not the values of legal obligations which govern them but love, trust and care. We should be wary of losing these virtues. Craig Lind, however, argues:

> If the intimate and caring relationships that people now form resemble friendship more closely than they do marriage, but fulfil functions—both at the social and personal level—which marriage traditionally fulfilled (or was, in an idealized way, meant to fulfil), it has become necessary, it is submitted, to bring friendship (or at least some attributes of friendship) into the realms of the regulation which we offer families and their members.[34]

He goes on to explain why legal intervention is important:

> Voluntarily assumed responsibility creates vulnerabilities and (inter)dependencies. These benefit our society while the relationships in which they are discovered continue. When those relationships end, the law's tendency to refuse recognition to those responsibilities—its refusal to acknowledge the vulnerabilities and dependencies

---

[31] N Barker. *Not the Marrying Kind* (Palgrave, 2012) 204.

[32] R Santorum, *It Takes a Family* (Intercollegiate Studies Institute, 2005) 28.

[33] J Eekelaar, *Family Law and Personal Life* (Oxford University Press, 2006).

[34] C Lind, 'Power and the Taking of Responsibility: Shifting the Legal Family from Marriage to Friendship' in C Lind, H Keating and J Bridgman (eds), *Taking Responsibility: Law and the Changing Family* (Ashgate, 2010) 76.

that are their result—places the onus on the side of the powerful and against the powerless.[35]

While therefore, as Eekelaar points out, there are dangers in legal intervention in relationships of care, there are also dangers in not doing so. Given that the legal interventions that are proposed in this chapter primarily operate at the end of the relationship, doing so is likely to protect those disadvantaged by relationships and is unlikely to pollute ongoing relationships.

To conclude, this section has argued that the focus of family law should be on the promotion of caring relationships. This requires a shift away from sexual relationships being the central focus. People do not need encouragement to engage in sex! This will be particularly marked in relation to the understanding of marriage, which will be considered next.

III. Marriage

Remarkably, the current marriage-centric law sees marriage in terms of its sexual, rather than caring features. Our current law is based on hetero-normative assumptions, which overemphasise reproduction and particular forms of sexual contact.[36] This can be seen by several of its key features. First, the fact that marriage must be between a man and a woman.[37] The definition of male and female in the law is largely tied to the capacity for heterosexual intercourse.[38] Some may seek to claim that the law is concerned with the production of children or some kind of essential good that is produced by the meeting of male and female, but the case law on sex for the purpose of marriage concentrates on the capacity to engage in heterosexual sex, rather than the production of children or relationships of care.[39] A couple who can engage in heterosexual sex with each other can get married, even if they are infertile.

Second, the significance of sex is also revealed by the fact that a lack of consummation is regarded as a ground to have a marriage annulled,[40] at least where the consummation is a result of the wilful refusal of the respondent to consummate the marriage, or where either party is incapable of consummating

---

[35] Ibid 76.

[36] S Ferlich Appleton, 'Towards a 'Culturally Cliterate' Family Law' (2008) 23 *Berkeley Journal of Gender, Law and Justice* 267.

[37] Matrimonial Causes Act 1973, s 11.

[38] J Herring and P-L Chau, 'Defining, Assigning and Designing Sex' (2002) 16 *International Journal of Law Policy and the Family* 327.

[39] Ibid.

[40] R Probert, 'Family Law—a Modern Concept?' [2004] *Family Law* 901.

the marriage.[41] Notably in English law, consummation is not a requirement for civil partnership.[42]

Third, the law on capacity to marry also reveals the fact that the law attaches significance to sex. The courts have held that a person who lacks the capacity to consent to sexual relations will automatically be said to lack the capacity to marry.[43] In *D Borough Council v AB* this was justified on the basis that 'a sexual component or dimension is, generally speaking, an intrinsic part of marriage'.[44] And so 'it would be an absurd state of affairs if a person had just sufficient intelligence to consent to marriage but insufficient capacity to consent to its (generally speaking) intrinsic component of consummation'.[45] In *Sheffield City Council v E and S*[46] it was explained that to have capacity to marry included an understanding of the obligation, inter alia, to 'love one another as husband and wife, to the exclusion of all others'. This is surprising because it elevates the sexual act to the heart of marriage. A person may have the capacity to understand the nature of a tender, loving relationship, but if they lack the capacity to understand about sex they thereby cannot understand marriage. This is all the more bizarre when it is explained in *D Borough Council v AB*[47] that the capacity to consent to sexual relations was said to involve an understanding of the mechanics of the act; that there were health risks involved; and that sex between a man and a woman could result in pregnancy. This raises a host of issues, which cannot be entered into here, but demonstrates that it is an understanding of the physical aspects of sex, rather than relational understanding, which is key.

As argued above, it should be care not sex which is central to marriage. I would advocate 'sexless marriage'![48] If there is a case for retaining marriage as a primary concept (and perhaps, I accept we would need a different name), it should be as a way of safeguarding or promoting caring relationships. This key issue seems hidden in some contemporary debates. There are some who argue that marriage should be restricted to its traditional heterosexual model.[49] Others argue that marriage should be extended to same-sex couples.[50] Yet others believe that we should apply the status of

---

[41] Matrimonial Causes Act 1973, s 12.

[42] See S Cretney, *Same Sex Relationships, from 'Odious Crime' to 'Gay Marriage'* (Oxford University Press, 2006) ch 3, for an extended discussion.

[43] *Westminster CC v IC* [2008] EWCA 198.

[44] [2011] EWHC 101 (Fam), para 14.

[45] Ibid, para 15.

[46] [2005] 1 FLR 965.

[47] [2011] EWHC 101 (Fam).

[48] S Nock, 'Time and Gender in Marriage' (2000) 86 *Virginia Law Review* 1971.

[49] R Santorum, *It Takes a Family* (ISI Books, 2005).

[50] W Eskridge, Jr, *The Case for Same-Sex Marriage* (Free Press, 1996).

marriage to cohabiting couples.[51] Of course, others argue that the state should remove itself completely from the business of regulating adult relationships.[52] I cannot deal with all of these arguments. But in response to all of these debates, I would ask what is it we are seeking to encourage or promote through marriage?

For some, marriage is properly linked with reproduction and a way of ensuring that the child has a biological mother and a father who is responsible for that child.[53] This produces an argument that in allowing same-sex marriage, children will be denied the 'birthright to two biological parents'.[54] This argument is very weak. There is no evidence that children born in heterosexual marital families are better cared for than those raised in gay families, indeed if anything the opposite is true.[55] Further, we do not limit access to marriage to those who are capable of raising children well. If gay couples are denied marriage because they are unsuitable raisers of children might not the same be said of those with low educational achievements, those who reject teetotalism, or those who do (or do not) have religious belief.[56] In any event not allowing gay couples access to marriage will not mean that they cannot produce and then care for children. Further, many marriages do not produce children. Only around 72 per cent do.[57] So to use marriage as a way of encouraging the production of children seems unlikely to succeed. Indeed, the current practice of prioritising and privileging marriage has not worked in the interests of women.[58] There has been a deep intertwining of heterosexual marriage and women's inequality in society.[59]

If, therefore, marriage is not about the production of children, what is it about? It should be about the care of dependants. To quote Maxine Eichner:[60]

> Because of its interest in the health, well-being, and dignity of its citizens, the liberal state has a vital interest in the success of relationships that foster caretaking,

---

[51] G Ganz Blumberg, 'Unmarried Partners and the Legacy of *Marvin v. Marvin*: The Regularization of Nonmarital Cohabitation: Rights and Responsibilities in the American Welfare State' (2001) 76 *Notre Dame Law Review* 1265.

[52] N Polikoff, *Beyond (Straight and Gay) Marriage: Valuing All Families under the Law* (Beacon Press 2008).

[53] D Blankenhorn, *The Future of Marriage* (Encounter Books, 2007).

[54] Ibid 3.

[55] C Patterson, 'Children of Lesbian and Gay Parents' (2006) 15 *Current Directions in Psychological Science* 241.

[56] M Eichner, *The Supportive State* (Oxford University Press, 2010) 95.

[57] P Laufer-Ukeles, 'Selective Recognition of Gender Difference in the Law: Revaluing the Caretaker Role' (2008) 31 *Harvard Journal of Law & Gender* 1.

[58] A Wilson, 'Feminism and Same-Sex Marriage: Who Cares?' (2010) 6 *Politics and Gender* 134.

[59] M Eichner, *The Supportive State* (Oxford University Press, 2010). For an excellent discussion of marriage see N Barker, *Not the Marrying Kind* (Palgrave, 2012).

[60] M Eichner, *The Supportive State* (Oxford University Press, 2010). For an excellent discussion of marriage see N Barker, *Not the Marrying Kind* (Palgrave, 2012).

and should provide these relationships with the institutional support that will help them flourish.

Marriage should be about the promotion of caring and ensuring justice within the sharing of caring obligations.[61] So understood limitations based on the gender of the parties or their sexual behaviour will be irrelevant.

IV. Parenthood

Traditionally in family law, parents play a crucial role in the law on children. Parents are given special rights which enable them to make decisions about children. Parents have particular responsibilities towards their children which can be legally enforced. The state's ability to intervene in family life and remove a child from his or her parents is restricted to the most severe of cases. In this legal regime parenthood has traditionally been understood in bio-logical terms. However, we have been seeing in recent years a move towards understanding parenthood in terms of the job of caring for the child, rather than the biological link. I will argue in this section that that is to be welcomed and should be developed.

The traditional approach has been that the biological link defines who the father is and who the mother is and thereby acquires, or has the potential to acquire, the rights and responsibilities of parenthood. In the past the bio-logical link was established by a series of presumptions that were needed, at least in the case of fatherhood. Hence the husband of the woman who gave birth was presumed to be the father of the child, even though there must have been plenty of cases where that was not so. Nowadays DNA tests can be used to determine paternity in cases where there is dispute and there is less need to rely on the presumptions. It would, however, be wrong to assume that it is biology that makes parenthood. Indeed it will be argued that it is care of the child that is the central thread of parenthood.

Looking first at the current state of the law, while it should be accepted that the law purports to emphasise the biological links, it is noticeable that it is generally reluctant to do this where doing so will give parenthood to a person who has no caring relationship with a child. This can be seen most obviously with the treatment of sperm and egg donors under the Human Fertilisation and Embryology Acts 1990 and 2008, where the donors are not treated as parents of a child, despite the biological link. We can see

---

[61] P Laufer-Ukeles, 'Selective Recognition of Gender Difference in the Law: Revaluing the Caretaker Role' (2008) 31 *Harvard Journal of Law & Gender* 1.

this further with the law's reluctance to order DNA tests in cases where the claimant father has no prospect of a relationship with the child.[62] There the 'truth' of the presumption, rendering the 'social father' the father, is preferred, rather than conducting tests to determine who the genetic father is. Perhaps we can see this most strongly by virtue of the fact that the law makes very little attempt to determine who the genetic parents of a child at birth are. It is for the mother to name the man who is to be the father of the child at his or her birth and the truth of that is accepted, unless challenged by the man. That is precisely the position one might expect if social parenthood was to be the marker of parenthood. If the law really did think the biological link was important it would do DNA tests on every child born, or at least every child born where paternity was at issue. While officially it is genetics that makes a man the father, in fact, the law operates in many cases so that a non-genetic father can have the title of father if that is the role he is to play in the child's life. Even where such a man cannot acquire the title of father, he can still claim parental responsibility for the child and acquire the rights and responsibilities of parenthood.[63]

The argument that having a caring relationship with a child should be the source of parental rights is not to deny that children may have some kind of claim to be entitled to know of their genetic origins,[64] but such a claim could be met by granting children access to the information without granting that person the status of parent. I would support what Judith Masson describes as parenting by doing. She explains:

> Parenting by doing acknowledges the reality of looking after children by recognising adult-child relationships. Parenting by being reflects a wish to identify for the child and the state people with responsibility for the child, regardless of the practical role they are playing or want to play in the child's life.[65]

This I suggest is appropriate. Parental status should be earned by the care and dedication to the child, something not shown simply by a biological link. It is the changing of the nappy; the wiping of the tear; and the working out of maths together that makes a parent, not the provision of an egg or sperm. Here are some of the reasons why parenthood should depend on care.

First, I argue that we should give parental status and parental rights in accordance with the principle of the promotion of the welfare of the child. Quite simply we should give parental status and rights to those who are

---

[62] J Fortin, 'Children's Right to know their Origins—too Far, too Fast?' (2009) 21 *Child and Family Law Quarterly* 336.

[63] For a detailed discussion of the law, see J Herring, *Family Law* (Pearson, 2011).

[64] Although I would question such a claim.

[65] J Masson, 'Parenting by Being; Parenting by Doing—In search of Principles for Founding Families' in J Spencer and A du Bois-Pedain, *Freedom and Responsibility in Reproductive Choice* (Hart, 2006).

likely to make the best decisions for the child in question. That will be the person who knows the child best; the person who is caring for the child day to day.

Second, parental status should not be seen as a right one can assert, but as a responsibility granted in recognition of the work one has done in respect of the child.[66] As Barbara Bennett Woodhouse claims, there is a danger that the law is 'intent on securing children for adults who claim them' rather than 'seeking to provide adults for children who need them'.[67] If we see parenthood in the nature of stewardship and parental status not as simply a source of power, but responsibilities with the child's interests at their heart, then, as Bennett Woodhouse argues, 'Stewardship must be earned through actual care giving, and lost if not exercised with responsibility'. Jo Bridgeman puts it this way:

> I suggest that a starting point is offered by the feminist ethic of care in which the responsibilities of parents arise from their relationship with their child, and which acknowledges the extent to which factors external to that relationship, including the law, have an impact upon the ability of parents to care. From this perspective the role of the law would be to support parents in the discharge of their responsibilities to their children and to foster the quality of the parent/child relationship, not to make parents meet their responsibilities.[68]

Third, there is much to be said in favour of the view that the law on the allocation of parenthood should match the perspective of the child. If the child regards an adult as a primary decision-maker, a parent figure, then that is a strong indication the law should follow suit. Step-parents; same-sex partners; grandparents and others[69] might be fully regarded by the child as a parent, and yet not be recognised as a parent by the law. By contrast, a person whom the child has little interaction with is unlikely to be regarded as a parent, however strong the biological link, and is unlikely to be seen by a child as a parent in a meaningful sense.

The current approach of the law is based on the heterosexual married model. The requirement that a child has one father and one mother reinforces that as a norm for parenthood. As we depart from the assumption that that model is the primary game in town, new vistas of what it means to be a parent

---

[66] J Wallbank, '(En)Gendering the Fusion of Rights and Responsibilities in the Law of Contact' in J Wallbank, S Choudhry and J Herring (eds), *Rights, Gender and Family Law* (Routledge, 2009). See further S Boyd, *Child Custody, Law and Women's Work* (Oxford University Press, 2003).

[67] B Bennett Woodhouse, 'Hatching the Egg: A Child-Centered Perspective on Parents' Rights' (1993) 14 *Cardozo Law Review* 1747, 1814.

[68] J Bridgeman, 'Parental Responsibility, Responsible Parenting and Legal Regulation' in J Bridgeman, H Keating and C Lind, *Responsibility Law and the Family* (Ashgate, 2008) 247.

[69] M Kavanagh 'Rewriting the Legal Family: Beyond Exclusivity to a Care-Based Standard' (2004) 16 *Yale Journal of Law and Feminism* 83, 143.

are opened up.[70] We can start to recognise the network of people that can play a role in a child's life. This includes recognition of the extent to which children care for other children.

Katherine Bartlett suggested that the law should recognise as parents all who

(1) have had custody of the child for at least six months;
(2) are understood to be a parent by the child; and
(3) began their relationship with the child with the support and consent of the child's legal parent.[71]

In a similar vein, Nancy Polikoff argues that legal parents would include 'anyone who maintains a functional parental relationship with a child when a legally recognised parent created that relationship with the intent that the relationship be parental in nature'.[72] It has been argued that this should even apply to those paid for care.[73]

While welcome as liberalisations, the difficulty with both these approaches is that they retain a stark parent/non-parent divide. A better approach, is it submitted, is to have a recognition of the range of adults who may be involved in a child's life, with particular focus on the nature of the relationship with the child. A teacher to whom a child is particularly close may thereby acquire a right to be involved in decision making about education. One benefit of such an approach is that it avoids the two opposite-sex parent norm which still has such a powerful influence in our law. The truth is that few families abide by such a straightforward model. As Laura Kessler suggests, the current law demonises 'difference, seeks to characterize as dysfunctional, disorganized, and deviant those families that do not conform with the nuclear, heterosexual, male-breadwinner, female-homemaker ideal'.[74] In doing so it puts enormous pressure on mothers so that motherhood becomes 'child-centred, expert-guided, emotionally absorbing, labour intensive and financially expensive'.[75]

So, to conclude, parenthood should shift from focusing on blood ties to focusing on the caring relationship between child and other. Rights should flow from the relationship with the child, not the blood tie. If this is recognised it has considerable significance. We move away from the idea that a child

---

[70] F Kelly, *Transforming Law's Family: The Legal Recognition of Planned Lesbian Families* (University of British Columbia Press, 2011).

[71] K Bartlett, 'Re-Thinking Parenthood as an Exclusive Status: The Need for Legal Alternatives when the Premise of the Nuclear Family has Failed' (1984) 70 *Virginia Law Review* 879.

[72] N Polikoff, *Beyond (Straight and Gay) Marriage* (Beacon Press, 2008) 23.

[73] P Laufer-Ukeles, 'Money, Caregiving, and Kinship: Should Paid Caregivers be Allowed to Obtain De Facto Parental Status?' (2009) 74 *Missouri Law Review* 25.

[74] L Kessler, 'Community Parenting' (2007) 24 *Journal of Law and Policy* 47.

[75] S Hays *Cultural Contradictions of Motherhood* (Yale University Press, 1998) 8–9.

can have only one parent. Further in terms of legal rights a range of adults might, depending on the context of their particular relationship, have a say in certain areas of the child's life. But the extent and nature of those rights will depend on the relationship.

V. Disputes over Children

When a court comes to resolve a dispute over the upbringing of children, English law is dominated by the 'welfare principle':

> When a court determines any question with respect to—
>
> (a) the upbringing of a child; or
> (b) the administration of a child's property or the application of any income aris-
> ing from it,
>
> the child's welfare shall be the court's paramount consideration.[76]

When considering applications under section 8 of the Children Act 1989, the court must take into account the checklist of factors in section 1(3), in deciding what is in the welfare of the child.[77] The court is required to consider all the different factors and weigh them in the balance, although the court can also take into account other factors not mentioned in the list.[78]

There is much to be said that is beneficial about the welfare principle: it ensures that the focus is on the child and enables an individual assessment of the needs of the child.[79] Using an ethic of care approach to interpret the principle is essential.

Under the welfare principle, as interpreted by the courts, the interests of adults and other children are only relevant in so far as they might affect the welfare of the child in question.[80] As was stated by the Court of Appeal in *Re P (Contact: Supervision)*,[81] 'the court is concerned with the interests of the mother and the father only in so far as they bear on the welfare of the child'. This followed the decision of the House of Lords in *J v C*,[82] which was especially significant because it was said that the interests of the children outweigh the interests of even 'unimpeachable' (perfect) parents. So whether an order is 'fair' or infringes the rights of parents is not relevant; all that

---

[76] Children Act 1989, s 1(1).
[77] Ibid, s 1(4).
[78] Baroness Hale in *Re G (Children) (Residence: Same-Sex Partner)* [2006] UKHL 43, para 40.
[79] J Herring, 'Farewell Welfare' (2005) 27 *Journal of Social Welfare and Family Law* 159.
[80] See eg, Lord Hobhouse in *Dawson v Wearmouth* [1999] 1 FLR 1167.
[81] [1996] 2 FLR 314, 328.
[82] [1970] AC 668.

matters is whether the order promotes the interests of children. It has been argued that the Human Rights Act 1998 requires the courts to reinterpret the word 'paramount' in section 1 to mean 'primary', so that the court can then take due account of the interests of parents and others.[83] But that argument has had little favour with the courts.

Although the way the courts have expressed the welfare principle might indicate that they are solely interested in the child, it is not surprising that, in fact, the English courts have been able to protect the interests of parents.[84] For example, there are some issues, such as the law on divorce, where the welfare principle does not apply. In other cases the courts have closely identified the interests of children and parents. Perhaps the best example to illustrate this is *Re T (A Minor) (Wardship: Medical Treatment)*.[85] This case concerned a dispute over whether life-saving medical treatment should be given to a child. The unanimous medical opinion was in favour, but the parents opposed it. The Court decided that it would not be in the child's best interests for the treatment to go ahead, bearing in mind the pressure that this would put on the parents. Butler-Sloss LJ reasoned:

> the mother and this child are one for the purpose of this unusual case and the decision of the court to consent to the operation jointly affects the mother and son and so also affects the father. The welfare of the child depends upon his mother.[86]

I think the courts are quite right to take into account the interests of parents when considering the interests of the child and that that is justified under the welfare principle. However, we need an understanding of welfare based on an ethic of care to justify that approach. I have developed an approach I have called 'relationship-based welfare'.[87]

Children, as we all do, live in the context of relationships. We cannot separate either the welfare or the rights of children from their parents. Their interests and rights are so intertwined and the parties so inter-dependent that to consider what order will promote the welfare of the child, as an isolated individual, and without consideration of the interests of the parents, as the courts suggest, is simply an impossibility.

---

[83] See S Choudhry and H Fenwick, 'Taking the Rights of Parents and Children Seriously: Confronting the Welfare Principle under the Human Rights Act' (2005) 25 *Oxford Journal of Legal Studies* 453. See J Herring, 'The Human Rights Act and the Welfare Principle in Family Law—Conflicting or Complementary? (1999) 11 *Child and Family Law Quarterly* 223 for an argument that the courts can retain the paramountcy notion, while taking into account parents' interests.

[84] J Herring, 'The Human Rights Act and the Welfare Principle in Family Law—Conflicting or Complementary?' (1999) 11 *Child and Family Law Quarterly* 223.

[85] [1997] 1 FLR 502.

[86] Ibid, 510.

[87] J Herring, 'The Human Rights Act and the Welfare Principle in Family Law—Conflicting or Complementary?' (1999) 11 *Child and Family Law Quarterly* 223.

A care-centred approach would require us to consider the child in the network of relationships within which they live. Relationship-based welfare[88] argues that children should be brought up in relationships which overall promote their welfare.[89] Relationships are central to the lives of children and so should be at the centre of decisions about their lives.[90] It is beneficial for a child to be brought up in a family that is based on relationships which are fair and just. A relationship based on unacceptable demands on a parent is not furthering a child's welfare. Indeed, it is impossible to construct an approach to looking at a child's welfare which ignores the web of relationships within which the child is brought up. Supporting the child means supporting the caregiver and supporting the caregiver means supporting the child.[91] So a court can legitimately make an order which benefits a parent, but not a child, if that can be regarded as appropriate in the context of their past and ongoing relationship.

A central aspect of relationship-based welfare is that we need to take a long-term view when considering welfare. The danger with the welfare principle is that it can lead to a snap shot approach being taken. The court looks at the pros and cons of a particular course of action at the time of the hearing and determines the correct result. The problem with this approach is that it focuses the courts' attention simply on the current issues and fails to locate it as part of an ongoing relationship between the parties. What has happened to date in the relationship and what will happen in the future between the parties drops out of the picture.

A good example of the problem can be seen in *Re S (A Child)*.[92] The case involved an attempt to prevent a mother moving to Cornwall with her daughter, Victoria, who was nine and a half years old and had Down's Syndrome. Victoria had mild learning difficulties and a range of other medical problems, requiring extensive levels of care. Her parents had separated when she was 18 months old and later divorced. She lived with her mother in South London, but had weekly contact with her father, who lived nearby and had remarried. The mother had met a new partner, who lived in Cornwall. His mother was dependent on him and lived there. The mother wished to move to Cornwall, but the father sought an order requiring her to remain in London. The Court granted the order, a decision affirmed on appeal. The key question, the Court held, was what was in the best interests of Victoria. The mother's strong

---

[88] Ibid. See also J Bridgeman, 'Children with Exceptional Needs: Welfare, Rights and Caring Responsibilities' in J Wallbank, S Choudhry and J Herring (eds), *Rights, Gender and Family Law* (Routledge, 2010).

[89] S Sevenhuijsen, 'An Approach through the Ethic of Care' in A Carling, S Duncan and R Edwards (eds), *Analysing Families* (Routledge, 2002).

[90] M Kavanagh, 'Rewriting the Legal Family: Beyond Exclusivity to a Care-Based Standard' (2004) 16 *Yale Journal of Law and Feminism* 83.

[91] Ibid.

[92] [2002] EWCA 1759.

desire to be with her new partner and the fact she had suffered depression after the initial refusal to leave London could not be relevant factors, save as they impacted on the welfare of the child. The expert evidence showed that Victoria would find the reduction in contact with the father confusing and it would cause her distress. It was, therefore, in her welfare to remain in London.

The difficulty with this decision is that it focused entirely on what was in Victoria's welfare at that moment. It failed to look at the broader timescale. In particular the fact this was a girl with considerable needs who had been given continuous intense care by her mother and would continue to receive that level of care for the rest of her life. The sacrifices made by her mother were enormous. While the father had been free to remarry and start his new life, the mother, through this order, was being deprived of the practical and emotional day-to-day support of her new partner. It is hard to see how, looking at this issue in the context of the relationships between the parties, this order promoted Victoria's welfare. It is in the nature of the relationships that there is give and take. That is what healthy relationships involve. Relationships in which one party does all the taking and none of the receiving is not beneficial. In this case allowing the move, even if that would have caused some harm, would have been productive of a beneficial ongoing relationship.

Arguments in favour of centreing care have already been made throughout this book, but some specific ones will be addressed in this context. First it is in tune with how children understand their lives. The excellent study by Carol Smart, Bren Neale and Amanda Wade[93] showed that children saw their lives and families in terms of love, care and relationships, rather than biological links. It was the quality of the relationship rather than the blood tie that matters.[94]

Second, the themes of responsibilities, within the context of relationships, are far more important to families than rights and rules. Few families are structured like law firms with careful accounting made of every minute and every pound. Responsibilities are owed and tasks undertaken within the context of the relationship. Family life is made up of people sacrificing their 'rights' for others. The rights of one member may predominate at particular moments, but it is the good of the family which is key.

Third, families make decisions generally based on what works for the individuals in that context. True, there may be some abstract principles that are occasionally followed, but it is daily experience and contextual solutions which are relied upon rather than universal abstract principles. This is what Smart and Neale have called the 'principle of actuality'.[95] Each family will

---

[93] C Smart, B Neale and A Wade, *The Changing Experience of Childhood* (Polity Press, 2001).
[94] Ibid 65.
[95] Ibid.

be treated as unique and universal assumptions about best interests of rights will be avoided. Not what is best for children, but rather what is best for their child. One benefit of this approach is that it requires carefully listening to the child to understand the context of their family life and their perspective on the relationships that matter.

It would be important to recognise that caring is a central activity of value and would show respect for those offering care. Care is not just a sad consequence of children's vulnerability, but deserves respect in its own right. Smart has argued that the law has traditionally undervalued caring *for* a child and has valorised caring *about* a child. She writes:

> Thus mothers, when they spoke about the work they did in caring for their children and the sacrifices they made, were hardly acknowledged. These actions were seen as being normal as breathing and thus as worthy of as much acknowledgment as such taken for granted activities usually generate. But when fathers articulated their care about their children, even if they had never really cared for them, their utterances seemed to reverberate around the courts with a deafening significance.[96]

Boyd suggests the following as factors to take into account when looking at the welfare of the child:

> past patterns of care and responsibility, including primary caregiving; the type of relationship each parent has with a child; whether there have been patterns of domination, or worse, a climate of coercion and fear between the adults or between the adult(s) and children; whether the parents have elected a shared arrangement; degree of geographical proximity between parental residences; ability of the parents to get along well and communicate; confidence in the other parent's parenting competence; and what the impact of proposed arrangements on a caregiver's ability to be emotionally available and attentive to a child and the child's views and needs would be.[97]

Basing our understanding of family on networks of care means that families are not centrally about individual rights, but are instead about relationships. The needs and relationships of children should be the centre of our understanding of the family, and there are ways, even within the legal system, to act upon this understanding. The proposals made here help us to shift our analysis away from recognising the assertions of individual adults of their rights to children and towards recognising caregiver-child relationships and the recognition and protection such relationships are due. This also allows us to move away from capitalist notions of ownership within the family and the tendency to view children as 'property'. Instead, by bringing children to the

---

[96] C Smart, 'Losing the Struggle for another Voice: The Case of Family Law' (1995) 15 *Dalhousie Law Journal* 173.

[97] S Boyd, 'Autonomy for Mothers? Relational Theory and Parenting Apart' (2010) 18 *Feminist Legal Studies* 137.

very centre of our analysis, we can build law and politics based on the needs of their day-to-day lives.

VI. Financial Orders

On divorce or dissolution, a court has authority to redistribute property and make orders for future payments. This is a remarkable power. Every last penny a person has can, in theory at least, be taken from them and handed over to someone else. Not only that, but every last penny they are to earn in the future can be taken too. Of course, it would be very unusual for a court to order that. Fairness, as we shall see, is regarded as the touchstone for the law in this area. From one point of view, ordering the transfer of ownership of property from one person to another in the absence of a contract or a tort is a major invasion of property rights. The spouse who has earned the money and 'kept' their partner should not be required to pay any more.[98] But from another point of view, it is just as outrageous that after a lengthy marriage the parties might be left with an enormous difference in their financial positions. To end a marriage, which typically involves an intertwining of their lives, with the wife having nothing and husband everything seems manifestly unfair. The financial orders on divorce, far from being an intrusion into property rights, are an essential aspect of fairness. Before exploring the theoretical issues and what a care-based law might look like, the current position will be summarised.

A. The Law

On divorce the court has a wide range of orders available. These include periodic payment orders[99] (eg that one spouse pay the other £100 per week); lump sum orders (eg that one spouse transfer to the other £30,000); transfer of property orders (eg that one spouse transfer to the other their share in the matrimonial home) to powers to order sale[100] (eg that the former matrimonial order be sold). The factors to be taken into account by a court in deciding which orders to make are listed in section 25 of the Matrimonial Causes Act 1973:

(1) It shall be the duty of the court in deciding whether to exercise its powers under section 23, 24, 24A or 24B above and, if so, in what manner, to have

---

[98] R Deech, 'What's a Woman Worth?' (2009) 39 *Family Law* 1140.
[99] Matrimonial Causes Act 1973 (MCA 1973), s 23.
[100] Ibid, s 24A.

regard to all the circumstances of the case, first consideration being given to the welfare while a minor of any child of the family who has not attained the age of eighteen.

(2) As regards the exercise of the powers of the court under section 23(1)(*a*), (*b*) or (*c*), 24, 24A or 24B above in relation to a party to the marriage, the court shall in particular have regard to the following matters—

  (a) the income, earning capacity, property and other financial resources which each of the parties to the marriage has or is likely to have in the foreseeable future, including in the case of earning capacity any increase in that capacity which it would in the opinion of the court be reasonable to expect a party to the marriage to take steps to acquire;

  (b) the financial needs, obligations and responsibilities which each of the parties to the marriage has or is likely to have in the foreseeable future;

  (c) the standard of living enjoyed by the family before the breakdown of the marriage;

  (d) the age of each party to the marriage and the duration of the marriage;

  (e) any physical or mental disability of either of the parties to the marriage;

  (f) the contributions which each of the parties has made or is likely in the foreseeable future to make to the welfare of the family, including any contribution by looking after the home or caring for the family;

  (g) the conduct of each of the parties, if that conduct is such that it would in the opinion of the court be inequitable to disregard it;

  (h) in the case of proceedings for divorce or nullity of marriage, the value to each of the parties to the marriage of any benefit ... which, by reason of the dissolution or annulment of the marriage, that party will lose the chance of acquiring.

A key point in understanding the current law is that judges are given a very wide discretion in how to use these factors. The Act deliberately has no one overall objective[101] and it is permissible for the court to take into account factors not listed in section 25, if it believes them to be relevant.[102] The House of Lords has accepted that different judges may quite properly reach different conclusions as to what the most appropriate order is in a particular case.[103] The courts have even been tentative about stating general principles about the application of the factors. The closest we have to a judicial interpretation of the overriding purpose of the jurisdiction is the suggestion of Lord Nicholls in the House of Lords in *White v White*[104] that it is fairness. But, fairness here means the judge's objective assessment of fairness, not the parties' subjective assessment of what they think might be fair.[105] Lord Nicholls accepted that this guidance was not of enormous assistance: as he put it, 'fairness, like

---

[101] *White v White* [2001] AC 596, 616–17.
[102] *Co v Co* [2004] EWHC 287 (Fam).
[103] *Piglowska v Piglowski* [1999] 2 FLR 763.
[104] [2000] 2 FLR 981, [2000] 3 FCR 555.
[105] *Lambert v Lambert* [2002] 3 FCR 673, para 39.

beauty, lies in the eye of the beholder'.[106] In *Miller v Miller; McFarlane v McFarlane* he said:

> Fairness is an illusive concept. It is an instinctive response to a given set of facts. Ultimately it is grounded in social and moral values. These values or attitudes, can be stated. But they cannot be justified, or refuted, by any objective process of logical reasoning.

> Baroness Hale was perhaps more helpful in suggesting that 'The ultimate objective is to give each party an equal start on the road to independent living'.[107]

It would, however, be wrong to suggest that in the vast majority of cases there is ambiguity over what order should be made. In nearly all cases the judge will simply distribute the meagre assets as best she or he can to meet the needs of the parties. I well remember giving a lecture on the law in this area to a group of practitioners and discussing the principle of division of assets. The first questioner at the end of the lecture was a legal aid solicitor who started his comments: 'Assets ... I haven't had a case involving assets for years. All my cases involve debts.' As the study by Chris Barton and Alistair Bissett-Johnson[108] showed, less than half of cases involve the making of any ancillary relief orders. For many couples there is no property the court can make an order over.

Many cases involve very few assets (if not at the time of separation, they do by the time of divorce) and any assets there are will be required for the care of children. So in many cases, the solicitors' job is simply to do what they can to ensure there is the most basic provision for the needs of the children and if that is possible to meet the needs of the spouses. For the vast majority of cases it is the meeting of needs, nearly always inadequately, which is at the heart of the lawyers' task. Any other principle, indeed arguably even fairness itself, goes out of the window when faced with substantial needs and negligible assets.

The truth is that for many couples suitable financial orders cannot be made. Neither party will be able to live at a standard of living they regard as acceptable. Both will feel they have been hard done by. As Pamela Symes explains:

> Quite clearly, marriage as it has traditionally been practised, is not intended to be ended by divorce. Indeed, traditional housewife marriage has a most potent feature of indissolubility built right into it—dependency ... The accumulation of responsibilities and obligations, the consequences of an unequal partnership based

---

[106] *White v White* [2000] 3 FCR 555, para 1.

[107] [2006] UKHL 46, para 144.

[108] C Barton and A Bissett-Johnson, 'The Declining Number of Ancillary Relief Orders' [2000] 30 *Family Law* 94.

on dependency—all mean that an absolute severance of the bond without massive adjustment would be manifestly unjust, more likely impossible.[109]

The academic and professional debates, however, surround cases involving the very wealthy. For it is really only in these cases that there is any argument to be had about what to do. The law is now dominated by two key decisions: *White v White*[110] and *Miller; McFarlane*.[111] Following these two decisions it has been generally accepted that in big money cases there are three key principles to be relied upon in determining the appropriate order:

— Needs.
— Sharing.
— Compensation.

The first is that the needs of the parties should be met. This is normally unproblematic given the sums of money involved. More needs to be said about the other two.

i. Sharing

The principle of equality was introduced by the decision of the House of Lords in *White v White*.[112] That case broke new ground. The Whites had assets of roughly £4.5 million when their marriage ended after 33 years together. The trial judge awarded the wife £800,000 which he assessed as meeting the wife's reasonable needs for the rest of her life. That followed the approach which had been adopted by the courts up until this date. A wife (typically) would be restricted to claiming a sufficient amount to meet her needs, while the husband (typically) would be entitled to the remainder. This reflected an assumption that the money-maker was entitled to the money he had made and the non-money-maker needed to show why she should have some of 'his' money. In the House of Lords this approach was rejected. Lord Nicholls argued:

> But there is one principle of universal application which can be stated with confidence. In seeking to achieve a fair outcome, there is no place for discrimination between husband and wife and their respective roles. Typically, a husband and wife share the activities of earning money, running their home and caring for their children. Traditionally, the husband earned the money, and the wife looked after the home and the children. This traditional division of labour is no longer the order of the day. Frequently both parents work. Sometimes it is the wife who is the money-earner, and the husband runs the home and cares for the children during

---

[109] P Symes, 'Indissolubility and the Clean Break' (1985) 48 *Modern Law Review* 44, 57.
[110] [2000] 3 FCR 555.
[111] [2006] 1 FCR 213.
[112] [2000] 3 FCR 555.

the day. But whatever the division of labour chosen by the husband and wife, or forced upon them by circumstances, fairness requires that this should not prejudice or advantage either party when considering paragraph (f), relating to the parties' contributions. This is implicit in the very language of paragraph (f): '... the contribution which each has made or is likely ... to make to the welfare of the family, including any contribution by looking after the home or caring for the family.' If, in their different spheres, each contributed equally to the family, then in principle it matters not which of them earned the money and built up the assets. There should be no bias in favour of the money-earner and against the home-maker and the child-carer.[113]

From this argument came the following central principle:

As a general guide equality should only be departed from if, and to the extent that, there is good reason for doing so. The need to consider and articulate reasons for departing from equality would help the parties and the court to focus on the need to ensure the absence of discrimination. This is not to introduce a presumption of equal division under another guise.[114]

The House of Lords made clear that this principle can be departed from where fairness requires it. On the facts of the case the wife ended up with less than half of their assets because of the significant contribution of the husband's family to the family business. In *Miller*[115] Lord Nicholls emphasised that the yardstick was intended as 'an aid, not a rule'. Indeed, given that in many cases there are insufficient assets to meet the needs of the couple and children, it will, in fact, be rare for there not to be a good reason for departing from the starting point of equal division.

It is notable that among the reported cases it is in fact rare for an equal division to be made. Reasons for departing from an equal division can include the needs of the parties;[116] an extra-ordinary contribution by one of the parties;[117] the fact that a part of the couple's wealth was inherited or donated by one of their parents;[118] that property was brought into the marriage;[119] that property was acquired after the marriage; in rare cases obvious and gross misconduct;[120] or to ensure adequate compensation for losses caused by the marriage; and the way the parties organised their marriage.[121] At the end of the day, given the range of factors that might be taken into account, it is difficult to say more than that the principle of equality will be departed from when it is considered fair to do so.

---

[113] Ibid, para 24.
[114] Ibid.
[115] [2006] UKHL 24, para 16.
[116] *Lambert v Lambert* [2002] 3 FCR 673, para 39.
[117] Ibid.
[118] *B v B (Ancillary Relief)* [2008] 1 FCR 613.
[119] *Miller; McFarlane* [2006] 2 FCR 213.
[120] *Clark v Clark* [1999] 4 FLR 498.
[121] In *J v J* [2009] EWHC 2654.

Further complexity surrounds the question of what property should be divided. The position the courts appear to have reached at present is that in principle all of a couple's property is available for redistribution, especially where the needs of the parties require it.[122] That is all of the assets the couple have at the time of the hearing.[123] But in a 'big money' case where there are sufficient funds to meet the parties' needs then the court may take into account that some property is non-marital. In other words, that it was acquired before the marriage started, or after it ended. Charles J in *J v J*[124] explained 'that property acquired and built up during the marriage through the respective efforts and roles of the couple should be shared equally. Such property is a product of the relationship'. The same could not be said of non-marital assets. In *Miller*, Baroness Hale and Lord Nicholls agreed that in a case of a lengthy marriage whether the assets were family assets or marital assets would become increasingly irrelevant and it would be likely that the Court would simply divide everything the couple had in half. But their lordships made it clear they were not setting down a hard and fast rule that in long marriages you divide all the property equally and in short marriages you divide only the marital property. In each case the judge must seek to determine what would be fair in the circumstances at hand.

In *Miller* there was a difference between the approach of Lord Nicholls and Baroness Hale. Lord Nicholls in *Miller* understood marital property[125] to be all assets acquired by either party during the marriage, save those acquired by gift or inheritance. He also included the matrimonial home as 'matrimonial property' even if one party had brought it into the marriage. Baroness Hale, by contrast, used a narrower understanding of 'marital assets', preferring the phrase 'family assets'. These were restricted to assets generated by the family: it could include the family home, family savings, income generated by a business organised by both parties. It would not include assets which were produced by the efforts of one party alone. She explained that in relation to non-family assets 'it simply cannot be demonstrated that the domestic contribution, important though it has been to the welfare of the family as a whole, has contributed to their acquisition'.[126] In *Charman v Charman*[127] Court of Appeal preferred Baroness Hale's approach, which Sir Mark Potter summarised in this way:

> a distinction fell to be made between 'family assets' and the fruits of a business in which both parties had substantially worked, on the one hand, and the fruits of a

[122] *Charman v Charman* [2007] EWCA Civ 503; *J v J* [2009] EWHC 2654.

[123] *H v H (Financial Provision)* [2009] 2 FLR 795; *J v J* [2009] EWHC 2654.

[124] [2009] EWHC 2654, para 304.

[125] He used the phrase 'matrimonial property', but later cases have preferred the terminology 'marital property'.

[126] [2006] 2 FCR 213, para 151.

[127] [2007] EWCA Civ 503.

business in which only one party had substantially worked, i.e. unilateral assets, on the other. The suggestion was that it was property only of the former character which was subject to the sharing principle.[128]

ii. Compensation

Intimate relationships often create disadvantage. Baroness Hale in *Miller v Miller*[129] explained that the Court is concerned with fairness not just at the time of divorce but also with the 'foreseeable (and on occasions more distant) future'. The unfairness of future inequality is particularly acute when one spouse has given up a career to pursue child care, leaving the other to generate substantial earning potential.[130] A good example is *McFarlane* where the couple's assets of £3 million were divided equally, but Mr McFarlane was earning around £1 million per year, while Mrs McFarlane had, early in the marriage, given up her very promising career to care for the child. A simple division of the assets would not ensure equality, even in the near future, nor would it provide adequate compensation for her lost career. The Court therefore ordered that the husband pay the wife periodic payments to make up her lost career for five years.[131] This enabled the Court to ensure that the economic disadvantage Mrs McFarlane had suffered during her marriage was compensated for.

iii. Balancing the Principles

What is to be done if the application of the principles of sharing, compensation and needs suggest different sums? Some guidance was supplied in *Charman v Charman*.[132] The Court of Appeal explained that if an assessment of the wife's needs was greater than the sum that she would be granted on the basis of sharing or compensation then she should be awarded that sum. If, however, the sum she would be awarded on the basis of sharing was greater than her needs, she should be awarded the sharing sum. In short, she should receive the sharing amount or the needs amount, whichever was greater. As regards what to do if the sum to be awarded under the principle of compensation was greater than the award based on needs or sharing, the Court decided that that question was best left to another case. Despite making these points,

---

[128] Ibid, para 82.
[129] [2006] 2 FCR 213, para 129.
[130] See also *Murphy v Murphy* [2009] EWCA Civ 1258.
[131] Subsequently this was extended until the date the husband was due to retire.
[132] *Charman v Charman* [2007] EWCA Civ 503, para 73; *Miller, McFarlane* [2006] 2 FCR 213, paras 11–13.

it was emphasised that, at the end of the day, the key issue is fairness. None of the Court of Appeal's comments were intended to be setting down a rule.[133]

B. What Approach Should the Law Take?

There has been extensive debate over financial orders on divorce. Although often overlooked, I will argue that care should be at the centre of this debate. In fact, the recognition of the importance of care has played an important role in the development of the law. In particular, in *White v White*, the recognition of the value of care work played a central role in the establishment of the principle of equality.

There are a number of ways that care can be used to justify an award. While sometimes the theoretical debates over financial orders on divorce are presented as a clash between different justifications, in fact there is no reason why the following arguments cannot be made as combined or multiple claims based on care.

C. Equal Contribution to a Partnership

According to this view, marriage should be regarded as analogous to a business partnership.[134] The husband and wife cooperate together as a couple as part of a joint economic enterprise.[135] It may be that one spouse is employed and the other works at home, but they work together for their mutual gain just as in a business. Therefore, on divorce each spouse should be entitled to their share of the profits of their enterprise, normally argued to be half each.[136] There are echoes of this kind of argument in the reasoning of Lord Nicholls's reasoning in *Miller v Miller*:[137]

> [in marriage] the parties commit themselves to sharing their lives. They live and work together. When their partnership ends each is entitled to an equal share of the assets of the partnership, unless there is a good reason to the contrary. Fairness requires no less.

---

[133] *C v C* [2007] EWHC 2033 (Fam).

[134] See the approach of the Canadian Supreme Court in *Moge v Moge* (1993) 99 DLR (4th) 456, discussed in A Diduck and H Orton (1994) 'Equality and Support for Spouses' (1994) 57 *Modern Law Review* 681.

[135] B Fehlberg, "With all my Worldly Goods I thee Endow'?: The Partnership Theme in Australian Matrimonial Property Law' (2005) 19 *International Journal of Law, Policy and the Family* 176.

[136] See C Burch, 'Of Work, Family Wealth and Equality' (1983) 17 *Family Law Quarterly* 99.

[137] [2006] 2 FCR 213, para 16.

For too long the caring contribution to a marriage was not valued or recognised. As Cynthia Starnes suggests, the law was beset by three myths: 'mothering just happens, mothering is free, and mothering is for babies'.[138] There needs to be a recognition of not only the value, but also the necessity for care, to a relationship. If care is at the heart of what we value about the relationship, then it is care which the primary activity and money-making enables it to happen. Prior to *White* it was the other way round, money-making was emphasised.

One of the more appealing aspects of the approach is the weight that it attaches to carrying out care giving obligations.[139] Notably the equal contribution to a partnership approach does not imply that the husband is giving the wife some of 'his' money. Rather it is regarding the matrimonial assets as the produce of both of their labour and fit for division between them.[140]

On first consideration it might be thought that this argument justifies redistributing assets that have accumulated during the marriage, but would not apply to assets owned by the parties before entering the marriage or assets acquired after the marriage breakdown. However, the approach can be developed to extend to future assets.

It is possible to argue that the partnership assets are not limited to tangible assets, but extend to the earning capacity of the parties.[141] So, if the wife had supported the husband at home while he developed his career, she could argue that he has only been able to reach the position where he is able to earn as much money as he does because of the help she provided. This argument would entitle the wife to a share in his future earnings, reflecting the increase in his earning potential acquired during the marriage.[142] This way of putting the argument is valid, but may prove difficult to utilise in practice because of the problem in identifying the extent to which a former spouse's contribution is still affecting current rates of pay. A stronger argument can be made based on the argument that if a caring enterprise is at the heart of a marriage, for example the care of children, that enterprise continues even after divorce and parties should contribute what they can to the success of that enterprise. That argument we will explore next.

---

[138] C Starnes, 'Mothers, Myths, and the Law of Divorce: One More Feminist Case for Partnership' (2006) 13 *William and Mary Journal of Women and Law* 203.

[139] L Glennon, 'The Limitations of Equality Discourses on the Contours of Intimate Obligations' in J Wallbank, S Choudhry and J Herring (eds), *Rights, Gender and Family Law* (Routledge, 2010).

[140] L Weitzman, *The Divorce Revolution* (The Free Press, 1985) 360.

[141] This argument is developed in C Frantz and H Dagan, 'Properties of Marriage' (2004) 104 *Columbia Law Review* 75.

[142] *H v H* [2008] 2 FCR 714.

D. Equality

It may be that the business model, just explained, that sees marriage as involving equal contributions is not the right one. Shari Motro argues:

> Marriage is not fundamentally about equal contribution of labor. It is about two people joining the risks and rewards of their lives: merging their fates, committing to be 'in the same boat,' to sink or swim together, to contribute unequally at times if that's what it takes to keep the union afloat.[143]

This way of putting the argument is interesting. It is not precisely an agreement to recognise as equal the contributions to the marriage, but rather an agreement to share the joys, slings and arrows of life. The model has considerable benefits. It views the family in the way we might assume that many couples do. The relationship may bring sickness, health, wealth or poverty, but the couple will share in that. Few families will seek to account for the contributions made.[144] We are, as they say, all in this together.

Let us start with the notion that an intertwining of life should lead to sharing the joys and disadvantages of that caring relationship. In some cases it may be that the relationship can be ended without a court order, because there is a fair share of these. But, particularly where there are caring responsibilities that result from the marriage, these will continue well beyond the marriage. Consider these comments of John Eekelaar, who seeks to restrict ongoing financial orders:

> [a] father who leaves a young child will, of course, retain the child support obligation. But his obligation to the mother should be less extensive than if he left a grown-up family, for he is more likely to take on new commitments, and the mother to enter a new relationship. In an era of no-fault divorce, the expectation of sharing in the resources of a partner on a long-term basis can no longer be held to be established immediately upon entering marriage, or on the making of a contractual undertaking. Instead, it should be seen as a gradual legal fructification of a social obligation which builds up in the context of extended mutual interdependence.

Notably this argument emphasises freedom to enter new relationships rather than recognising the responsibilities that attach when family life has become intertwined.

The intertwining of lives explanation provides the response to a potential criticism of the partnership model. Some complain that the partnership model suggests that the child care of the wife of a multi-millionaire is equal to millions of pounds; while the wife of an impoverished academic may be

---

[143] S Motro, 'Labor, Luck, and Love: Reconsidering the Sanctity of Separate Property' (2008) *102 Northwestern University Law Review* 1623.

[144] Alicia Brokars Kelly, 'Money Matters in Marriage: Unmasking Interdependence in Ongoing Spousal Economic Relations' (2008) 47 *University of Louisville Law Review* 113.

just a few thousand. This seems particularly odd as the wife of the millionaire is likely to have a veritable bevvy of assistance in terms of cleaners, nannies and the like. This argument, however, perhaps fails to fully appreciate the nature of intimate relationships. Care is not about counting the hours and pennies. It is a throwing together of lives, without calculating the costs.[145] As Carolyn Frantz and Hanoch Dagan put it:

> The unique goods of 'communal' marriage—intimacy, caring, and commitment—are collective in a crucially different way. A mercenary understanding of these goods is hopelessly misguided, corrupting the community ideal of marriage. A self-centered quest to capture these marital goods—cooperating to achieve solely individual ends—will not ultimately be successful. Rather, to secure these unique goods of marriage, what is good for one spouse must affect what is good for the other. This partial fusion, at the core of communal marriage, is achieved when spouses perceive themselves at least partially as a 'we,' a plural subject, that is in turn a constitutive feature of each spouse's identity as an 'I'.[146]

If caring is a central aspect of this intertwining of lives, then when there are children or other dependants involved, this continues post marriage. This deals with a further concern from a care-based perspective with the partnership approach, which is that, as Lisa Glennon points out, it only rewards care work performed within the context of the marriage and does not recognise the post-divorce care of children.[147] An approach which puts a caring relationship at its heart can do this. It sees financial orders on divorce as ensuring that the primary purpose of the marriage, the caring of dependants, continues to thrive despite the divorce.

E. Compensation

The extent of disadvantage for women on divorce[148] is closely related to their employment history during marriage.[149] There is convincing evidence that following divorce those who have undertaken primary care of the child

---

[145] A Alsott, 'Private Tragedies? Family Law as Social Insurance' (2010) 4 *Harvard Law and Policy Review* 3.

[146] C Frantz and H Dagan, 'Properties of Marriage' (2004) 104 *Columbia Law Review* 75, 82.

[147] P Laufer-Ukeles, 'Selective Recognition of Gender Difference in the Law: Revaluing the Caretaker Role' (2008) 31 *Harvard Journal of Law & Gender* 1.

[148] K Funder, 'Women, Work and Post-Divorce Economic Self-Sufficiency: An Australian Perspective' in M Meulders-Klein and J Eekelaar (eds), *Family, State and Individual Economic Security* (Kluwer, 1988).

[149] For a useful discussion of compensation claims see A Murray, 'Guidelines on Compensation' (2008) 38 *Family Law* 756.

(normally the wife) suffer significantly.[150] The conclusions of a recent study of the impact of divorce on women were blunt:

> The stark conclusion is that men's household income increases by about 23 per cent on divorce once we control for household size, whereas women's household income falls by about 31 per cent. There is partial recovery for women, but this recovery is driven by repartnering: the average effect of repartnering is to restore income to pre-divorce levels after nine years. Those who do not repartner ... the long term economic consequences of divorce are serious.[151]

Child care responsibilities mean that women are far more likely to have given up employment than men; where they are employed, mothers are more often in part-time, low status, poorly paid jobs.[152] Even where they have returned to full-time employment, the time taken out to care for children will have set back their earning potential.[153] In part, ex-wives' financial hardships also reflect the wage differences which exist generally between men and women: average earnings of women are 22 per cent lower than men.[154] Women face discrimination in finding employment, both on the basis of their sex and on the basis that they are caring for children and therefore in a weaker position to advance their careers.[155] It is not just child care that can restrict a woman's ability to advance her career. Women still carry the primary duty of housework.[156] In one survey 48 per cent of men did little or no housework.[157] The impact of this becomes particularly apparent on retirement where women suffer particular poverty as compared with men.[158]

In response to facts such as these the compensation theory focuses on the disadvantages that the parties have suffered as a result of the marriage.[159] Typically this will involve one spouse giving up their career to care for the children. However, it could involve a spouse sacrificing career-

---

[150] S Dex, K Ward, and H Joshi, (2006) *Changes in Women's Occupations and Occupational Mobility over 25 Years* (Centre for Longitudinal Studies, 2006); W Sigle-Rushton, 'Great Britain: "Things Can Only Get Better ..."' in H-J Andreß and D Hummelsheim (eds), *When Marriage Ends* (Edward Elgar, 2009).

[151] H Fisher and H Low, 'Who Wins, Who Loses and Who Recovers from Divorce?' in J Miles and R Probert (eds), *Sharing Lives, Dividing Assets* (Hart, 2009) 254. See also A Wax, 'Bargaining in the Shadow of the Market: Is there a Future for Egalitarian Marriage?' (1998) 84 *Virginia Law Review* 509; E Steiner, 'Why Are Divorced Mothers Economically Disadvantaged? And What Can Be Done About It' (2007) 17 *Texas Journal of Women and Law* 131.

[152] J Scott and S Dex, 'Paid and Unpaid Work' in J Miles and R Probert (eds), *Sharing Lives, Dividing Assets* (Hart, 2009).

[153] Ibid.

[154] National Statistics, *Gender Pay Gap* (ONS, 2009).

[155] M Maclean, *Surviving Divorce* (Oxford University Press, 1991).

[156] J Trew and S Drobnic, *Dividing the Domestic* (University of Stanford Press, 2010).

[157] Mintel, *Mintel Housework Survey* (Mintel, 2004). C Geist, 'Men and Women's Reports about Housework' in J Trew and S Drobnic (eds), *Dividing the Domestic* (University of Stanford Press, 2010) notes that in surveys men tend to exaggerate the amount of housework they do.

[158] See J Herring, *Older People in Law and Society* (Oxford University Press, 2009).

[159] In *VB v JP* [2008] 2 FCR 682, the wife refused to take up a promotion because the husband did not want to move. This was regarded as an economic disadvantage due to the marriage.

developing opportunities, so that the other spouse can peruse their career. The compensation principle was accepted in *Miller v Miller*,[160] where Lord Nicholls explained:

> [Compensation] is aimed at redressing any significant prospective economic dispar- ity between the parties arising from the way they conducted their marriage. For instance, the parties may have arranged their affairs in a way which has greatly advantaged the husband in terms of his earning capacity but left the wife severely handicapped so far as her own earning capacity is concerned. Then the wife suffers a double loss: a diminution in her earning capacity and the loss of a share in her husband's enhanced income.

The claim shares a benefit with the equal contribution to the partnership approach in that it puts the wife's claim in term of an entitlement, rather than classifying her as in especial need.[161] It is, however, notably different from the sharing approach in that the claim is not tied to the gains made by the husband. So the argument is likely to produce a lower award in cases where the husband has been especially economically productive, but a higher award where he has not.

Ultimately I do not find the compensation argument attractive. It has practical problems in attempting to predict what salary a person would have earned had they not married. More significantly, while it does recognise that caring causes loss, it finds the value of the care in terms of the economic career given up, rather than in terms of the value of the care work itself. The focus is on replacing the economic damage that care causes, rather than recognising its value.[162]

F. The State's Interests

Most people who have written on the issue of justifications for redistribution of property on divorce have assumed that the issue is about achieving fair- ness between the parties themselves.[163] However, it is arguable that financial orders on divorce can be justified by interests of the state, regardless of what would be fair or just between the parties.[164] So what state interests are there here? These might include ensuring that, if possible, neither spouse becomes

---

[160] [2006] 2 FCR 213, para 13.

[161] J Eekelaar 'Back to Basics and Forward into the Unknown' (2001) 31 *Family Law* 30.

[162] L Glennon, 'The Limitations of Equality Discourses on the Contours of Intimate Obligations' in J Wallbank, S Choudhry and J Herring (eds), *Rights, Gender and Family Law* (Routledge, 2010).

[163] Many commentators make the assumption that redistribution of property on divorce is a private matter: see eg, S Cretney, 'The Family and the Law – Status or Contract?' (2003) 15 *Child and Family Law Quarterly* 403.

[164] J Herring, 'Why Financial Orders on Divorce should be Unfair' (2005) 19 *International Journal of Law, Policy and the Family* 218.

dependent on welfare payments or promoting the stability of the family.[165] Here I will focus on the state's interests in promotion of caring relationships.

The response of society to the disadvantage will have an impact on the way parents are likely to organise their child care arrangements. Obviously a system that provided no kind of financial compensation or support to a spouse who lost out financially through child care or other forms of care would be discouraging people from undertaking child care. By contrast, a society which did provide some kind of compensation would be making that a more attractive option. The availability of financial orders on divorce is one way a state could seek to do that. It is not the only way. Others would be to provide state sponsored funding for those who undertake care work or to restructure work around the norms of family care.[166] Of course, a combination of these could be offered. Joan Williams argues:

> If we as a society take children's need for parental care seriously, it is time to stop marginalizing the adults who provide it. The current structure of work is not immutable: it was invented at a particular point in time to suit particular circumstances. Those circumstances have changed.[167]

Part of taking care seriously involves making appropriate orders on separation. As Joan Williams asserts:

> Today a man can overinvest in his career secure in the knowledge that if his marriage fails, he can walk away with his wallet and enter another marriage with his financial assets substantially intact. He can put his prior marriage behind him in a way his marginalized wife and children cannot ... Mothers always have understood that having children decreases future freedom. Fathers need to learn the same lesson. Men today know they can overinvest in work and create a family premised on their absence from daily life, secure in the knowledge that if at any point they want to reverse their priorities, they can walk with their wallets, get a younger wife and reinvest in a new and improved family, taking with them the asset that embeds not only their market work but their ex-wife's family work as well.[168]

These points have received judicial recognition. In *SRJ v DWJ (Financial Provision)*,[169] Hale J (as she was then) in the Court of Appeal stated:

> It is not only in [the child's] interests but in the community's interests that parents, whether mothers or fathers, and spouses, whether husbands or wives, should have a real choice between concentrating on breadwinning and concentrating on homemaking and child-rearing, and do not feel forced, for fear of what might happen

---

[165] Ibid.
[166] J Williams, 'Toward a Reconstructive Feminism: Reconstructing the Relationship of Market Work and Family Work' (1998) 19 *North Illinois University Law Review* 89.
[167] Ibid.
[168] Ibid 139–40.
[169] [1999] 2 FLR 176, 182.

should their marriage break down much later in life, to abandon looking after the home and the family to other people for the sake of maintaining a career.

How the law provides for financial orders on divorce will directly impact on the decisions couples may make. It also contributes more widely to the societal response to care giving and how it is regarded.[170] Not everyone will be convinced by these arguments. There are three particular issues to address.

First, Lucinda Ferguson has argued that the state has over-extended the appropriate interpersonal obligations owed between spouses and by parents to children in order to deal with poverty, which should be resolved by state support:

> The notion of interpersonal obligation has been distorted in both contexts in an attempt to respond to social inequality. More concerning than this distortion, however, is the fact that neither of these support obligations manages to successfully respond to social inequality anyway. Separated and divorced women and children raised in single-parent families represent a disproportionate percentage of those Canadians[171] living below the low income cut-off. Focus on expanding and strengthening these interpersonal obligations has distracted us from the urgent need to address the root causes of the inequality that these obligations have been adapted to address.[172]

Ferguson's argument is that if we accept these state-based justifications (a recognition of care; reduction of gender-based disadvantage) for intervention we should not impose the burden on the other spouse, but on the Government.

There is much to be said in favour of Ferguson's argument. One of the difficulties with the current law is the extent to which the claims of the spouse may be met or the goals of the state furthered, depends on the wealth of the husband. For the vast majority of cases they are fine sounding words of no practical significance. Putting the burden on the state to recognise the value of care work; promote equality and limit disadvantage to employment patterns caused by family responsibilities is more likely to ensure these aims are met.

But, and it's an enormous but, the costs of doing this through state funds would be enormous. In the current economic climate it is especially hard to imagine it being taken on. Further, it would not capture the fact that the losses caused to the wife have resulted in the gains to the husband in terms of home and family life.[173]

---

[170] A Brokars Kelly, 'Money Matters in Marriage: Unmasking Interdependence in Ongoing Spousal Economic Relations' (2008) 47 *University of Louisville Law Review* 113.

[171] The point could equally well be made about this in England.

[172] L Ferguson, 'Family, Social Inequalities and the Persuasive Force of Interpersonal Obligation' (2008) 22 *International Journal of Law, Policy and the Family* 61, 75.

[173] L Glennon, 'The Limitations of Equality Discourses on the Contours of Intimate Obligations' in J Wallbank, S Choudhry and J Herring (eds), *Rights, Gender and Family Law* (Routledge, 2010).

A second argument is that rather than using financial orders to address these issues, it would be better to improve the extent of child care undertaken by men. That would ensure that the burden of child care is shared equally. Although there is evidence of fathers seeking to play an increased role in child care,[174] the vast majority is still undertaken by women.[175] The question must be the extent to which the state can affect the distribution of care within households. The current trend is for those working to be working for longer and longer hours, making it harder for couples to share child care and work.[176] The alternative is to encourage both parties to work and for ever greater use to be made of day care. However, this raises the debate over whether day care or care at home is preferable for children. This is a heated debate. Although the evidence suggests that there are some advantages and disadvantages to both, there is controversy as to whether one is preferable overall.[177] While ensuring a fair distribution of child care is a worthy aim, it is not a reason against ensuring that where the distribution is unequal the burdens of that distribution should all fall on one party.

Third, financial orders on divorce will reflect the norms that are said to underlie the marital relationship. The orders made can seek therefore to reinforce certain norms or to downplay others.[178] There may be some who will wish to privilege independence and autonomy. We saw earlier, for example, the importance John Eekelaar attaches to giving parties the freedom to form new relationships. However, I would emphasise rather the value and vulnerability that care work gives rise to. As Milton Regan explains:

> The ideas of autonomy as independence and obligation as consensual rest upon the valorization of the realm of the market in which men traditionally have been the primary agents, and the marginalization of a realm in which women traditionally have been the primary actors.[179]

Through financial orders on divorce, determined by the values of the law, our community is able to recognise the value and importance of care work. There is much more that our society needs to do to properly value that work, but this is a starting point.

---

[174] S Maushart, *Wifework* (Bloomsbury, 2001) 129.

[175] See eg J Eekelaar and M Maclean, *The Parental Obligation* (Hart, 1997) 137.

[176] P Moen, *It's About Time* (Cornell University Press, 2003).

[177] J Ermisch and M Francesconi, *Working Parents: The Impact on Kids* (Institute for Social and Economic Research, 2003) argue that children whose parents both work suffer in a variety of ways. The Daycare Trust, *Towards Universal Child Care* (The Daycare Trust, 2003) paints a much more positive view of day care.

[178] C Smith, 'Philosophical Models of Marriage and their Influence on Property Division Methods at Divorce' (2000) 11 *Journal of Contemporary Legal Issues* 214.

[179] M Regan, *Alone Together: Law and the Meaning of Marriage* (New York, Oxford University Press, 1999) 166.

G. Pre-Nuptial Agreements

Historically it was seen as contrary to public policy for spouses to make a contract that determined what should happen to their finances on separation.[180] There were three public policies that were seen to be in play. The first was that rendering such an agreement enforceable could be seen as amounting to an encouragement to separate.[181] Presumably the argument is that if a spouse knows exactly what they will receive financially in the event of a divorce they may be thereby encouraged to separate. The second was that it was seen as contrary to public policy that a couple contemplate separation at the very time they are meant to be contemplating what is intended to be a life-long union.[182] The third is that it was seen to deprive the courts of their Parliament-given jurisdiction to determine how property disputes should be resolved on divorce.[183]

In recent years the courts have been giving increasing weight to pre-nuptial agreements.[184] They were recognised as having evidential weight[185] and guiding the court.[186] If the pre-nuptial agreement was within the range of orders a court might give then that might sway the court to making an order in those terms. The law is now dominated by *Radmacher v Granatino*,[187] where it was held that it 'should accord respect to the decision of a married couple as to the manner in which their financial affairs should be regulated'.[188] The Court held that:

> '[t]he court should give effect to a nuptial agreement that is freely entered into by each party with a full appreciation of its implications unless in the circumstances prevailing it would not be fair to hold the parties to their agreement.[189]

In effect, once it is shown that the agreement was freely entered into, the Justices have placed on the party who is seeking to avoid the agreement the burden of proving to the court that it would be unfair to give effect to it. In future cases, therefore, two key questions will arise:

— Is the agreement valid? Was it 'freely entered into by each party with full appreciation of its implications'?[190]

— Is the agreement fair?

---

[180] See J Scherpe (ed), *Marital Agreements and Private Autonomy in Comparative Perspective* (Hart, 2012) for a helpful discussion.

[181] *Cocksedge v Cocksedge* (1844) 14 Sim 244, 13 LJ Ch 384; *H v W* (1857) 3 K & J 382.

[182] Rejected by Connell J in *M v M (Prenuptial Agreement)* [2002] *Family Law* 177.

[183] *Hyman v Hyman* [1925] AC 601.

[184] Resolution *A More Certain Future: Recognition of Pre-Marital Agreements in England and Wales* (Resolution, 2011).

[185] *N v N (Jurisdiction: Pre-nuptial agreement)* [1999] 2 FLR 745, 752.

[186] *M v M(Prenuptial Agreement)* [2002] 1 FLR 654, para 44.

[187] [2010] UKSC 42.

[188] Ibid, para 78.

[189] Ibid, para 75.

[190] Ibid, para 75.

It seems from the judgment that the following factors will be considered in deciding whether the contract is unfair:

(1) 'A nuptial agreement cannot be allowed to prejudice the reasonable requirements of any children of the family'.[191]
(2) If events occurred which were not foreseen by the parties at the time of the agreement, then these have the potential to render it unfair.
(3) The agreement fails to meet the needs of one spouse and leaves the spouse 'in a predicament of real need'.[192]
(4) 'If the devotion of one partner to looking after the family and the home has left the other free to accumulate wealth, it is likely to be unfair to hold the parties to an agreement that entitles the latter to retain all that he or she has earned'.[193]

There is a strong dissenting judgment in *Radmacher*, written by the only specialist family lawyer in the Supreme Court, Lady Hale. She rejected the view that the starting point should be giving effect to the pre-nup, referring to the principles established in the earlier case law:

> It seems to me clear that the guiding principle in *White, Miller* and *McFarlane* is indeed fairness: but it is fairness in the light of the actual and foreseeable circumstances at the time when the court comes to make its order. These circumstances include any marital agreement made between the parties, the circumstances in which the agreement was made, and the events which have happened since then.[194]

The approach of the courts to pre-nups has generated substantial disagreement. I won't go into all of the issues here.[195] But there are several which are significant, given the themes of this book. It was noticeable that the majority of their Lordships in *Radmacher* emphasised the importance of autonomy:

> The reason why the court should give weight to a nuptial agreement is that there should be respect for individual autonomy. The court should accord respect to the decision of a married couple as to the manner in which their financial affairs should be regulated. It would be paternalistic and patronising to override their agreement simply on the basis that the court knows best. This is particularly true where the parties' agreement addresses existing circumstances and not merely the contingencies of an uncertain future.[196]

---

[191] Ibid, para 77.
[192] Ibid, para 81.
[193] Ibid, para 81.
[194] Ibid, para 169.
[195] See R George, P Harris and J Herring, 'Pre-Nuptial Agreements: For Better or For Worse?' (2009) *Family Law* 934; R George, J Herring and PG Harris, 'Ante-Nuptial Agreements: Fairness, Equality, and Presumptions' (2011) 127 *Law Quarterly Review* 335.
[196] [2010] UKSC 42, para 78.

I would argue that this argument is flawed for two primary reasons. First, it assumes that the agreement is a matter for the two parties alone and is their decision. Second, it is hard enough to assess what is a fair distribution of the assets when the facts are known. Trying to predict what will happen in the future is impossible. How can a couple negotiate a fair division of assets when they don't know what life will bring them? One may become seriously disabled; their children may be disabled; the wealth of one may be decimated in a stock market crash: the imponderables are too many. The economically weaker party is also likely to be the one who will suffer most in the event of unexpected occurrences during the marriage, where they involve caring responsibilities. If the child is born disabled or a parent needs extra care, this is most likely to fall on the woman. Relationships are unpredictable and messy. The sacrifices called for can be unpredictable and obligations without limit. Ask any partner caring for their demented loved one. To seek to tie these down at the start of the relationship in some form of 'once and for all' summation of their claims against each other ignores the realities of intimate relationships.[197] We need to ensure a fair sharing of the risks of caretaking.[198] These cannot be predicted in advance and only assessed at the end of a relationship.

H. Conclusion

Lady Hale has argued:

> Do we want to encourage responsible families [and, I would add, societies] in which people are able to compromise their place in the world outside the home for the sake of their partners, their children and their elderly or disabled relatives [and again I would add society], and can be properly compensated for this if things go wrong? I continue to hope that we do.[199]

That claim is central to the argument in this section. We need financial orders on divorce that recognise the value of care; that ensure the consequences of care are shared equally; and appreciate the intertwining of interests that takes place in intimate relationships.

The problems identified in this discussion are significant. The difficulties that arise reflect broader problems of gender equality and distribution of child care and housework roles.[200] If there is to be financial fairness between

[197] J Herring, 'Relational Autonomy and Family Law' in J Wallbank, S Choudhry and J Herring, (eds), *Rights, Gender and Family Law* (Routledge, 2010) 270.
[198] T Metz, 'Demands of Care and Dilemmas of Freedom: What We Really Ought to be Worried About' (2010) 6 *Politics and Gender* 120.
[199] B Hale, 'Equality and Autonomy in Family Law' (2011) 33 *Journal of Social Welfare and Family Law* 3, 4.
[200] A Diduck, 'What is Family Law For?' (2011) 64 *Current Legal Problems* 287.

spouses on divorce, some fundamental change in society is required. Diduck and Orton look forward to a better future:

> Along with true equality in employment and pay and affordable good quality child care, an adequate valuation of domestic work would mean it would not be necessary that each partner play exactly the same role in wage earning ... Roles in marriage could be adopted based on the partners' actual interests and skills. Maintenance on divorce would still sometimes be necessary, then, but it would no longer overwhelmingly be women who require it and it would no longer result in economic disadvantage for the recipient. Maintenance would be seen as a right, expected and earned, rather than as a gift, act of benevolence or based on a notion of women's dependency on men.[201]

The real problems are social: a society with gendered inequalities in terms of distribution of child care; housework; wages and access to the employment market; and a society that fails to adequately recognise the value of care work. Given these issues, any attempt to produce a 'fair' law on ancillary relief is doomed to fail.

VII. Unmarried Couples and Property Disputes

The law on cohabiting couples who have separated is complex.[202] In short, at the end of a relationship which is neither marriage nor civil partnership, the couple cannot claim financial orders. The court has no power to redistribute property, nor to make maintenance orders. The couple can only seek an order as to who owns what. This means that property disputes between cohabitants are resolved by reference to the existing law of land or trusts, rather than there being any discretion.

There is widespread unhappiness with the current law.[203] The Law Commission has stated that:

> Current property law rules are generally agreed to be highly complicated and uncertain. In addition to the technical difficulties they present, the nature of the evidence required to prove the elements of a claim makes it difficult in practice to predict the likely outcome of cases. Most significantly, the rules lead to outcomes which many people would consider to be unfair.[204]

---

[201] A Diduck and H Orton, 'Equality and Support for Spouses' (1994) 57 *Modern Law Review* 680, 686–87.

[202] B Sloan, *Informal Carers and the Law* (Hart, 2012) provides an invaluable guide to the law in this area, focused on carers.

[203] See G Douglas, J Pearce and H Woodward, 'Money, Property, Cohabitation and Separation' in J Miles and R Probert (eds), *Sharing Lives, Dividing Assets* (Hart, 2009); S Gardner, 'Family Property Today' (2008) 122 *Law Quarterly Review* 422.

[204] Law Commission, *Consultation Paper (Overview)* (Law Commission) 15.

I will not go into the detail of the law on this area, which is dominated by the law on constructive trusts.[205] To establish a constructive trust there are two essential elements: the intention of the parties to share the property and acts in reliance on the common intention. Great difficulty has centred on the establishment of the common intention.[206] Less difficult cases are those where there is clear evidence as to the fact the parties intended to share and in what proportions. However, such cases are rare. Where there is no such intention, the court will try to infer of impute intention from what the parties said and the way they lived their lives. The complexities involved are well discussed elsewhere, but the following two points are particularly relevant in focusing on caring.

First, the law can lead to great injustice for unmarried cohabitants. Injustice was revealed in the following *dicta* of Johnson J in *T v S (Financial Provision for Children)*:[207]

> the sadness here is that, after a long and seemingly happy relationship, this mother of five children, never having been married to their father, has no rights against him of her own. She has no right to be supported by him in the short term, still less in the long term; no right in herself to even have a roof over her head.

This injustice can be particularly harsh on a woman who has contributed significantly to the family through child care and housework, who will leave the relationship with many of the economic disadvantages that flow from it, and none of the economic gains.

Second, the current law on constructive trusts places significant weight on the agreements the parties have reached.[208] In fact, it is unrealistic to expect all couples to discuss the legal ownership of their property. The cases demonstrate that the courts have had to pick up on casual comments made during the relationship,[209] even where there is clear evidence. Where there is no evidence of conversations, economic contributions to the house count as evidence of an intention to share, but it is generally thought that non-financial ones do not.[210] The problem here is that the law focuses on irrelevant factors. As argued in the context of financial orders on divorce, it is the care work performed by the parties, and the intertwining of their lives which creates the strongest case for creating a share in the properties.[211] Notably, in relation to

---

[205] See J Herring, *Family Law* (Pearson, 2011) ch 4, for a detailed discussion.

[206] J Miles, 'Property Law v Family Law: Resolving the Problems of Family Property' (2003) 23 *Legal Studies* 624.

[207] [1994] 2 FLR 883.

[208] S Gardner, 'Family Property Today' (2008) 122 *Law Quarterly Review* 422.

[209] P Rippon, 'Mistresses I Have Known – Unmarried Cohabitants and Land Ownership' (1998) 28 *Family Law* 682.

[210] There may be some slight relaxation on that following *Jones v Kernott* [2011] UKSC 53 (SC).

[211] S Wong 'Caring and Sharing: Interdependency as a Basis for Property Redistribution' in A Bottomley and S Wong, *Changing Contours of Domestic Life, Family and Law* (Hart, 2009).

the redistribution of property of married couples on divorce, the House of Lords has held that there should be no discrimination between the money-earner and the homemaker or child-carer.[212]

Ruth Deech opens her recent discussion of financial orders on separation by asking her readers to consider three sisters:

> One is very pretty and marries a national footballer; they have no children and it is a short marriage before she leaves him for an international celebrity. The second sister marries a clergyman and has several children; the marriage ends after 30 years as he is moving into retirement. The third sister never marries; she stays at home and nurses first their mother, who has a disability, and then their father, who has Alzheimer's, and dies without making a will. Which of the three sisters will get the windfall: an amount sufficient to keep her in luxury for the rest of her days, when her relationship with a man comes to an end? And which one most needs and deserves financial support, even of the bare minimum? The message is that getting married to a well-off man is an alternative career to one in the workforce.[213]

Her implied message is that the current law on financial orders on separation has gone badly wrong. The undeserving footballer's wife ends up with millions, the carer of the demented mother ends up with nothing. She is right that this seems unfair. But, of course it does not follow that the problem is the award to the footballer's wife. It may be the real issue is the lack of provision for carers, rather than excessive awards to wives. And the way resources are distributed in the world is generally unfair. As argued above, if caring is at the heart of what we value about family life and it is caring that we should be seeking to uphold, value and enable in our law, then we should prize caring wherever it is found. That is so whether the relationships involve people who are married or unmarried; same-sex or opposite sex; living together or not.

VIII. Autonomy and Family Law

Autonomy appears to be playing an ever greater role in family law. As discussed in chapter three, autonomy at its most simple is a recognition that individuals should be allowed to make decisions for themselves. We can see the growing significance of autonomy in family law in the greater emphasis placed on mediation, rather than litigation; restrictions on legal aid; a move to no fault divorce; and increased weight attached to pre-nuptial agreements and cohabitation contracts.

---

[212] *White v White* [2001] AC 596.
[213] R Deech, 'What's a Woman Worth?' (2009) 39 *Family Law* 1140.

Family law, at least until recently, has placed relatively little weight on the idea of autonomy and it is easy to see why. It fits uncomfortably with what are commonly thought to be the central themes of family law: the responsibilities of parents; the state interest in upholding marriage; the enforcement of obligations between spouses. None of these are readily reconcilable with the freedom to forge one's life story which is at the heart of individualist models of autonomy.

This emphasis on autonomy is influenced by a number of factors, and not just a straightforward philosophical approach. It fits in well with the Government's continued attempts to reduce expenditure. Cutbacks in legal aid are attractively packaged as they encourage people to avoid the adversarial courts and prefer cosy mediation instead. It might also reflect the fact the Government is feeling the heat from complaints about the way courts and state bodies make decisions in relation to family matters. This is true particularly of the court's response to applications by non-resident fathers for contact with their children and the operation of the Child Support Agency. In both cases the responses have involved attempts to shift decision making away from state agencies or courts and towards the couples themselves.[214]

In chapter three I argued that individualistic autonomy which regards freedom to live as one chooses; a separation from others; and respecting an individual's choice is simply inconsistent with family life as it is understood and experienced by most. As Pamela Scheininger puts it:

> Because the law is conceived of in its application to the isolated individual rather than in its application to the individual's various associations and relationships, the law does not accurately reflect the reality of human existence. The legitimacy of the law is thus challenged. Individual persons do not operate as independent, separate entities, but as interdependent, connected parts of larger groups. In failing to deal with laws as they affect human relationships, lawmakers ignore a fundamental aspect of our humanity ...[215]

The traditional approach is particularly inappropriate in family cases. It disguises the fact that in families the interests of different parties cannot be separated.[216] This, however, is predicated on the basis that we *can* separate out the interests of a parent and a child. But one cannot separate out the interests of a parent and a child or the interests of intimate partners. They

---

[214] Children and Adoption Act 2007; Child Maintenance and Other Payments Act 2008.

[215] P Scheininger, 'Legal Separateness, Private Connectedness: An Impediment to Gender Equality in the Family' (1998) 31 *Columbia Journal of Law and Social Problems* 283.

[216] M Eichner, 'Principles of the Law of Relationships among Adults' (2007) 41 *Family Law Quarterly* 433.

are intertwined.[217] To harm a child is to harm the person caring for the child; and to harm the carer is to harm the child.

Also, family life practices inevitably raise important social and community issues. It is not possible to consider the significance of family practices in isolation from those practices. Quite simply many family disputes are not essentially private matters. Running through this book we have seen the many public ramifications that flow from the treatment and practice of care. Fineman argues:

> [T]he family in [the traditional 'separate spheres' understanding of society] is positioned as a unique and private arena. I argue that this is an incorrect and unsustainable conception. The family is contained within the larger society, and its contours are defined as an institution by law. Far from being separate and private, the family interacts with and is acted upon by other societal institutions. I suggest the very relationship is not one of separation, but of symbiosis. It is very important to understand the roles assigned to the family in society—roles that otherwise might have to be played by other institutions, such as the market or the state.[218]

Third, if autonomy is about developing and living out a vision for one's own flourishing, for many, if not all, that involves being in relationships with others. The state is required to create the conditions where a person can exercise their autonomy by entering a relationship which receives support and protection by society; and ensures a person is not disadvantaged by entering such a relationship. As Jennifer Nedelsky argues, the state must attend to 'conditions that foster people's capacity to form caring, responsible and intimate relationships with each other—as family members, friends, members of a community, and citizens of a state'.[219]

Finally, privileging individualist autonomy can operate in a way that disadvantages women. It promotes the unattached, unencumbered person as the norm. In advocating autonomy as the ideal, the obligation and responsibility of care work is downplayed. Indeed it is seen as antagonistic to the autonomous ideal. As women undertake the majority of care work, it disadvantages them. As Pamela Laufer-Ukeles puts it:

> Revaluing nurture work does not mean that women must or should perform such work; rather, it is in the interest of society that such work be given proper accord. Gender makes a difference, and ignoring that difference creates unfairness. This unfairness must be addressed. An alternative to the gender neutral paradigm of divorce law must be identified. Gender difference in the context of divorce should be recognized by advocating support for the different and important contribution

---

[217] J Herring, 'The Human Rights Act and the Welfare Principle—Conflicting or Complimentary?' (1999) 11 *Child and Family Law Quarterly* 223.

[218] M Fineman, *The Autonomy Myth* (New Press, 2004) xviii.

[219] J Nedelsky, 'Property in Potential Life? A Relational Approach to Choosing Legal Categories' (1993) 6 *Canadian Journal of Law and Jurisprudence* 343, 343.

of caretaking. Such recognition will begin to address the hardships caretakers face at divorce.[220]

In most, if not all, intimate relationships parties invest in varying ways and extents to the relationship. Putting central value on the autonomy of the parties to leave the relationship and pursue their own life goal will disadvantage the party who has invested more in it and has suffered economic or social disadvantage as a result.

These arguments do lead me to abandon the benefit of autonomy altogether, but rather promote a relational approach of autonomy. The notion of relational autonomy has already been outlined in chapter two. It seeks to move away from individualism, which ignores the complex web of relations and connections which make up most people's lives. The reality for everyone, but in our society particularly women, is that it is the values of inter-dependence and connection, rather than self-sufficiently and independence, which reflect their reality. People do not understand their family lives as involving clashes of individual rights or interests, but rather as a working through of relationships. The muddled give and take of everyday family life where sacrifices are made and benefits gained, without them being totted up on some giant familial star chart, chimes more with everyday family life than the image of independent interests and rights. We need, therefore, to be wary of approaches to family life that elevate autonomy to a high position. Family life should be about the fulfilment of responsibilities that arise from relationships and fashioning responses to problems that enable the relationship to continue.

IX. Conclusion

This chapter has argued for a refocusing of family law on the promotion of care. There are, in fact, moves in this direction already. It has argued that approaching family law through an ethics of care lens provides some invaluable perspectives. It encourages family law to focus on caring relationships as its central focus rather than sexual ones. It means that when considering the welfare of children, they must be considered in the context of the relationships they are in. In addition, in resolving disputes over money at the end of the relationship, the focus would be on acknowledging the significance of the responsibilities that flow from a relationship of a care between the parties.

---

[220] P Laufer-Ukeles, 'Selective Recognition of Gender Difference in the Law: Revaluing the Caretaker Role' (2008) 31 *Harvard Journal of Law and Gender* 1.

In its paper, *Beyond Conjugality*, the Law Commission of Canada[221] calls for relational equality and equality within relationships. Relational equality involves not discriminating against people unfairly based on the status of their relationship. Whether couples are same-sex or opposite sex; married or not; sexual or not; does not, I suggest, affect the contribution they make to the social good. They deserve the same support and protection. The principle of equality within relationships seeks to address disparity of income, wealth and power within relationships. These are valuable principles around which to reshape family law.

---

[221] Law Commission of Canada, *Beyond Conjugality* (Law Commission of Canada, 2001).

7

Caring and General Law

I. Introduction

In this chapter I will explore several areas of law in so far as they affect caring relationships. This does not purport to a definitive guide to the law on caring relationships in all these areas of law, but rather to provide further examples of how an ethic of care approach can impact on a wide range of areas of the law. To start, I will consider the human rights claims by those in caring relationships.

II. Human Rights and Caring Relationships

Carers could seek to rely on human rights claims to bolster their legal position in a range of legal cases. A number of different articles of the European Convention on Human Rights (ECHR) could be relied upon, through the Human Rights Act 1998.

A. The Right to Respect for Private and Family Life

A caring relationship is protected by article 8 of the ECHR, which protects the right to respect for family and private life. Where it involves relatives then there will be no difficulty in arguing that their relationship falls within the category of family. But even if they are not relatives, there is a good argument that they can still be regarded as having family life where there are 'close personal ties'.[1] The European Court of Human Rights (ECtHR) has,

[1] *Lebbink v The Netherlands* 45582/99, para 36; *Kautzor v Germany* [2012] 2 FCR 197, para 61.

for example, accepted that foster carers and the children they look after can have family life.[2] Even if a claim to family life fails, a strong case can be made for their relationship to be protected by the right to respect private life. This part of article 8 has been said to include the right to 'establish and develop personal relationships', and is wider than the concept of family life.[3]

Article 8 contains both positive and negative aspects. In negative terms, the state must not interfere in an individual's private and family life unless to do so is necessary under the terms of article 8(2)—for example it is necessary to protect the interests of others. More significant is the positive obligation under article 8.[4] This can require the state to provide services or otherwise act in a way to enable a person to maintain a family relationship. This is, of course, limited. A state is only required to take reasonable steps to respect those relationships. Article 8, therefore, imposes a duty on the state not to interfere in a caring relationship, unless there is a sufficiently good reason for doing so. Not only that, it requires the state to take reasonable steps to enable a caring relationship to continue.[5]

This is particularly relevant when local authorities have concerns about caring relationships. In *A Local Authority v A (A Child)*,[6] Munby J emphasised the significance of article 8 when criticising the overly-interventionist approach of the local authority in one case (concerning a child (A) and vulnerable adult (C)), which saw its role as simply to protect the vulnerable person. He explained that that assertion:

> ... betrays a fundamental misunderstanding of the nature of the relationship between a local authority and those, like A and C and their carers, who it is tasked to support—a fundamental misunderstanding of the relationship between the State and the citizen. People in the situation of A and C, together with their carers, look to the State—to a local authority—for the support, the assistance and the provision of the services to which the law, giving effect to the underlying principles of the Welfare State, entitles them. They do not seek to be 'controlled' by the State or by the local authority. And it is not for the State in the guise of a local authority to seek to exercise such control. The State, the local authority, is the servant of those in need of its support and assistance, not their master ...[7]

The primary duty of the state under article 8 in a case where intense care is involved is, therefore, to support and enable that relationship to continue.

---

[2] *Rieme v Sweden* (1992) 16 EHRR 155; *Cyprus v Turkey* (1976) 4 EHRR 282.

[3] A Mowbray, *The Development of Positive Obligations under the European Convention on Human Rights by the European Court of Human Rights* (Hart, 2003).

[4] Department of Health, *Carers and Disabled Children Act 2000. Practice Guidance* (The Stationery Office, 2001).

[5] *R (Hughes) v Liverpool City Council [2005]* EWHC 428 (Admin); *R (Bernard) v Enfield LBC [2002]* ECHC 2282 Admin.

[6] [2010] EWHC 978 (Fam).

[7] Ibid, para 27. For a detailed discussion of this case see J Herring and M Dunn, 'Safeguarding Children and Adults: Much of a Muchness?' [2011] *Child and Family Law Quarterly* 528.

Another telling example of a local authority misunderstanding its role is a case which became public following a complaint to the Ombudsman. Due to a service failure, a mother of children with considerable needs was not offered bathing assistance for the children and so she had to hose them down in the back garden. When the council was aware of that she was accused of being abusive and warned that steps would be taken against her. As the Ombudsman said this involved 'breath-taking insensitivity' and 'institutionalised indifference' by a council.[8] What is so revealing here is that the local authority was blind to its own responsibilities to support this family and turned the blame entirely on the mother. The positive obligations on the state towards caring relationships are explored further in chapters four and eight.

B. The Right to Protection from Torture or Inhuman or Degrading Treatment

This right is protected by article 3 of the ECHR. It also imposes positive and negative obligations on the state. Not only must the state not torture or inflict inhuman or degrading treatment on its citizens, it must protect citizens from torture or inhuman or degrading treatment at the hands of other people, in so far as it is reasonable.[9] This is particularly important in cases where people are being abused within the context of intimate relationships.

Hence, if the state is aware that children are suffering abuse and fails to take reasonable steps to offer them protection, the state is said thereby to infringe the children's rights under article 3.[10] The same would be true of anyone suffering serious harm in a caring relationship. It has been used to argue that the state is under an obligation to ensure protection for victims of domestic violence[11] or elder abuse.[12] This is discussed further in chapter eight.

There may be cases where the burdens of a caring relationship are such that they can claim they are suffering torture or inhuman or degrading treatment. One can imagine 24-hour-a-day care with no respite readily falling into such a category. In such a case a failure to offer state support could breach article 3. Similarly, the state may be under an obligation to ensure that services are offered so that a disabled person's article 3 rights are not infringed. Indeed, the case mentioned above of the children being hosed down in the garden may fall into this category.

---

[8] Complaint no 07/C/03887 against Bury MBC, 14 October 2009.

[9] *E v UK* [2002] 3 FCR 700.

[10] Ibid.

[11] S Choudhry and J Herring, 'Righting Domestic Violence' (2006) 20 *International Journal of Law, Policy and the Family* 95.

[12] J Herring, 'Elder Abuse: A Human Rights Agenda for the Future' in I Doran and A Soden (eds), *Beyond Elder Law* (Springer, 2012).

C. The Right to Protection from Discrimination

While discrimination on the basis of sex, race and age is now well established, discrimination on the grounds of carer status has received little attention. Article 14 of the ECHR states that the rights protected by the ECHR 'shall be secured without discrimination on any ground such as sex, race, colour, language, religion, political or other opinion, national or social origin, association with a national minority, property, birth or other status'.

The use of the words 'such as' in that article indicate that the list of prohibited grounds of discrimination is not closed.[13] Three arguments could be made that carers should be added to this list.

First, discrimination on the grounds of disability is now rightly regarded as unacceptable[14] and article 14 has been interpreted by the ECtHR to cover it.[15] It could be said that discrimination against those in caring relationships with disabled people is a form of discrimination against disabled people. Anything that disadvantages the carers of disabled people will disadvantage the disabled people themselves; and disadvantages to disabled people will disadvantage the carers. This argument has been considered and accepted by the European Court of Justice in the context of protection in employment law from discrimination.[16] In *Coleman v Attridge Law*[17] it was held that discrimination in employment against a carer of a disabled person was discrimination on the grounds of disability, even though the carer was not themselves disabled. It was discrimination by association with a protected group. That, with respect, seems right. A person who is discriminated against because their spouse is a certain race, is discriminated against on the grounds of race, even though it is not their race that has caused the issue. It should be emphasised that even if either of these arguments is accepted, article 14 can only be relied upon if one of the other rights in the ECHR was engaged. The most obvious claim would be that a carer's right to respect for her private or family life was interfered with in a way which was discriminatory on the grounds of her caring status.

The argument, against this way of putting the argument is that it does not protect the interests of the carer in their own right. It relies on the disadvantages faced by the 'cared for' as the route of legal redress for the 'carer'.[18] As the Government White Paper puts it, we should 'treat carers as equals, not as an extension of the person for whom they care'.[19] On the

---

[13] *Da Silva Mouta v Portugal* [2001] 1 FCR 653.

[14] Equality Act 2010.

[15] *Kityutin v Russia*, application 2700/10.

[16] Council Directive 2000 (2000/78/EC) of 27 November 2000.

[17] Case C-303/06.

[18] L Waddington, *Carers, Gender and Employment Discrimination* (University of Maastricht, 2010).

[19] HM Government, *Caring for our Future* (The Stationery Office, 2012) 62.

other hand, it might be said to recognise that in a caring relationship the interest of the parties become merged so that discrimination against either impacts on both. These issues have been explored in chapter two. Another concern may be that it limits the protection of carers of people who do not have a disability.

Second, Laura Kessler suggests the argument for caring rights can be put in terms of gender equality:

> If women assert that they deserve rights because they are equal to men, they are likely to be afforded rights only when they are in fact equal. If women assert that they deserve rights because gender socialization or biological forces dictate their caregiving, they will receive rights only during the limited circumstances when society considers their agency to be bounded. But if women assert that they deserve rights because caregiving work is at least in part an assertion of the legitimacy of their identity and equality as citizens, then women and men for that matter will be afforded rights when they engage in caregiving.[20]

This argument is that an essential part of combating sex discrimination is to ensure caring does not cause disadvantage. By disadvantaging carers, one is engaging in indirect sex discrimination. This way of putting the argument might be preferable to some than the first because it covers all carers, not just those caring for a disabled person. It also may be thought to recognise the claim of the individual carer in his or her own right. However, it may be said to sideline male carers.

Third, the argument could be made that carers as a group are vulnerable and disadvantaged and need protection as a group in their own right. Luke Clements writes:

> Carers should have the same life chances as anyone else. The mere fact they are providing care should not disentitle them to opportunities available to people who do not have caring responsibilities. To argue otherwise would be to suggest that it is legitimate to discriminate against carers in a way that would not be acceptable for any other group.[21]

The Equality and Human Rights Commission has recognised that there is a need to 'increase autonomy, choice and control for both carers and those who receive care'.[22] A state keen to promote autonomy and freedom could rely on such an argument to recognise the rights of those in caring relationships.

The difficulty in making this claim is that being in a caring relationship (unlike race or sex) is not an 'immutable characteristic'; rather it is a role

---

[20] L Kessler, 'Is there Agency in Dependency? Expanding the Feminist Justifications for Restructuring Wage Work' in M Fineman and T Dougherty (eds), *Feminism Confronts Homo Economicus* (Cornell University Press, 2005).

[21] L Clements, *Carers and the Law* (Carers UK, 2008) para 4.40.

[22] Equality and Human Rights Commission, *How Fair is Britain?* (EHRC, 2010) 46.

a person has chosen to undertake.[23] Further, unlike other grounds of discrimination, carers are not a category of people with a clear group identity. In response, it can be argued that it is doubtful whether 'immutability' or 'group identity' are required for a ground of discrimination. Illegitimacy and marital status do not fall under either of these headings and yet are accepted as grounds of discrimination. Sandra Fredman, rejecting the view that immutability is a requirement for a ground of discrimination, argues that the central requirement is that 'a person or group has been discriminated against when a legislative distinction makes them feel that they are less worthy of recognition or value as human beings, as members of society'.[24]

Another argument would be to challenge the assumption that caring is 'chosen'. As explored in chapter three, caring responsibilities should be seen as a given: a norm into which we are born and cannot escape.

A fourth possibility, and one I would support, would be to recognise that those in caring relationships are disadvantaged. All of the arguments made above have validity but all of them have difficulties. These flow from the individualised nature of rights. The full wrong of the discrimination against a person in a caring relationship cannot neatly be captured by identifying this as just a wrong against the 'carer'. It is a wrong against the relationship. The difficulty in identifying this discrimination reveals the individualistic tendencies of the law described in chapter three.

From a broader perspective, in Martha Fineman's *The Autonomy Myth*,[25] the claim is made that as carers provide much benefit to society there is a debt owed to them by society. She argues:

Caretaking thus creates a 'social debt', a debt that must be paid according to principles of equality that demand that those receiving social benefits also share the costs when they are able. Far from exemplifying equal responsibility for dependency, however, our market institutions are 'free-riders', appropriating the labour of the caretaker for their purposes.[26]

Fineman's arguments were explored in chapter three. They could be used in this context to bolster a claim for rights for protection.

D. Carers and the Equality Act 2010

The Equality Act 2010 prohibits less favourable treatment based on a number of characteristics including age and disability. Being a carer is not one of the list characteristics and the Act gives no scope for adding to the list through

---

[23] S Fredman, *Discrimination Law* (Oxford University Press, 2011) ch 1.

[24] Ibid 43.

[25] M Fineman, *The Autonomy Myth* (New Press, 2004).

[26] Ibid.

judicial interpretation, unlike the ECHR. But there are provisions in the Act which can be used to help those in caring relationships. Perhaps most significant is the concept of 'associative discrimination'.

i. Associative Discrimination

Section 13 of the Equality Act 2010 sets out the key concept of direct discrimination:

'(1) A person (A) discriminates against another (B) if, because of a protected characteristic, A treats B less favourably than A treats or would treat others.'

Crucially, this does not require that the person being discriminated against has the characteristic. So the parent of a disabled child who is treated differently because her child is disabled (eg an employer allows other parents time off for child-related reasons, but not the disabled parent because her child is disabled) would be able to bring a case under section 13.[27] Although she is not disabled, she is being treated differently 'because of a protected characteristic' (her child's) and so is being discriminated against. The Equality and Human Rights Commission gives this example:

The guest at a club dinner is the full-time carer of a disabled child with learning difficulties. The club excludes her and the child from the association's main dining room. The carer could complain of direct discrimination because of disability—in this case based on the disability of the child with whom she is associated.[28]

In *Coleman v Attridge Law*[29] the European Court of Justice held that discriminating against a person caring for a disabled person was prohibited under legislation protecting disabled people from discrimination.[30] The significance of this is that if an employee requests flexible working and is refused by an employer this could amount to discrimination on the basis of disability, if he or she can be shown to have been treated less favourably than other requests for flexible working. It also means that there should be no discrimination between the benefits and treatments for those caring for children and those caring for adults with disabilities.[31] This has been described as discrimination by association or, perhaps better, 'transferred, discrimination'.[32]

---

[27] Equality and Human Rights Commission Services, *Public Functions and Associations* (EHRC, 2010) para 4.19.

[28] Ibid para 12.40.

[29] Case C 303/06.6.

[30] European Framework Directive 2000 (2000/78/EC).

[31] P Robertson, 'Caring for the Disabled? New Boundaries in Disability Discrimination' (2009) 72 *Modern Law Review* 635.

[32] S Honeyball, 'Discrimination by Association' [2007] 4 *Web Journal of Current Legal Issues*; C O'Brien, 'Equality's False Summits: New Varieties of Disability Discrimination, 'Excessive' Equal Treatment and Economically Constricted Horizons' (2011) *European Law Review* 49.

ii. Carer Discrimination and Indirect Discrimination

The Equality Act covers not only direct discrimination, but also indirect discrimination. Section 19 states:

(1) A person (A) discriminates against another (B) if A applies to B a provision, criterion or practice which is discriminatory in relation to a relevant protected characteristic of B's.

(2) For the purposes of subsection (1), a provision, criterion or practice is discriminatory in relation to a relevant protected characteristic of B's if—

    (a) A applies, or would apply, it to persons with whom B does not share the characteristic,

    (b) it puts, or would put, persons with whom B shares the characteristic at a particular disadvantage when compared with persons with whom B does not share it,

    (c) it puts, or would put, B at that disadvantage, and

    (d) A cannot show it to be a proportionate means of achieving a legitimate aim.

This, then, covers apparently neutral provisions (eg over height) which in fact are harder for people with 'protected characteristics' to satisfy than others. An employer might be able to justify having the neutral provision if it is 'a proportionate means of achieving a legitimate aim'.

If a particular provision was harder for those with caring responsibilities to satisfy than others, it could not be argued that this was discriminatory against carers per se, because being a carer is not a protected characteristic. However, it could be argued that because most carers are women, that provisions that are harder for carers to satisfy are thereby indirectly discriminatory against women.[33] The Equality and Human Rights Commission provide a good example:

> When a local council holds its consultation meetings on a weekday evening, it discovers that fewer women than men attend. A woman complains that this is because some women, including herself, cannot come because of childcare responsibilities. This is enough to demonstrate disadvantage and she does not have to show that the absence of women is attributable in particular cases to childcare responsibilities.[34]

It should be emphasised that indirect discrimination may be easier to justify than direct discrimination. An employer, for example, may be able to show that for a particular job working outside school hours is necessary, even though that will be discriminatory of carers.

---

[33] L Clements, *Carers and their Rights* (Carers UK, 2010) para 13.10.

[34] Equality and Human Rights Commission Services, *Public Functions and Associations* (EHRC, 2010) para 5.11.

III. Carers and Tort

The law of tort covers those in caring relationships just as any other. In chapter eight we will look generally at the way extra obligations are taken on by those who undertake care of another. Here we will look at some of the specific issues that arise in relation to the law of tort and caring relationships.

A. Duties of Care

There have, remarkably, been very few cases where children have successfully sued their parents under the law of tort.[35] As so often in the law of tort there is a special exception in relation to car accidents where universal car insurance skews the operation of the law. Outside that context, litigation is rare. Of course, that is partly because the child will have little to gain (outside the context of insured risks) in suing his or her own parents. However, there may be ideological reasons for this too.

Lord Woolf in *Barrett v Enfield LBC* explained:

> If a parent when driving a car injures his child who is a passenger, then of course as is the case with any other driver there is no reason why he should not be liable for damages. However parents are daily making decisions with regard to their children's future and it seems to me that it would be wholly inappropriate that those decisions, even if they could be shown to be wrong, should be ones which give rise to a liability for damages.[36]

In the House of Lords, Lord Hutton agreed, stating, 'it would be wholly inappropriate that a child should be permitted to sue his parents for decisions made by them in respect of his upbringing which could be shown to be wrong'.[37]

As Jo Bridgeman[38] suggests, it seems that the courts are not necessarily denying that parents owe their children a duty of care, it is just that rarely, if ever, will a court be willing to find that parents have fallen below the standard expected. This is part of the law's general willingness to allow parents a broad

---

[35] J Bridgeman, 'Caring for Children: Risks and Responsibilities in the Law of Tort' in M Freeman (ed), *Law and Childhood Studies* (Oxford University Press, 2012).

[36] *Barrett v Enfield LBC* [1998] QB 367, 377.

[37] *Barrett v Enfield LBC* [2001] AC 550.

[38] J Bridgeman, 'Caring for Children: Risks and Responsibilities in the Law of Tort' in M Freeman (ed), *Law and Childhood Studies* (Oxford University Press, 2012).

discretion in deciding how to raise their children.[39] But Jo Bridgeman goes on to make a more profound observation:

> Failure to extend the protective reach of the civil law to children, in the belief that it would be an 'intrusion' which could 'disturb family harmony', is to fail to recognize harm to children and reinforces a construction of children as becoming not being. Where a child is injured, it will be the child's parents who assume the burden of caring for the child. As such not only the cause but also the consequences of injury are privatized; confined to the home. Responsibility for children is thus individualised and privatized. The responsibility for children rests with their parents, the responsibility to care for children rests with their parents. Parents are responsible for, rather than to, their children.

She is not seeking necessarily to extend the scope of tort law into parenthood or caring more generally, but is noting its role in rending caring a private matter, and the harms that result from parenting decisions likewise private.

B. Recovery for Carers' Loss of Earnings

If A is injured by X's negligence and, as a result, A's partner, B, has to give up work to care for him, it might be expected that the law would say that X has, as a result of her negligence, caused B a loss and is liable to pay him damages. But no. X is liable to pay damages for B's loss, but these are payable to A, although A will then hold them on trust for B.[40] The use of the trust might be thought just a technical issue. After all, at the end of the day, the carer receives the damages, should it matter exactly how the law formulates this? It is suggested that it should matter for two reasons. First, the carer is at the mercy of the claimant suing for damages.[41] If the claimant does not wish to sue, for example she cannot face the effort of litigation, the carer has no remedy in her own right.[42] Second, there is the symbolic effect of the message sent by the law. The loss to the carer is not explicitly acknowledged: the loss is seen as the loss to the claimant who will have to pay for care.[43]

Even where damages are paid under the principles just outlined, the carer will not necessarily get the actual loss of earnings she has suffered.[44] The Law Commission reports that the general approach is to award the amount

---

[39] See J Herring, *Family Law* (Pearson, 2011) ch 8.

[40] *Hunt v Severs* [1994] 2 All ER 385. A useful summary and discussion of the law is found in the Law Commission, *Damages for Personal Injury: Medical, Nursing and Other Expenses; Collateral Benefits* (Report No 262, 1999).

[41] Law Commission, *Damages for Personal Injury: Medical, Nursing and Other Expenses; Collateral Benefits* (Report No 262, 1999) para 3.47.

[42] S Degeling, *Restitutionary Rights to Share in Damages* (Cambridge University Press, 2003).

[43] Ibid.

[44] B Braithwaite 'The Significance of Family Care for Injured People' [2005] *Personal Injury Compensation* 10.

it would cost to pay for the care on the open market, less one third. The one-third reduction is to reflect the fact that National Insurance and tax costs are not incurred.[45] Colin McEachran QC, referring to these cases, states that gratuitous care is 'grossly undervalued by the courts'.[46] It does not necessarily reflect the actual loss of income suffered by the carer. It might be said that where the would-be carer is currently earning more than a paid carer would be, the claimant should mitigate the loss and rely on paid care, rather than their high-earning relative or friend providing the care. However, surely it is reasonable to prefer care to be provided by a person close to you. Supporters of the current tort law approach to carers might argue that it is appropriate because the carer has no 'right to provide care' and so should not be able to seek damages in respect of it. A carer should not be able to receive damages for care which the injured person may decide they would rather receive from someone else. This argument may have carried weight in the past. But, in these days of structured settlements where damages can be paid in variable instalments over time, the argument is weaker. The instalments can be paid to the person who has been providing care (or is likely to provide care) for the relevant period of time and payments can cease if they stop providing the care.

C. Loss of Care

In *Sklair v Haycock*[47] a car accident injured the claimant who at the time of the accident had Asperger's syndrome and obsessive compulsive disorder. If it hadn't been for the accident, his family would have given him care out of love and affection. The accident severely affected his mobility and psychological well-being. The family stated that following the deterioration of his condition they could not provide the 24-hour-a-day care that he needed. The Court held he did not need to take that into account in calculating his claim against the defendant. So he was entitled to the full damages and not a reduction in them by the saving of the amount of care that had been provided anyway. Edwards-Stuart LJ explained:

> ... where the claimant would have continued to enjoy care and attention given out of love and affection which he now cannot enjoy because of the accident, I see no reason in either logic or justice why he should be required to place a value on that care and attention and then be made to give credit for it against his claim. In this case the claimant has not gained by the absence of his father's care and attention—indeed he would say that he is now worse off because he is without

---

[45] Law Commission, *Damages for Personal Injury: Medical, Nursing and Other Expenses; Collateral Benefits* (Report No 262, 1999) para 3.83.
[46] Ibid para 3.84.
[47] [2009] EWHC 3328.

it—and I do not believe for one moment that his father would feel that he has achieved a saving as a result of the accident: far from it, I am sure that he would have much preferred to continue to care for the claimant for as long as he is able to do so. I therefore reject the submission of the defendant that I should place a value on these services and give the defendant the benefit of it. To do that would be to add insult to injury.[48]

D. Significance of Local Authority Assistance

One argument which has fortunately been rejected by the courts is that if a local authority contributes to the payment of care costs, this should lead to a reduction in the level of damages. The rejection of this argument in *Freeman v Lockett*[49] is welcome because local authority payments can be variable and cannot be guaranteed, a point acknowledged in *Crofton v NSH Litigation Authority*.[50] In *Burton v Kingsbury*[51] the problem was dealt with by ordering the defendant to pay the proportion of the cost of care not funded by the local authority. A claimant cannot seek damages if currently receiving care by the local authority nor for NHS care provided free. More problematic is whether a failure to utilise local authority care will mean a failure to mitigate.

E. Private Care Costs

Another way to deal with the issue of the unreliability of local authority care is to hold that it is reasonable for a claimant to use private care. In *Sowden v Lodge*[52] the Court of Appeal accepted the issue must be seen from the point of view of the claimant. The test is not what was in a claimant's best interests but whether the private care and accommodation were reasonable. If the private care was significantly short of that which was offered by the local authority (augmented by extra private care if needed), it should be met.[53] Notably, one reason why private care may be seen as a reasonable choice is if the care offered by the local authority has been uncertain.[54] This might be

---

[48] Ibid, para 35.
[49] [2006] EWHC 102.
[50] [2007] 1 WLR 923.
[51] [2007] EWHC 2091.
[52] [2005] 1 WLR 2129.
[53] See also *Massey v Tameside Glossop Acute Services NHS Trust* [2007] EWHC 317 QB (Admin).
[54] *Crookdake v Drury* [2005] 1 WLR 2129.

that it is unclear how long the local authority care will be provided[55] or how much care will be available.[56]

Perhaps the most striking case in favour of permitting a claimant to utilise private care was *Freeman v Lockett*[57] where the claimant was receiving direct payments from her local authority to provide for her care. The claimant wished to move to private funding of care to give her greater control over her resources, which would contribute to her sense of independence and well-being. This was approved, with emphasis placed on the fact that direct payments from the local authority could not be guaranteed, especially if she were to move. Similarly in *Peters v East Midlands Strategic Health Authority*[58] a disabled child was receiving what the Court regarded as excellent care provided by the local authority. It was accepted that the local authority was paying substantial expenses. It was said that due to the cost and the strain on local authority resources there could be no certainty that it could continue to meet the need. The Court of Appeal went further, with Dyson LJ stating

> We can see no reason in policy or principle which requires us to hold that a claimant who wishes to opt for self-funding and damages in preference to reliance on the statutory obligations of a public authority should not be entitled to do so as a matter of right.[59]

The key concern, of course, was over double recovery, but it was held that if a claimant's affairs were administered by the Court of Protection then that Court could be given a copy of the judgment and seek an order that no application for public funding under the claimant's care under the National Assistance Act 1948 could be made without further order.

F. Where the Carer is Injured

In *Decoy v William Doxford*,[60] Mr Decoy had been exposed to asbestos dust and as a result developed a malignant mesothelioma and died aged 68. His 63-year-old widow suffered from Parkinson's disease, osteoporosis and a spinal condition. She claimed that prior to her husband's illness she had been dependent upon him for most things, save personal hygiene. She was, after his death, given care by family and friends, and later paid carers. She sought an extra award due to her husband's reduced ability to care for her until her death and the cost of replacement services. The past care provided by friends and relatives was valued at the rate of payment for a home help, with a

---

[55] *Godbold v Mahmood* [2005] Lloyd's Rep. Med. 379.
[56] *Walton v Calderdale Healthcare NHS Trust* [2005] Lloyd's Rep. Med. 398.
[57] [2006] LS Law Med. 151.
[58] [2008] LS Law Med. 370.
[59] [2010] QB 48.
[60] [2009] EWHC 1598 (QB).

25 per cent reduction because they were friends or relatives.[61] There was no real explanation for this reduction. She was able to recover for the costs of the care her husband would have provided; and also for the loss of love and affection.[62] Claims for replacements for gratuitous services in fact have a long history in tort law.[63] Husbands have long been able to recover the costs of procuring the services of a housekeeper[64] following the negligent harm to their wives. Where reasonable, a husband who gives up his job to care for children can recover lost income.[65] However, in *Batt v Highgate Private Hospital*[66] it was held not reasonable for a father to give up his well paid job to care for his daughter, care which could be bought commercially for less than his salary. Similarly, where a relative has to give up her job, as did the aunt in *Cresswell v Eaton*,[67] she was entitled to the loss of earnings as a travel warden, notably at a level less than a commercial nanny.

G. Conclusion

We can see from these cases on tort law the courts struggling to fit caring into traditional forms of legal thought. The absence of the law of tort in enforcing formal duties of care reflects the assumptions that care should be seen as a private matter in which it is not appropriate for the law to intervene. The difficulties in dealing appropriately with issues around care in the law of tort reflect the failure to value care and the fixation on economic productivity as the sole marker of significance.

IV. Carers' Employment Law Protection

In chapter four we looked at some of the ways the state can support those involved in caring relationships. While welfare support for caring relationships is essential in some cases, there are inevitably limits on the extent of state financial support. Not surprisingly the Government has sought to enable and encourage people to combine their caring responsibilities with paid employment. As we saw in Chapter four, concerns over work life balance have led to calls to produce a labour market which is not based on a

---

[61] Ibid, para 63.
[62] See also *Beesley v New Century Group Ltd* [2008] EWHC 3033.
[63] *Berry v Humm and Co* [1915] 1 KB 627.
[64] *Jeffery v Smith* [1970] RTR 279.
[65] *Mehmet v Perry* [1977] 2 All ER 529.
[66] [2005] PIQR Q1, paras 24 to 32.
[67] [1991] 1 WLR 1113.

model designed for a 'husband' who dedicates his life to work, while his wife looks after the caring responsibilities, nor its more modern manifestation of the male earner and female part-time earner, part-time carer.[68] Nicole Busby discusses the conflict between wishing to care and needing to have sufficient income in these terms:

> The main source of this conflict is the inability of those engaged in the non-negotiable work of caring to conform to the practices ascribed by established and apparently unyielding structures surrounding paid work which dictate how, where, and when it should take place. This non-conformance has resulted in the exercise of 'alternative' strategies, such as the growth in part-time work, which are often accompanied by a reduction in legal protection against the vagaries of the market which is heralded as the determinant of what are deemed to be appropriate standards of behaviour.[69]

The Government Carers' Strategy encourages carers to undertake employment.[70] The Carers (Equal Opportunities) Act 2004 and Work and Families Act 2006 give protection under employment law to carers.[71] However, as we shall see these are somewhat limited.[72] Not only are there few legal rights that workers with caring obligations have, but these are unevenly distributed. Protection for parents, especially maternity rights, is notably stronger than that for those caring for, for example, elderly parents or older children with disabilities.[73]

The difficulties facing carers who wish to remain in employment was recognised in the Government's paper on carers in 2010:

> It is crucial that we place a much higher priority on supporting people of working age with caring responsibilities to remain in work, if they wish to do so. The Government wants to empower carers to fulfil their work potential, to protect their own and their family's current and future financial position and to enjoy the health benefits and self-esteem that paid employment or self-employment can bring. Yet many carers currently feel forced to give up work because they feel they have no other options available to them.[74]

Before exploring the legal rights that carers have, it is worth summarising the impact of caring on employment opportunities.

---

[68] R O'Brien, *Bodies in Revolt: Gender, Disability and a Workplace Ethic of Care* (Routledge, 2005).

[69] N Busby, *A Right to Work?* (Oxford University Press, 2011) ch 3.

[70] HM Government, *Carers at the Heart of 21st-Century Families and Communities* (The Stationery Office, 2008); HM Government, *Recognised, Valued and Supported* (The Stationery Office, 2010).

[71] J Lewis, 'The Changing Context for the Obligation to Care and to Earn' in M Maclean (ed), *Family Law and Family Values* (Hart, 2005).

[72] S Himmelweit and H Land, *Reducing Gender Inequalities to Create a Sustainable Care System* (Joseph Rowntree Foundation, 2008).

[73] P Smith, 'Parental-Status Employment Discrimination: A Wrong in Need of a Right?' (2002) *University of Michigan Journal of Law Reform* 569.

[74] HM Government, *Recognised, Valued and Supported* (The Stationery Office, 2010).

A. Carers and Employment

Considerable pressure is experienced by those who seek to combine paid work with caring responsibilities.[75] Heavy caring responsibilities can severely impact employment.[76] Around 80 per cent of carers are of working age and it has been suggested that 12 per cent of the workforce are seeking to combine employment with heavy caring responsibilities. Caring responsibilities particularly impact upon the employment position of women. Twenty five per cent of female carers are in part-time employment, while only 15 per cent of male carers are. However, 37 per cent of male carers are in full-time employment, while only 26 per cent of female carers are.[77] It has been suggested that 80 per cent of carers below the pension age would return to work if they could.[78] Sixty per cent of carers providing substantial amounts of care have given up paid work to care and of these 70 per cent find themselves financially worse off as a result.[79] It has been estimated there are a million carers who have given up work due to their caring responsibilities.[80]

The current law is based on a major review by the Department of Health in 2000, entitled *Carers and Employment*.[81] It created a series of measures designed to improve the employment rights of carers. We shall discuss these now.

B. Emergency Leave

Under section 57A(1) of the Employment Rights Act 1996:

(1) An employee is entitled to be permitted by his employer to take a reasonable amount of time off during the employee's working hours in order to take action which is necessary—

    (a) to provide assistance on an occasion when a dependant falls ill, gives birth or is injured or assaulted,

    (b) to make arrangements for the provision of care for a dependant who is ill or injured,

---

[75] S Cunningham-Burley, K Backett-Milburn and D Kemmer, 'Constructing Health and Sickness in the Context of Motherhood and Paid Work' (2006) 28 *Sociology of Health and Illness* 385.

[76] Department of Health, *Shaping the Future of Care Together* (The Stationery Office, 2009); HM Government, *Recognised, Valued and Supported* (The Stationery Office, 2010) 15.

[77] Department of Health, *Shaping the Future of Care Together* (The Stationery Office, 2009).

[78] L Clements, *Carers and their Rights* (Carers UK, 2010) para 4.54.

[79] Carers National Association, *The True Cost of Caring, Caring Costs* (Carers National Association, 1996).

[80] Carers UK and Ipsos MORI, *One Million People Give Up Work To Care* (Carers UK, 2009)

[81] Department of Health, Carers and Employment (The Stationery Office, 2000).

    (c)   in consequence of the death of a dependant,

    (d)   because of the unexpected disruption or termination of arrangements for the care of a dependant, or

    (e)   to deal with an incident which involves a child of the employee and which occurs unexpectedly in a period during which an educational establishment which the child attends is responsible for him.

This is not as generous a provision as might first appear. Only 'a reasonable amount of time off' is permitted. The Government Guidance explains:

> There's no set amount of time allowed to deal with an unexpected event involving a dependant—it will vary depending on what the event is but for most cases one or two days should be sufficient to deal with the problem.[82]

An employer is unlikely to accept that this provision could be used to allow for regular caring commitments, indeed it is specifically designed to cover emergency need. Crucially under (d) the need for care must be 'unexpected', which greatly restricts the width of that provision.

C. Flexible Working

For many with caring responsibilities, it is the difficulty of combining full-time work and care which is the problem and flexible working hours provide the solution. The Government's strategy on carers acknowledges this:

> Those carers who are looking to return to paid work cite flexible working as the most important component in their job search. While opportunities for flexible working have grown, this has not happened consistently across types of flexible working, and availability varies across different types of organisations, sectors and job levels. The availability of flexible work is particularly low for those looking for work, compared with existing employees. For people who have growing caring responsibilities, or have those responsibilities suddenly thrust upon them, the ability to change their working patterns is particularly important, and where it does not exist this may compel them to leave their job.[83]

Section 12 of the Work and Families Act 2006 does not offer a right to flexible working, but does offer a right to apply for it, which some might think is hardly worth the legislative effort in setting out, as there is nothing to stop an employer considering the request and then turning it down. The most that can be said is that the employer must consider the request seriously and refuse if there is a clear business reason or the request has been made in the past 12 months. A request can be made by a parent of a disabled child under the

[82] Directgov, *Time Off for Dependants*, available at www.direct.gov.uk/en/parents/moneyand-workentitlements/workandfamilies/dg_10026555.

[83] HM Government, *Recognised, Valued and Supported* (The Stationery Office, 2010) 15.

age of 18 or a person with a caring responsibility for an adult.[84] The request could involve working a different total number of hours; or a change to the time they work or to work from home. If such arrangements are accepted by an employer, they may lead to a change in salary.[85]

In *London Underground Ltd v Edwards (No. 2)*,[86] the Court of Appeal was sympathetic to a claim made by a mother that a change in the way her shifts worked made it much more difficult to combine her work with her child care. She alleged this was sex discrimination as the change in shift patterns worked against the interests of single parents, who were predominantly women. Ultimately the case turned on whether the new shift system created requirements which were 'such that the proportion of women who can comply with it is considerably smaller than the proportion of men who can comply with it'. This kind of argument will be all the more effective because of the Equality Act 2010, which extends these arguments to those caring for disabled people and also through the notion of associative discrimination, explained above.

As already mentioned, flexible working hours are attractive to carers. It enables them to work around the unpredictable needs that can arise in a caring relationship. There has been much talk by the Government and others in promoting 'flexicurity'.[87] This is designed to encourage employers to provide work which is flexible, but also provides a good degree of job security. Despite the hype surrounding it, Sandra Fredman argues that its result has not matched the hype. Indeed, she suggests the result of promotion of the policy is

> a precarious workforce, characterised by low pay, low status and little job security. Nor is it an accident that the precarious workforce is made up predominantly of women. Women are now both homeworkers and breadwinners, constantly traversing the boundary between unpaid and paid work.[88]

She explains why:

> that the dissonance between the ideal and the reality is a result of the tenacity of these two fundamental assumptions. The first is that 'work' encompasses paid work only, and particularly, only work which is the subject of market exchange. The

---

[84] To be a carer the employee must be a spouse, partner, relative or living with the person needing care: The Flexible Working (Eligibility, Complaints and Remedies) Regulations 2002 (SI 2002 No 3236) reg 3B (as amended).

[85] The Flexible Working (Eligibility, Complaints and Remedies) Regulations 2002 (SI 2002 No 3236) as amended by The Flexible Working (Eligibility, Complaints and Remedies) (Amendment) Regulations 2006 (SI 2006 No 3314), The Flexible Working (Eligibility, Complaints and Remedies) (Amendment) Regulations 2007 (SI 2007 No 1184) and The Flexible Working (Eligibility, Complaints and Remedies) (Amendment) Regulations 2009 (SI 2009 No 595).

[86] [1999] ICR 494 (CA).

[87] S Fredman, 'Women at Work: The Broken Promise of Flexicurity' (2004) 33 *Industrial Law Journal* 299.

[88] Ibid.

second is that employers' social responsibility only arises as a quid pro quo for the worker's full commitment to the individual employing enterprise. An employment relationship which gives the worker the apparent freedom to choose not to take on a particular task at a particular time need not give rise to responsibilities on the part of the employer. Nor do employers' responsibilities extend beyond the strictly bilateral relationship. Thus the reality of the dual burden of paid and unpaid work exacts a double cost. Family and domestic work is not only invisible, but counts against workers struggling to maintain the difficult balance between paid and unpaid obligations. The result is that employers are able to pass the risks of the enterprise onto the most vulnerable workers.

As part of its strategy on carers, the Government says it will consult on encouraging employers to offer flexible working practices.[89] However, it may well take more than encouragement to change employers' attitudes.

D. Parental Leave

Parents can be entitled to parental leave of up to 18 weeks to care for children they are responsible for. However, this is subject to significant limitations:

— It is only available to parents who have worked for their employee for more than a year.
— It is only available if a child is disabled[90] or under the age of five.
— A maximum of 18 weeks is available for disabled children and 13 weeks for children under five years old.
— The leave is unpaid, unless the employer has a special scheme.
— It is only available to parents with parental responsibility.

In addition, time off is permitted for antenatal care. For maternity leave 26 weeks is permitted and a further 26 weeks with notification requirements. On return there is the possibility of returning to part-time work, but this must be requested and need not be granted. The first six weeks of statutory maternity leave are 90 per cent of weekly earnings and 33 weeks at the statutory rate.

At the moment there is real concern that more generous protection for fathers is needed. The mother is now allowed to give some of 'her' leave to the father, but it is seen as dependent on her agreement.

There is a right to request flexible working arrangements. It is necessary to show that the parent is an employee with 26 weeks continuous employment history and expects to have responsibility for the child's upbringing. It is not an automatic right and employers have a wide discretion to reject such a claim on the grounds of it having a detrimental impact on work

---

[89] HM Government, *Recognised, Valued and Supported* (The Stationery Office, 2010) 18.
[90] Defined as those for whom Disability Living Allowance is paid.

quality or leading to additional costs, for example. A claim can be made to an employment tribunal, but only on the procedural issues and the validity of the grounds provided.[91]

As mentioned earlier, the Government has suggested it will encourage employers to be more open to allowing carers to work flexible hours.[92] The Government is clearly concerned that taking a harder line in carers' rights in this area might deter employers from employing carers or might cause economic hardship. Charlotte O'Brien[93] has helpfully suggested that an analogy could be drawn with the notion of 'reasonable adjustment' that is used in the law governing disabled employees. This does not require employers to do everything imaginable to enable a disabled employer to work, but does require them to make 'reasonable adjustments'. The same approach could be used for any in a caring relationship: an employer must make reasonable adjustments to enable their employment. O'Brien accepts this is a compromise between those who would wish to see a stronger right to flexible employment and those who wish to protect the freedom of employers to set down the terms of employment. It offers a realistic next step for the law to take.

E. Difficulties in Employment Protection

The issues raised in discussing employment protection give rise to some broader questions.

i. Parents and Carers

There is a stronger protection under employment law for parents who seek leave than for carers. It may be that this simply reflects the time it has taken to appreciate the significance that is attached to care work more generally. It may be that many of the carers are older women and are less likely long term to return to the market place and so may explain the lesser effort compared to mothers.[94] There may even be a continuing suspicion around disability. It has even been claimed that the increased rates of abuse of disabled people in public are linked to allegations that disabled people are 'scroungers' on

---

[91] *Hussain v Consumer Credit Counselling* ET Case No 1804305/04.

[92] HM Government, *Recognised, Valued and Supported* (The Stationery Office, 2010) 15.

[93] C O'Brien, 'Confronting the Care Penalty: The Case for Extending Reasonable Adjustment Rights along the Disability/Care Continuum' (2012) 34 *Journal of Social Welfare and Family Law* 5.

[94] S Himmelweit and H Land, *Reducing Gender Inequalities to Create a Sustainable Care System* (Joseph Rowntree Foundation, 2008).

the benefits system.[95] This kind of attitude does not apply to childhood. However, there is no particular reason why the caring of one kind of dependant should be seen as any less important than the caring of any other.[96] Indeed, there is the danger of privileging those engaged in standard forms of care, such as parenthood, and disadvantaging those doing work which is just as significant, but not traditionally recognised, such as a gay partner caring for a child.[97]

ii. 'Carer Stigma'

There is a concern that the emphasis on care might cause 'special term stigma',[98] specifically that employers may be more reluctant to hire caregivers because of their legal rights. There may also be resentment from employees who are not care giving. The latter is particularly common where co-workers feel that they (rather than society generally or the company) are bearing the burden for the care-giving work. Such arguments commonly rely on the principle of equal treatment: workers should be treated equally. The difficulty with such an approach is that if the starting points are different equal treatment is not equal.

This leads some to argue that to ensure there is equal outcome there should be special treatment. The difficulty with this approach is that it leads to an emphasis on the 'male norm'. This is seen as the ideal worker: a person with no family commitments and free to be dedicated to the workplace. Those who are unable to comply with this norm are seen as in need of 'special treatment'. It is the standard of the independent worker who is free to commit him or herself to the firm which is the norm we should question. If we started with the norm of the family—committed worker, there would be no special treatment on offer. In Fineman's analysis, this is not 'special treatment' but instead is part of the 'basic right of accommodation due to all members of society as they engage in society-enhancing or -preserving tasks'.[99]

The best response is to focus on the real lives of the people involved. Are they in fact experiencing the treatment as equal? Even in a formal, legal sense, there may be an equal requirement of employment, if in the reality of the

---

[95] 'Benefit Cuts are Fuelling Abuse of Disabled People Say Charities' *The Guardian* 5 February 2012.

[96] J Williams and S Bornstein, 'Caregivers in the Courtroom: The Growing Trend of Family Responsibilities Discrimination' (2006) 41 *University of San Francisco Law Review* 171.

[97] N Dowd 'Bringing the Margin to the Center: Comprehensive Strategies for Work/Family Policies' (2004) 73 *University of Cincinnati Law Review* 433.

[98] N Porter, 'Why Care about Caregivers? Using Communitarian Theory to Justify Protection of "Real 2 Workers"' (2010) 58 *University of Kansas Law Review* 355.

[99] M Fineman, *The Autonomy Myth* (New Press, 2004).

lives of employees these are experienced differently, that should cause us to question whether there is a meaningful equality. Christine Littleton proposes 'equality as acceptance' so that 'difference between human beings, whether perceived or real, and whether biologically or socially based, should not be permitted to make a difference in the lived-out equality of those persons'.[100] However, differences carry costs and they must be borne by someone. If we are to use the law to try and ensure the costs do not fall on the individual, they must fall on something. Hence the argument that care is a valuable activity for all of society and it is essential to ensure that it should not be a cause of disadvantage in employment.

iii. Choice

As discussed in chapter two, some commentators believe we are seeing a move to a more individualistic society.[101] A more positive spin may be that an individual's self-fulfilment is growing in importance.[102] Certainly there seems to be an increased emphasis on the notion of choice and less on ideas associated with responsibility. Nevertheless, perceptions about what is expected of a mother, a father or a child has impacted upon decisions about arrangements of child care. As Grace James notes:

> Traditionally, the ideology of motherhood has constructed women as predominantly and inevitably responsible for providing consistent and selfless nurturing and, where necessary, abandoning any desire for self-fulfilment and independence that might be achieved through participation in the labour market. Nurturing was often considered to be an essential and exclusive part of a woman's identity and has had a powerful impact on the labour market participation decisions of, and attitudes towards, mothers with young children.[103]

In part, the question is whether we need to see greater access to work as the key. Vicki Schultz, for example, argues that we need to create viable working conditions to enable everyone to work and become financially self-sufficient. For her full employment is the goal, coupled with living wage legislation and job training and creation, combined with a reduction of the full time work week. She thus sees employed work as a platform for equal citizenship. This issue falls into the well documented debate between those who seek to increase the number of women in paid employment and those

[100] C Littleton, 'Reconstructing Sexual Equality' (1987) 75 *California Law Review* 1279, 1295–96.

[101] A Giddens, *The Transformation of Intimacy* (Polity Press, 1992).

[102] J Lewis, 'Marriage and Cohabitation and the Nature of Commitment' (1999) 11 *Child and Family Law Quarterly* 355.

[103] G James, 'Mothers and Fathers as Parents and Workers: Family-Friendly Employment Policies in an Era of Shifting Identities' (2009) 31 *Journal of Social Welfare and Family Law* 217.

who seek to improve the recognition and weight attached to women who work at home.[104]

Joan Williams argues:

[S]ocial forces ... get encoded as womens' choice to devote themselves to caregiving rather than to market work. These [include] objective factors such as the lack of affordable, high quality child care, employers, entitlement to marginalize anyone who does not live up to the ideal-worker norm, and fathers felt entitlement to perform as ideal workers. These objective factors create strong force fields pulling mothers toward marginalization ... [M]en and women live in different force fields, and so experience very different social cues. As a result, most well adjusted people become gendered. Consequently, women develop various skills and traits required for the modern caregiving role, such as the ability to do six things at once, family executive skills ... and the ability to sustain is there agency in dependency?[105]

F. New Models

How could the law on the employments rights of carers be improved? From the discussion above, a number of key points emerge:

First, care work needs to be valued by employers. This involves a recognition that caring makes an employee a good employee. Employers will be aware of the costs of paid leave not only in the financial sense, but depreciation in human capital, perhaps increased retraining time and reorganisation costs during the employee's absence.[106] However, care friendly policies can decrease absenteeism and attrition and encourage recruitment.[107] There is, therefore, a business case for granting workers the opportunity to combine employment with meeting care responsibilities.[108]

Second, as Sandra Fredman argues, employers need to be seen in the context of the broader social structures. Employers succeed and operate in the society which functions only because of the performance of care work by employees generally and others.[109] Employers gain much from broader social structures, which create costs for carers. As part of their broader social obligations they need to support the right of those employees who

---

[104] R Arnow-Richman, 'Accommodation Subverted: The Future of Work/Family Initiatives in a 'Me, Inc.' World' (2003) 12 *Texas Journal of Women and Law* 345, 395–96; P Smith, 'Parental-Status Employment Discrimination: A Wrong in Need of a Right?' (2002) 35 *University of Michigan Journal of Law Reform* 569, 598–99.

[105] J Williams, *Reshaping the Work-Family Debate* (Harvard University Press, 2010) 287.

[106] G Lester, 'In Defense of Paid Family Leave', available at http://ssrn.com/abstract=607984.

[107] J Williams and N Segal, 'Beyond the Maternal Wall: Relief for Family Caregivers who are Discriminated Against on the Job' (2003) *Harvard Women's Law Journal* 77.

[108] HM Government, *Recognised, Valued and Supported* (The Stationery Office, 2010) appendix 2.

[109] S Fredman, 'Women at Work: The Broken Promise of Flexicurity' (2004) 33 *Industrial Law Journal* 299.

have carer obligations.[110] As Gillian Lester points out, just arguing that caring benefits society may not be enough:

> These arguments have some force, but they beg the question of why *paid leave* policies, as opposed to other policies that might advance the same ends, would be desirable. Society might enjoy the benefits listed above to an even greater degree if social policy were designed to encourage single-earner partnerships: a financially supported adult, staying in the home, could devote greater time than a worker could to child and elder care. Alternatively, we might create a more comprehensive infra-structure for externally-provided caregiving, such as publicly provided daycare, or state subsidized home healthcare and elder care provision. Paid leave, although it may well facilitate parent-child bonding and family health, may not, in fact, be the best method for maximizing these goods. My defense of paid family leave instead rests principally on other normative goals: increasing labor market equality and enhancing women's autonomy.[111]

Third, the issue of carers' employment rights needs to be understood in the context of the changing social attitudes towards work and caring obligations. We are witnessing the demise of traditional model of the breadwinner and the stay at home mother/housewife.[112] Many men and women are seeking to combine their work and caring responsibilities.[113] Work practices and expectations are currently failing to keep up with these changes.[114]

Fourth, some commentators, in particular Nicole Busby, have argued that a right to care needs to be recognised as an important part of employment law.[115] As she acknowledges, one of the difficulties in recognising such a claim is that it does not neatly fit within models of rights. This is partly because by its nature it is imprecise and partly because it involves a complex interaction of social policy and private law and these do not neatly come together. However, if we accept the argument made above that employers gain from the current social structures, we can see a case for employers playing their role in sharing the costs of those structures which currently fall particularly harshly on those in caring relationships.

Fifth, there is a danger in separating gender discrimination issues from work/family divides in the workplace. In fact these two issues are insepa-rable.[116] The difficulty is that until broader social attitudes and practices

---

[110] R Arnow-Richman, 'Public Law and Private Process: Toward an Incentivized Organizational' (2007) *Utah Law Review* 25.

[111] G Lester, 'In Defense of Paid Family Leave', available at http://ssrn.com/abstract=607984.

[112] G James, 'Mothers and Fathers as Parents and Workers: Family-Friendly Employment Policies in an Era of Shifting Identities' (2009) 31 *Journal of Social Welfare and Family Law* 217.

[113] R Arnow-Richman, 'Accommodation Subverted: The Future of Work/Family Initiatives in a 'Me, Inc.' World' (2003) 12 *Texas Journal of Women and the Law* 235.

[114] G James, 'Mothers and Fathers as Parents and Workers: Family-Friendly Employment Policies in an Era of Shifting Identities' (2009) 31 *Journal of Social Welfare and Family Law* 217.

[115] N Busby, *A Right to Care?* (Oxford University Press, 2011).

[116] L Kessler, 'Keeping Discrimination Theory Front and Center in the Discourse Over Work and Family Conflict' (2007) 34 *Pepperdine Law Review* 313.

are resolved in relation to care work, a full feminist solution will not be found.[117]

V. Conclusion

In this chapter I have undertaken a wide ranging look at the significance of caring relationships in the law. The case has been made for recognising the promotion of caring relationships as a human right. Where law affects those in caring relationships unfairly, this should be recognised as a form of discrimination.

This chapter has also used tort law as an example of how, particularly in the area of remedies, caring is recognised in only a limited way. This is a potent sign of the law's failure to appreciate the value and importance of care.

Employment law demonstrates most visibly the lack of value attached to care. It seems much is still based on assumptions of a 'male unattached worker' model.[118] Joan Williams[119] argues that the law assumes:

> that is natural for women to take sole responsibility for child care, that doing so fulfils women's deepest nature and so makes them happy, that men are competitive and ambitious and thus naturally suited to employment but not to caregiving, and that homemakers' economic vulnerability in breadwinner-homemaker households is no big deal.

This is re-enforced in recent times in greatly increased assumptions about what it is to be a mother. Mothers' time is totally absorbed with ensuring that they provide every opportunity for their children and are constantly at children's side to protect them from the manifest dangers posed by society. This is well captured in Judith Warner's book, *Perfect Madness: Motherhood in the Age of Anxiety*.[120] With increased pressures and expectations on those caring and an increasingly insecure workplace environment, the case for an effective employment law for those in caring relationships is overwhelming. The goal we should be seeking has been set out by Sandra Fredman:

> The most fundamental change necessary to accommodate the combination of participative parenting and paid work would be to relax the rigidity of the working day

---

[117] R Arnow-Richman, 'Accommodation Subverted: The Future of Work/Family Initiatives in a 'Me, Inc.' World' (2003) 12 *Texas Journal of Women and the Law* 235.

[118] See the excellent S Fredman, *Women and the Law* (Oxford University Press, 1998).

[119] J Williams, *Reshaping the Work-Family Debate* (Harvard University Press 2010) 4.

[120] J Warner, *Perfect Madness: Motherhood in the Age of Anxiety* (Riverhead, 2005).

and the working year. The current situation, in which flexible work is of low pay and low status, only reinforces inequalities and disadvantage.

This change would entail more than just protection of women against prejudice and the facilitation of a return to paid work after childbirth. It would also bring about change in the nature of work and working to allow parents to become full participants in paid work and in parenting.[121]

She writes there about parenting, but what she says is applicable to all forms of caring. She wrote those words nearly 15 years ago and if anything we seem to have moved further from that ideal, not closer to it.

---

[121] S Fredman, *Women and the Law* (Oxford University Press, 1998) 40.

Caring and Abuse

I. Introduction

I was once at a meeting of lawyers discussing the law of inheritance. I brought up the issue of carers. One solicitor immediately muttered 'carers … awful greedy people'. I was astonished. No doubt his experience was of people claiming to be carers and eligible for an order under the Inheritance (Provision for Family and Dependants Act) 1975. The event brought home the point that it is all too easy to write about caring relationships in a glowing, positive light. It is easy to think that caring is like crème brûlée, no one could possibly argue against it. But, of course, caring relationships can involve abuse as well as the many positive attributes we have discussed in this book. As suggested in chapter two, it is possible to define a caring relationship in such a way as to exclude the possibility of an abusive caring relationship. As that chapter recognised, there are serious dangers in that an ethic of care can be misused in a way that can lead to exploitation.[1] Any responsible proponent of an ethic of care must address its dark side and ensure there is necessary legal protection from abuse.

Abuse in caring relationships is often hidden. Hidden in several senses: hidden from the public view; hidden from the parties themselves; and hidden from the legal discourse. Caring is typically carried out in private, given its intimate nature. This means there are usually few, if any witnesses, apart from the parties themselves. This makes it difficult to detect abuse and to prove that it exists. It is hidden from the public imagination. Because the home and family are seen as a 'haven in a heartless world',[2] the public can find it hard to imagine them as sites for abuse. Hidden too because victims, and perpetrators, of abuse can fail to recognise the abusive nature of their relationship. This is why it has taken so long to recognise domestic violence and child

---

[1] B Houston, 'Caring and Exploitation' (1990) 5 *Hypatia* 115.
[2] C Lasch, *Haven in a Heartless World* (Basic Books, 1979).

abuse. And we are only now acknowledging elder abuse and the abuse of vulnerable adults.[3] Gradually, the extent of abuse within the setting of intimate relationships is being uncovered. Recent events in the UK have brought to the fore the fact that even within formal caring relationships, terrible abuse can occur. We will start by looking at these.

II. Recent Scandals

The abuse of children by their parents and in care homes has been acknowledged in recent decades,[4] although in recent years it has been abuse in the context of the care of vulnerable adults which has grabbed the headlines.

Between March and June 2011, the Care Quality Commission (CQC) undertook 100 unannounced inspections of acute NHS hospitals in England.[5] These focused on the standards of dignity and nutrition on wards caring for older people. Of the 100 hospitals inspected, two were found to be putting people at unacceptable risk of harm. Less than half the hospitals (45) were fully compliant with the standards required for nutrition or dignity. Thirty five met the standards in both, but needed to improve on one or both. Twenty did not meet one or both standards.

The picture painted in the report was grim and, in particular, what the report noted about the standard of nursing care for older people. It is worth quoting from the introduction by Dame Jo Williams at length:

> Time and time again, we found cases where patients were treated by staff in a way that stripped them of their dignity and respect. People were spoken over, and not spoken to; people were left without call bells, ignored for hours on end, or not given assistance to do the basics of life—to eat, drink, or go to the toilet.

> Those who are responsible for the training and development of staff, particularly in nursing, need to look long and hard at why 'care' often seems to be broken down into tasks to be completed—focusing on the unit of work, rather than the person who needs to be looked after. Task-focused care is not person-centred care. It is not good enough and it is not what people want and expect. Kindness and compassion costs nothing.[6]

In fairness, it is worth quoting what Dame Williams went on to say about resources.

---

[3] House of Commons Health Committee, *Elder Abuse* (The Stationery Office, 2004) 1.
[4] See J Herring, *Family Law* (Pearson, 2010) ch 11, for a discussion of these.
[5] Care Quality Commission, *Dignity and Nutrition for Older People* (Care Quality Commission, 2011).
[6] Ibid 3.

... resources have a part to play. Many people told us about the wonderful nurses in their hospital, and then said how hard pressed they were to deliver care. Having plenty of staff does not guarantee good care (we saw unacceptable care on well-staffed wards, and excellent care on understaffed ones) but not having enough is a sure path to poor care. The best nurses and doctors can find themselves delivering care that falls below essential standards because they are overstretched.

Staff must have the right support if they are to deliver truly compassionate care that is clinically effective. In the current economic climate this is easy to say and far harder to deliver, but as the regulator our role is to cast an independent eye over care and reflect on what we see. There are levels of under-resourcing that make poor care more likely, and those who run our hospitals must play their part in ensuring that budgets are used wisely to support front line care staff.[7]

In the report a long list of inappropriate conduct is listed, including:

— call bells being out of patients' reach;
— curtains not being properly closed when personal care was being given;
— staff speaking to patients in a rude or condescending manner;
— patients not being given the help to eat;
— patients being interrupted during meals and having to leave their food unfinished;
— patients not being able to clean their hands before meals.

The report noted the following comments from patients and their relatives:

— 'The patient constantly called out for help and rattled the bedrail as staff passed by... We noted that 25 minutes passed before this patient received attention. When we spoke with the patient we observed that their finger-nails were ragged and dirty.'
— 'We saw a staff member taking a female patient to the toilet. The patient's clothing was above their knees and exposed their underwear. The staff member assisted them to the toilet in full view of other patients on the ward, only closing the door when they left the toilet room.'
— 'When we spoke to one member of staff about how they managed to meet the needs of people on the ward, they said that they did not have enough time to care for patients. They said that when they are rushed they cannot always meet people's needs and some things have to be delayed as a result.'

What is particularly chilling about this report is there is little that is new. We have known for a long time that too many older people are infantilised or ignored in hospital; that too often they fail to receive adequate hydration or nutrition; and that their dignity is not protected. And the remedies to some of the complaints appear so easy to provide. Yet it seems care is so low down as a priority that it gets overlooked in favour of more tangible goals such as cost saving and queue shortening.

---

[7] Ibid 4–5.

Reports from the Alzheimer's Society;[8] Equality and Human Rights Commission[9] and the Health Service Ombudsman[10] paint a similarly grim picture. The pictures of neglect and abuse can be found in mental health services,[11] care homes[12] and social care.[13] These reports are deeply depressing. In part because of the enormous pain caused by things which could be so easily remedied: 'An abiding memory is of a woman who cried out each morning for her grapefruit spoon. It was her one possession from her own home and invariably it was missing from the breakfast trolley.'[14] Such a small thing... but such a big thing.

What many reports highlight is that it is not so much a problem with complex cases or mistakes being made in emergencies, it is the day-in day-out basics of care. The Ombudsman report, for example, found not only shocking treatment but that staff in dealing with complaints were 'dismissive' and showed 'a disregard for process and procedure and [an] apparent indifference ... to deplorable standards of care'.[15] It is the absence of respect and relationality which I identified in chapter two as central to a good notion of care which is so striking.

III. Statistics

It cannot be denied that abuse takes place within the broad sweep of caring relationships. Here are some of the leading statistics on child abuse:

— A study by the NSPCC, the highly respected children's charity, found that 38 per cent of children suffered serious or intermediate level maltreatment.[16] A quarter (25 per cent) of children experienced one or more forms of physical violence during childhood.[17] Thirty one per cent of children claim to have experienced bullying.[18]

---

[8] Alzheimer's Society, *Counting the Cost: Caring for People with Dementia on Hospital Wards* (Alzheimer's Society, 2009).

[9] Equality and Human Rights Commission, *Close to Home* (Equality and Human Rights Commission, 2011).

[10] Health Service Ombudsman, *Care and Compassion?* (The Stationery Office, 2011).

[11] Department of Health, *Securing Better Mental Health for Older Adults* (Department of Health, 2005).

[12] Help the Aged, *My Home Life* (Help the Aged, 2008). See also Office of Fair Trading, *Survey of Older People in Care Homes* (Office of Fair Trading, 2005).

[13] Health Committee, UK Parliament, *Social Care* (The Stationery Office, 2012).

[14] Help the Aged, *My Home Life* (Help the Aged, 2008). See also Office of Fair Trading, *Survey of Older People in Care Homes* (Office of Fair Trading, 2005). See Age Concern, *Delivering Dignity* (Age Concern, 2012).

[15] Health Service Ombudsman, *Care and Compassion?* (The Stationery Office, 2011) 10.

[16] P Cawson, *Child Maltreatment in the Family* (NSPCC, 2002) 52.

[17] NSPCC, *Key Child Protection Statistics* (NSPCC, 2007).

[18] Ibid.

— Fretwell Wilson[19] claims that in Great Britain between 12 and 24 per cent of girls[20] and eight to nine per cent of boys experience sexual abuse before their sixteenth birthday.[21] Eleven per cent of children suffer sexual abuse from someone known to them but unrelated to them; four per cent are sexually abused by a parent or relative; and five per cent by a stranger.[22]

— There is a common misperception that children are at greater risk of abuse from strangers than families. On average, five or six children die a year at the hands of strangers, while between 70 and 100 will die at the hands of their families.[23]

The statistics on domestic violence make for grim reading too:

— Domestic violence is the largest cause of morbidity worldwide in women aged 19–44, greater than war, cancer or motor vehicle accidents.[24]

— The British Crime Survey found that one in four women and one in six men had been or will be physically assaulted by a current or former partner at some point in their lives.[25]

— Twenty eight per cent of people aged 16 to 59 had experienced domestic (partner or family) abuse since the age of 16.[26] In 2009/10, seven per cent of women in that age group had suffered domestic abuse, as had four per cent of men.[27]

— An incident of killing, stabbing or beating takes place on average every six minutes in a home in Britain.[28]

— Around two women a week are killed by a current or former partner.[29] Forty seven per cent of all female murder victims are killed by a current or former partner.[30]

— One in five of all violent crimes reported are related to domestic abuse.[31]

---

[19] R Fretwell Wilson, 'Fractured Families, Fragile Children—the Sexual Vulnerability of Girls in the Aftermath of Divorce' (2002) 14 *Child and Family Law Quarterly* 1.

[20] Whether it is 12% or 24% depends on the definition of sexual abuse used.

[21] See S Smallbone, W Marshall, and R Wortley, *Preventing Child Sexual Abuse* (Willan, 2008) for a discussion of the nature and extent of child sexual abuse.

[22] NSPCC, *Key Child Protection Statistics* (NSPCC, 2007).

[23] C Lyon, 'Children's Rights and Human Rights' (2001) 31 *Family Law* 329.

[24] The first two statistics are found in Home Affairs Select Committee, *Domestic Violence, Forced Marriage and 'Honour' Based Violence* (Hansard, 2008) 1.

[25] G Thompson, *Domestic Violence Statistics* (Hansard, 2010).

[26] D Povey, *Homicides, Firearm Offences and Intimate Violence 2006/07* (Home Office, 2008).

[27] J Flatley, C Kershaw, K Smith, R Chaplin, and D Moon, *Crime in England and Wales 2009/10* (Home Office, 2010).

[28] E Stanko, *Press Release* (Reuters, 2000).

[29] Home Affairs Select Committee, *Domestic Violence, Forced Marriage and 'Honour' Based Violence* (Hansard, 2008) 1.

[30] G Thompson, *Domestic Violence Statistics* (Hansard, 2010).

[31] J Flatley, C Kershaw, K Smith, R Chaplin, and D Moon, *Crime in England and Wales 2009/10* (Home Office, 2010).

Less research is available in relation to abuse of elders and abuse of adults.[32] We now have the benefit of a major recent study of elder abuse carried out for Comic Relief and the Department of Health.[33] It found that 2.6 per cent of people aged 66 or over who were living in their own private household reported mistreatment involving a family member, close friend or care worker in the past year. If the sample is an accurate reflection of the wider older population, it would mean 227,000 people aged over 66 are suffering mistreatment in a given year. The figures rise to four per cent or 342,400 people in incidents involving neighbours or acquaintances.[34] Three quarters of those interviewed said that the effect of mistreatment was either serious or very serious. The researchers believed these figures to be on the conservative side as they did not include care home residents in their survey and some of those most vulnerable to abuse lacked the capacity to take part. Also, even among those interviewed there may have been those who, for a variety of reasons, did not wish to disclose abuse.[35] A recent literature review looking at evidence of elder abuse around the world concluded that six per cent of older people had suffered significant abuse in the last month. 5.6 per cent of older couples had experienced physical violence in their relationships. Twenty five per cent of older people had suffered significant psychological abuse.[36] Finding evidence on the levels of abuse in a residential setting is even harder. Professionals assert that, for example, 'the institutional abuse of older people is common'.[37] Although there is widespread anecdotal evidence to support this there is little hard empirical evidence.[38] Care homes are more heavily regulated than domestic care and that may be thought to reduce the likelihood of abuse.

[32] J Manthorpe, B Penhale, L Pinkney, N Perkins and P Kingston, *A Systematic Literature Review in Response to Key Themes Identified in the Report of the House of Commons Select Committee on Elder Abuse* (Department of Health, 2004).

[33] M O'Keeffe, A Hills, M Doyle, C McCreadie, S Scholes, R Constantine, A Tinker, J Manthorpe, S Biggs and B Erens, *UK Study of Abuse and Neglect of Older People Prevalence Survey Report* (Department of Health, 2008). See also A Mowlam, R Tennant, J Dixon and C McCreadie, *UK Study of Abuse and Neglect of Older People: Qualitative Findings* (Department of Health, 2008) and C Cooper, A Selwood and G Livingston, 'The Prevalence of Elder Abuse and Neglect: A Systematic Review' (2008) 37 *Age and Ageing* 151.

[34] M O'Keeffe, A Hills, M Doyle, C McCreadie, S Scholes, R Constantine, A Tinker, J Manthorpe, S Biggs and B Erens, *UK Study of Abuse and Neglect of Older People Prevalence Survey Report* (Department of Health, 2008) 4.

[35] Ibid para 7.4

[36] C Cooper, A Selwood, G Livingston, 'Prevalence of Elder Abuse and Neglect: A Systematic Review' (2008) 37 *Age and Ageing* 151.

[37] J Garner and S Evans, 'An Ethical Perspective on Institutional Abuse of Older Adults' (2002) 26 *Psychiatric Bulletin* 166.

[38] S Hussein, J Manthorpe, B Penhale, *Public Perceptions of the Neglect and Mistreatment of Older People: Findings of a United Kingdom Survey* (Kings College, 2005).

Official statistics of allegations of abuse on vulnerable adults (adults of any age who are vulnerable) found 96,000 reported cases in England in 2010/11.[39] Around a third of those involved physical abuse. Of the allegations which were investigated, 41 per cent were found wholly or partially substantiated; 28 per cent inconclusive or not determined and 31 per cent not substantiated. These only related to officially reported cases and can only represent a portion of actual cases.

IV. Defining Intimate Relationship Abuse

Defining abuse in the context of a caring relationship is enormously complex. One commentator has suggested that there are 43 different forms of abuse.[40] The Department of Health's document *No Secrets* restricts itself to the following six:

— *Physical abuse*, including hitting, slapping, pushing, kicking, misuse of medication, restraint, or inappropriate sanctions;
— *Sexual abuse*, including rape and sexual assault or sexual acts to which the vulnerable adult has not consented, could not consent to or was pressured into consenting;
— *Psychological abuse*, including emotional abuse, threats of harm or abandonment, deprivation of contact, humiliation, blaming, controlling, intimidation, coercion, harassment, verbal abuse, isolation or withdrawal from services or supportive networks;
— *Financial or material abuse*, including theft, fraud, exploitation, pressure in connection with wills, property or inheritance or financial transactions, or the misuse or misappropriation of property, possessions or benefits;
— *Neglect and acts of omission*, including ignoring medical or physical care needs, failure to provide access to appropriate health, social care or educational services, the withholding of the necessities of life, such as medication, adequate nutrition and heating; and
— *Discriminatory abuse*, including racist, sexist, that based on a person's disability, and other forms of harassment, slurs or similar treatment.

Given the complexity of these different kinds of abuse, and the range of victims in a caring relationship, it will become apparent that we cannot

---

[39] BBC News Online, 'Vulnerable Adults: 96,000 Alleged Abuse Cases Reported' 3 November 2011.
[40] P Hall, 'Elder Maltreatment Items: Subgroups and Types: Policy and Practice Implications' in J Hendricks (ed), *The Ties Of Later Life* (Baywood, 1995) 97.

meaningfully talk about 'abuse in caring relationships' as some kind of catch-all topic. There are very specific issues that arise in dealing with child abuse, which are not present in cases of elder abuse, for example. Nevertheless, there are some common aspects which is helpful to bring out.

Not surprisingly, it is enormously difficult to define abuse within a caring relationship.[41] The abuse can take many forms.[42] As Phillipson and Biggs argue in relation to elder abuse:

> Attempts to define and map the extent of elder abuse indicate that it should not be seen as a single monolithic phenomenon, but that it takes a variety of forms in different settings and in different kinds of relationships.[43]

One way forward would be to offer definitions within different professional spheres; for example it has been suggested[44] that we need separate legal, care management and research definitions of abuse. The difficulty in seeking to define the concept is that the different professions are using the notion of abuse for different purposes. A medical professional seeking to see if there is abuse requiring medical intervention is likely to rely on a very different definition from a police officer wanting to know if it is appropriate to investigate a possible crime. The medical professional is more likely to focus on the perspective of the abused person and the impact on their well-being of the conduct in question, while the police officer will be interested in the blameworthiness of any alleged perpetrator. That said, there are, of course, certain forms of conduct which would on any definition, and for any purpose, be abuse.

There is a real difficulty in seeking to define abuse in any context. A narrow definition, for example, focusing on physical harm, may be regarded as inappropriately downplaying other forms of abuse, such as emotional abuse or neglect which can be regarded as serious as physical harm. But extending the term to cover all forms of unpleasant behaviour may stretch the definition to such an extent that it loses any real meaning. What is more useful than seeking to produce a single definition that is appropriate for all purposes is to set out the factors that need to be considered by anyone seeking to analyse the abusive nature of the conduct and the factors that would need to be taken into account in producing a definition of elder abuse in a particular context.

Any act of violence or abuse is wrong in itself. What I will seek to do here is to explore the particular wrong that occurs when abuse takes place within

---

[41] A Brammer and S Biggs, 'Defining Elder Abuse' (1998) 20 *Journal of Social Welfare and Family Law* 385.

[42] R Hawks, 'Grandparent Molesting: Sexual Abuse of Elderly Nursing Home Residents and its Prevention' (2006) 8 *Marquette Elder's Advisor* 159.

[43] C Phillipson and S Biggs, *Elder Abuse in Perspective* (Open University Press, 1995) 202.

[44] G Bennett, P Kingston, and B Penhale, *The Dimensions of Elder Abuse* (Macmillan, 1997).

a supposed caring relationship. I suggest that can be done by exploring three features of intimate abuse:[45]

— Harmful acts in an intimate relationship.
— Acts perpetuating relational inequality.
— Act perpetuating societal disadvantage.

I do not argue that in order to amount to abuse all of these features will be present. Nor even that the greater the number of these features the 'worse' the abuse will be. Rather that by considering these aspects of the conduct, we can bring to the fore the precise nature of the wrongs in the abuse.

A. Harmful Acts in an Intimate Relationship

This first requirement is that the abuse involves harmful acts in an intimate relationship. By intimacy I mean to indicate a close relationship. This need not contain a sexual element, nor cohabitation, nor emotional warmth, but requires regular contact and a degree of dependency. It can, therefore, cover a relationship between a care home resident and care assistant; as well as others in a caring relationship. However, it would exclude cases of abuse where the 'carer' was not in an ongoing relationship with the victim. So excluded from the definition would be cases where a person shoves an older person in the street or carries out a distraction burglary[46] on a vulnerable adult. I restrict intimate abuse to those in intimate relationships for three reasons.[47]

First, in cases of intimacy abuse, the ability of the victim to escape from the violence is restricted.[48] That will most obviously be so where the parties are living together, but the victim may be dependent on the perpetrator even where they are living separately. Elder abuse, for example, is commonly committed by someone not living with the victim.[49]

Second, intimate violence can be seen as a breach of trust.[50] Intimate relationships involve becoming physically and emotionally vulnerable. The trust which is central to close relationships creates special obligations not to

---

[45] I am building upon M Madden Dempsey, 'What Counts as Domestic violence? A Conceptual Analysis' (2006) 12 *William and Mary Journal of Women and the Law* 301.

[46] These are burglaries where a person pretends to be acting in an official capacity and thereby gain entry to someone's house, where they then steal property.

[47] J Herring, 'No More Having and Holding: The Abolition of the Marital Rape Exemption' in S Gilmore, J Herring and R Probert (eds), *Landmark Cases in Family Law* (Hart, 2011).

[48] H Reece, 'The End of Domestic Violence' (2006) 69 *Modern Law Review* 770.

[49] J Herring, *Older People in Law and Society* (Oxford University Press, 2010) ch 3.

[50] J Herring, 'The Serious Wrong of Domestic Abuse and the Loss of Control Defence' in A Reed and M Bohlander (eds), *Loss of Control and Diminished Responsibility* (Ashgate, 2011).

misuse that vulnerability. Intimate relationships rely on trust so that we can flourish.[51]

Third, and linked to the second point, the harm in an abusive intimate relationship goes particularly deep. It is through our intimate relationships that we form our identity and sense of self.[52] Intimate abuse strikes at the very conception of the self for the victim. Intimate relationship abuse, therefore, turns what should be a tool for self-affirmation and self-identification into a tool for alienation and self-betrayal. The victim almost becomes used as a tool against herself.[53]

These arguments seem to point to the 'intimacy' requirement better understood as not a point about the location of the incident so much as the nature of the relationship between the parties. Whether the parties are living together or whether they are related is much less relevant than whether their relationship is of the kind where there is trust and vulnerability.

B. Acts Perpetuating Relational Inequality

The second element of intimacy abuse is acts which perpetuate relational inequality. Before exploring this further it is worth emphasising that I am using the terminology of harm rather than violence. There has been much debate among those writing on domestic violence on whether violence is an essential element of domestic violence.[54] At first sight it seems obvious that violence should be at the heart of domestic violence. The clue is in the name. Indeed it is noticeable that, as this chapter has done, the term domestic abuse has been relied upon rather than domestic violence, to capture the fact that a broader concept is intended. Indeed it is interesting that the Supreme Court has held that domestic violence under the Housing Act 1996 is not limited to assaults.[55]

Helen Reece has argued against the view that domestic violence should include conduct which is not physical assault. She argues it 'represents a remarkable downplaying of the physical'.[56] This raises the controversial issue whether a physical injury should necessarily be regarded as more serious than an emotional or psychological one. Certainly the law has traditionally taken

---

[51] J Eekelaar, *Family Law and Personal Life* (Oxford University Press, 2007) 44–47.

[52] O Rachmilovitz, 'Bringing Down the Bedroom Walls: Emphasizing Substance Over Form in Personalized Abuse' (2007) 14 *William and Mary Journal of Women & Law* 495.

[53] L Arnault, 'Cruelty, Horror, and the Will to Redemption' (2003) 18 *Hypatia* 155.

[54] Michael P Johnson, 'Patriarchal Terrorism and Common Couple Violence: Two Forms of Violence against Women' (1995) 57 *Journal of Marriage and Family* 283.

[55] *Yemshaw v LB Hounslow* [2011] UKSC 3, discussed in J Herring, 'The Meaning of Domestic Violence' (2011) 33 *Journal of Social Welfare and Family Law* 297.

[56] H Reece, 'Feminist Anti-Violence Discourse as Regulation' in E Jackson et al (eds), *Regulating Autonomy: Sex, Reproduction and Families* (Hart, 2009) 46.

the view that physical injuries are the focus of the criminal law and emotional injuries are not covered.[57]

The argument against restricting intimate abuse to physically violent acts is as follows. The experiences of victims of domestic abuse show that it is best understood not as simply a series of violent or abusive acts, but rather as a program of 'coercive control' (to use Evan Stake's[58] phrase) or 'patriarchal terrorism' or 'intimate terrorism' (to use Michael Johnson's[59] phrase). Michael Johnson distinguishes intimate terrorism from what he calls 'situational couple violence' or 'mutual violence'. Patriarchal terrorism is 'violence enacted in the service of taking general control over one's partner'.[60] By contrast, in the situational couple violence or mutual violence case, there is violence but there is no attempt to control the relationship. Rather, there is an incident of violence that arises in a moment of conflict during an intimate relationship with is not generally marked with inequality. It involves a lashing out in self-defence, anger or frustration, rather than an attempt to exercise control. As this distinction shows, it is not whether or not there is violence which matters so much as whether there is a pattern of control.

The 'coercive control' model of intimate violence argues that understanding the impact of domestic abuse requires an appreciation of its controlling intent and impact. This can only be understood by looking at the relationship between the parties as a whole. Psychologist Mary Ann Dutton[61] explains:

Abusive behaviour does not occur as a series of discrete events. Although a set of discrete abusive incidents can typically be identified within an abusive relationship, an understanding of the dynamic of power and control within an intimate relationship goes beyond these discrete incidents. To negate the impact of the time period between discrete episodes of serious violence—a time period during which the woman may never know when the next incident will occur, and may continue to live with on-going psychological abuse—is to fail to recognize what some battered woman experience as a continuing 'state of siege'.

The whole aim of the behaviour of the abuser is to dominate the victim and diminish her sense of self-worth. This is done by restricting the victim's access to work; isolating her from friends; manipulating the victim emotionally; and using physical attacks. Physical violence, then, is but one tool

---

[57] M Burton, 'Commentary: *R v Dhaliwal*' in R Hunter, C McGlynn and E Rackley (eds), *Feminist Judgements* (Hart, 2010).

[58] E Stark, *Coercive Control* (Oxford University Press, 2007).

[59] M Johnson, 'Apples and Oranges in Child Custody Disputes: Intimate Terrorism vs. Situational Couple Violence' (2005) 2 *Journal of Child Custody* 43.

[60] Ibid.

[61] M Dutton, 'Understanding Women's Response to Domestic Violence' (2003) 21 *Hofstra Law Review* 1191, 1204.

used in the relationship to keep one party inferior.[62] From this perspective, it is intimidation, isolation and control which should be the hallmarks of domestic violence rather than the means to achieve them, which may, or may not, involve violence.[63]

Seeing intimate abuse as coercive control has important implications. It means that an assessment of whether there is domestic violence must look at the whole relationship between the parties, rather than assessing the severity of individual attacks. Incidents which might appear trivial can be seen as having a significant impact when appreciated in their broader context. Coercive control abuse may involve physical attacks, and often does, but the abuser may not need to resort to those. The abuser intimidates, isolates and controls through a range of means. These effects, rather than physical violence, should be seen as the hallmarks of intimate abuse.

C. Acts Perpetuating Societal Disadvantage

We have seen that intimate abuse is best seen as part of an inequality within the relationship. However, it also reflects broader inequalities within society. Madden Dempsey argues:

> Structural inequalities are functions of social structures, the 'sets of rules and principles that govern activities in the different domains of social life'. When social structures sustain or perpetuate the uneven distribution of social power, they can be understood as structural inequalities.[64]

Madden Dempsey's point is that abuse within the relationship can be a tool used to maintain the dominance of one party in the relationship, usually the man. Domestic violence may also, alongside a range of other social pressures, be seen as working against the interests of women generally. So, domestic violence is linked to inequalities within the relationship and within society more widely. Madden Dempsey explains:

> the patriarchal character of individual relationships cannot subsist without those relationships being situated within a broader patriarchal social structure. Patriarchy is, by its nature, a social structure—and thus any particular instance of patriarchy takes its substance and meaning from that social context. If patriarchy were entirely eliminated from society, then patriarchy would not exist in domestic arrangements and thus domestic violence in its strong sense would not exist... Moreover, if patriarchy were lessened in society generally then *ceteris paribus* patriarchy would be

---

[62] O Rachmilovitz, 'Bringing Down the Bedroom Walls: Emphasizing Substance over Form in Personalized Abuse' (2007) 14 *William and Mary Journal of Women & Law* 495.

[63] N Jacobson and J Gottman, *When Men Batter Women: New Insights into Ending Abusive Relationships* (Simon & Schuster, 2007).

[64] M Madden Dempsey, *Prosecuting Domestic Violence* (Oxford University Press, 2009) 112.

lessened in domestic relationship as well, thereby directly contributing to the project of ending domestic violence in its strong sense.[65]

The same is true for intimate violence generally. It does not only impact on the couple themselves. It reinforces and relies upon power exercised by men over women in society more generally. As the Parliamentary Assembly, Council of Europe, Committee on Equal Opportunities for Women and Men[66] puts it:

> Violence against women is a question of power, of the need to dominate and control. This in turn is rooted in the organization of society, itself based on inequality between the sexes. The meaning of this violence is clear: it is an attempt to maintain the unequal relationship between men and women and to perpetuate the subordination of women.

One example of this point is that domestic violence commonly involves attempts by the male perpetrators of abuse to prevent their female partners entering the workplace or public arena. These reinforce and reflect general restrictions on women's access to the workplace.

On such a view, intimate violence must be seen in its broader context as part of a set of power relationships which enable men to exercise control over women. The broader context is relevant for several reasons. It explains how domestic violence gets its power: the woman is disadvantaged not only by the abuse in the home, but by the lack of power outside the home. It may also explain why the law has been so reluctant and ineffective to respond to it. According to Currie, '(A)lthough experienced and more easily recorded as an episode or event, violence is an extreme expression of one moment in on-going processes through which heterosexual relationships are "negotiated".'[67]

Taking such a view sees the genders of the parties as crucial to an understanding of intimate violence. It is true that the vast majority of domestic violence takes place against women,[68] although many men are also subject to violence from their partners.[69] But, most violence by women against men is quite different from violence by men against women because women's

[65] M Madden Dempsey, 'What Counts as Domestic Violence' (2006) 13 *William and Mary Journal of Women and the Law* 301; M Madden Dempsey, 'Towards a Feminist State' (2007) 70 *Modern Law Review* 908, 938.

[66] Parliamentary Assembly, Council of Europe, Committee on Equal Opportunities for Women and Men, *Domestic Violence* (2002) para 12.

[67] D Currie 'Violent Men or Violent Women? Whose Definition Counts?' in R Bergen (ed), *Issues in Intimate Violence* (Sage, 1998).

[68] For a discussion of violence in lesbian relations, see M Eaton, 'Abuse by Any Other Name: Feminism, Difference and Intralesbian Violence' in N Fine and R Myktiuk (eds), *The Public Nature of Private Violence. The Discovery of Domestic Abuse* (Routledge, 1994).

[69] C Mirless-Black, *Home Office Research Study 191: Domestic Violence* (Home Office, 1999). Where men are abused the degree of violence tends to be less: E Buzawa and C Buzawa, *Domestic Violence: The Criminal Justice Response*, 3rd edn (Sage, 2003).

violence is often in self-defence rather than being an aspect of an ongoing oppressive relationship,[70] and that where men are the victims the injuries involved tend to be less serious.

A similar analysis can be made of the abuse of older people, children and vulnerable adults. Abuse of older people reflects wider societal attitudes towards elder people. Elder abuse reflects and reinforces attitudes about older people in a way which interacts with the attitudes about them. Many of the victims are women and then we see the interaction of both ageism and sexism in creating and reinforcing the structures that enable abuse to take place.[71] As the Toronto Declaration on the Global Prevention of Elder Abuse puts it, 'Ultimately elder abuse will only be successfully prevented if a culture that nurtures intergenerational solidarity and rejects violence is developed'.[72]

Any response to elder abuse must put it in the context of the wider social problems facing older people.[73] Inadequate housing, difficulties accessing social activities and transport can have an effect on the quality of life of older people. At the moment our society often restricts the access of older people to many public spaces. This can be through the practical difficulties or transport, but also by the attitudes of the public generally. Older people are too often excluded from sections of public life.[74] This not only enables elder abuse to take place, but is itself a form of elder abuse.[75]

D. Conclusion on Definition of Intimate Abuse

This discussion has highlighted the importance of taking a relational approach to a consideration of intimate abuse. Doing so helps bring out three key elements of the abuse. First, it illustrates the fact that it is the intimate nature of the relationship, rather than the details of the living arrangements which is key to the wrong of the abuse. In particular it highlights the abuse of trust which is a central element of the wrong of intimate abuse. Second, it reveals the importance of appreciating that it is coercive control of the relationship which is at the heart of intimate abuse, rather than individual acts of violence. Third, it shows how abuse within intimate relationships is an aspect

[70] R Dobash and R Dobash, 'Women's Violence to Men in Intimate Relationships' (2004) 44 *British Journal of Criminology* 324, 343.

[71] For further exploration and discussion see J Herring, *Older People in Law and Society* (Oxford University Press 2010) ch 3.

[72] World Health Organisation, *The Toronto Declaration on the Prevention of Elder Abuse* (World Health Organisation, 2002).

[73] Action on Elder Abuse, *Placing Elder Abuse within the Context of Citizenship* (Action on Elder Abuse, 2004).

[74] Ibid.

[75] D Schuyler and B Liang, 'Reconceptualizing Elder Abuse: Treating the Disease of Senior Community Exclusion' (2006) 15 *Annals of Health Law* 257.

of wider structures and forces within society, which disadvantage women and perpetuate other inequalities within society, including in relation to disabled people and older people.

V. The Causes of Intimate Abuse

Given the wide range of intimate abuse, it is unsurprising that there is no general consensus over its causes. Writing in the context of domestic violence, Joanna Miles[76] has usefully separated out 'micro causes' and 'macro causes'. 'Micro causes' refer to issues related to the individual perpetrator and victim. They may include, for example, claims that abuse is caused by character flaws of the perpetrator. 'Macro causes' are those that rely on wider social forces, for example the position of women in society. She argues that a proper understanding of domestic violence requires an appreciation of both these factors. It is suggested that a similar comment is true in the context of intimate abuse.

For some, the causes of intimate abuse are found in the characteristics of the victim,[77] while others have sought to identify characteristics of the abuser[78] and yet others focus on aspects of the relationship between the abuser and victim.[79] For example, the Public Health Agency of Canada, in the context of elder abuse, saw the causes of elder abuse as being the following:[80]

(1) Victims of psychological and physical abuse usually have reasonably good physical health, but suffer from psychological problems. Their abusers have a history of psychiatric illness and/or substance abuse, live with the victim, and depend on them for financial resources ...

(2) Patients with dementia, who exhibit disruptive behaviour and who live with family caregivers, are more likely to be victims of physical abuse. Their abusive caregivers may suffer from low self-esteem and clinical depression ...

---

[76] J Miles, 'Domestic Violence' in J Herring (ed), *Family Law: Issues, Debates, Policy* (Willan, 2001).

[77] R Wolf, 'Major Findings from Three Model Projects on Elder Abuse' in K Pillemer and R Wolf (eds), *Elder Abuse: Conflict in the Family* (Auburn House, 1986).

[78] E Hocking, 'Caring for Carers: Understanding the Process that Leads to Abuse' in M Eastman (ed), *Old Age Abuse: A New Perspective*, 2nd edn (Chapman and Hall, 1994); K O'Leary, 'Through a Psychological Lens: Personality Traits, Personality Disorders, and Levels of Violence' in R Gelles and D Loeske (eds), *Current Controversies on Family Violence* (Sage, 1993).

[79] A Homer and C Gilleard, 'Abuse of Elderly People by their Carers' (1990) 301 *British Medical Journal* 1359.

[80] Public Health Agency of Canada, *Abuse and Neglect of Older People: A Discussion Paper* (Public Health Agency of Canada, 2005) 5.

(3) There may not be a 'typical' victim of financial abuse; however, when the abused person is dependent on the abuser, the financial abuse may be more serious ...

(4) Victims of neglect tend to be very old, with cognitive and physical incapacities. Their dependency on their caregivers serves as a source of stress ...

As these indicate, supporters of the micro causes explanation focus on matters personal to the individuals or their relationship. Hence there is emphasis on the personality of the abuser;[81] 'situational stresses' facing the caregiver;[82] childhood abuse of the abuser;[83] or the lack of social support provided to carers. These problems can be exacerbated if the caregiver turns to alcohol[84] or other drugs.[85] Some studies suggest that abuse is caused when the abuser feels they lack power.[86] There is some evidence to suggest that perpetrators are often heavily dependent on the person they are mistreating.[87] A little more will be said about 'caregiver' stress as it is most commonly relied on micro-cause abuse of intimates.

A. 'Caregiver Stress'

In the public imagination, abuse in a care setting is popularly regarded as caused by carer stress.[88] A loving carer lashes out in desperation, driven to the point of despair in physical and emotional exhaustion. This claim has been described by academic specialists in the field as a 'persistent characterization'[89] and 'widely accepted'.[90] Professors Rainey and Payne state that

---

[81] K Pillemer and D Finkelhor, 'Causes of Elder Abuse: Caregiver Stress versus Problem Relatives' (1989) 59 *American Journal of Orthopsychiatry* 179.

[82] M Lee and S Kolomer, 'Design of an Assessment of Caregivers' Impulsive Feelings to Commit Elder Abuse' (2007) 17 *Research on Social Work Practice* 729.

[83] E Rathbone-McCuan, 'Elderly Victims of Family Violence and Neglect' (1980) 61 *Social Casework* 296.

[84] There are consistent findings of links between alcohol and elder abuse: A Reay and K Browne, 'Risk Factor Characteristics in Carers who Physically Abuse or Neglect their Elderly Dependants' (2001) 5 *Aging and Mental Health* 56.

[85] G Anetzberger, J Korbin and C Austin, 'Alcoholism and Elder Abuse' (1994) 9 *Journal of Interpersonal Violence* 184.

[86] K Pillemer and J Suitor, 'Violence and Violent Feelings: What Causes them Among Family Caregivers?' (1992) 47 *Journal of Gerontology* 165.

[87] K Pillemer, 'Elder Abuse is Caused by the Deviance and Dependence of Abusive Caregivers' in D Loseke, R Gelles and M Cavanaugh (eds), *Current Controversies on Family Violence* (Sage, 2004); J Greenberg, M McKibben and J Raymond, 'Dependent Adult Children and Elder Abuse' (1990) 2 *Journal of Elder Abuse Neglect* 73.

[88] J Pritchard, *Working with Adult Abuse: A Training Manual* (Jessica Kingsley, 2007) 310.

[89] National Center on Elder Abuse, *Preventing Elder Abuse by Family Caregivers* (National Centre on Elder Abuse, 2002).

[90] K Pillemer and D Finkelhor, 'Causes of Elder Abuse: Caregiver Stress versus Problem Relatives' (2006) 19 *Journal of Health Human Services Administration* 245.

caregiver burden is the most cited explanation for elder abuse.[91] Three leading English academics in one of the leading works on elder abuse describe that as a 'widespread view'.[92]

Much work has been done in seeking to expound on these claims and explain the theory in more detail.[93] It has been said that caregiver stress causes depression and mood disturbances which lead to abuse in uncharacteristic outbursts of anger.[94] Emphasis is placed on empirical evidence that carers who have to live with the dependant are particularly likely to be abusive.[95] Indeed some research suggests that the greater the number of hours per day the carers must care, the greater the risk of abuse.[96] Further, it has been claimed that the lower the functioning of the 'victim', the higher the likelihood of abuse.[97] Carers of those suffering from dementia are particularly prone to commit abuse.[98] 'Victims' who are violent towards caregivers are more likely to suffer abuse at the hands of the caregiver.[99] Evidence has been produced which, it is said, shows that when the 'victim' engages in certain forms of behaviour these cause the carer stress, which can lead the carer to abuse. Such behaviour includes verbal aggression, refusal to eat or take medications, calling the police, invading the caregiver's privacy, noisiness, 'vulgar habits,' disruptive behaviour, embarrassing public displays and physical aggression.[100] Others refer to the 'difficult personality' of the dependant causing carer stress and hence abuse.[101] As can be seen there are real dangers of the arguments leading to the abused person being said to be the real cause of the abuse.

Despite its hold on the public imagination, most recent studies strongly downplay the relevance of carer stress as a cause of elder or vulnerable adult

[91] R Gainey and B Payne, 'Caregiver Burden, Elder Abuse and Alzheimer's Disease: Testing the Relationship' (2006) 2 *Journal of Health and Human Services* 245.

[92] G Bennet, P Kingston and B Penhale, *The Dimensions of Elder Abuse* (Macmillan, 1997) 54.

[93] L Nerenberg, *Caregiver Stress and Elder Abuse* (National Centre on Elder Abuse, 2002).

[94] J Garcia and J Kosberg, 'Understanding Anger: Implications for Formal and Informal Caregivers' (1992) 4 *Journal of Elder Abuse & Neglect* 87; M Bendik, 'Reaching the Breaking Point: Dangers of Mistreatment in Elder Caregiving Situations' (1992) 4 *Journal of Elder Abuse & Neglect* 39.

[95] L Nerenberg, *Caregiver Stress and Elder Abuse* (National Centre on Elder Abuse, 2002).

[96] M Bendik, 'Reaching the Breaking Point: Dangers of Mistreatment in Elder Caregiving Situations' (1992) 4 *Journal of Elder Abuse & Neglect* 39.

[97] A Coyne, W Reichman, and L Berbig, 'The Relationship between Dementia and Elder Abuse' (1993) 150 *American Journal of Psychiatry* 643.

[98] K Pillemer and J Suitor, 'Violence and Violent Feelings: What Causes them Among Family Caregivers?' (1992) 47 *Journal of Gerontology* S165–72.

[99] A Coyne, W Reichman and L Berbig, 'The Relationship between Dementia and Elder Abuse' (1993) 150 *American Journal of Psychiatry* 643.

[100] K Pillemer and J Suitor, 'Violence and Violent Feelings: What Causes them Among Family Caregivers?' (1992) *Journal of Gerontology* 165-172.

[101] L Phillips, 'Theoretical Explanations of Elder Abuse: Competing Hypotheses and Unresolved Issues' in K Pillemer and R Wolf (eds), *Elder Abuse: Conflict In The Family* (Auburn House, 1986).

abuse. There is now a substantial body of research suggesting that care-giver stress plays a very minor role in causing elder abuse.[102] The House of Commons Health Select Committee when looking at the issue of elder abuse received evidence from several bodies working in the field which all agreed that carer stress was rarely a factor in elder abuse.[103] Help the Aged in its evidence stated: 'few incidents of abuse are committed by loving, supportive people who have lashed out as a consequence of the burden of their caring responsibilities'.[104] This is certainly not to say that the evidence suggests that carers do not suffer stress, quite the opposite. It is clear that caring is extraordinarily hard work.[105] But there is no evidence that the stresses of caring are linked to abuse in any significant way.

The problem with seeing intimate abuse as caused by caregivers' stress is that it creates an image of a victim who is vulnerable and problematic.[106] We cannot expect them to help themselves, indeed it is their behaviour and condition which has created the stressful situation. The best response to abuse is, therefore, seen to be to offer support and assistance to the carer, and medical support to the dependant, rather than offering protection or services to the person being abused.[107] Indeed, as Simon Biggs points out, the carer stress model neatly fits into the logic of community care, with the support of carers in the home with a care package being the solution to the problems of the older person. The caregiver stress model also clearly indicates that criminal punishments are not appropriate because the abuser is not to blame and is responding in an understandable way to an extremely difficult situation.[108]

B. Macro Causes

One of the consequences of the carer stress explanation is that it hides all the wider social factors which contribute to the practice, perpetuation and lack of recognition of intimate abuse. In particular, the significance of

---

[102] K Pillemer, 'The Abused Offspring are Dependent: Abuse is Caused by the Deviance and Dependence of Abusive Caregivers' in R Gelles and D Loeske (eds), *Current Controversies on Family Violence* (Sage, 1993); B Brandl and L Cook-Daniels, 'Domestic Abuse in Later Life' (2002) 8 *The Elder Law Journal* 302; L Bergeron, 'An Elder Abuse Case Study: Caregiver Stress or Domestic Violence? You Decide' (2001) 34 *Journal of Gerontological Social Work* 47.

[103] House of Commons Health Committee, *Elder Abuse* (The Stationery Office, 2004) para 36.

[104] Ibid.

[105] R Gainey and B Payne, 'Caregiver Burden, Elder Abuse and Alzheimer's Disease: Testing the Relationship' (2006) 29 *Journal of Health and Human Services* 245.

[106] L McDonald and A Collins, *Abuse and Neglect of Older Adults* (NCFV, 2002).

[107] R Bergeron, 'An Elder Abuse Case Study: Caregiver Stress or Domestic Violence? You Decide' (2001) 34 *Journal of Gerontological Social Work* 47.

[108] R Pain, *Theorising Age in Criminology: The Case of Home Abuse* (British Criminology Conferences, 1999).

ageism and patriarchy.[109] No better indication of the failure to appreciate the significance of gender in the context of intimate abuse is the very existence of the 'carer stress' theory itself. The fact that the vast majority of those caring are women, but the vast majority of those abusing are men should have immediately demonstrated that the link was not as strong as had been assumed.[110]

Discrimination against people with disabilities and ageism play a crucial role in intimate abuse. Ageism creates preconceptions and norms of the behaviour and attitudes expected of older people.[111] Disablism does the same thing. These are reinforced by a range of subtle means including characterisations in the media, advertising, language and social norms. Those who transgress these norms are subject to ridicule.

Society portrays older people and disabled people as lacking capacity or being of doubtful capacity. This can restrict their access to power, public spaces and their role in the community. These all have significant impact on carer abuse. First, ageism and disablism work hard to keep disabled and older people in their homes or restricted to a few specific public places. This means that more time is spent at home and therefore the scope of intimate abuse is increased. Further, the lack of access to support from others, or public services, means that abuse goes undetected.

Second, disablist and ageist attitudes create and reinforce attitudes among older people about themselves. The ageist notion that older people are a 'waste of space' and always complaining about things, deter victims of elder abuse from seeking help or indeed even lead them to believe that the behaviour is not abusive. Such attitudes belittle and sap the confidence of those suffering abusive relationships.

Third, the lack of alternative facilities for disabled and older people both in terms of housing and social support can make the alternatives to the abusive situation as terrifying as the abuse itself. Financial barriers to seeking help or leaving the relationship can be even greater among older women than younger victims of domestic violence.[112]

Fourth, those in need of care are often dependent on their carers.[113] There are little alternative forms of care. This leads to little opportunity for alternative care.

Fifth, there are ageist and disablist attitudes about men that affect perpetrators. Is elder abuse in part an attempt by men to assert power in the home

---

[109] T Whittaker, 'Violence, Gender and Elder Abuse' in B Fawcett, B Featherstone, J Hearn, and C Toft (eds), *Violence and Gender Relations: Theories and Interventions* (Sage, 1996).

[110] D Hines and K Malley-Morrison, *Family Violence in the US* (Sage, 2004) 247.

[111] J Herring, *Older People in Law and Society* (Oxford University Press 2009) ch 3.

[112] S Straka and L Montminy, 'Responding to the Needs of Older Women Experiencing Domestic Violence' (2006) 12 *Violence against Women* 251.

[113] D Wilke and L Vinton, 'The Nature and Impact of Domestic Violence Across Age Cohorts' (2005) 20 *Affilia* 316.

when ageism means they are losing it in other areas of their life?[114] We cannot know, but it is interesting to note the evidence that perpetrators of abuse tend to be those who are themselves highly dependent on the victim.[115]

The 'macro causes' of intimate abuse seek to find the causes of abuse outside the relationship between the parties. One explanation is that the way our society is arranged tends to mean that older people are outside the 'public sphere'. They live their lives in nursing homes, or in their own homes, but are not free to leave. The fact their lives are largely spent 'behind closed doors' means that their abuse is readily undetected and that because older people tend to be dependent on their carers for their basic needs their options in seeking to escape from the abuse are limited. The lack of social inclusion; dependency on others; lack of access to information and remedies can all contribute to the social circumstances that enable elder abuse to take place.[116]

A wider point is the failure of society to effectively integrate older people into mainstream society.[117] Social structure and attitudes towards the elderly marginalise them[118] and this encourages and enables the abuse to take place.[119] The Royal College of Psychiatrists suggested that dehumanisation is at the root of most abuse.[120] Although notions of dehumanisation and a lack of respect are vague, the benefit of emphasising them is that they play an important role in explaining not all the attitudes which may cause abuse, but also how the abuse is perceived by the older person and society at large.

So then, intimate abuse can reflect some powerful social forces. Negative attitudes towards women, older people and disabled people are all manifested in intimate abuse and the response to abuse in the law and society more generally.

VI. Rights to Protection

I will now develop an argument that those suffering intimate abuse have a human right to protection. Establishing this is central to developing the law's response to intimate abuse. It might seem surprising to turn to human rights at

---

[114] S Biggs, C Phillipson and P Kingson, *Elder Abuse in Perspective* (Open University Press, 1995) 21.

[115] J Ogg and C Munn-Giddings, 'Researching Elder Abuse' (1993) 13 *Ageing and Society* 381.

[116] Department of Health, *Safeguarding Adults* (Department of Health, 2005).

[117] D Schuyler and B Liang, 'Reconceptualizing Elder Abuse: Treating the Disease of Senior Community Exclusion' (2006) 15 *Annals of Health* 275.

[118] M Quinn and S Tomita, *Elder Abuse and Neglect: Causes, Diagnosis and Intervention Strategies* (Springer, 1986).

[119] Social Exclusion Unit, *Social Exclusion Among Older People* (The Stationery Office, 2005).

[120] Royal College of Psychiatrists, *Institutional Abuse of Older Adults* (Royal College of Psychiatrists, 2000).

this point, given that an ethic of care has tended to avoid the notion of rights. In part I do so because they provide a powerful legal basis for the claims I will make. More importantly, as argued in chapter two, a central aspect of a caring relationship is one that demonstrates respect for each party. Any legal system that wishes to ensure that relationships flourish must have an effective protection from abuse within them. Otherwise people will be deterred from entering relationships, and/or relationships marked by abuse, not care, will prevail. I will outline the key rights in the European Convention on Human Rights (ECHR), protected through the Human Rights Act 1998, before exploring in detail the practical consequences of protecting these rights.[121]

A. The Right to Life: Article 2

Article 2 of the ECHR not only prohibits the state from intentionally and unlawfully taking life, it requires the state to take appropriate steps to safeguard the lives of people living within the jurisdiction.[122] This requires there to be effective criminal law to deter violent crimes and an effective mechanism for law enforcement.[123] In some cases, this extends to taking specific measures to protect individuals from 'a real and immediate risk to life'[124] at the hand of another.[125] That obligation must be interpreted in a way so that the burden on the state is not disproportionate or impossible.[126] In *Opuz v Turkey* it was explained:

> For a positive obligation to arise, it must be established that the authorities knew or ought to have known at the time of the existence of a real and immediate risk to the life of an identified individual from the criminal acts of a third party and that they failed to take measures within the scope of their powers which, judged reasonably, might have been expected to avoid that risk.[127]

Of course, only the most extreme cases of intimate abuse are likely to give rise to right to life issues.

B. The Right not to Suffer Torture and Inhuman or Degrading Treatment: Article 3

Serious intimate abuse could constitute an infringement of the right to protection from inhuman or degrading treatment under article 3 of the ECHR:

---

[121] For a more detailed analysis see S Choudhry and J Herring, *European Human Rights and Family Law* (Hart, 2010) chs 8 and 9.

[122] *LCB v the United Kingdom*, 9 June 1998, § 36, Reports 1998-III.

[123] *R (AP) v HM Coroner For The County Of Worcestershire* [2011] EWHC 1453 (Admin).

[124] Ibid.

[125] *Osman v the United Kingdom*, 28 October 1998, § 115, Reports 1998-VIII.

[126] *Opuz v Turkey* [2009] ECHR 33401/02.

[127] Ibid, para 129.

'No one shall be subjected to torture or to inhuman or degrading treatment or punishment.'

Of the three kinds of prohibited conduct, torture is seen as worse than inhuman or degrading treatment.[128] The phrase 'inhuman treatment' in article 3 includes actual bodily harm or intense physical or mental suffering.[129] 'Degrading treatment' includes conduct which humiliates or debases an individual; or shows a lack of respect for, or diminishes, human dignity. It also includes conduct which arouses feelings of fear, anguish or inferiority capable of breaking an individual's moral and physical resistance.[130] In considering whether treatment is 'degrading', the court will have regard to whether its object was to humiliate and debase the victim and the effect on the victim. Hence corporal punishment can fall within this category, even if the physical injuries caused are relatively minor.[131] Clearly serious physical assaults will fall into this category. But less serious incidents, especially when occurring over a prolonged period of time, can too. In *Pretty v UK*[132] it was held that 'fear, anguish *or* inferiority' could be involved in degrading treatment. Depression, learned helplessness and alienation, post-traumatic stress disorder, guilt and denial have been cited as resulting from elder abuse.[133] This suggests that an ongoing relationship in which the victim is subject to a series of incidents, which seen individually might appear minor, could amount to a breach of article 3. A lack of respect of a person's humanity can be included.[134] In serious cases, persistent infantilisation and emotional abuse could, therefore, fall within article 3.

Article 3 not only prohibits the state from inflicting torture or inhuman or degrading treatment on its citizens, it also requires the state to protect one citizen from torture or inhuman or degrading treatment at the hands of another.[135] A state will infringe an individual's right under article 3 if it is aware that she or he is suffering the necessary degree of abuse at the hands of another and fails to take reasonable,[136] adequate[137] or effective[138] steps to protect that individual.[139] There is a particular obligation on the state to protect the article 3 rights of vulnerable people, such as children.[140] The obligations

---

[128] *Ilascu and others v Moldova and Russia* [GC], no 48787/99, 08 July 2004, para 440.

[129] *Ireland v the United Kingdom* 2 EHRR 25.

[130] See *Price v the United Kingdom*, no 33394/96, para 24–30 and *Valašinas v Lithuania* [2001] ECHR 479.

[131] *Campbell and Cosans v UK* (1982) 4 EHRR 293; *Tyrer v UK* (1978) 2 EHRR 1.

[132] [2002] ECHR 423, para 52.

[133] R Wolf, 'Elder Abuse and Neglect: Causes and Consequences' (1997) 31 *Journal of Geriatric Psychiatry* 153.

[134] *Albert and Le Compte v Belgium*, judgment of 10 February 1983, Series A, no 58, para 22.

[135] *A v UK* [1998] 3 FCR 597; *E v UK* [2002] 3 FCR 700.

[136] *Z v UK* [2001] 2 FCR 246.

[137] *A v UK* [1998] 3 FCR 597, para 24.

[138] *Z v UK* [2001] 2 FCR 246, para 73.

[139] *E v UK* [2002] 3 FCR 700.

[140] *A v UK* [1998] 3 FCR 597, para 20.

imposed on the state include ensuring that there is an effective legal deterrent to protect victims from abuse; to ensure that there is proper legal investigation and prosecution of any infringement of the individual rights; and where necessary to intervene and remove a victim from a position where she or he is suffering conduct which is prohibited by article 3.[141] Hence states have been found to infringe article 3 when they have been aware that children are being abused but have not taken steps to protect them;[142] where the law on sexual assault required proof that the victim had physically resisted the sexual assault;[143] and where the police failed to properly investigate or take steps to prosecute men alleged to have committed sexual assaults.[144] These obligations can arise in cases of intimate abuse, just as they do in cases of child abuse or domestic violence.

The recent decision in *Opuz v Turkey*[145] is particularly revealing. There a woman who was in a violent relationship with her husband complained to the police on several occasions about domestic violence against her and her mother (who lived with the couple). However, each occasion she subsequently withdrew her complaint and the police halted intervention. Tragically her mother was killed by the husband and the woman seriously injured. The woman complained that the state had failed to protect her and her mother's rights. The state claimed it was proper to stop proceedings when the complaints were withdrawn. The Court found against the state and explained:

> In the Court's opinion, it does not appear that the local authorities sufficiently considered the above factors when repeatedly deciding to discontinue the criminal proceedings against H.O. [the man]. Instead, they seem to have given exclusive weight to the need to refrain from interfering in what they perceived to be a 'family matter'... Moreover, there is no indication that the authorities considered the motives behind the withdrawal of the complaints.[146]

This makes it clear that it is insufficient for the state simply to rely on the victim's withdrawal of a complaint or a failure to complain as a justification for non-intervention in cases where rights under articles 2 or 3 are concerned.

The right under article 3 is an absolute one.[147] Unlike many of the other rights mentioned in the European Convention there are no circumstances in which it is permissible for the state to infringe this right. This makes it clear that the rights of another party cannot justify an infringement of someone's article 3 rights. So, for example, it cannot be successfully argued

---

[141] See S Choudhry and J Herring, *European Human Rights and Family Law* (Hart, 2010) chs 8 and 9.

[142] *E v UK* [2002] 3 FCR 700.

[143] *MC v Bulgaria* (2005) 40 EHRR 20.

[144] Ibid.

[145] [2009] ECHR 33401/02.

[146] Ibid, para 143.

[147] M Addo and N Grief, 'Does Article 3 of the European Convention on Human Rights Enshrine Absolute Rights?' (1998) 9 *European Journal of International Law* 510.

that a family's right of privacy justifies non-intervention by the state if that non-intervention is an infringement of one family member's article 3 rights. Indeed, and perhaps this is more controversial, it is suggested that other rights of the victim cannot justify an infringement of article 3. In other words, in an intimate abuse case the state cannot justify its failure to protect a victim's article 3 rights by referring to that person's right to respect for private life.[148] Of course, the fact that the victim is 'happy' with the abuse might mean it falls short of amounting to inhuman or degrading treatment in borderline cases. However, where it does not, I would argue that article 3 is automatically engaged. Further, it should be emphasised that although article 3 is drafted in absolute terms, the state's obligations towards its citizens in respect of article 3 are only to take *reasonable* measures to protect an individual's article 3 rights.[149] Again, where a victim of abuse is 'happy' with being in the abusive relationship that may mean that it is not reasonable to expect the state to intervene. However, I would argue that would be very rare where the victim is facing inhuman or degrading treatment.

C. The Right to Respect for Private and Family Life: Article 8

Article 8 of the ECHR states that

(1)   Everyone has the right to respect for his private and family life, his home and his correspondence.
(2)   There shall be no interference by a public authority with the exercise of this right except such as in accordance with the law and is necessary in a democratic society in the interests of national security, public safety or the economic well-being of the country, for the prevention of disorder or crime, for the protection of health or morals, or for the protection of the rights and freedoms of others.

Included within the right to respect for private life is the right to bodily integrity and this includes 'psychological integrity' and 'a right to personal development, and the right to establish and develop relationships with other human beings and the outside world'.[150] Like article 3, article 8 has been interpreted to mean that not only must the state not infringe someone's bodily or psychological integrity, but also the state must ensure that one person's integrity is not interfered with at the hands of another. In other words it is not just a 'negative right' inhibiting state intrusion into citizens' private lives, it places 'positive obligations' on the state to intervene to protect

---

[148] Although the state may argue that the victim's views make it unreasonable for the state to intervene.
[149] *E v UK* [2002] 3 FCR 700.
[150] *Pretty v UK* [2002] ECHR 423, para 61.

individuals.[151] However, unlike article 3, this is a qualified right. It is permissible for the state to fail to respect an individual's right to respect for private life under article 8(1) if paragraph 2 is satisfied. So, if the level of abuse is not sufficient to engage article 3 but falls within article 8 then it is necessary to balance the article 8 rights and interests of other parties. It would therefore be possible to make an argument that the rights of the abuser, or perhaps even the victim, justify the state in not intervening in an article 8 case.

So, how can these competing rights and interests under article 8 be balanced? Rachel Taylor and I[152] have suggested that in a case of clashing rights the court should look at the values underpinning the right.[153] In the case of article 8 the underlying value is that of autonomy: the right to pursue your vision of the 'good life'. A judge could then consider the extent to which the proposed order would constitute a blight on each of the party's opportunities to live the good life and make the order which causes the least blight. Applying that in this context I would argue that although removing the victim from intimate abuse from an abusive carer will infringe the carer's autonomy, it will do so to a much lesser extent than leaving the victim to suffer abuse would do. But what if the victim does not want the assistance?

Here there is a balance between protecting the current autonomous wish of the victim, with the increase in autonomy they may experience if they were removed from the abuse. That controversial issue will be looked at later, but I will conclude that in most cases intervention is still appropriate.

VII. Criminal Law

Of course, the normal criminal law provisions apply to those in caring relationships and these, in part, help ensure the rights of protection. Offences of assault, theft and the like apply to those in caring relationships, as in other cases. I shall focus on offences of particular relevance in caring relationships. Rather than considering crimes separately, I wish to draw out three themes relating to those in caring relationships.

---

[151] S Choudhry and J Herring, 'Domestic Violence and the Human Rights Act 1998: A New Means of Legal Intervention' [2007] *Public Law* 752.

[152] J Herring and R Taylor, 'Relocating Relocation' (2006) 18 *Child and Family Law Quarterly* 517; S Choudhry and H Fenwick, 'Taking the Rights of Parents and Children Seriously: Confronting the Welfare Principle and the Human Rights Act' (200 5) 25 *Oxford Journal of Legal Studies* 453.

[153] This seeks to develop a dicta of Lord Steyn in *Re S (A Child) (Identification: Restrictions on Publication)* [2005] 1 AC 593, para 17, which refers to the need to consider the values underlying the right when considering cases of clashing rights.

A. Relational Wrongs

As explored in chapter two, we are essentially relational beings. The criminal law, however, is typically bad at recognising relational wrongs. The definition of crimes tends to abstract the kind of wrong that is performed against the victim: there is an actual bodily harm; there is a non-consensual sexual penetration and so forth. These are seen outside the context of the overall relationship between the parties. Yet seeing what is done in the light of the broader context of the relationship between the parties is key to properly understanding the nature of the wrong against the victim.

A striking example is *R v Dhaliwal*, where a husband by a sustained campaign of abuse drove his wife to commit suicide. Because all that could be proved were his abusive comments, his conviction for constructive manslaughter was overturned. Looked at individually his unpleasant remarks were not unlawful. The sustained campaign of behaviour did not fit neatly into the tools of legal analysis.

In fact, the criminal law is beginning to get better at recognising these relational wrongs. The Protection from Harassment Act 1997, for example, recognises that a course of conduct which causes harassment can be a criminal offence. Indeed it has been suggested that in *Dhaliwal* itself the prosecution, with some imagination, could have obtained a conviction.[154] It is crucial that the law gets better at recognising the wrongs done in their broader context if it is to protect people from intimate abuse.

Another good example is the law of theft. There is a widespread concern that vulnerable people can be taken advantage of by unscrupulous 'carers' and be persuaded to give over their money.[155] The issue comes to a head in cases where a vulnerable person has given a gift to a carer or changed a will in their favour while there is doubt over the older person's ability to understand what they have done.[156] Such a case can create a clash between the principles of property law and those of criminal law. A criminal lawyer may focus on the dishonesty of the person receiving the money. For property lawyers it is important that ownership of property passes with possession. So that where a transfer has been made only in the most unusual of circumstances should the ownership not pass. An example will explain why. If a rather confused person buys 10 Kit-Kats from a corner shop, we may take the view that if they were rather befuddled and had not fully understood what they were doing then the transfer would be invalid. But saying that would cause a host of problems

---

[154] J Horder and L McGowan, 'Manslaughter by Causing Another's Suicide' [2006] *Criminal Law Review* 1035.

[155] C Dessin, 'Financial Abuse of the Elderly: Is the Solution a Problem?' (2003) 34 *McGeorge Law Review* 267.

[156] J Langan, 'In the Best Interests of Elderly People? The Role of Local Authorities in Handling and Safeguarding the Personal Finances of Elderly People with Dementia' (1997) 19 *Journal of Social Welfare and Family Law* 463.

for property lawyers. It means the money handed to the shop keeper remains the property of the befuddled person and that in turn means that the shop keeper does not have ownership. Problems will arise if the shop keeper gives the money as change to the next customer and the problems could go on. It is not surprising then that a property lawyer would rather say, although a bit confused, the person knew they were buying something and so the confusion is insufficient to upset the transaction.

The case of *R v Hinks*[157] highlights the issues well. A 38–year-old woman (Karen Hinks) befriended a 53-year-old man (John Dolphin), who was described as of limited intelligence. In the period of eight months £60,000 was given to Ms Hinks. Her conviction for theft was upheld. Although it appeared that no threats or deceptions had been used (which would have made the case an easy one), it was felt she had behaved dishonestly in receiving the money. What is notable about the case is the House of Lords willingness to find that there was theft, even though there was no civil wrong (in other words the gifts may have been valid under the law of property). Lord Steyn noted the possible differences between civil and criminal law as mentioned above. He saw this justifying a finding that a criminal offence had taken place, even though there may have been an effective transfer of ownership.[158]

As this example demonstrates, there is much to be gained from the criminal law not simply focusing on the moment of the crime and defining the wrong in terms of a particular act and state of mind. Rather, we should look at the act within the broader context of the relationship. Only then, for example, can the wrong in *Hinks* be identified. Another good example of that point is the offence of rape where the focus of the law is on whether there was consent at the particular moment in time. I have argued that a better approach would be to look at the sexual encounter in the context of the relationship. Not just was there a 'yes' at the time of the intercourse, but what was the context of that 'yes'? How was the act understood within the context of the relationship of the parties? Only by answering these questions can a proper assessment of the effect of 'consent' be made.[159]

There is a broader point. If we are people constructed through our relationships then the wrong and abuse of those relationships are particularly serious, both to us as individuals and to a society dedicated on care. The current law fails to capture the abuse of those relationships. The wrong at the heart of intimate violence is not properly captured by the current law. Behaviour such as bullying; trolling and infliction of emotional distress are

---

[157] [2000] UKHL 53.

[158] The case has generated much debate among criminal lawyers. This is summarised in J Herring, *Criminal Law: Text Cases and Materials* (Oxford University Press, 2012) ch 8.

[159] J Herring, 'Relational Autonomy and Rape' in S Day Sclater, F Ebtehaj, E Jackson and M Richards (eds), *Regulating Autonomy* (Hart, 2009).

inadequately covered. We see again the assumption about protection of the isolated individual, rather than of caring relationships.

B. Special Obligations under the Criminal Law

It is noticeable that entering a caring relationship can generate responsibilities under the criminal law. For example, there are statutory offences which can only be committed by those responsible for caring for another.[160] Under the common law, entering into an intimate relationship may generate an obligation to summon help, whereas generally one is not under an obligation to help others under the criminal law.

While there must be concerns over adding to the responsibilities of carers who are a marginalised group,[161] I believe these can be justified.[162] In part this reflects the emphasis in an ethic of care on the importance of responsibilities. Acknowledging and giving effect to these is an important part of valuing relationships.[163] However, there is debate over whether or not the criminal law is the best mechanism for doing this.[164] The main concerns are the following.

i. Concerns over the Broader Support

There are a number of issues here. The first is that given the lack of state and social support for those undertaking care, it might be seen as unfair to punish those that undertake care. The issues are well illustrated by *R v Stone and Dobinson*,[165] which involved two defendants: John Stone described as below average intelligence, partially deaf and almost blind and Gwendoline Dobinson, described as 'ineffectual and inadequate'. They had Stone's 50-year-old sister, Fanny, who was suffering from anorexia nervosa, come to live with them. Fanny regularly refused food and grew very weak. The defendants failed to summon help, despite requests from neighbours. Fanny was later found dead in squalid conditions. The appellants were convicted of manslaughter and their convictions were upheld by the Court of Appeal. The Court of Appeal emphasised the fact they had taken on care of a person

---

[160] Eg Mental Capacity Act 2005, s 44 creates an offence of ill-treatment or neglect of a person lacking capacity.

[161] M O'Hear, 'Yes to Nondiscrimination, No to New Forms of Criminal Liability: A Reply to Professors Collins, Leib, and Markel' (2008) 88 *Boston University Law Review* 1437.

[162] E Leib, D Markel and J Collins, 'Voluntarism, Vulnerability, and Criminal Law: A Response to Professors Hills and O'Hear' (2008) 88 *Boston University Law Review* 1449.

[163] D Markel, J Collins and E Leib, *Privilege or Punish: Criminal Justice and the Challenge of Family Ties* (Oxford University Press, 2009).

[164] M O'Hear, 'Yes to Nondiscrimination, No to New Forms of Criminal Liability: A Reply to Professors Collins, Leib, and Markel' (2008) 88 *Boston University Law Review* 1437.

[165] [1977] QB 354.

who was unable to care for herself and that they had been negligent in the performance of that care.

The decision has proved controversial. The defendants were of low capacity. It appears they had enough difficulty looking after themselves, yet alone anyone else. Notably the Court of Appeal confirmed the use of the negligence standard for cases of this kind. In other words, guilt flowed from the fact their level of care fell below that expected and there was no need to show any kind of intention or recklessness. The fact they had done the best that might be expected of them was irrelevant. The concern here is that the criminal law is being used to impose higher standards than the defendant is capable of. That seems inherently unjust. Even taking the point that these defendants had assumed responsibility for the victim, they cannot be taken to have assumed responsibility to do more than they were capable of.

The law should impose only limited obligations imposed on carers. Informal carers, unlike professionals, are unlikely to have ready access to a code of conduct on how they can behave. Indeed, informal care may arise without a person being consciously aware that they are thereby taking on legal obligations. Further, the precise extent of what is expected of an informal carer is far from clear.[166] It should be limited to requiring carers to do what they are capable of and only then to what would be widely known principles of basic good care.

The second reason for the controversy is that there seems to be multiple failings in the care offered to Fanny. Her doctor, other relatives, social services, and neighbours all could have offered care and arguably failed in their caring responsibilities to Fanny. Yet it was Stone and Dobinson alone, who at least attempted to meet their responsibilities, who faced the censure of the law.

Carers, the courts have assumed, are different because they have 'voluntarily' assumed caring responsibilities. Neil Cobb, in an important article, has questioned this assumption.[167] He talks of 'compulsory care-giving', where a person undertakes care because of the failings of the state or others to provide adequate care of a loved one. Social, emotional and familial pressures can mean that women particularly are assumed to be responsible for care. This questions whether the 'assumption' of care should be regarded as a voluntary undertaking which justifies imposing especial obligations on carers.

---

[166] H Biggs and R Mackenzie, 'End of Life Decision-Making, Policy and the Criminal Justice System: Untrained Carers Assuming Responsibility [UCARes] and their Uncertain Legal Liabilities' (2006) 2 *Genomics, Society and Policy* 118.

[167] N Cobb, 'Compulsory Care-Giving: Some Thoughts on Relational Feminism, the Ethics of Care and Omissions Liability' (2008) 39 *Cambrian Law Review* 11.

ii. A Failure to Recognise the Relational Reality

The law, in punishing those who fail to live up to the standards expected of carers, sometimes fails to appreciate the relational context in which they are acting. A good example is the offence of causing or allowing the death of another. Section 5 of the Domestic Violence, Crime and Victims Act 2005 criminalises a person who fails to take reasonable steps to protect a child they were living with from a significant risk of significant harm from someone else in the household.

In a study of some of the prosecutions for an offence, I expressed concerns that those prosecuted for these offences were often themselves the victims of violence at the hands of an abuser.[168] For example, the first reported conviction concerned Sandra Mujuru, aged 21, who allowed her partner, Jerry Stephens, to murder their four month old baby (Ayesha). Ms Mujuru was sentenced to a two year community order, although while awaiting trial she had served the equivalent of more than a year in jail. The Court of Appeal justified her conviction in this way:

> There was also evidence before the jury capable of supporting a finding that Miss M knew that S had broken A's arm, or had good reason to think that he might have done so, and that she was, or ought to have been, aware that there was a significant risk that he might deliberately harm A again. If they made those findings, the jury could go on to find that by leaving A in his care while she went to work Miss M failed to take such steps as she could reasonably have been expected to take to protect her.[169]

It was noted that Ms Mujuru must have known of Stephens's potential for violence because she had visited him while he was serving time in prison for an attack on his previous girlfriend.

These explanations fail to give sufficient weight to the circumstances in which Ms Mujuru found herself. She was an asylum seeker escaping violence in Zimbabwe. In sentencing her, the judge commented that she was a 'decent young woman in a vulnerable position'. The judge noticed that Stephens was twice her age and was a 'self-centred and dangerous man with a dangerously short fuse'. As a young asylum-seeker should she really have been expected to know from which authorities to seek advice and how to access the appropriate services? Could she have done this without endangering her child and herself by igniting her partner's 'dangerously short fuse'? On the day the child's body was found Stephens had assaulted his previous girlfriend, hitting her on the head with a frying pan and a vase. So, were her fears that she would be attacked if

---

[168] J Herring, 'Home Made Apple Pie and Allowing Children to Die' *Durham Law Review* 4 November 2010.

[169] *R v Stephens and Mujuru* [2007] EWCA 1249.

she sought help for her and her child really so ill-founded? As this case demonstrates, in the calm of the court room and in retrospect it is easy to say that a mother could easily have saved her child from this violent man. Rebecca Lewis was sentenced to six years in prison because she had left her child with her partner, knowing him to be violent. She explained at the trial that she had not sought help because he would kill her if she left. Six years is a little less than the average sentence for rape. Notably in this case social services had been warned about the dangers the child faced. Their only attempt to rescue the child was to send a letter seeking an appointment to the incorrect address. Needless to say they did not face a criminal prosecution.

It is not my case that prosecutions under section 5 for failure to protect are never justified. However, I do believe that there should be a specific defence to a charge under section 5 for the defendant to show she was subject to domestic violence from the person who killed the child. This will commonly apply. The links between domestic violence and child abuse are well established. It is not hard to believe that a man willing to kill or do serious violence to a child would do the same to his partner if he thought she was 'informing on him' to the authorities. Further, domestic violence nearly always has highly adverse psychological impact on the victim. The victim can lose all self confidence, can feel completely trapped, and even become emotionally dependent on the abuser and believe that she is to blame for her own abuse. Inevitably this will significantly impact on her understanding of the situation, the risks to the child and the alternatives open to her. The dangers posed by the man, and the ease of rescue which can seem so obvious to the outside world may not be to the woman in the particular situation. An abused woman may well decide that for herself and her children the violence to which she has become accustomed is safer than the violence that may be provoked by an attempt to leave or seek assistance. Can we be confident that such an assessment is wrong? The 'reasonable' course of seeking help from authorities when a child is in danger is not always reasonable. It can be an extremely dangerous course of action for a woman. As studies have consistently shown, it can be more dangerous for a victim of domestic violence to leave her partner than to remain with him. If they do manage to leave, our society still offers woefully little assistance by way of housing, financial or emotional support. The 'reasonable' course of protecting the child expected by the law in fact requires something quite extraordinary from mothers in some cases.[170]

In *R v Khan*,[171] the Court of Appeal thought that the concerns were addressed by the fact the defendant could only be convicted if the jury were

---

[170] J Herring, 'Familial Homicide, Failure to Protect and Domestic Violence: Who's the Victim?' (2007) *Criminal Law Review* 923.

[171] [2009] EWCA Crim 2.

persuaded that she had failed to take reasonable steps to protect her child. In considering whether reasonable steps were taken the jury would be able to take into account any violence that she faced. However, this I believe to be inadequate. First, it is assumed that the jury is aware of the impact of domestic violence on a defendant and unless there is good expert evidence of that it may not. Second, the case law referred to above demonstrates that juries are willing to convict in cases where the defendant has been subject to a regime of violence. Third, I ask simply in what case is it appropriate to convict a victim of domestic violence living with a violent man who is a serious danger to his child and partner for not protecting herself or her child? Especially given the woeful lack of state support for those seeking protection and escape from violence. I believe such a case cannot be imagined. Hence my proposal that the Act be amended to provide a specific defence in cases where the defendant was herself subject to violence from the killer.

Another example of the failure to appreciate the relational context is the law on assisted suicide. The issues of assisted suicide are complex and cannot be dealt with in detail here.[172] While the academic debates have tended to focus, understandably, on abstract principle such as the sanctity of life or the right to die, many of the cases have involved individual carers.

The current law states that assisting or encouraging suicide is an offence but following the decision in *R (Purdy) v Director of Public Prosecutions*[173] the Director of Public Prosecutions produced new guidance on when a prosecution would be brought.[174] The guidance seems particularly designed to ensure that carers acting out of compassion will not be liable.[175] So a factor in favour of prosecution is:

> (6) The suspect was not wholly motivated by compassion; for example, the suspect was motivated by the prospect that he or she or a person closely connected to him or her stood to gain in some way from the death of the victim;[176]

Whereas a factor against prosecution is:

> (2) The suspect was wholly motivated by compassion;[177]

---

[172] See J Herring, 'Mum's Not the Word: An Analysis of Section 5, Domestic Violence, Crimes and Victims Act 2004' in C Clarkson and S Cunningham, *Criminal Liability for Non-Aggressive Death* (Ashgate, 2008).

[173] [2009] UKHL 45.

[174] Director of Public Prosecutions, *Policy for Prosecutors in Respect of Cases of Encouraging or Assisting Suicide* (Director of Public Prosecutions, 2010).

[175] A Mullock, 'Overlooking the Criminally Compassionate: What are the Implications of Prosecutorial Policy on Encouraging or Assisting Suicide?' (2010) *Medical Law Review* 442.

[176] Director of Public Prosecutions, *Policy for Prosecutors in Respect of Cases of Encouraging or Assisting Suicide* (Director of Public Prosecutions, 2010).

[177] Ibid.

Indeed, Alexandra Mullock goes so far as to claim:

> the Policy has precisely the effect of sanctioning compassionately motivated assisted suicide, with compassion as the key determining factor which potentially places an act which remains criminal beyond the reach of the criminal courts.[178]

She accepts that this might be seen as a surprise, given that the autonomy of the victim might be thought to be the central factor, she explains that 'the very concept of compassion, in this context, assumes autonomy on the part of the victim'.[179]

It is submitted that this approach is the best way of understanding the current approach of the law. The law continues to make it an offence to assist or encourage suicide, but it acknowledges that the motivation of those doing so may be good, especially in the context of a caring relationship. The law can then maintain the line that prima facie it is a criminal offence to assist or encourage suicide, but that an individual motivated by compassion should not be subject to prosecution.[180] This neatly sidesteps the question of why: is it that the compassionate act, while wrong, does not deserve the stigma of a punishment? Or is it that the compassionate act is a good one?

These reforms do nothing for those who actually kill those they are caring for and are prosecuted, even if motivated by compassion.[181] For them the charge is murder. The leading case is *R v Inglis*.[182] Frances Inglis was the mother of Thomas Inglis, a young man who when being taken to hospital in an ambulance, fell out and suffered catastrophic head injuries. Two months later she tried to kill him with heroin, but he survived. A year later she managed, in breach of a bail condition, to inject him with heroin and he died. She was convicted of murder and given the mandatory life sentence. It was accepted that she was enormously distressed by her son's condition. There was evidence that after his condition became apparent, she was constantly crying.[183] She had become convinced it would be better for him if he was dead. One psychiatrist explained her mental state:

> She believed that she needed to relieve Thomas of his suffering, which in her mind was being prolonged and exacerbated by the interventions of the medical team. She had convinced herself that she was the only person who had his interests at heart or who genuinely cared for him.[184]

---

[178] A Mullock, 'Overlooking the criminally compassionate: what are the implications of prosecutorial policy on encouraging or assisting suicide?' (2010) *Medical Law Review* 442.

[179] L Van Zyl, *Death and Compassion: A Virtue-based Approach to Euthanasia* (Ashgate Publishing, Aldershot, 2000) 165.

[180] K Greasley, 'R(Purdy) v DPP and the Case of Wilful Blindness' (2010) 30 *Oxford Journal of Legal Studies* 301.

[181] H Keating and J Bridgemen, 'Caring Responsibilities, Harm and 'Compassionate' Acts?' in J Bridgeman, H Keating, and C Lind, *Regulating Family Responsibilities* (Ashgate, 2011).

[182] [2010] EWCA 2637.

[183] Ibid, para 14.

[184] Ibid, para 15.5.

Although the Court of Appeal acknowledged the case was a tragedy, it held that there were 'sensitive and difficult' issues of the public interest. It emphasised that 'the law of murder does not distinguish between murder committed for malevolent reasons and murder motivated by familial love'.[185] This is a revealing comment. It shows the narrowness of the criminal law's attempts to ascertain blame. By focusing on intention to kill as the mental state for murder, rather than taking a broader, more contextual approach to the incident, with a particular consideration of the relationship between the parties. This reveals a highly skewed view of the kinds of emotions and circumstances in which a killing might be excused or justified. The law on loss of control (previously provocation) permits a killing in anger following a grave wrong, but cannot account for a defendant overcome with compassion who calmly decides to kill a loved one. Killing another to protect oneself from a serious attack is justified; killing another to protect them from a painful medical condition is not.[186] The criminal law needs a far more sophisticated approach to understanding the relational context within which crimes are committed.

iii. The Glorification of Carers

The use of the criminal law against carers in some cases reflects the 'glorification of carers', particularly women carers. The mother, in particular, is expected to be the paragon of selfless care: the all-knowing, all-giving mother. The fall of such a mother from grace is seen in the harshest light.

Looking at familial homicide, for example, there is evidence from the United States that fathers are readily believed when they say they did not notice the mother was harming the child or would not have known where to go for help, whereas such claims by the mother are readily dismissed.[187] Similarly in cases of child neglect it is often the mother who is prosecuted, even though the father may have the same level of legal responsibility to protect the child.[188] As we have seen, such an approach leads with the blame ending up on the mother, not the true villain of the piece, the killer. When we say that parents ought to protect children from harm, where does this expectation come from? What standard of motherhood are these women departing from so far as to justify the intervention of the criminal law? Is

---

[185] Ibid, para 37.

[186] H Biggs and R Mackenzie 'End of Life Decision-Making, Policy and the Criminal Justice System: Untrained Carers Assuming Responsibility [UCARes] and their Uncertain Legal Liabilities' (2006) 12 *Genomics, Society and Policy* 118.

[187] See J Herring, 'Mum's Not the Word: An Analysis of Section 5, Domestic Violence, Crimes and Victims Act 2004' in C Clarkson and S Cunningham, *Criminal Liability for Non-Aggressive Death* (Ashgate, 2008).

[188] B Daniel and J Taylor, 'Gender and Child Neglect: Theory, Research and Policy' (2006) 26 *Critical Social Policy* 426.

this the standard of the ideal mother who cooks wonderful apple pies and transports her dears to their ballet lessons? Or is the standard expected that of a mother struggling under the oppression and dehumanising effect of domestic abuse? How easily the abused becomes seen as the abuser. The media coverage of these cases is revealing: 'Woman lets boyfriend kill her baby';[189] 'Mother allowed baby son's murder';[190] and 'Mother first to be convicted of failing to stop violent lover killing her baby'. In one popular daily newspaper we read:

> For her dereliction of the most basic motherly instinct, 23-year-old Hayley is now the first woman ever to be convicted of the new charge of familial homicide, or allowing the death of a child. And hurrah for that: frankly, if it were left to me, I'd throw away the key.[191]

Notice in these headlines that it is the mother who is targeted for blame, rather than the man who actually killed the child. *Attorney General's Reference (No.35 of 2005)*[192] is a striking case. The father admitted ill treatment of the child which had involved bruises on various parts of her body, partial hair loss and a possible cigarette burn on her foot. He received a conditional discharge. The mother (at a separate hearing) who admitted neglect on the basis that she had not sought medical attention for the injuries was given a six month prison sentence, albeit it was suspended for 18 months. Such is the opprobrium who fails in her 'motherly duties' that the real abuser disappears from the picture.

iv. The Responsibility of the State

The enthusiasm for prosecuting mothers in these cases in fact disguises the failures of the state. As we have seen, section 6 of the Human Rights Act 1998 puts an obligation on public authorities to protect children and vulnerable adults from violence. In many of the cases where there have been prosecutions, the state authorities have been aware of the dangers to the child and have done nothing. For the state to fail in its own obligations and fail to protect children, to then prosecute mothers who fail to protect is hard to justify. The use of section 5 is an attempt to divert attention away from the failures of public authorities to protect vulnerable adults and children.

---

[189] BBC News Online, 'Woman Let Boyfriend Kill her Baby' 11 April 2006.

[190] BBC News Online, 'Mother Allowed Baby Son's Murder' 13 March 2007.

[191] Quoted in J Herring, 'Mum's Not the Word: An Analysis of Section 5, Domestic Violence, Crimes and Victims Act 2004' in C Clarkson and S Cunningham, *Criminal Liability for Non-Aggressive Death* (Ashgate, 2008).

[192] [2006] EWCA Crim 378.

Consider, for example, *R (Jenkins) v HM Coroner for Portsmouth and South East Hampshire and Cameron and Finn*[193] where a man died after an injury to his foot was left untreated. Although his condition gradually deteriorated until his death, none of his friends sought medical help for him. The case arose as an appeal against the verdict of a coroner who had refused to find unlawful killing. The relatives complained that a Ms Cameron, who was a particularly close friend of the deceased and was with him when he died, should have summoned help. She, the deceased and his friends were all members of the Quiet Mind Centre who sought to avoid the use of traditional medicine and preferred alternative therapies.

For Pitchford J the case was relatively straightforward. As the deceased had made it clear he did not want to receive medical treatment he could not be forced to.[194] Therefore, the friends could not have breached a duty in failing to summon help for the deceased. The only argument that could be made was that when the deceased lost consciousness, he could not refuse treatment and at that point treatment, which was in his best interests, could have been provided. However, the judge found by that point even if help had been summoned it would not have arrived in time to save the deceased's life.

Inevitably given the nature of the court procedures, there was no attention paid to the wider social responsibilities for his death. What Mr Jenkins's doctor, and thereby the NHS, was aware of was that he was a diabetic who had failed to keep in contact with medical advisers. Is there not responsibility owed by the NHS to patients who are vulnerable to life threatening conditions to ensure that they are receiving appropriate and regular medical care? Were there other professionals involved with him who should have been alert to the dangers he faced? Should the Quiet Mind Centre have been subject to some form of regulation or inspection?

C. Conclusion on the Criminal Law

There are undoubtedly dangers that abuse can occur within a caring relationship.[195] Consider, for example, the evidence of elder abuse.[196] There is certainly a place for the criminal law to punish those who fail to care

---

[193] [2009] EWHC 3229 (Admin); discussed in J Herring, 'The Legal Duties of Carers' (2010) 18 *Medical Law Review* 248.

[194] This was well established in eg *Re B (Conmsent to Treatment: Capacity)* [2002] EWHC 429 (Fam).

[195] A Burke, 'When Family Matters' (2010) 119 *Yale Law Journal* 1210.

[196] M O'Keeffe, A Hills, M Doyle, C McCreadie, S Scholes, R Constantine, A Tinker, J Manthorpe, S Biggs and B Erens, *UK Study of Abuse and Neglect of Older People Prevalence Survey Report* (Department of Health, 2008).

adequately.[197] However, it is a limited one and must be based on three principles. First, criminal obligations of carers can only be justified when an adequate level of support and recognition is given for the role of carers. Second, any criminal obligation must recognise the realities of care work. That can be frustrating, exhausting and be perceived as imprisoning. Third, there must be a recognition that the state has an obligation to care for vulnerable people in our society. That should not be shirked by placing overly onerous obligations on those who undertake care work.[198]

VIII. Civil Law

Earlier we mentioned the rights of protection that are provided under the Human Rights Act 1998. In part, the state's obligations flowing from these rights are met by the criminal law provisions. But the state is also required under the civil law to ensure that people's rights are protected.[199] It is in the area of intimate relations where the kind of abuse that people are likely to need intervention is most relevant. The civil law can involve a range of remedies:

— Advice, assistance and services. It may be that the individual requires accommodation, services or money to protect themselves from the abuse.[200] These are discussed in chapter four.
— Civil remedies can be utilised by people seeking to protect themselves, such as injunctions. The civil remedies under the Family Law Act 1996 are a good example of these.
— Steps may be brought by the state to protect individuals from intimate abuse. These are likely to be used in cases involving children or where an individual has lost their capacity or are vulnerable and therefore unable to bring proceedings in their own name.

A full survey of the relevant law on protection is not possible.[201] The relevant areas of law will be sketched out in only the briefest of terms, before an exploration of some of the underlying issues.

---

[197] Mental Capacity Act 2005, s 44 creates an offence of ill-treatment or neglect of a person lacking capacity.

[198] D Markel, J Collins and E Leib, *Privilege or Punish: Criminal Justice and the Challenge of Family Ties* (Oxford University Press, 2009).

[199] *Council of Europe Convention on Preventing and Combating Violence against Women and Domestic Violence* (The Istanbul Convention).

[200] *Re Z (Local Authority: Duty)* [2004] EWHC 2817.

[201] Social Care Institute for Excellence (SCIE), *Safeguarding Adults at Risk of Harm* (SCIE, 2011) provides a thorough guide to the law.

A. Protection of Children

The law on child abuse is complex and cannot be dealt with in detail here. The law provides a way whereby the state can remove a child from his or her parents or intervene in the family life in order to protect him or her. The Children Act 1989 places on local authorities obligations to care for children in their area who are in need. This can include the provision of services or of accommodation.[202] More drastic intervention can remove taking a child away from the parents and placing the child in alternative care, which can be done through a care order or ordering a social worker to offer advice and assistance to a family through a supervision order.[203] Before making a care or supervision order, the court must under section 31 be satisfied:

(1) that 'the child concerned is suffering, or is likely to suffer, significant harm'.[204]

(2) '[t]hat the harm, or likelihood of harm, is attributable to: (i) the care given to the child, or likely to be given to him if the order were not made, not being what it would be reasonable to expect a parent to give him; or (ii) the child's being beyond parental control.'[205]

(3) the making of the order would promote the welfare of the child.[206]

This power is one of the greatest that the state has. For many parents, having their children compulsorily removed by the state would be one of the worst things that could happen to them. On the other hand, the appalling harm that children can suffer at the hands of their parents means that the state must intervene if children's rights are to be protected.[207]

One of the great problems in the law concerning the protection of children is that if the wrong decision is made, enormous harm can be caused. Imagine that a social worker visits a home where a child has a broken arm and bruises. The social worker suspects this may have been caused by the parents, while the parents claim that the injuries were caused by a fall down the stairs. If the parents' explanation is untrue, but the social worker decides to believe it, she would be leaving the child with abusive parents and there would be a danger that the child could suffer serious injury or even death. On the other hand, if the explanation is true and the social worker decides to remove the child, then the child and parents may suffer great harm through the separation. The

---

[202] Children Act 1989, pt 3.

[203] For a magnificent discussion see L Hoyano and C Keenan, *Child Abuse: Law and Policy Across Boundaries* (Oxford University Press, 2007).

[204] Children Act 1989, s 31(2)(a).

[205] Ibid, s 31(2)(b).

[206] Ibid, s 1(1).

[207] For a disturbing account of the long term effects of child abuse, see eg F Colquhoun, *The Relationship between Child Maltreatment, Sexual Abuse and Subsequent Suicide Attempts* (NSPCC, 2009).

history of the law on child protection reveals tragedies resulting from excessive intervention in family life, as well as gross failure to intervene.[208] The difficulty is that it is only with hindsight that it would be apparent that in a particular case the approach was inappropriate.

B. Domestic Violence

In a family situation a victim may choose to bring civil proceedings. Indeed it has been a common complaint of victims of domestic violence that the police have told them to seek civil remedies rather than 'bother' the police. If the victim seeks a remedy under civil law the application can be brought under the Family Law Act 1996 or the Protection from Harassment Act 1997. The Family Law Act 1996 provides a complex set of provisions which mean that the criteria for granting orders, and the range of orders available, depends on whether the applicant is married to the respondent, whether the applicant and/or respondent has a property interest in the home in question. It is not possible here to provide a complete analysis of the Family Law Act 1996 and its interpretation, but it is notable that the courts have described the making of an occupation order, removing the respondent from his home, as 'Draconian' and requiring 'exceptional circumstances' in order to justify it.[209]

C. Mental Capacity Act 2005

If an individual lacks capacity, the court can make orders under the Mental Capacity Act 2005 to determine where that person should live. While the court will assume that they should remain with their family, the court has the power to remove the individual if that would be in their best interests. There is no formal requirement of proof of significant harm, equivalent to section 31 of Children Act 1989. In other words, it is a straightforward question of what is in the best interests of the individual concerned.[210] However, the courts are likely to take the common sense point of view that a person lacking capacity is best cared for by those in caring relationships with him unless there is clear evidence otherwise. More significantly the court will bear in mind the right to respect of family and private life in article 8 of the ECHR, which requires any interference in family life to be justified.[211]

---

[208] L Hoyano and C Keenan, *Child Abuse: Law and Policy Across Boundaries* (Oxford University Press, 2007).

[209] For detail of the law see J Herring, *Family Law* (Pearson, 2011), ch 6.

[210] *IIBCC v LG* [2010] EWHC 1527 (Fam).

[211] *A Local Authority v A and B* [2010] EWHC 978 (Fam).

In *A Local Authority v A and B*,[212] there was considerable concern over the intervention of a local authority in the care of two people with Smith Magenis Syndrome, one a child and one an adult. The local authority were concerned about the way their families were locking them into their bedrooms at night. The Court was clear that the local authority had extensive duties to provide care services and support, which are discussed in chapter four. There may also be a duty at common law to investigate vulnerable adults under the law of tort or under the *No Secrets* policies.[213] Munby J, while accepting the responsibility of the state to protect, emphasised that its first role must be to support:

> People in the situation of A and C, together with their carers, look to the State—to a local authority—for the support, the assistance and the provision of the services to which the law, giving effect to the underlying principles of the Welfare State, entitles them. They do not seek to be 'controlled' by the State or by the local authority. And it is not for the State in the guise of a local authority to seek to exercise such control. The State, the local authority, is the servant of those in need of its support and assistance, not their master.[214]

D. Section 47 National Assistance Act 1948

National Assistance Act 1948, section 47 allows a local authority to apply for an order to remove a person to 'suitable premises' (such as a hospital). This power applies to any person who is:

(1) suffering from grave chronic disease, or being aged, infirm or physically incapacitated, is living in insanitary conditions; and

(2) unable to devote to themselves, and is not receiving from other persons, proper care and attention.

Before an order can be granted, a 'medical officer of health' must certify that the removal is necessary in the interests of the person or for the prevention of injury to the health of or serious nuisance to, other persons. The Law Commission[215] has questioned whether this power is much used. In its consultation no one claimed to have used it, at least since the Mental Capacity Act 2005 was implemented. It even questioned whether its use would involve a breach of article 5 ECHR rights. It recommended its repeal but accepted there may be a case for adding an alternative power.

---

[212] Ibid.
[213] Department of Health and Home Office, *No Secrets* (Department of Health, 2000).
[214] Ibid para 52.
[215] Law Commission, *Adult Social Care, Report 326* (Law Commission, 2011) para 9.65.

E. Vulnerable Adults

Where there are concerns about the abuse of a child or an adult without capacity, the provisions under the relevant legislation (Children Act 1989 or Mental Capacity Act 2005) should be used.[216] However, the courts have kept open the inherent jurisdiction to be used in cases concerning 'vulnerable adults' who have capacity, but are in need of protection. The existence of this jurisdiction has questioned, but was recently confirmed by the Court of Appeal in *DL v A Local Authority*.[217] There the Court of Appeal approved Munby J's approach in *Re: SA (Vulnerable adult with capacity: marriage)*:[218]

> the inherent jurisdiction can be exercised in relation to a vulnerable adult who, even if not incapacitated by mental disorder or mental illness, is, or is reasonably believed to be, either (i) under constraint or (ii) subject to coercion or undue influence or (iii) for some other reason deprived of the capacity to make the relevant decision, or disabled from making a free choice, or incapacitated or disabled from giving or expressing a real and genuine consent....

> I would treat as a vulnerable adult someone who, whether or not mentally incapacitated, and whether or not suffering from any mental illness or mental disorder, is or may be unable to take care of him or herself, or unable to protect him or herself against significant harm or exploitation, or who is deaf, blind or dumb, or who is substantially handicapped by illness, injury or congenital deformity. This, I emphasise, is not and is not intended to be a definition. It is descriptive, not definitive; indicative rather than prescriptive.

Where the inherent jurisdiction is used the court will make the order based on what is in the best interests of the individual. Indeed it seems from *DL v A Local Authority*[219] that there will be no difference in the way a case will in result be dealt with under the inherent jurisdiction and under the Mental Capacity Act.

I will now look at some of the broader issues raised by the law's response to abuse in intimate relationships.

IX. Compulsory Intervention

The primary legal response to intimate violence in England and Wales is the availability of criminal proceedings brought by the state and civil proceedings

---

[216] *IIBCC v LG* [2010] EWHC 1527 (Fam).
[217] [2012] EWCA Civ 253.
[218] [2005] EWHC 2942 (Fam), para 77, 82.
[219] [2012] EWCA Civ 253.

brought by the victim. However, the development of positive obligations on the state, as set out above, arguably reveals certain gaps in the English criminal justice systems. There is certainly a sufficient range of offences that exist to cover intimate violence, at least where it results in physical injury. The primary difficulty is in the police and prosecution response to such cases. A report by Her Majesty's Inspectorate of Constabulary and Crown Prosecution Service Inspectorate admitted in relation to domestic violence:

> Until relatively recently, for example, dominant police culture depicted violence in the home as 'just another domestic' a nuisance call to familiar addresses that rarely resulted in a satisfactory policing outcome. To the service's credit, tremendous efforts have been made in the last five years or so to overturn this stereotype and ensure that domestic violence is treated as a serious incident, requiring a high standard of professional investigation. The CPS too has raised the profile of domestic violence, issuing revised policy and guidance and setting up a network of Area domestic violence coordinators. But all too often, policies and rhetoric are not matched on the ground by effective responses and solid investigative practice.[220]

As these comments indicate, although at present much work is being done to change attitudes, for too long the attitude of the police was that 'domestics' were not proper crimes which warranted a thorough investigation. Further, the prosecution authorities were reluctant to take such cases to court unless there was a very high chance of success. Indeed the report noted that there was a 50 per cent attrition rate at each stage of the process (the police being called; the making by the police of a potential crime report; the making of a full crime report; the making of an arrest; the charging of the defendant; the conviction). As a result only a tiny percentage of domestic assaults were ending up in court. There is a determination within the police to change the attitudes of officers towards domestic violence and within the Crown Prosecution Service to pursue, where appropriate, prosecutions for domestic abuse. It remains to be seen what success these measure will have.

One issue which generates considerable controversy is the extent to which it is appropriate to prosecute an intimate violence case or bring civil proceedings on their behalf, where the victim does not support the prosecution.[221] It is clear that even if the victim does not want there to be a prosecution the state can still prosecute.[222] The views of the victims will be taken into account, but the prosecution is taken on behalf of the public at large and not the individual victim. Of course, there can be practical difficulties facing prosecutors seeking to bring a case where the victim is reluctant to give

---

[220] Her Majesty's Inspectorate of Constabulary/Crown Prosecution Service Inspectorate, *A Joint Inspection of the Investigation and Prosecution of Cases Involving Domestic Violence* (Her Majesty's Inspectorate of Constabulary, 2004) 6.

[221] See eg M Madden Dempsey, *Prosecuting Domestic Violence: A Philosophical Analysis* (Oxford University Press, 2011).

[222] Ibid para 9.5.

evidence, although there can be ways around these, such as relying on written statements of victims or relying on the evidence of others.[223]

Some commentators emphasise the autonomy of the victim and argue that to prosecute despite the victim's objections is to infringe the autonomy of the victim. On the other hand, there are those who argue that a prosecution is brought by the state not the victim and where there has been an incident of domestic violence the state should prosecute in order to show society's opposition to domestic violence.[224] The debates over compulsory intervention using the criminal or civil law raise the following issues.

A. Autonomy

What relevance is attached to the views of the individual seeking protection? I would argue that the right under article 3 is an absolute one. Unlike many of the other rights mentioned in the European Convention, there are no circumstances in which it is permissible for the state to infringe this right. This makes it clear that the rights of another party cannot justify an infringement of someone's article 3 rights. So, for example, it cannot be successfully argued that a family's right of privacy justifies non-intervention by the state if that non-intervention is an infringement of one family member's article 3 rights. Indeed, and perhaps this is more controversial, it is suggested that other rights of the victim cannot justify an infringement of article 3. In other words, in a domestic violence case the state cannot justify its failure to protect a victim's article 3 rights by referring to that person's right to respect for private life. Where article 3 is engaged, the state must take reasonable steps to protect the victim, regardless of her wishes.

However, unlike article 3, article 8 is a qualified right. It is permissible for the state to fail to respect an individual's right to respect for private life under article 8(1) if paragraph 2 is satisfied. So, if the level of abuse is not sufficient to engage article 3 but falls within article 8, then it is necessary to balance the article 8 rights and interests of other parties. It would therefore be possible to make an argument that the rights of autonomy of the victim justify the state in not intervening in an article 8 case. I will argue that in most cases this balancing of rights will still fall down in favour of intervention.

First, a strong pro-prosecution approach would not necessarily reflect the autonomous wish of the victim. It may be that she has been pressurised into withdrawing her cooperation in proceedings. It should not be forgotten what the impact of domestic violence can be: low self-esteem; dependence upon

---

[223] Ibid ch 9.

[224] S Choudhry and J Herring, 'Righting Domestic Violence' (2006) 20 *International Journal of Law, Policy and the Family* 95; M Madden Dempsey, 'Towards a Feminist State: What Does 'Effective' Prosecution of Domestic Violence Mean?' (2007) 70 *Modern Law Review* 908.

the perpetrator; feelings of hopelessness about ending the violence; and a tendency to minimise or deny the violence. If we do attach weight to the views of the victim in deciding whether or not to prosecute, all we will do is open up victims to further abuse as the defendant seeks to pressurise the victim into withdrawing her complaint. The *Opuz v Turkey*[225] case is a good example of where, although the victim made complaints to the police, the victim withdrew them in the face of threats from the defendant.

Second, even if there is a genuine request for non-intervention, there is a balance between protecting the current autonomous wish of the victim, with the increase in autonomy they may experience if they were removed from the abuse. Many victims in these cases have conflicting wishes. They want to remain in the relationship, but they want the abuse to stop. In such a case it is not easy to determine what is promoting their autonomy. It is not possible to respect these two conflicting desires. I suggest that where the abuse is low level, the infringement on autonomy in remaining in the relationship will be limited. However, in more serious cases the autonomy arguments will be in favour of removal. It must be remembered that being in an abusive relationship is itself undermining of autonomy. Leaving a person to suffer abuse, because they do not want to be protected, is not necessarily justified in the name of autonomy.

It may be argued that my approach is giving insufficient respect for the notion of a private life. Katherine O'Donovan,[226] before criticising the argument, suggests, 'Home is thought to be a private place, a refuge from society, where relationships can flourish uninterrupted by public interference.' Some therefore consider it essential that the law should 'stay out of the home'. This argument must be resisted. Catharine Mackinnon characterised the ideology of privacy as 'a right of men "to be let alone" to oppress women one at a time'.[227] Even if there is value in the notion of the privacy of the family life, I argue there are good reasons in favour of state intervention in cases of domestic violence.

A good starting point for rethinking the nature of privacy is to ask: Why should the state respect the private life of its citizens? One popular answer lies in the concept of autonomy. Each person should be entitled to develop her or his own understanding of the 'good life'. We could have a state that attempted to enforce a beneficial lifestyle on each citizen, telling her or him what to read, eat and do, but most people would find such a society repellent. Not least because living in a society of 'clones' would be boring indeed. So, the notion of privacy plays a role in allowing us to develop our lives and intimate relations in the ways we wish. This produces a wide range of different personalities and lifestyles which provide part of the enjoyment of life.

---

[225] [2009] ECHR 33401/02.
[226] K O'Donovan, *Family Law Matters* (Pluto, 1993) 107.
[227] C Mackinnon, *Feminism Unmodified* (Harvard University Press, 1987) 32.

But, so understood, privacy is not necessarily a negative concept about state non-intervention, but rather about an enabling of each individual to flourish as a person. As Elisabeth Schneider argues,[228] the state needs to promote 'a more affirmative concept of privacy, one that encompasses liberty, equality, freedom of bodily integrity, autonomy and self-determination, which is important to women who have been battered'. For those with power, that may be possible with little intervention from the state. However, for the less powerful, state intervention may be necessary to enable a person (or groups of people) to live their lives fully. Adopting such an approach means that privacy is not a concept which prevents state intervention in incidents of domestic violence but which in fact requires it. Without state intervention, a victim of domestic violence will be prevented from pursuing her vision of the good life. As we have seen, domestic abuse is typically about the control of a woman's life. So, then, if the state wishes to promote privacy in this sense, the ability to thrive in one's attempt to do what one wishes with one's life then protection from violence is required. To leave a person in an abusive relationship which is restricting her ability to develop her life as she wishes is not respecting her privacy, quite the opposite. Properly understood, therefore, privacy is a reason in favour of intervention, not against it.

Third, there are strong state reasons which can justify prosecuting a case of domestic violence, even where the victim does not want intervention. There are the interests of the community in expressing a clear message that domestic violence is unacceptable and will be taken very seriously by the state.[229] It is important to remember that prosecutions are brought by the state and not the victim. Battering can be seen as causing public harm: it can cause increased costs to the state; extensive loss to the economy of police time, victims having to take time off work, etc. In the UK, it has been estimated that domestic violence alone costs the economy £5.8 billion per year.[230] More than this, domestic violence is caused by and reinforced by patriarchy. As the state upholds and maintains patriarchy, it has responsibility for it and so is under a duty to mitigate its effects. To rely on Schneider's words:

> [H]eterosexual intimate violence is part of a larger system of coercive control and subordination; this system is based on structural gender inequality and has political roots... In the context of intimate violence, the impulse behind feminist legal arguments [is] to redefine the relationship between the personal and the political, to definitively link violence and gender.[231]

---

[228] E Schneider, 'The Violence of Privacy' in M Fineman and R Myktiuk (eds), *The Public Nature of Private Violence* (Routledge, 1994).

[229] M Madden Dempsey, *Prosecuting Domestic Violence* (Oxford University Press, 2009) describes how effective prosecution of domestic violence can exhibit the characteristics of a feminist state.

[230] S Walby, *The Cost of Domestic Violence* (London, Home Office, 2004).

[231] E Schneider, 'The Violence of Privacy' in M Fineman and R Myktiuk (eds), *The Public Nature of Private Violence* (Routledge, 1994) 5–6.

Fourth, even if these arguments are not accepted, the issue cannot be categorised as private where children are involved.[232] A UNICEF report suggests that up to one million children in the UK are living with domestic violence.[233] There is widespread acceptance that children raised in a household where there is domestic violence suffer in many ways, as compared to households where there is not.[234] This includes psychological disturbance and often a feeling that they are to blame for the violence.[235] The impact of the domestic violence on the mother may itself harm the child.[236] Indeed, one study of children who had suffered abuse showed that 39 per cent of them had come from families in which there was domestic violence.[237] Marianne Hester found that children were present in 55 per cent of cases of domestic violence.[238] Ten per cent of children who witnessed domestic violence witnessed their mother being sexually assaulted.[239]

Even if these arguments are accepted, it may be argued that there are insurmountable problems in putting a strong pro-prosecution policy into practice. One of the difficulties of domestic violence is that often the only witnesses to the violence are the two parties themselves. In many cases it is one person's word against another's. This requires the courts to make orders that may infringe important rights of either party on the basis of meagre evidence. If the court makes the wrong decision, an innocent person may be removed from his or her home, or a victim may be denied protection from further violence. An obvious objection to a pro-prosecution approach is that without the evidence of the victim, it is going to be extremely difficult to obtain a conviction. The incident is often only witnessed by the victim: so, in a practical sense, is it possible to prosecute where the victim opposes the prosecution? Those who wish to see more extensive prosecution in this area might suggest two solutions.

One would be to compel victims of domestic violence to testify under pain of imprisonment for contempt of court. This has few supporters. As the primary justification offered for intervention is the protection of the rights

---

[232] M Hester, C Pearson and N Harwin, *Making an Impact—Children and Domestic Violence: A Reader* (Jessica Kingsley, 2007).

[233] UNICEF, *Behind Closed Doors: The Impact of Domestic Violence on Children* (UNICEF, 2006).

[234] K Kitzmann, N Gaylord, A Holt and E Kenny, 'Child Witnesses to Domestic Violence: A Meta-Analytic Review' (2003) 71 *Journal of Consultative Clinical Psychology* 339.

[235] Barnado's, *Bitter Legacy* (Barnado's, 2004).

[236] L Radford and M Hester, *Mothering through Domestic Violence* (Jessica Kingsley, 2006).

[237] E Farmer and S Pollock, *Substitute Care for Sexually Abused and Abusing Children* (John Wiley & Sons, 1998).

[238] M Hester, *Who Does What to Whom? Gender and Domestic Violence Perpetrators* (Northern Rock, 2009). According to a study by the charity Barnardo's, in 9 out of 10 cases of domestic violence children are in the room of, or in the room next door to, the violence (Barnado's, *Bitter Legacy* (Barnado's, 2004)).

[239] A Mullender, *Tackling Domestic Violence: Providing Support for Children Who Have Witnessed Domestic Violence* (Home Office, 2005).

of the victim and any children, to imprison the victim would undermine that aim. The second alternative has more support. This involves a prosecution without the involvement of the victim. At present it is very rare for this to happen.[240] Louise Ellison[241] has argued that 'victimless prosecution' is the way forward.[242] She argues that, although it is often assumed that without victim involvement a prosecution is not possible, more imaginative policing and prosecution techniques would make it feasible. She discusses, for example, the use of cameras as soon as the police arrive on the scene, to capture objective evidence of injuries. She recommends that police procedure in domestic violence cases should be premised on the assumption that there will be a 'victimless prosecution'.[243] There may also need to be changes to the law of evidence—and in particular the hearsay rule and the admissibility of previous convictions—to assist in victimless prosecution. The advantages of victimless prosecution are clear: it involves less invasion of the victim's autonomy if the victim is opposed to it; the victim can avoid the pressures associated with giving evidence in these kinds of cases; and it can prevent threats or other pressures being used to dissuade victims from participating in litigation. Of course none of this should be seen as seeking not to prosecute with the victim's consent; much more should be done to enable and encourage the victim to support the litigation. The use of specialist domestic violence police, advisors,[244] prosecutors and courts might assist in these procedures.[245] The pilot studies to date indicate that in specialist domestic violence courts victimless prosecutions have been successfully brought.[246]

To summarise, I am not arguing in favour of a mandatory prosecution policy. However, wherever there is a reasonable chance of success a prosecution should be brought in all cases, save in cases of the least serious domestic abuse, where the victim strongly opposes the prosecution. This approach is in fact required under the ECHR to ensure protection of the rights of victims.

---

[240] S Edwards, *Briefing Note: Reducing Domestic Violence* (Home Office, 2000).

[241] L Ellison, 'Responding to Victim Withdrawal in Domestic Violence Prosecutions' (2002) *Criminal Law Review* 760; L Ellison, 'Prosecuting Domestic Violence without Victim Participation' (2002) 65 *Modern Law Review* 834.

[242] See also S Edwards, *Briefing Note: Reducing Domestic Violence* (Home Office, 2000) arguing for a greater willingness to use victims' written statements in cases where victims are unwilling to give evidence in court.

[243] Crown Prosecution Service, *Policy for Prosecuting Cases of Domestic Violence* (CPS, 2009).

[244] E Howarth, L Stimpson, D Baran, and A Robinson, *Safety in Numbers* (Hestia Fund, 2009).

[245] Crown Prosecution Service, *Policy for Prosecuting Cases of Domestic Violence* (CPS, 2009).

[246] M Burton, *Domestic Violence: Literature Review* (LSC, 2009).

B. The Views of Those Lacking Capacity

Considering next, cases where the victim lacks capacity. The decision on whether proceedings should be brought will involve an assessment of their best interests, which will include an assessment of their views.[247] The courts acknowledge that vulnerable people, like other competent people, are entitled to make decisions which others might regard as foolish. The problem was well put in *Re MM (an adult)*[248] by Munby J:

> ...The fact is that all life involves risk, and the young, the elderly and the vulnerable, are exposed to additional risks and to risks they are less well equipped than others to cope with. But just as wise parents resist the temptation to keep their children metaphorically wrapped up in cotton wool, so too we must avoid the temptation always to put the physical health and safety of the elderly and the vulnerable before everything else. Often it will be appropriate to do so, but not always. Physical health and safety can sometimes be bought at too high a price in happiness and emotional welfare. The emphasis must be on sensible risk appraisal, not striving to avoid all risk, whatever the price, but instead seeking a proper balance and being willing to tolerate manageable or acceptable risks as the price appropriately to be paid in order to achieve some other good—in particular to achieve the vital good of the elderly or vulnerable person's happiness. What good is it making someone safer if it merely makes them miserable?

As this quote indicates, forcing a vulnerable person out of a potentially abusive situation against their wishes may remove them from abuse, but doing so will create harms of its own. Munby J went on to say that the vulnerable adult's wishes and feelings were 'one of the most important factors' to be taken into account.[249] What he does not explain is whether the vulnerable adult's wishes are to be taken into account in ascertaining his or her best interests; or whether to operate outside of that assessment so that a judge must decide whether the proposed order is sufficiently beneficial to the individual that it justifies making an order against their wishes.[250] Munby J's comments are especially welcome given that we are dealing with people who, although vulnerable, do have capacity. The law is significantly infringing in the right to autonomy in these cases and it should only do so where there is very strong justification.[251] Of course, in other cases the views of the individual may simply not carry weight because they are based on a delusion. In *IIBCC v LG*,[252] a 96-year-old woman suffering dementia stated she wanted to 'go home' but the Court determined that this referred to her childhood home.

---

[247] *Hillingdon LBC v Neary* [2011] EWHC 1377 (Fam).

[248] [2007] EWHC 2003 (Fam), para 120 (Munby J).

[249] Ibid, para 121.

[250] See chapter three for further discussion of this issue.

[251] M Dunn, I Clare and J Holland, 'To Empower or to Protect? Constructing the 'Vulnerable Adult' in English Law and Public Policy' (2008) *Legal Studies* 234.

[252] [2010] EWHC 1527 (Fam).

Such a wish could not carry weight because it could not be carried out and was based on a misunderstanding of her current position.

Many of these cases are seen as a clash between the autonomy interests and the welfare interests of the individual.[253] Of course, in other cases intervention will enhance the autonomy of a vulnerable adult. This is a point emphasised in *DL v A Local Authority*[254] by Macfarlane LJ. He explained[255] that a person who is subject to coercion or constraint will have their autonomy enhanced, rather than restricted, if they are taken away from the abusive relationship. For the reasons in the previous section, this means that in all cases, save those of low level abuse, protective proceedings should be instigated, regardless of the views of the individual.

C. Interests of Carers

Any removal by the state of someone from their family or carers will automatically constitute an infringement of article 8, but this may be justified by taking into account the welfare of the child.[256] Paragraph 2 of article 8 permits an infringement of the right if it is necessary in the interests of others, and this would clearly include the interests of the child.[257] In deciding whether the infringement is necessary, the consideration of the welfare of the individual to be protected is 'crucial'.[258] There is little difficulty justifying an intervention in family life in order to protect someone from serious abuse.[259]

Fox Harding, looking at the issue of child protection, has outlined four basic approaches that the law could take:[260]

— *Laissez-faire and patriarchy*. Here, the core approach is that the role of the state should be kept to a minimum. The privacy of the original family should be respected. This is an 'all or nothing' approach. Family privacy should be protected unless it is absolutely necessary to remove a child. Critics argue that the approach promotes non-intervention except in the most extreme cases of violence, enabling men to exercise control over women and children within their families.

— *State paternalism and child protection*. This approach favours the intervention of the state in order to protect the child. It encourages state intervention, to whatever extent is necessary, to promote the welfare

---

[253] *Dorset CC v EH* [2009] EWHC (Fam) 784.

[254] [2012] EWCA Civ 253.

[255] Ibid, para 54.

[256] Although see the argument in J Herring, 'Respecting Family Life' (2008) 75 *Amicus Curiae* 21 that abusive forms of family life may not be entitled to respect under art 8.

[257] See chapter eight for a general discussion.

[258] *K and T v Finland* [2000] 2 FLR 79; *L v Finland* [2000] 2 FLR 118.

[259] *Re B* [2008] 2 FCR 339, para 77.

[260] L Fox Harding, *Family, State and Social Policy* (Macmillan, 1996).

of children. Opponents of this policy claim that the approach places insufficient weight on the rights of birth families. The approach, they claim, can too easily slip into 'social engineering', and presumes that the state knows what is best for the child.

— *The defence of the birth family and parents' rights.* The emphasis in this approach is on the benefits of psychological and biological bonds between children and parents. The birth family is seen as the 'optimal context' for bringing up children. Even where parents fail, the state should see its role as doing as much as possible to preserve the family ties. The approach is not opposed to state intervention, but argues that such intervention should be aimed at supporting the family as much as possible. Even where children do have to be removed, contact with the family should be retained and the aim should be to reunite the family if at all possible. Opponents of such an approach argue that it does not provide adequate protection for children.[261] Given the levels of abuse within families, we cannot assume that children are always best cared for by their families.

— *Children's rights and child liberation.* Here the emphasis is on the child's viewpoints, feelings and wishes. There is a range of approaches focusing on children's rights. At one extreme it could be argued that the state should intervene only if the child requests it. In areas of suspected abuse placing weight on children's views must be treated with great caution, given the complex psychological interplay that can exist between a child and his or her abuser.[262]

These four approaches could be adopted in relation to adults in cases of suspected abuse too. Of course, depending on the capacity of the individual concerned more weight may be attached to their wishes than in other cases. For the arguments made above, in cases of more serious abuse the protectionist element should always prevail.

There is a striking difference between procedures involving the removal of a child from his or her parents and cases involving adults from their caring relationships. While the cases involving children are subject to detailed legislative provision, described above, the position involving adults receive little detailed legislative attention. It has now been established that an adult cannot be removed from their caring relationships with their consent or the consent of those caring for them, without a court order.[263] Under both the Mental Capacity Act 2005 and the inherent jurisdiction, decisions about

---

[261] See *Re R (Care: Rehabilitation in Context of Domestic Violence)* [2006] EWCA Civ 1638 for a case where the Court of Appeal thought that the judge's attempts to rehabilitate the parents and child were unrealistic.

[262] E Jones and P Parkinson, 'Child Sexual Abuse, Access and the Wishes of Children' (1995) 9 *International Journal of Law, Policy and the Family* 54.

[263] *A Local Authority v A and B* [2010] EWHC 978 (Fam).

vulnerable adults must be based on what is in their best interests. This at first sight indicates that there are no 'threshold criteria' which need to be satisfied before an order can be made. There is, in other words, nothing equivalent to the 'significant harm' test in child protection which needs to be satisfied before an order removing an adult from their home can be made.[41] Although the interests of the vulnerable person's family members or carers might be affected by the removal, the sole factor for decision making is the interests of the vulnerable adult.[42] The only way the well-being of carers or family members is relevant is in so far as it might affect the welfare of the vulnerable adult.[43]

However, it is submitted this issue is not that straightforward. First, the ECHR rights of the carers and family members must be considered by the courts when making orders under either the Mental Capacity Act 2005 or the inherent jurisdiction.[44] A removal of an incapacitated person from her family will inevitably impact on the article 8 rights of the family members. In considering such an argument, Munby J had this to say in *Re MM (An Adult)*:[45]

> In domestic law the governing consideration is the welfare of the child or vulnerable adult. So it is under the Convention. Strasbourg jurisprudence has long recognised that, in the final analysis, parental rights have to give way to the child's—that the case may be one of sufficiently pressing necessity as to justify, in the interests of the child's welfare, the supercession and assumption by the State of parental rights and responsibilities. The answer can be no different where the child, although now an adult, remains unemancipated because mentally incapacitated. Parental rights and responsibilities, and the rights and responsibilities of partners or other carers, have in the final analysis to give way to the best interests of a vulnerable adult.

Here Munby J adopts the now familiar, if much criticised, judicial line that there is no conflict between a welfare-based approach and one based on human rights. It is not necessary to re-enter that well-worn territory.[46] Indeed, it is clear that human rights arguments can succeed in this context. In *G and E v Manchester CC*,[264] the local authority had removed E from F, a foster carer, with whom he had lived. In one hearing[265] it was held that the local authority had infringed article 8 rights by removing E from F without proper authorisation. E's article 5 rights were also infringed by placing him at a residential unit without authorisation under the Deprivation of Liberty Safeguards in schedule A1 of the Mental Capacity Act 2005 or an order of the Court of Protection. An order was made that E be reunited with F.

---

[264] [2010] EWHC 2512(COP) (Fam).
[265] [2010] EWHC 621 (Fam), [2010] 2 FLR 294.

Whether through human rights arguments or assumptions, it is clear that a straightforward best interests test is not automatically applied in this area.[266] Wood J in *London Borough of Ealing v KS*[267] held:

> we should not lightly interfere with family life. If the State—typically, as here, in the guise of a local authority—is to say that it is the more appropriate person to look after a mentally incapacitated adult than her own partner or family, it assumes, as it seems to me, the burden—not the legal burden but the practical and evidential burden—of establishing that this is indeed so.

Still, the judiciary prefers not to talk in terms of a presumption. In *A Local Authority v E, D and A*,[268] Sir Mark Potter stated:

> I start ... from the position that, while there is no presumption that mentally incapacitated adults will be better off if they live with a family rather than in an institution, however benign and enlightened the institution may be, and however well integrated into the community, it is nonetheless the normal assumption that mentally incapacitated adults who have been looked after within their family will be better off if they continue to be looked after within the family rather than by the state.[269]

While supporting Munby J's 'common sense' comments (quoted above), he added:

> ... This commonsense approach is in no way inconsistent with proper adherence to the unqualified principle that the welfare of the incapacitated person is, from beginning to end, the paramount consideration.[270]

This was recently echoed in *K v LBX*[271] where the Court of Appeal concluded that the human rights arguments or talk of presumptions should not interfere in the central task of assessing what the best interests of a person are.

D. Statutory Regime for Intimate Abuse

In a speech on 13 March 2006, Liam Byrne, the Parliamentary Under-Secretary of State for Care Services, said that he was considering whether it would be appropriate to introduce adult abuse equivalent of the protection from child abuse.[272] Nothing further was heard about that until the 2012 White Paper, which promised the Government would 'put action to protect

---

[266] Although see *Re S (Adult Patient) (Inherent Jurisdiction: Family Life)* [2003] 1 FLR 292 where Munby J noted the importance of the European Convention on Human Rights.

[267] [2008] EWHC 636 (Fam).

[268] [2007] EWHC 2396 (Fam).

[269] Ibid, para 66.

[270] Ibid, para 67.

[271] [2012] EWCA Civ 79.

[272] Speech by Liam Byrne MP, 13 March 2006, Action on Elder Abuse Conference.

people from abuse and neglect on a statutory footing, with clear duties on local authorities, the police and the NHS to work together to keep people safe'.[273] There will be consultation on how to do that. What we desperately need is a specific statutory regime to deal with the issue of the abuse of older people, and vulnerable people more generally.[274]

Currently, local authorities lack powers to investigate and act against intimate abuse involving adult victims.[275] A stark contrast can be made with the multitude of duties and powers a local authority has to investigate child abuse and then seek court orders to deal with it. There is no express duty on local authorities to deal with cases of intimate abuse and, as we have seen, although court orders may be available, they often have to be applied for under the inherent jurisdiction, which lacks any clear structure or guidelines.[276] There are four circumstances, summarised by the Law Commission, in which a duty might arise:

(1)   the duty to assess under section 47 of the NHS and Community Care Act 1990 and provide services under community care legislation;
(2)   local authority statutory powers to take or initiate compulsory action under section 47 of the National Assistance Act 1948, the Mental Health Act 1983 and the Mental Capacity Act 2005;
(3)   the statutory guidance *No Secrets* and *In Safe Hands* which establish social services as the lead co-ordinating agency for safeguarding; and
(4)   public law requirements, including those imposed by the European Convention on Human Rights (ECHR).[277]

However, a more effective general duty is required. The Law Commission[278] called for a law which put a duty on social services authorities to make enquiries where there is reason to believe a vulnerable adult in their area is suffering or is likely to suffer significant harm; a power to gain access to premises where it is believed a person at risk is living; the power to arrange a medical examination; the power to arrange the removal of the vulnerable person from

---

[273] HM Government, *Caring for our Future* (The Stationery Office, 2012) 36.

[274] J Manthorpe 'Local Responses to Elder Abuse: Building Effective Prevention Strategies' in A Wahidin and M Cain (eds), *Ageing, Crime and Society* (Willan, 2006).

[275] The National Health Service and Community Care Act 1990, s 47 gives a right to be assessed if one is in need and the Mental Health Act 1983, s 135 gives an approved social worker the right to apply to remove to a place of safety a person suffering from a mental disorder. But neither of these offer effective protection in most cases of elder abuse: J Williams, 'State Responsibility and the Abuse of Vulnerable Older People: Is there a Case for a Public Law to Protect Vulnerable Older People from Abuse' in J Bridgeman, H Keating and C Lind (eds), *Responsibility, Law and the Family* (Ashgate, 2008).

[276] The Care of Older and Incapacitated People (Human Rights) Bill 2006 which would have given local authorities some powers and duties was defeated in Parliament.

[277] Law Commission, *Adult Social Care, Report 326* (Law Commission, 2011), para 9.3.

[278] Law Commission, *Report on Mental Incapacity* (HMSO, 1997).

the home; and the power to apply for temporary and long term protection orders.[279] Currently none of these are available.

If one were to start to draft legislation along these lines, the obvious analogy is with the protection of abused children. The key issue would be setting the threshold at which the state intervenes to protect a victim of intimate abuse. If we were to adapt the regime in part IV of the Children Act 1989 to apply to adults, we could permit a court to make a care order or supervision order in respect of a vulnerable adult if the court is satisfied that making the order is in their best interests and that:

(a)   the vulnerable adult concerned is suffering or is likely to suffer, significant harm; and

(b)   that the harm, or likelihood of harm, is attributable to—the care given to the vulnerable adult or likely to be given to him or her if the order were not made, not being what it would be reasonable to expect a carer to give to him or her.[280]

Looking at this proposal, a number of issues would arise.

First, state intervention would only be justified if there was significant harm. Proof of lower levels of harm would be insufficient. Is this appropriate in the case of intimate abuse? I suggest so for two reasons. First, we must recall that the provision of residential care for vulnerable adults is far from satisfactory in many cases and inevitably impacts on rights of self-determination.[281] In the absence of significant harm it is unlikely that removal will be justified. Second, it should be recalled that we are dealing with cases where the vulnerable adult has not chosen to be taken into care. So there needs to be extremely good reasons to override their wishes, or to make up for their lack of consent.

Second, the Children Act 1989, section 31 includes a reference to the harm the child is suffering being attributable to the care being given to the child. Should any intimate abuse statute include a similar provision? It might be argued that in the case of children this reference protects the rights of parents so that if a parent has behaved reasonably they will not have their children taken away.[282] This has no application in relation to intimate abuse. However, this may overlook the interests of spouses, partners and carers whose relationship with the vulnerable adult will be seriously affected if the older person is removed. It is argued that this provision will also mean that if the real cause of the vulnerable adult's harm is the lack of social support,

---

[279] See also Action on Elder Abuse, *Consultation Paper on the Potential for Adult Protection Legislation in England, Wales and Northern Ireland* (Action on Elder Abuse, 2008).

[280] (b) refers to a child being beyond parental control, which is not relevant.

[281] Equality and Human Rights Commission, *Close to Home* (Equality and Human Rights Commission, 2012); D Wanlass, *Securing Good Care for Older People* (Kings Fund, 2006).

[282] J Herring, 'The Suffering Children of Blameless Parents' (2000) *Law Quarterly Review* 550.

rather than the quality of the care, then their removal into care would be unjustified.

Third, and most significantly, section 31 attaches no weight to the wishes of the individual. Their wishes would, however, be relevant in assessing their best interests. However, to some that may be insufficient. Vulnerable people's rights to choose how to wish their lives should be respected, whether or not they are the victims of elder abuse.[283] However, for the reasons given earlier, when discussing autonomy in the area of abuse the autonomy rights of the victim should not necessarily rule the day.

X. Prevention and Regulation

Of course, preferable to taking steps to protect people from abuse, is the use of measures to prevent abuse arising in the first place.

A. Protection of Vulnerable Adults List

It is extraordinary that before 2000 there was virtually no regulation or control of those working with vulnerable adults.[284] Traditionally, care assistants have been largely untrained and badly paid. There have been difficulties in recruiting and retaining suitable staff.[285] There is now in place a system for the registration and regulation of professional social workers. Since 1 April 2003, such staff have to be accredited with an NVQ level 2 within three years of being registered.[286]

One important limb of the current law protecting older people from abuse is the creation of the Protection of Vulnerable Adults List, which was introduced in July 2004 through the Care Standards Act 2000.[287] This requires employers to check whether an individual is on the List when employing workers or volunteers who are in regular contact with vulnerable adults. This is in addition to the need to do a Criminal Records Bureau Check.

---

[283] J Pritchard, *The Needs of Older Women* (Joseph Rowntree Foundation, 2000).

[284] There is a lack of training for care home owners: S Furness 'Recognising and Addressing Elder Abuse in Care Homes' (2006) 8 *Journal of Adult Protection* 33.

[285] Help the Aged, *My Home Life* (Help the Aged, 2008).

[286] There are concerns about the availability of places: House of Commons Health Committee, *Elder Abuse* (The Stationery Office, 2004).

[287] Department of Health, *Protection of Vulnerable Adults Scheme in England and Wales for Care Homes and Domiciliary Care Agencies, A Practical Guide* (Department of Health, 2004); M Stevens and J Manthorpe, *POVA Referrals—the First 100* (Kings College London, 2005).

B. Multi-Agency Work

Local authorities are required to set up multi-agency policies and practices to tackle the abuse of vulnerable people in their area.[288] In the past a failure by different agencies to communicate their concerns about vulnerable adults left them open to abuse. Although such multi-agency approaches are now standard, there is considerable diversity in how these arrangements work and the level of resources allocated to their work.[289]

The notion of agencies involved in the care of vulnerable adults 'talking to each other' seems straightforward. But in this area, as in others, it has proved complex. Different professional approaches and even language can impede effective communication.[290] There can even be conflicts between different professions, either based on monetary concerns over who should pay for an investigation or intervention, or disputes over what kind of intervention is appropriate.[291]

Safeguarding Adults provides the Government's guidance on the issue on inter-agency cooperation in cases of abuse of vulnerable adults. It requires a 'zero-tolerance' of abuse. However, the report states:

> The wishes of an adult with mental capacity should normally be respected. However, statutory agencies must act to uphold the human rights of all citizens and where others are at risk this duty will take precedence.

> Any action taken by an organisation to safeguard an adult should meet Human Rights standards. It should be proportionate to the perceived level of risk and seriousness. Intervention should not be arbitrary or unfair. It must have a basis in law: e.g. acting with the consent of the adult or, under duty of care, acting in the best interest of the adult; undertaken to secure a legitimate aim (i.e. to prevent a crime or protect the public) and be necessary to fulfil a pressing social need.

This indicates that normally if a vulnerable adult has mental capacity but does not want to have protection, then it should not be forced upon them. However, the guidance leaves open the possibility that there may be cases where it is appropriate to intervene to protect a vulnerable adult, even without their consent.

---

[288] Department of Health, *Safeguarding Adults, A National Framework of Standards for Good Practice and Outcomes in Adult Protection Work* (Department of Health, 2005); House of Commons Health Committee, *Elder Abuse* (The Stationery Office, 2004) 1.

[289] M O'Keeffe, A Hills, M Doyle, C McCreadie, S Scholes, R Constantine, A Tinker, J Manthorpe, S Biggs, and B Erens, *UK Study of Abuse and Neglect of Older People Prevalence Survey Report* (Department of Health, 2007).

[290] J Manthorpe, B Penhale, L Pinkney, N Perkins and P Kingston, *A Systematic Literature Review in Response to Key Themes Identified in the Report of the House of Commons Select Committee on Elder Abuse* (Department of Health, 2004).

[291] M Preston-Shoot and V Wigley, 'Closing the Circle: Social Workers Responses to Multi-Agency Procedures on Older Age Abuse' (2002) 32 *British Journal of Social Work* 299.

Not surprisingly, professionals in the area have found that the guidance offers little help in defining precisely when they should intervene. The Government intends more detailed policies to be developed at a local authority level. The difficulty is that the different agencies involved have a different understanding about what abuse is and how it is best to deal with it. The cultures of the different professions and even the language used can make communication between the different bodies troublesome. There is much to be said for wider use of inter-agency training.[292] The bureaucratic, organisational and historical barriers to interagency cooperation should not be underestimated. There has been concern expressed that risk assessments are carried out by agencies primarily to protect them from complaints or legal liability, rather than being a genuine attempt to ascertain whether or not there is a problem.[293]

C. Inspection and Regulation

The Care Quality Commission has the task of inspecting and regulating adult care services. These include ensuring that care homes meet the required standards in the following areas:

— treating people with dignity and respect;
— making sure food and drink meets people's needs;
— making sure that the environment is clean and safe; and
— managing and staffing services.

The Health and Social Care Act 2008 gives the Care Quality Commissioner a number of sanctions if a care home is failing to comply with a request for action.[294] These range from an emergency closure order to a variation of condition of registration, to a fine.[295]

There have been serious concerns about the effectiveness of the Care Quality Commission's inspection. The House of Commons Public Accounts Committee has branded the Commission a failure after scandals revealing major failures which it had not uncovered in its inspections.[296]

[292] P Cambridge and T Parkes, 'The Management and Practice of Joint Adult Protection Investigations between Health and Social Services: Issues Arising from a Training Intervention' (2006) 25 *Social Work Education* 824.

[293] C McCreadie, D Mathew, R Filinson and J Askham, 'Ambiguity and Cooperation in the Implementation of Adult Protection Policy' (2008) 42 *Social Policy and Administration* 228.

[294] Health and Social Care Act 2008, ss 26–32.

[295] S Furness, 'A Hindrance or a Help? The Contribution of Inspection to the Quality of Care in Homes for Older People' (2007) *British Journal of Social Work* 1.

[296] BBC News Online, 'Care Quality Commission Has Long Way to Go Says MPs' 30 March 2012.

A significant aspect of the Act is that it will ensure that the Human Rights Act applies to all publicly arranged care, whether that is in fact provided in the voluntary or private section. In *YL and Others v Birmingham City Council and Others (Secretary of State for Constitutional Affairs intervening)*,[297] it was held that a privately owned care home was not a public authority and so was not subject to the duties in the Human Rights Act[298] to act in a way which complied with the ECHR. The key argument was whether a private body running a care home was performing a 'function of public nature'.[299] The significance of the decision was short lived because under the Health and Social Care Act 2008 the decision will be reversed and all care homes, whether public or private will be covered. Section 145(1) states:

> A person ('P') who provides accommodation, together with nursing or personal care, in a care home for an individual under arrangements made with P under the relevant statutory provisions is to be taken for the purposes of subsection (3)(b) of section 6 of the Human Rights Act 1998 (c. 42) (acts of public authorities) to be exercising a function of a public nature in doing so.[300]

An action can therefore be brought under section 7 of the Human Rights Act against the owners of a care home complaining that they have failed to protect the rights of a resident.[301] This could lead to a court ordering the home to act, or not act, in a particular way in order to protect the person's rights. An award of damages could also be made.[302]

XI. Conclusion

This chapter has argued that it is essential for supporters of an ethic of care to promote an effective legal protection from abuse within intimate relationships. As defined in chapter two, caring relationships are those marked by respect and rationality. Abusive relationships will not have those characteristics and so are not protected by an ethic of care. If we are to promote caring relationships we must recognise that those entering intimate relationships make themselves vulnerable to abuse. Without an effective legal regime of protection, people will be deterred from entering intimate relationships.

---

[297] [2007] UKHL 27.

[298] s 6.

[299] s 6(3)(b).

[300] Section 145 does not apply to care where the services are provided in the older person's home.

[301] Although see *R (Thomas) v Havering LBC* [2008] EWHC 2300 (Admin) where a resident failed in claiming that a closure of a nursing home interfered with her right to life under article 2.

[302] Human Rights Act 1998, s 8.

Some have questioned whether an ethic of care can provide an effective protection against abuse. I argue it can, indeed it is uniquely well placed to do so.[303] Because an ethic of care places such weight on the importance of the quality of the relationship, it is able to recognise the severity of the wrong that takes place in intimate abuse. The wrongs discussed in this chapter of breach of trust and coercive control can only be fully appreciated by a deeply relational approach. Further, the appreciation of the significance of relationships brings out the difficulties in placing the correct weight on the wishes of the victim in cases of abuse.

This chapter has argued that the current legal structure is inadequate. The current criminal law fails to adequately protect people from relational abuse. There is still much work to be done on ensuring the crimes between people in an intimate relationship are prosecuted effectively. We desperately need a proper legal structure governing the duties on local authorities to investigate and protect vulnerable adults from abuse.

---

[303] V Held, 'Can the Ethics of Care Handle violence?' (2010) 4 *Ethics and Social Welfare* 115.

9

Conclusions

I. Introduction

Imagine a society where care is central. Where its primary purpose is to care for those who are dependent on others to meet their needs. Where all activities are assessed on what they contribute to the care of others. Economic productivity would be valued in so far as it produces what is needed to support care and in so far as it is consistent with care. Those with needs would be recognised for all they contribute and would not be seen as an expensive burden. Employees would be expected to combine their employment with meeting their caring responsibilities. Workplaces would expect workers to have caring responsibilities and so have flexible hours of work and leave, and would encourage working from home where possible. The work of women and men would be valued equally. It would be a society with a low GDP compared with others no doubt. But one where older people were left with a decent standard of life; disabled people were empowered through caring relationships to live the lives they wish; and where children spend more time with people caring for them, than with characters on computer games.

Imagine a society in which the generation of wealth is the primary goal. Where success is measured solely by income. Children are left uncared for by parents obsessed with generating more income. Older people are left in squalid conditions, provided with the minimum level of care by the lowest paid workers. Those who could not face leaving their parents or children in these dire situations and undertook care themselves are left in poverty and social exclusion. Exhaustion, loneliness and hardship are the order of the day for these carers, even if cheered by the rewards of the caring itself. Women who undertake the majority of care and make up the larger portion of older people suffer significantly more than men. The ever increasing number of older people is seen as a nightmare scenario, a route to catastrophe, rather than a cause for celebration. Disabled people are viewed as a burden and inconvenience. A society in which the highest court in the land accepts that someone would have to wear incontinence pads and spend the night soaked in urine and excreta because it is too expensive to provide a night time carer.[1] Any suggestion that her human rights were breached are brushed aside because doing so was justified by the difficulties in funding care.

II. Social Justice and Societal Well-Being

One of the major breakthroughs in theories of social justice and ethical analysis in recent years has been the work of Amartya Sen and Martha Nussbaum.[2] They have challenged the assumption that economic well-being automatically correlates to social justice or societal well-being. They emphasise the idea of capabilities: what people are able to do. Gender plays a key role in both of their writing. A nation may be economically well off, but women severely restricted in what they can do. To describe such a society as having social justice or a high quality of life would be clearly incorrect. Economic success does not reveal how the deprived people in that society are doing. It is the things people are capable of doing which is the most useful indication of a successful society.

One particular benefit of this approach is that it emphasises that the legal rights people have in a free market economy are not helpful if they do not manifest in real options. As Nussbaum argues:

> A further advantage of the capabilities approach is that, by focusing from the start on what people are actually able to do and to be, it is well placed to foreground and address inequalities that women suffer inside the family: inequalities in resources and opportunities, educational deprivations, the failure of work to be recognized as work, insults to bodily integrity.

> Traditional rights talk has neglected these issues, and this is no accident, I would argue: for rights language is strongly linked with the traditional distinction between a public sphere, which the state regulates, and a private sphere, which it must leave alone.[3]

---

[1] *Cf R(Macdonald) v Kensington and Chelsea* [2011] UKSC 33.

[2] Eg A Sen, *Commodities and Capabilities* (North-Holland Press, 1985); M Nussbaum, *Women and Human Development: The Capabilities Approach* (Cambridge University Press, 2000).

[3] M Nussbaum, 'Capabilities as Fundamental Entitlements: Sen and Social Justice' (2003) 9 *Feminist Economics* 33, 37.

Nussbaum goes on to list the 10 capabilities which she sees as central:

(1)   Life. Being able to live to the end of a human life of normal length; not dying prematurely, or before one's life is so reduced as to be not worth living.

(2)   Bodily Health. Being able to have good health, including reproductive health; to be adequately nourished; to have adequate shelter.

(3)   Bodily Integrity. Being able to move freely from place to place; to be secure against violent assault, including sexual assault and domestic violence; having opportunities for sexual satisfaction and for choice in matters of reproduction.

(4)   Senses, Imagination, and Thought. Being able to use the senses, to imagine, think, and reason—and to do these things in a 'truly human' way, a way informed and cultivated by an adequate education, including, but by no means limited to, literacy and basic mathematical and scientific training. Being able to use imagination and thought in connection with experiencing and producing works and events of one's own choice, religious, literary, musical, and so forth. Being able to use one's mind in ways protected by guarantees of freedom of expression with respect to both political and artistic speech, and freedom of religious exercise. Being able to have pleasurable experiences and to avoid nonbeneficial pain.

(5)   Emotions. Being able to have attachments to things and people outside ourselves; to love those who love and care for us, to grieve at their absence; in general, to love, to grieve, to experience longing, gratitude, and justified anger. Not having one's emotional development blighted by fear and anxiety. (Supporting this capability means supporting forms of human association that can be shown to be crucial to one's development.)

(6)   Practical Reason. Being able to form a conception of the good and to engage in critical reflection about the planning of one's life. (This entails protection for the liberty of conscience and religious observance.)

(7)   Affiliation:
   A.   Being able to live with and toward others, to recognise and show concern for other human beings, to engage in various forms of social interaction; to be able to imagine the situation of another. (Protecting this capability means protecting institutions that constitute and nourish such forms of affiliation, and also protecting the freedom of assembly and political speech.)
   B.   Having the social bases of self-respect and nonhumiliation; being able to be treated as a dignified being whose worth is equal to that of others. This entails provisions of nondiscrimination on

the basis of race, sex, sexual orientation, ethnicity, caste, religion, national origin.

(8) Other Species. Being able to live with concern for and in relation to animals, plants, and the world of nature.

(9) Play. Being able to laugh, to play, to enjoy recreational activities.

(10) Control Over One's Environment:

    A. Political. Being able to participate effectively in political choices that govern one's life; having the right of political participation, protections of free speech and association.

    B. Material. Being able to hold property (both land and movable goods), and having property rights on an equal basis with others; having the right to seek employment on an equal basis with others; having the freedom from unwarranted search and seizure. In work, being able to work as a human being, exercising practical reason, and entering into meaningful relationships of mutual recognition with other workers.[4]

Amartya Sen and Martha Nussbaum have developed their approaches with considerable sophistication. I will not seek to explore all of the ramifications, and difficulties, of them. But the point I want to emphasise is how central care is to producing capabilities. The meeting of basic needs is essential if people are to have the capabilities to live as they wish. Support and recognition for those caring for the needs of others is essential if they are to have the capabilities. A society which does not support caring relationships will not be one which produces the capabilities Nussbaum relies upon. She recognises this:

> Any real society is a caregiving and care-receiving society, and must therefore discover ways of coping with these facts of human neediness and dependency that are compatible with the self-respect of the recipients and do not exploit the caregivers. This, as I have said, is a central issue for gender justice.

I would put this point in more positive terms. It is not a matter of 'coping' with needs and care. These are at the heart of humanity. Vulnerability and care need to be celebrated, not merely endured.

This book has argued that caring relationships should be at the heart of law. Law, legal procedure and legal remedies should be designed with the aim of upholding, enabling, encouraging and maintaining caring relationships. This has consequences not only in the more obvious areas of family law and state benefits and services for carers, but more widely. It has an impact on the nature of law, on how legal rights are formulated and understood. The key points made in the book are detailed in the sections that follow.

---

[4] Ibid 41–42.

III. The Nature of Care

Chapter two suggested the following four markers of care:

— Meeting needs
— Respect
— Responsibility
— Relationality

I have rejected the view that care is about emotion, and instead emphasised it is an act. However, it is an act that must be understood in its relational context. Acts of care take their meaning from an ongoing relationship. Only in the context of the relationship can responsibility and respect be developed. Too often care is treated in market terms as a task. Reports that one dementia patient had 106 carers in one year[5] show the dangers of seeing care as simply a series of tasks. Hence it is caring relationships, marked by the meeting of central needs, responsibility and rationality, that we need to promote.

IV. The Relational Self

Central to much jurisprudential and political thought is the assumption that our starting point is the individual person. In issues ranging from debates over the definition of personhood to the concept of legal rights, the arguments assume as a given an isolated individual. We ask whether he has the attributes that we look for to grant him a legal status or conceive of his rights. His rights are seen as arranged to protect his freedom from intervention from others, to keep him free from unwanted obligations.

This book has argued in favour of an ethic of care, where the starting point is caring relationships. Our legal rules and approaches should be based on the inevitably and goodness of care. Far from legal rights being designed to promote freedom, legal rights should be designed to enable us to undertake our caring responsibilities. Our legal status should not be based on individuals but on relationships. So rather than asking what rights or status this individual has, we ask what rights and status flow from this relationship. This is not to downplay the significance of the individual, but to recognise that our identities and value is found not in ourselves but in our relationships. It is these that give sense to individual lives.

---

[5] See www.telegraph.co.uk/health/healthnews/9276052/106-carers-in-a-year-took-away-dementia-patients-right-to-dignity-says-wife.html.

Sandra Fredman[6] has referred to six tenets that hold great sway over the current law: 'rationality; autonomy; individualism; equality; a neutral State and legal system; and a free market.' She argues that these have operated to undermine the concerns of women and downplay the importance of care. By contrast an ethic of care valorises caring relationships; recognises the importance of emotions; seeks out solutions that operate in the day-to-day realities of peoples' lives; and emphasises our mutual independence.[7]

V. Gender Care and Power

Throughout this book the impact of the downgrading of care on women has been emphasised. It is women who undertake the majority of caring activities. A key aspect of, and even explanation for, the devaluing of care is its highly gendered nature. As Joan Tronto argues, the distribution of care is an exercise of power:

> Relatively more powerful people in society have a lot at stake in seeing that their caring needs are met under conditions that are beneficial to them, even if this means that the caring needs of those who provide them with services are neglected. More powerful people can fob caregiving work on to others: men to women, upper to lower class, free men to slaves. Care work itself is often demanding and inflexible, and not all of it is productive. People who do such work recognize its intrinsic value, but it does not fit well in a society that values innovation and accumulation of wealth.[8]

As we have seen in this book, the failure to recognise the value of care is apparent in financial orders on divorce; remedies in tort; and the welfare system. Care is not valued in itself and women are denied access to a workplace which is largely premised on an employee who has no caring responsibilities. Women are often restricted to low paid and low status part-time employment in an attempt to meet their caring responsibilities and employment aspirations.

While there have been some very gradual improvements in this area, it is wealthier women who have been able to take advantage of them. Traci Levy,[9] writing in the American context, explains:

> Caregiving is often treated solely as an issue of personal responsibility. Its burdens, moreover, fall disproportionately on those at the bottom of the 'traditional' gender,

---

[6] S Fredman, *Women and Law* (Oxford University Press, 1997) 32.
[7] See also T Kröger 'Care Research and Disability Studies: Nothing in Common?' (2009) 29 *Critical Social Policy* 398.
[8] J Tronto, 'The Value of Care', *Boston Review*, 6 February 2002.
[9] T Levi, 'The Relational Self and the Right to Give Care' (2006) 28 *New Political Science* 547.

race, and class hierarchies. The ability to make caregiving arrangements that do not greatly increase the vulnerability of the caregiver is often reserved for the most affluent families, although even these families can struggle in some respects.

VI. The Promotion of Caring Relationships

Chapter four analysed the state's response to caring relationships. We are beginning to see a shift away from the straightforward assumption that care should be regarded as women's work that is private and of no concern to the state. We are seeing a gradual increase in state involvement in care.[10] Not only that, we are also seeing a gradual acceptance that the state has a responsibility to provide care. It is in the area of child care where it is most evident, with the Government seeing provision of child care as an essential part of encouraging lone parents to enter the workplace. However, at the same time, through the restrictions on funding for local authority care services and moves to increase the use of personal budgets, we are seeing in other areas a withdrawal of state-provided care.

The Government rhetoric at least is that care is now recognised as being of significance and in need of reform:

> We all want to live a full and active life, to live independently and to play an active part in our local communities. Supporting people to live this way is a central ambition of the Coalition Government. It is also the purpose of this White Paper.
>
> The unfortunate truth is that this is not the life lived by many of those with care and support needs. For them, the daily reality can be a life of dependence, of struggling with daily tasks, of loneliness and isolation.
>
> …
>
> Our system of care and support, developed in a piecemeal fashion over more than six decades, is broken and in desperate need for reform. Individuals and their carers should have far better support and they need to be in control of the services they use. People need to have the peace of mind that if they or their loved ones need care they will be treated with respect, safe from abuse and neglect, and that it will be simple to arrange. We are putting in place radical changes to make this a reality.[11]

In chapter four I explored some of the proposals seeking to address the issue. The sad truth is that, despite the fine words, without a substantial investment of money for those in caring relationships the situation continues to be dire.

---

[10] S Sevenhuijsen, 'The Place of Care. The Relevance of the Feminist Ethic of Care for Social Policy' (2003) 4 *Feminist Theory* 179.
[11] HM Government, Caring for our Future (The Stationery Office, 2012), 3.

Care is currently hugely underfunded and people are left in appalling circumstances without proper care. Julia Neuberger[12] quotes one woman:

> I feel unclean half the time. I felt deprived when social services cut me down from two to one bath a week in 2004—deprived of feeling like a normal adult. Then they told me I had to stop having the one bath a week I have now because my care was taking longer than the one hour I was allocated. I told them I was doubly incontinent and why on earth couldn't I have a bath? Wasn't I entitled to be properly clean? They told me that time and money wouldn't allow it. But we're talking about fifteen minutes.

The standard of care in too many care homes is dismally low, as highlighted in a range of reports, discussed in chapter four.

The response of the state towards care needs to change. Sandra Fredman writes:

> To go beyond liberalism requires a sensitivity to the real distributions of power in society as well as the close interaction between power on the one hand, and gender, race and wealth on the other. It replaces the ethic of self-interest with one of responsibility, both by people for each other, and by the State for its citizens. Most urgently, the responsibility and care for children need to be both valued and accommodated within the public as much as the private sphere. The result would be a relaxation of the rigid boundary between unpaid and paid work, between the family and the market place, with the duty on formal structures to accommodate responsibilities towards children and others. In this way both men and women, and the broader community, are made to take responsibility and share the cost of ensuring the continuity of the human species.[13]

VII. Care and Health

In chapter five I argued for a refocusing in medical law. For too long medical law and ethics has focused on the interaction between the patient and the doctor as the central health care practice. Quite rightly it has been pointed out that this ignores the other medical professionals. It also ignores those involved in caring. The work of caring, formally or informally, should be seen as central to the medical care. Health related interventions should be designed to promote not individual patients, but rather patients in the context of their relationships with others. Our bodies and our health are deeply

---

[12] J Neuberger, *Not Dead Yet* (Harper Collins, 2008) 197.
[13] S Fredman, *Women and Law* (Oxford University Press, 1998).

interconnected and the traditional medical paradigms individualise health in a dangerous way.

VIII. Refocusing Family Law on Care

In chapter six I argued in favour of a refocusing of family law. I argued that for too long it has been focused on sexual or blood relationships. I have argued that while sexual relationships may be fun for the individuals involved, even deeply meaningful, they do not provide a benefit to the state. Nor do blood links deserve any political attention or weight. It is relationships of care which the state should promote through family law. Flowing from this I have argued that the allocation of parental rights and responsibilities should flow from an adult having a close relationship with the child, not from merely having a genetic link. Financial orders on relationship breakdown are best justified as a way of encouraging and rewarding care and of ensuring that the disadvantages and gains flowing from a cared relationship are shared between the parties fairly. I have argued that these orders should flow from all caring relationships, not just marriage.

IX. Care and Employment

Employment law and practice is structured around a model of an individual employee with no, or only limited, caring responsibilities. This may hark back to the time of the male employee supported at home by his wife who takes on his caring responsibilities. Although that is a hopelessly dated model to be based on, labour law has struggled to move away from it. There are currently very few measures designed to protect employees with caring responsibilities, and these are very limited.

We need a fundamental restructuring of the integration of care and employment. These include steps to encourage mothers and fathers to share parental leave; the provision of high quality care provision; equal pay for women and for part-time workers; flexible working conditions that can accommodate caring provision; and effective equal provisions. If necessary, the financing of these may require state support to employers.[14]

---

[14] S Fredman, *Woman and the Law* (Oxford University Press, 2004) 416.

X. Care and Protection from Abuse

I believe that protection from abuse must be central to any ethic of care. Intimate relationships generate vulnerability and can be used to perpetuate abuse. Indeed the severity of the abuse can only properly be understood in the context of the relationship. If we are to encourage people to enter caring relationships, there must be an effective protection from abuse. That is why any ethic of care must take the protection issues seriously. It would be most wrong to think that an ethic of care would take a lax view in relation to abuse if it occurs in an intimate relationship. That is because where there is abuse there would not be care, because the relationship would not have the markers of respect and relationality which I spelled out in chapter two. In chapter nine I explained how the current law has failed to offer sufficient protection from abuse in intimate relationships and how the law needs to take a more proactive approach to ensure that adequate protection is provided.

XI. Final Thoughts

There is no escaping the issue of care. It won't go away by claiming it is too expensive. Our collective failure to give adequate recognition and support of care means that some people are having their basic needs unmet and others are left in poverty and isolation. When it is said that care is too expensive to deal with we are making a decision about the distribution of the burdens of care. We are leaving those burdens on those with great needs and those sacrificially providing care. Those people are predominantly women. We should not accept that. We need the law (and more widely) to prioritise caring. Our central focus should be to provide social and legal regimes which promote, enable and protect relationships of care.

Index